THE VIETNAM WAR

**Recent Titles in
Contributions in Military Studies**

THE VIETNAM WAR

Teaching Approaches and Resources

EDITED BY
Marc Jason Gilbert

Contributions in Military Studies, Number 109

Greenwood Press
New York • Westport, Connecticut • London

Library of Congress Cataloging-in-Publication Data

The Vietnam war : teaching approaches and resources / edited by Marc
Jason Gilbert.
   p. cm. – (Contributions in military studies, ISSN 0883-6884
; no. 109)
  Includes index.
  ISBN 0-313-27740-0 (alk. paper)
  1. Vietnamese Conflict, 1961-1975 – Study and teaching – United
States.   I. Gilbert, Marc Jason.   II. Series.
DS557.74.V54 1991
959.704'3'071173 – dc20   90-20674

British Library Cataloguing in Publication Data is available.

Library of Congress Catalog Card Number: 90-20674
ISBN: 0-313-27740-0
ISSN: 0883-6884

First published in 1991

Greenwood Press, 88 Post Road West, Westport, CT 06881
An imprint of Greenwood Publishing Group, Inc.

Printed in the United States of America

The paper used in this book complies with the
Permanent Paper Standard issued by the National
Information Standards Organization (Z39.48-1984).

10 9 8 7 6 5 4 3 2 1

Contents

Abbreviations

ARVN	Army of the Republic of Vietnam
ASEAN	Association of Southeast Asian Nations
CIA	Central Intelligence Agency
CORDS	Civil Operations and Revolutionary Development Support
COSVN	Central Office for South Vietnam (Hanoi's field command in South Vietnam)
DRV (DRVN)	Democratic Republic of Vietnam
GVN	Government of Vietnam (South Vietnam)
MAAG	Military Assistance Advisory Group
MACV	Military Assistance Command, Vietnam
NLF (NLFSV)	National Liberation Front (of South Vietnam)
NVA	North Vietnamese Army (same as PAVN)
OSS	Office of Strategic Services
PAVN	People's Army of Vietnam
RVN	Republic of Vietnam

SAM	Surface-to-air missile
SAR	Search and rescue
SRV	The Socialist Republic of Vietnam
USIA	The United States Information Agency
USIS	The United States Information Service

Preface

Today, a generation too young to remember the Vietnam War has entered America's classrooms. Many of these students are intensely curious about both how and why the war was fought. Educators at all levels of instruction have responded to this surge in interest by increasing the number of courses devoted to that war and expanding the treatment afforded it in courses in American, Asian and military studies. They have also acted in concert with professional associations, such as the American Historical Association and the Association for Asian Studies, and with interested institutions, such as The National Endowment for the Humanities and the United States Air Force Academy, to sponsor workshops designed to identify teaching approaches and classroom resources that can be effectively employed by those instructors who will bear the burden of interpreting the war for this generation and those that will follow.

Among the institutions most active in the effort to improve the quality of instruction on the Vietnam War has been the Southeast Conference of the Association of Asian Studies (SEC/AAS) which, acting in cooperation with numerous colleges and universities in that region, supported teaching workshops at regular intervals from the earliest days of that war. This volume would not have been possible without the encouragement of the Publications Committee of the SEC/AAS and the financial support provided by North Georgia College, whose engraved marble wall memorial to those of its students who perished in Vietnam is no less poignant than its larger counterpart in Washington D. C. The editor is also indebted to Mildred Vassan and Catherine Lyons of Greenwood Press and Kenneth Berger, Margaret Fussel, Catherine M. Hall, Jane Hooper, Ellen Milholland, Craig Lockard and Robert McLean for their assistance in the preparation of the manuscript. He also wishes to express his thanks to his parents, Nat and Lottie, veterans of the Second World War, who taught him to value the study of war and peace.

The editor owes a special debt of gratitude to Professors Damodar R. SarDesai and Stanley Wolpert of UCLA and Professor Martin Yanuck, the late chairman of the Department of History at Spelman College. While teaching the history of South and Southeast Asia on some of this country's most tumultuous campuses during the Vietnam War, each earned the respect not only of both the opponents and proponents of the war, but also of those of its veterans who came to them as graduate students and left as friends and colleagues. At that time and since, these three scholars championed the scholarly and fair-minded approach to the war that is evinced in SarDesai's *Vietnam: Struggle for National Identity* (Boulder, Colo.: Westview, 1991) and in each of the contributions to this volume.

THE VIETNAM WAR

Introduction

MARC JASON GILBERT

There are over four hundred courses on the subject of the Vietnam War currently offered at American institutions of higher learning. The subject is also widely taught in American secondary schools. These courses vary in scope, focus and academic discipline, yet most share a common characteristic: they seek to lend perspective to a conflict that was, and in some public forums continues to be, perceived in narrow terms. Classroom discussions of the war, once largely limited to American foreign policy or military operations, now also address the social, cultural and economic dimensions of that conflict. Whereas the war was formerly studied chiefly as an episode in American history, it is today also examined as an episode in Southeast Asian and world history. Further, the "home front" in America and in the former two Vietnams, once so divisive an issue in the classroom, is now usually addressed in a manner too balanced to allow the search for heroes, villains and, above all, scapegoats to dictate the parameters of classroom debate. Finally, most instructors are now in the process of abandoning the ideologically-driven confrontational style that characterized the teaching of the war in the 1960s, 1970s and early 1980s in favor of teaching methodologies that promote the acquisition of knowledge and the development of analytical skills that are necessary if students are to formulate a truly informed opinion of America's involvement in the affairs of Southeast Asia and render a fair assessment of its still hotly debated lessons.

The broad perspective now sought, together with the inherent complexities of the war, can test the limits of the skills and knowledge of even the most experienced instructor. Scholars and publishers are attempting to help teachers address this challenge by producing new texts and curriculum development materials. This volume contributes to this effort by identifying and evaluating a variety of teaching approaches and resources. It is designed to serve the needs of instructors who are planning to teach the course for the first time or are considering modifying an existing course to take advantage of fresh alternative strategies and new classroom resources. Each of its constituent essays reflects the thoughts of those whose command of their subject has been acquired through long service to American, Asian and Vietnam War studies. The contributing authors display tolerance for views contradictory to their own and express ideas consistent with the growing consensus about major issues that was apparent at symposia for scholars recently held at George Mason University, the United States Air Force Academy and the Georgia Institute of Technology.

The volume opens with an examination by Larry E. Cable of the interpretive stances that can be employed by instructors responsible for courses on the Vietnam War. Cable identifies three such stances: the war as an expression of America's arrogance as a world power, the war as a successful military crusade betrayed by weak-willed politicians at home (which Cable calls the "stab in the back thesis"), and the war as the application of a rational policy that failed. After establishing that only the third option provides a variety of instructional opportunities and allows for a broad based analysis of the war, Cable identifies several issues teachers employing this interpretive stance can utilize as a focus or as foci for their courses. Among these issues are: the background to American involvement in Southeast Asia, including Vietnam's colonial past and independence movement and the evolution of the Cold War in Asia; America's conduct of the war; and the nature and course of the decision-making process of the Kennedy and Johnson administrations, which led to the large-scale commitment of American ground forces in South Vietnam. Cable concludes by tendering several reasons why instructors might choose instead to concentrate on the political culture of South Vietnam, or on the anti-war movement, or on the media's possible impact on American and Vietnamese politics.

Earl H. Tilford, Jr., and Cecil B. Currey address in greater detail two of the chief issues identified by Cable: the air war and American misconceptions regarding its opponent's military strategy. Tilford describes two ways of organizing material on the air war, episodical and chronological, and evaluates the merits of each approach. He also examines several thematic components of United States Air Force policy in Vietnam and discusses the myths about the air war that permeate both writing and teaching about the war. In addition, he provides a discussion of sources and an outline of the air war prepared with a view toward addressing classroom needs. Cecil B. Currey notes that during the Vietnam War the terms "conventional warfare," "unconventional warfare," "guerilla warfare," "partisan operations" and "insurgency" were applied interchangeably by American strategists to a pattern of North Vietnamese and Viet Cong military activity that refused to conform to the American definition of any of these rubrics. America's enemy described its activities in terms associated with the concept of a "people's war of national liberation." Edward Lansdale was one of the very few Americans to understand the nature of people's wars, and Cecil B. Currey, Lansdale's biographer, employs Lansdale's own words to introduce the subject, trace its origins and analyze America's inability or unwillingness to adopt an appropriate counterstrategy. After placing the concept of people's wars in its historical perspective, Currey reviews the methods by which students can be brought into the lively debate that still surrounds this issue. He favors a classroom role-playing exercise that allows students to appreciate the mind-set and the actions of participants in a people's war. He also provides a description of sources for the use of instructors and students engaged in an analysis of the impact of people's wars in the shaping of Vietnamese anti-colonialism and Vietnamese opposition to American and allied forces in Vietnam.

John James MacDougall and Melford Wilson, Jr., favor another of those issues recommended by Cable as a focus for the teaching of the Vietnam War: the evolution of American policy toward Southeast Asia. Employing techniques appropriate to their discipline, political science, each seeks to demonstrate the effectiveness of decision-making and foreign policy-making analysis as classroom learning techniques. MacDougall and Wilson maintain that an emphasis on the formation of government policy and public opinion allows an instructor to convey a considerable amount of material about the war without oversimplifying it. MacDougall demonstrates the utility of his chosen approach through a detailed description of a course that permits students to explore the role of the technocratic or managerial mind-set that was alleged to have influenced the formation of American policy in Vietnam between 1960 and 1968. This description includes comments on sources, examples of course discussion questions and sample term paper topics. Wilson further exemplifies this approach through the description of a course designed to expose students to the wide variety of opinions that Americans voiced in regard to the war's origin, conduct and purpose. Wilson offers a list of course readings structured in a manner that allows the student considerable flexibility in choosing the sources he or she will examine.

MacDougall and Wilson's contributions are followed by an essay by this writer that supports Cable's suggestion that the political culture within the former Republic of Vietnam constitutes a legitimate focus for a course on the Vietnam War, but argues that this focus be extended to include the political culture of Vietnam generally and, also that of neighboring Cambodia and Laos. It identifies the American War in Vietnam as but the second of three wars that have attended the Vietnamese journey to independence and revolution in this century and contends that even courses restricted to that conflict should examine its aftermath in Vietnam,

Southeast Asia and the United States. This essay also demonstrates that the employment of global as well as national and regional points of analyses are essential to the study of the origins, nature and impact of the war. It concludes with a discussion of resources that can be used by instructors to master the many dimensions and the global reach of war and revolution in modern Southeast Asia.

Gerald Berkley, Jonathan Goldstein, Catherine Calloway and Kali Tali explore the use of strategies and resources derived from one or more of three related sources that can be used in conjunction with any teaching approach, discipline or focus: literature, film and the voice of the veteran. These scholars argue that the use of literary sources in a course on the Vietnam War is similar to the function literature plays in other academic courses: the illumination of personal and group behavior and the identification of friend and enemy, self and "other."

Gerald Berkley and Jonathan Goldstein emphasize the benefits that can be obtained by using Asian, European and American literary sources to gain insight into the historical experience of the Vietnamese people. Gerald Berkley, a pioneer in this field, introduces the subject with a brief essay describing the benefits that can be obtained by assigning students readings in popular novels that lend insight into the thoughts and motives of America's opponents in the war. Jonathan Goldstein follows with a systematic discussion of how and why such novels and other literature can be used to enrich offerings on the Vietnam War in any academic discipline. Catherine Calloway devotes her attention to the American experience of the Vietnam War as reflected in American literature and film. She cites a number of works that can be used effectively in the classroom and discusses classroom exercises and critical sources that may be of value to those employing this material. Kali Tal explores the most intimate means of addressing the American experience in Southeast Asia: the testimony of veterans. Employing methodology drawn from anthropology as well as history, she identifies both the pitfalls and the advantages of classroom visits by veterans and offers a guide to the creation of a context for such visits that can most effectively enrich a course in history or literature.

These contributions are followed by surveys of teaching techniques and resources that, like literature and film, can be used regardless of an instructor's chosen academic discipline or teaching approach. In the first of these surveys, this writer contends that exercises designed to develop students' analytic or critical-thinking skills can greatly increase the effectiveness and comprehensiveness of any course on the Vietnam War. This essay demonstrates how these exercises can supply the means to address complex or elusive topics, such as the anti-war movement, the role of the American media in the war, and issues of race and gender. In the second essay in this section, Steve Potts treats in some detail one of the most widely used exercises for developing the critical-thinking skills of students enrolled in courses that address the war: the analysis of primary sources. Potts identifies readily available sources of documents suitable for this purpose and advances innovative ways of employing them in the classroom. In the final essay of this section, Joe P. Dunn couples a stimulating, personalized review of leading textbooks and monographs on the war with an invaluable survey of Vietnam War bibliographies and reference works. Dunn's bibliographical essay and the sources referenced in each of the previous essays constitute a significant resource for those seeking to expose students to a wide variety of views and interpretations.

The volume concludes with a guide to further resources for the teaching of the Vietnam War and a collection of course syllabi drawn from scholars active in the field. The guide identifies monographs, periodical literature, an instructional video program, maps and other materials that may aid in the development of Vietnam War courses. It also identifies those centers for Southeast Asian Studies and other institutions that maintain teacher outreach programs. The collection of course syllabi, presented in the form of an appendix, includes syllabi that further exemplify how the many teaching approaches and materials described in this volume can be effectively used in a variety of classroom settings. The syllabi describe courses ranging in focus from the American experience in Vietnam as reflected in literature to courses on the government and politics of Vietnam in which the American experience in Vietnam is but one of the subjects discussed. They provide examples of courses structured as undergraduate surveys and graduate seminars, multidisciplinary team-taught courses and courses designed to suit short-term or evening classes. Collectively, these syllabi reference a wide variety of main text choices, supplementary readings, exercises and student evaluation instruments, and they offer solutions to many common problems, such as how to best utilize the Public Broadcasting System's *Vietnam: A Television History*. Their chief value and that of the preceding essays, however, lies in their presentation and analysis of many alternative course strategies, structures and resources available to instructors seeking solutions to the unique challenges posed by their own teaching environments.

1
Running the Sweep Line: The Search for an Interpretive Stance

LARRY E. CABLE

Whether dealing with the Vietnam conflict in the context of a survey study of American history, as a subject within an American or modern military history course, or as the sole focus of a quarter or a longer effort, the most perplexing task is the selection of an overall interpretive stance. While this fundamental operation is not substantially different from that undertaken in the development of any course, it is made more difficult by the emotionalism surrounding the subject, the absence of well-defined historiographic traditions and the convoluted nature of the many faces of the war itself. Focal points and interpretive stances must be selected, but the absence of any consensus on these factors within the scholarly community does nothing to assist the process. When dealing with a traditional conflict such as the American Civil War or the Second World War, where the parameters of debate and the alternative points of focus are well established and major revision based upon new evidence is a remote possibility, the historian need only choose stances and foci of personal interest and have at it. He might demonstrate that the North's victory over the Confederacy was based upon superior generalship or superior industry; he might decry the Allied strategic bombardment campaign in Europe or wax eloquent concerning the development by the United States Navy of the carrier task force in the Pacific theater. All of these stances are logical and defensible and are imbued with enough historical controversy to prevent terminal ennui from setting in. The debate may be lively, but the field of play is well marked and the rules are understood. This happy scene does not apply to the war in Vietnam.

GOLDILOCKS GAMBIT

The literature of the Vietnam War period constitutes a minor growth industry for American publishers with the result that now some semblance of order might be imposed upon the welter that has emerged to date. Loosely, there are three major interpretive assemblages ("school" is entirely too structured a term to be applicable): the United States as behemoth, the stab in the back, and the rational policy that failed. This trinity is open to debate, the borders between these approaches are loose and ill defined, and an author may change his or her affiliation may change from one category to another. The division, however, remains useful as a preliminary organizing tool.

Adherents of the "United States as behemoth" approach argue that the American policy choices leading to involvement in the Vietnamese revolution were inherently fatally flawed for reasons ranging from Cold War myopia to the assumed moral supremacy of nationalistic insurgents or the perceived tactical superiority of guerrillas over high tech warriors delivering massive quantities of external stores from Mach 1 fighter-bombers. Partisans of the second theory, the stab in the back, argue that the American policy was rational and justifiable, American goals were both moderate and realizable, and American methods were equal to the task. They argue that micro-management by successive administrations, a meddling media and a species of moral cowardliness by Americans generally served to fatally undercut the efforts of military men to execute the initial policy.[1] These individuals regard the military as W. S. Gilbert described the English law in *Iolanthe*: "the true embodiment of everything that's excellent." Members of the third interpretive assembly accept that the decision-train leading first to a political commitment on the part of the United States to South Vietnam and subsequently to the use of American ground troops was rational within the context of the Cold War, but assert that the decision resulted in failure because of a variety of features endogenous to the American military forces and civilian assets employed in Vietnam.[2]

Having set up the choice of interpretive stances in the finest traditions of the "Goldilocks gambit," one option being "too hot" and another "too cold," there remains only one "just right" choice: the third. While each of the three interpretive stances mentioned has some, even much, merit, only the third allows for a broad-based analysis of the war and a treatment of that conflict which is not overly pejorative nor unduly laudatory. If, as Thucydides asserted, a valid use of history is the instruction of generations of statesmen and generals yet unborn, the third option seems to provide the greatest opportunity for so doing without at the same time operating to perpetuate the myths of wartime.

CONTEXTUAL FOCUS: HISTORICAL BACKGROUND

One major alternative focus within the third option is the historical background to the decision to invest American support and combat potential. Under this heading is to be found a significant list of topics: the nature, character and history of the Vietnamese society itself; the nature and quality of the French colonial administration; the Indochinese War from both the French and Vietnamese perspectives; the inducements and constraints of the Cold War period which resulted in American decisions to support the French and to invest in the Diem regime in the post-partition period; and the nature, goals and motivations of the revived insurgency within South Vietnam in the early 1960s as well as the precursors and external aids to this insurgency.[3]

CONTEXTUAL FOCUS: DECISION-MAKING

Another focus of major importance is the history of the decision-making within the Kennedy and Johnson administrations that led first to the use of American air power and later to the deployment of ground troops. While all the standard treatments of the war consider this chain of events, and many of the participants have written some form of more or less exculpatory memoir, the sad fact remains that the public literature is less than satisfyingly accurate. A prolonged period of research in the Kennedy and, more importantly, the Johnson libraries has convincingly demonstrated that previous treatments of the decision-making procedure are in need of major revision. Among the more important aspects of this revisionist approach would be the elucidation of how the Americans drove the escalatory process: how the use of air power in an attempt to solve a problem which did not exist (the ground infiltration of men and material from North Vietnam to the South) created a problem that could never be solved (the introduction of this infiltration in response to the air campaign). Unfortunately, the examination of the connection between military doctrine, both conventional and nuclear, and the decisions made at the highest echelons has only just begun. The difficulty that presents itself is simply that the raw decisions regarding the employment of American air and ground combat forces makes little sense unless seen in the context of prevalent military doctrine on the subject of both counterinsurgency and continental war.

CONTEXTUAL FOCUS: MILITARY STRATEGY

Indeed, a very meaningful focus that is generally ignored is that of the evolution of an American view of guerrilla war and how to fight it. While there are a number of books on that subject dating from the early 1960s, these are not sufficient to address the underlying central question: how accurate and historically valid was the American conceptualization and the specific derived doctrine?[4] There are strong reasons to argue that the American view of guerrilla war was both simplistic and historically invalid, being predicated upon incorrect appreciations of the German anti-partisan campaigns in the East during World War II as well as the American experiences in the Greek Civil War, the partisan war aspects of the Korean War, the Huk Insurrection and the British conduct of the Malayan Emergency. The central error of the Americans may have been the failure to differentiate between the two major subsets of guerrilla war: partisan and insurgent. This was compounded by the insistence that all guerrilla conflicts were not only of the partisan species but were generally the harbinger of conventional cross-border invasions. Thus the Americans were all too ready to see the activities of the Viet Cong in South Vietnam in the period from 1959 to 1965 as paralleling the partisan activities of the South Korean Labor Party in the year before the invasion by North Korea. These two deceptively simple but quite fundamental errors combined to fatally erode the accuracy and structural integrity of the American "theory of victory" regarding guerrilla war.

Further compounding the underlying errors of perception was the reality that the army had become configured, trained and equipped for a hypothetical armored conflict upon the presumably nuclear battlefield of Europe against a numerically superior and heavily mechanized opponent.[5] The thrust of the developments surrounding the replacement of older organizational structures and the heavy emphasis upon tactics of dispersion predicated upon new technologies of command, control and communications, and the new maneuver potentials conferred by the helicopter was due to the embedding of the idea that a single, general-purpose ground combat force was equally capable of handling an armored opponent upon the nuclear fields of Europe and the guerrilla in the bush on the world's periphery. As a corollary, such thinking assured that the Clausewitzian doctrine underpinning all American operational formulations would be employed against an opponent whose logic and grammar of war owed far more to Sun Tzu. The emphasis upon firepower killing and helicopters transporting and the dedication to searching out the enemy, fixing him in place and destroying him through heavy fire in a set piece conventional battle might have had a genuine utility in the environment and against the opponent originally envisioned as the most likely threat, but produced disastrous results when transferred to a far different arena and against a far different adversary.

When considering this contextual focus and its effect upon both the decisions leading to troop commitment and the course of the war thereafter, it is interesting to examine how the military viewed the noncombat use of combat and support forces. While this gradates into the matter of pacification and nation building, the so-called other war, the doctrinal roots are not without interest. Civil affairs and psychological warfare received great attention on paper. The field manuals are lengthy and well written, reflecting a proper understanding of the Huk Insurrection and the Malayan Emergency. The reality of application, however, was far removed from the theoretical model of the manuals.[6] Clearly, these less muscular activities were considered secondary or even tertiary extra duty with the inevitable implication that American military doctrine was to win the hearts and minds of the people by way of a strong hold upon the gonads. This set of priorities is to be seen as well in the documents of the Johnson Presidential Library: the nonmilitary programs are consistently subordinated to the conventional use of armed force, and the Vietnamese government is given the same message.

So far the discussion of focal points has been limited to factors that might be best described as contextual or background in nature. Matters such as military doctrine and the nature or historical character of Vietnamese society, while not central to a discussion of the war per se, are essential to understanding why American policy developed as it did and had the results it had. Indeed, it might be fairly argued that the historically invalid American view of guerrilla war and the perception that a true general-purpose ground combat force could and did exist conspired to issue every United States Marine at Red Beach in March 1965 with an invisible white flag so that the next seven years simply constituted a bloody, prolonged anti-climax.

OPERATIONAL FOCUS

Be that as it may, the central reality of the Vietnam conflict was the war itself. There are several major alternative foci that call for attention, chief among which is the ground campaign. While much of the meat of the ground war is not yet accessible, or at least not easily so, there is a large, if not altogether satisfying, body of literature available.[7] Critical points for evaluation include the efficacy of search and destroy missions, the effects of the one year tour on combat efficiency, the real effect of air mobility upon the conduct of combat operations, the actual numbers of combat-capable troops available for aggressive operations, the correctness of Westmoreland's decision to order the marines in I Corps to discontinue the Combined Action Platoons and related civic action programs, the utility of close air support and the utility of the refugee generation program. Although reliable data is quite sparse, an evaluation of the competence of the Army of the Republic of Vietnam (ARVN) should be attempted, as should an assessment of the accuracy of the pervasive accounts of American racism, counterproductive cultural insensitivity and the use of torture.

In connection with this last term, the Phoenix program might be mentioned. Phoenix and its components grew from the Quang Ngai Special Platoons of 1964-65, about which nothing has been written. Phoenix itself was a multi-faceted activity that incorporated the use of counterterror and deceptions such as those employed by the "pseudo-gangs" of the Mau-Mau Emergency and the Huk Insurrection. While the dictum of Huey Newton, chairman of the Black Panther Party, "them what knows don't talk and them what talks don't know," applies in abundance to the Phoenix operations, hints both true and mythic appear throughout the literature. From this perspective, myth far outweighs fact.

Another subject rife with legend is the air war, or more properly air wars, despite the best efforts of Guenter Lewy, in particular, to act the role of myth buster. The air campaigns over both North and South Vietnam bode well to produce as much controversy as the strategic bombardment campaign against Germany. While there is little doubt that the air war in the North was not highly productive and may well have been counterproductive, this has not been demonstrated in a rigorous and well-documented fashion. The same statement cannot be made with the same degree of certainty as regards the aerial operations in the South. Throughout the literature references occur regarding the results of inappropriate targeting and the inefficacy of the free-fire zone, but there is not yet a coherent and documented evaluation of the successes and failures of the aerial operations in the south. The consensus, such as it exists, holds that close air support, particularly that delivered by marine and navy pilots, was very good; the use of B-52s in tactical roles as in the ARCLIGHT strikes was more spectacular than effective; and indiscriminate employment of tactical air power in harassment and interdiction roles generated more hostile peasants in formerly friendly villages than dead bodies of formerly hostile personnel.

At the antipodes from the sanitary, detached and massively destructive air war was the "other war," the struggle in the villages for the hearts and the minds of the population in the context of the pacification effort. As previously mentioned, the documents in the Johnson Presidential Library demonstrate that, while there was a genuine concern for pacification and a genuine realization that it was necessary to demobilize popular sentiment from support of the insurgents and remobilize it in support of the Saigon government, the task of pacification had a secondary priority when compared to military operations. The justification for this was simply that pacification could occur only in districts that were secure from large-scale hostilities, districts from that first-line insurgent forces had been ejected. Given the highly localized and particularistic nature of Vietnamese society, with its long standing distrust of remote, central authority and the consequent difficulties of documentation and analysis presented to historians, it is not surprising that the complex and inherently frustrating task of pacification has not yet gained the attention that it so richly deserves.[8]

One of the major reasons for the relative failure of the pacification program was the inability of the American planners to understand and relate positively to the Vietnamese pattern of government. Another reason was the inability of the villagers to see any particular benefit that might accrue to them from actively collaborating with the central government in Saigon. Whether they lived in the old, traditional villages or had been forced to move into the new strategic hamlets, the Vietnamese peasants retained their traditional hierarchy of loyalties, which revolved about the family, secret society, clan and village in that order. Despite the fondest desires of the true believer proselytizers of the strategic hamlet, such as Roger Hillsman, who saw the use of such hamlets not simply as a tactic in a war but as a whole new and definitive answer to Marxist insurgency, the Vietnamese villagers stolidly saw no reason to become involved with the central government. Thus, the central government in the post-Diem days constitutes a legitimate focus of discussion.

FOCUS ON VIETNAMESE POLITICS

If our ignorance of Vietnamese political culture does not seem to be enough reason to look closely at the rats' nest of Saigon politics with its Byzantine gavotte of coups, countercoups, and rumors of coups and its regimes of ephemeral tenure and revolving personalities, consider that the need to bolster the will to resist of one or another new Saigon governments by the concrete exhibition of American will was the major reason the Johnson administration initiated the bombing of the supposed but virtually nonexistent infiltration routes. This action was the first slippery step onto the path of escalation. The political dynamics of South Vietnam in the post-Diem period are not easily accessible to contemporary readers as the basic scholarship has not yet been accomplished.[9]

Unresolved questions include those of cultural conflict, the linguistic incompetence of so many American personnel detailed to work with government offices and similar narrow gauge technical matters. Of a larger nature is the question of what might be called the "Levittown syndrome," the smug American conviction that all people everywhere really want to live in a Long Island suburb with access to all its delights, including a highly evolved and maturely stable system of representative democracy, both local and national. The accuracy of the Levittown model as describing the ultimate in desirability for Vietnamese peasant society is open to debate, a debate with relevance.

TET AND AFTER

When focusing upon the end game period of the war, including the Tet Offensive, the withdrawal of American troops, the conclusion of the Paris Accords, the Easter Offensive and the final fall of the South in 1975, it is clear that the questions far outweigh the certainties. The resolution of key questions, such as the policy intent of the Nixon administration in the peace talks in Paris, the nature and character of the Vietnamization process, the nature and extent of the residual American commitment following the withdrawal, the effect (and effectiveness) of the Christmas bombing campaign and the mining of Haiphong, the intent and results of the "secret" bombing campaign of Cambodia as well as the 1970 Cambodian incursion must await the opening of the Nixon Archives and the declassification by the State Department and the Joint Chiefs of the relevant papers under their jurisdiction. It is clear that the published Nixon and Kissinger recollections are, by their very nature, less than completely reliable and that the third-party literature to date is often contradictory, highly speculative and pejorative.[10]

IMPLICATIONS

Leaving the conflict itself to one side, it is proper to shift the focus to ramifications and implications of the war. There were a number of important direct effects upon American foreign policy. Indeed, it does not do violence to the truth to assert that the entirety of American diplomacy was held hostage to the war, particularly during the Johnson administration. Two examples of the magnetic power of the war serve to underscore this contention. In 1965 President Johnson, acting against the uniform and well-reasoned advice of the Joint Chiefs of Staff, reversed long-standing American policy and authorized the sale of first-line main battle tanks to the Israelis. The reason for this was the perceived need to "buy his peace" with the already vocal opposition to the war which involved not only a significant number of Jewish Americans, but an even larger, more influential number of supporters of the state of Israel. In 1965 the United States undertook a remarkably short and, in the near term, surprisingly effective intervention in the Dominican Republic. While the details of that intervention fall outside the scope of the present inquiry, suffice it to say that the American intervention was short by compulsion: compulsion imposed by the programmed increase of troops in Vietnam scheduled for the summer of 1965. Without this impetus it is doubtful that the United States would have so quickly and so effectively sought not only hemisphere support, but the supplanting of American forces by hemispheric contingents and the effecting of an internal Dominican compromise which fell short of traditional American goals and conditions for disengagement.

Another key focus involving the implications of the war is to be found in the attitudes of the media toward the war and the accuracy of the reportage. An interlocking series of questions must be asked, including whether or not it was the media, more than the spokesmen for Military Assistance Command, Vietnam (MACV) and the administration, that caused the celebrated "Credibility Gap", and to what degree did the media's initial attitude of unquestioning and even fervent support of the war cause the later backlash against it? From the military's perspective it is important to examine the question of whether or not the Department of Defense and MACV provided too much access and too much support to the members of the working press in Vietnam. Were these "working" media representatives too oriented toward the superficial aspects of the war, accounting for both their initial "gee whiz" attitude (Walter Cronkite reporting from the back seat of a B-57 during an actual combat strike against very dubious targets), as well as their later seizure of the appearance of U. S. defeat in the Tet Offensive of 1968? Did not the nature of the war itself cut across the grain of media strengths and couple all too well with its weaknesses? Is there a proper role for the media in a war zone, acceptable to the military, the media and the public they serve?[11]

In connection with the matters of media are to be found those of public opinion concerning the war and the nature, character and influence of the anti-war movement. While there are a number of books and articles that treat the subject of public opinion about the war and the political consequences of shifts in that opinion, a better vehicle for tracing not simply opinions but perceptions is to be found in the body of films and television treatments of the conflict.[12] Chronologically ranging from *Go Tell the Spartans* to the lamentable epic *Green Berets*, through *The Deerhunter* and *Apocalypse Now* to the spate of Chuck Norris and Sylvester Stallone blood and gore flag-wavers of recent vintage, films have portrayed the war in Vietnam in a manner that tends to mirror and reinforce public perceptions in a fine example of a positive feedback loop. The same is true with regard to television whether the treatment was documentary or fictional (who can forget the long period in the early and mid 1970s when no television police drama could do without the convenient presence of a deranged Vietnam veteran going berserk or strung out on drugs?).

A consideration of the peace movement is essential particularly when testing the stab in the back theory for accuracy of fit. The literature concerning anti-war activists is large, elderly and much more likely to demonstrate the political predilections of the author than to say anything of substance concerning the movement and its effects. It is important to note that the documentation concerning the possibility of foreign (Russian) sponsorship, guidance or control of the movement conclusively demonstrates that such control was absent: the Central Intelligence Agency (CIA) had its feet held to the Nixonian and Johnsonian fires alike when it was unable to prove any foreign connection, much to the disgust of the higher authorities. Neither saints nor subversive villains, the peace activists served two vital functions: they kept a portion of the Constitution alive and well at a time when many in power would have liked to see it atrophy, and they provided a political and organizational matrix for the large number of previously neutral or pro-war Americans who came into the anti-war milieu following the Tet Offensive. Thus, they helped to make the war stoppable, although to assert that they stopped the war is to overstate the case. A note of caution is in order: much of the social-political history of the 1960s, particularly as concerns the Vietnam generation, is a species of seamless garment. The anti-war movement took place in the context of the civil rights movement and other high-profile aspects of the 1960s such as rock and roll, drugs, and the counterculture generally. To go far into the draft protest and anti-war activist scene, however, may be to risk the same type of broadening commitment as the United States undertook in Vietnam.

The United States lost the war in Vietnam. This is a harsh statement, but to attempt to modify or soften its impact by asserting that the Americans were never militarily beaten and could never have been is to play a species of semantic legerdemain: the mere ability to avoid military defeat does not equal victory. To refrain from facing the reality that the Americans were defeated is to exhibit a lack of intellectual courage and to dishonor the more than 50 thousand people whose names are inscribed on the low wall on the Mall in Washington. Only through accepting this starting point of defeat can meaningful questions as to how and by whom and why be posed. By undertaking the inquiry, even if not answering with certainty and finality, the burden imposed upon historians by Thucydides will be carried another step: the war will serve not as a looming mythic presence but as an assimilable lesson, and therefore the Americans killed will not have died as much in vain.

NOTES

1.   Some of the purest adherents are frankly exculpatory in their writings, for example, William Westmoreland, *A Soldier Reports* (Garden City, N. Y.: Doubleday, 1976) and U. S. Sharp, *Strategy for Defeat: Vietnam in Retrospect* (San Rafael, Calif.: Presidio, 1978). Others, of a more recent origin, such as Harry Summers, *On Strategy: A Critical Analysis of the Vietnam War* (San Rafael, Calif.: Presidio, 1983), have become not only well known and highly influential, but quite literally the "school solution." One final recent example which in many ways is superior to Colonel Summers's work is Bruce Palmer, *The 25-Year War: America's Military Role in Vietnam* (Lexington, Ky.: University of Kentucky, 1984).

2.   Quite new and quite exhaustive in its treatment of battlefield operations is Shelby L. Stanton, *The Rise and Fall of an American Army: U. S. Ground Forces in Vietnam, 1965-1975* (San Rafael, Calif.: Presidio, 1985). Unsurpassed in the area of Vietnamese history are two works by Joseph Buttinger, *The Smaller Dragon* (New York: Praeger, 1958) and *Vietnam: A Dragon Embattled*, 2 volumes (New York: Praeger, 1967). On the French war, all of Bernard Fall's works have stood the test of time quite well, particularly *Street Without Joy* (New York: Praeger, 1961); *The Two Vietnams* (New York: Praeger, 1963, 1967), and *Hell in a Very Small Place: The Seige of Dien Bien Phu* (Philadelphia: Lippincott, 1967). Good from a French perspective is Jules Roy, *Battle of Dien Bien Phu* (New York: Harper and Row, 1965). Now quite elderly but still useful is Ellen Hammer, *The Struggle for Indochina* (Stanford, Calif.: Stanford University, 1954). For good insight on the American commitment to Diem as well as the personality of that controversial leader Denis Warner, *The Last Confucian* (New York: Praeger, 1963) is useful. Regarding the earliest American view of Ho Chi Minh and his insurgent movement, one cannot do better than Archimedes Patti, *Why Vietnam?* (Berkeley: University of California, 1980), as Patti was the head of the Office of Strategic Services (OSS) team in direct, daily association with Ho and the Viet Minh at the close of World War II. For the policy constraints and inducements operating on decision makers from Truman through Johnson, several works provide an excellent starting point: Douglas Blaufarb, *The Counterinsurgency Era* (New York: Free Press, 1977); Chester Cooper (who is quite valuable, but self-serving on a number of points), *Lost Crusade* (New York: Dodd, Mead, 1970) and John Gaddis, *Strategies of Containment* (New York: Oxford, 1982). For the insurgents, Douglas Pike, *Viet Cong* (Cambridge, Mass.: Massachusetts Institute of Technology, 1966) has never been equalled and is usually overlooked, as it was, tragically, at the time of its publication.

3. A classic of this genre is Guenter Lewy, *America in Vietnam* (New York: Oxford, 1978). This treatment is now showing its age and could well profit from revision on the basis of more recently declassified documentation. Of a more political if not metaphysical inclination is Norman Podhoretz, *Why We Were in Vietnam* (New York: Simon and Schuster, 1982). Focusing on military command structure and personnel policy problems to the exclusion of other considerations but still useful as examples of this third classification are the complementary works by Cecil B. Currey, *Self-Destruction: The Disintegration and Decay of the United States Army during the Vietnam Era* (New York: Norton, 1981) and Richard Gabriel and Paul Savage, *Crisis in Command* (New York: Hill and Wang, 1978). For a broader-based evaluation of errors in doctrine and decision making that falls squarely in this classification, see Larry E. Cable, *Conflict of Myths: The Development of US Counter-insurgency Doctrine and the Roots of the Vietnamese Commitment* (New York: New York University, 1988).

4. Among the more influential works of that day were Clark Osanka, *Modern Guerrilla War,* (New York: Free Press, 1962); T. N. Green, *The Guerrilla and How to Fight Him* (New York: Praeger, 1962); David Galula, *Counterinsurgency Warfare: Theory and Practice*, (New York: Praeger, 1962); Otto Heilbrunn, *Partisan Warfare* (New York: Praeger, 1962) and *Warfare in the Enemy's Rear* (New York: Praeger, 1965); Cecil Aubrey Dixon and Otto Heilbrunn, *Communist Guerrilla Warfare* (New York: Praeger, 1955); Paul A. Jureidini, *Casebook on Insurgency and Revolutionary Warfare* (Washington, D. C.: American University Press, 1962); John McCuen, *The Art of Counter-Revolutionary War* (Harrisburg, Penn.: Stackpole, 1966) and Virgil Ney, *Notes on Guerrilla War: Principles and Practices* (Washington, D. C.: Command Publications, 1961). There are other works on this subject, many of which are discussed by Cecil B. Currey and Marc Jason Gilbert in their contributions to this volume, but these sources were widely read within the defense community.

5. In addition to the relevant field manuals and a very substantial professional journal literature, the following might be perused with profit: Theodore Mataxis, *Nuclear Tactics* (Harrisburg, Penn.: Military Service Publishing Company, 1958); G. C. Rinehardt, *Atomic Weapons in Land Combat* (Harrisburg, Penn.: Military Service Publishing Company, 1954); Marvin Worley, *A Digest of New Developments in Army Weapons, Tactics, Organization and Equipment* (Harrisburg, Penn.: Military Service Publishing Company, 1958).

6. In addition to the field manuals, the following are of use: Murray Dyer et al., *The Developing Role of the Army in Civil Affairs* (Bethesda, Md.: Operations Research Office, 1961); Alfred Hausrath, *Civil Affairs in the Cold War* (Bethesda, Md: Operations Research Office, 1961); Gerald Higgens, *Civil Affairs in Future Armed Conflicts* (Bethesda, Md.: Operations Research Office, 1960); and Paul Linebarger, *Psychological Warfare* (New

York: Hawthorne, rev. ed., 1954). Linebarger was particularly influential as the psychological warfare guru of the Central Intelligence Agency. The *Final Composite Report of the Draper Committee*, dated 1959, is also of great interest.

7.   Two volumes of articles originally appearing in *Infantry in Vietnam: Small Unit Actions in the Early Days, 1965-66* (Nashville, Tenn.: Battery Press, 1982) and *A Distant Challenge: The US Infantryman in Vietnam 1967-1972* (Nashville, Tenn.: Battery Press, 1982) are of use in understanding the face of battle. In looking at the United States Marines in I Corps, two books by Francis West, *The Village* (New York: Harper and Row, 1972) and *Small Unit Action in Vietnam, Summer 1966* (New York: Arno, 1967), present a good starting point; also to be commended in this connection are the several volumes of official history brought out by the History and Museums section of the Marine Corps Headquarters. Lewis Walt, the commander of the III Marine Amphibious Force and I Corps, has offered an interesting treatment of his experiences and sense of "lessons learned" in *Strange War, Strange Strategy* (New York: Funk and Wagnalls, 1970), as has the Corps' first real specialist in counterinsurgency, Victor Krulak, *First to Fight* (Annapolis, Md.: Naval Institute Press, 1984). Although long past his prime when he wrote them, S. L. A. Marshall has offered four books of interest, if used with caution: *Battles in the Monsoon* (Nashville, Tenn.: Battery Press, 1966, 1967); *Ambush and Bird* (Nashville, Tenn.: Battery Press, 1968, 1969); *West to Cambodia* (Nashville, Tenn.: Battery Press, 1969) and *Fields of Bamboo* (Garden City, New York: Doubleday, 1971). While combat memoirs are usually a risky proposition, the best are of definite assistance. Examples include Charles Anderson, *The Grunts and Vietnam: The Other War* (San Rafael, Calif.: Presidio, 1982) and James McDonough, *Platoon Leader* (San Rafael, Calif.: Presidio, 1985). An excellent overall impression of the war that serves to accurately and convincingly convey the sound, sight and smell of the war can be found in Michael Herr, *Dispatches* (New York: Knopf, 1977). A treatment with general utility that both considers the ground war and serves as a bridge to the policy level and the air war is David Richard Palmer, *Summons of the Trumpet: US-Vietnam in Perspective* (San Rafael, Calif.: Presidio, 1978).

8.   An early and highly influential devotee of the strategic hamlet as the sovereign remedy was Roger Hilsman, whose book *To Move A Nation* (New York: Doubleday, 1964) recounts how he developed a born-again fervor for the originally British idea. His mentor in this conversion experience was the "old Malaya hand" Robert Thompson, author of several books such as *Defeating Communist Insurgency* (New York: Praeger, 1966). Another early and overly sanguine treatment of the pacification program is George Tanham et al., *War Without Guns* (New York: Praeger, 1967). A very worthwhile and more recent treatment is Stuart Herrington, *Silence Was a Weapon: The Vietnam War in the Villages* (San Rafael, Calif.:

Presidio, 1982). Also useful is Jeffrey Race, *War Comes to Long An: Revolutionary Conflict in a Vietnamese Province* (Berkeley: University of California, 1972).

9. Two rather opposing views of politics and government in South Vietnam are to be found in analyses by political scientists, one Vietnamese and the other American: Nghiem Dang, *Vietnam: Politics and Public Administration* (Honolulu: East-West Center Press, 1966) and Charles A. Joiner, *The Politics of Massacre: Political Processes in South Vietnam* (Philadelphia: Temple University, 1974). A duo of long active South Vietnamese political leaders have written memoirs of use in this connection: Nguyen Cao Ky, *Twenty Years and Twenty Days* (New York: Stein and Day, 1976) and Tran Van Don, *Our Endless War: Inside Vietnam* (San Rafael, Calif.: Presidio, 1978). Maxwell Taylor's memoirs are the useful and perceptive insights of a seasoned "Saigon watcher" in much of the critical commitment period, but they are too brief when considered in light of his telegrams and kindred materials in the Johnson Presidential Library.

10. In addition to the Kissinger and Nixon memoirs and the Porter and Issacs works previously mentioned, the following are of assistance in considering various aspects of the endgame period: Allan E. Goodman, *The Lost Peace: America's Search for a Negotiated Settlement of the Vietnam War* (Stanford, Calif.: Stanford University Press, 1978); Stuart Herrington, *Peace with Honor? An American Reports on Vietnam 1973-75* (San Rafael, Calif.: Presidio, 1983); Stephen Hosmer et al., *The Fall of South Vietnam: Statements by Vietnamese Military and Civilian Leaders* (New York: Crane Russak, 1980); William Shawcross, *Sideshow: Kissinger, Nixon and the Destruction of Cambodia* (New York: Simon and Schuster, 1979); Frank Snepp, *Decent Interval* (New York: Random House, 1977) and G. H. Turley, *The Easter Offensive: The Last American Advisors in Vietnam, 1972* (San Rafael, Calif.: 1985).

11. Peter Braestrup, *Big Story* (Boulder, Colo.: Westview, 1977) remains the best overall treatment of the accuracy of the reportage, although its primary focus is on the Tet Offensive. In addition, there is a virtually limitless journal literature of much greater bulk than wisdom. [Editor's Note: Until recently, little was written on this subject that possessed any degree of scholarly balance. This pattern has been broken by William Hammond's contribution to the *United States Army in Vietnam* series entitled *Public Affairs: The Military and the Media, 1962-68* (Washington, D. C.: U. S. Army Center for Military History, 1988). This volume, which has earned Braestrup's praise, and its forthcoming sequel, *Public Affairs: The Military and the Media, 1968-73*, are solid scholarly efforts, free of the "finger pointing" that characterize earlier efforts. Daniel C. Hallin, *The Uncensored War: The Media and Vietnam* (New York: Oxford, 1986) is also a reliable resource.

12.   Among the best works dealing with the subject are Louis Harris, *The Anguish of Change* (New York: Norton, 1973); Samuel Lubell, *The Hidden Crisis in American Politics* (New York: Norton, 1971); John Mueller, *War, Presidents and Public Opinion* (Lanham, Md.: University Press of America, 1973).   On the public and personal effects of the war, the following are useful: Robert Stevens, *Vain Hopes, Grim Realities: The Economic Consequences of the Vietnam War* (New York: New Viewpoints, 1976) and Gloria Emerson, *Winners and Losers* (New York: Random House, 1976). The latter is a particularly bitter book of downbeat vignettes that perhaps says more concerning the journalist than her subjects.   More recent is Thomas Powers, *Vietnam: The War at Home, Vietnam and the American People 1964-1968* (Boston: G. K. Hall, 1984).

2

An Approach to Teaching the Air War

EARL H. TILFORD, JR.

In *War Without Fronts: The American Experience in Vietnam*, operations analyst Thomas C. Thayer argues that in terms of resource expenditure, the American war in Vietnam "was first and foremost an air war . . . and second, a ground attrition campaign."[1] American strategy revolved around the air war in two ways: first as a coercive instrument to affect the behavior of the Hanoi regime, and second, as a substitute for the expenditure of the lives of American soldiers. To these ends, the weight of the effort was immense, with over four million combat sorties flown and eight million tons of bombs dropped throughout Indochina between 1962 and 1973. As Thayer indicates, the air force built up its forces the fastest and remained in Southeast Asia the longest of any of the services, not closing down its Thailand headquarters until January 1976. In terms of resources, in 1969, at the height of the American commitment, $9.3 billion dollars went to support air operations (including the navy, marine corps, and army aviation), while $5 billion dollars was spent to sustain ground and sea forces.[2] The air force, however, suffered fewer casualties than the army, navy, or marine corps, with approximately 2,700 killed and 3,500 wounded. The air force lost 2,257 aircraft between 1961 and 1975, and the total number of aircraft lost, including fixed-wing craft and helicopters, for all the services, came to over 8,500.[3] For all that, the air war is probably the least understood portion of that conflict.

Myths about the air war abound. Partly this is the fault of the air force, which has not addressed the Vietnam War adequately. It has been reluctant to ask the difficult questions about strategy and the appropriateness of its doctrines because, since air power played such a large role in the war, the ultimate failure of the United States in Vietnam could be construed as a failure of air power. As such, it might lead some to question the efficacy of strategic or independent bombing as well as the need for an independent air force. Furthermore, officers who made up the senior leadership of the air force during the war, and many of those who have risen to leadership positions since 1975, remain convinced that the Linebacker II air campaign, the bombing of North Vietnam from 18 to 29 December 1972, brought victory. Even today, many officers still believe that if air power had been applied with equal resolve earlier, the war could have been concluded on terms favorable to the United States as soon as 1965.[4]

It is unfortunate that the air force has not invested more in critical, scholarly appraisals of the air war, because there is within the service a readily available supply of scholars who understand historical methods of investigation as well as the complexities and subtleties of aerial warfare. Many in the civilian academic community are not prepared to deal with the technical aspects of aerial warfare and they sometimes accept exaggerated statements as truth. For instance, H. Bruce Franklin, the John Cotton Dana Professor of English and American Studies at Rutgers University, stated in a review essay of James William Gibson's *The Perfect War: Technowar in Vietnam*, that "the United States dropped between eight and fifteen million tons of aerial munitions on Vietnam . . . during the 1972 Christmas bombing of North Vietnam, Hanoi alone was hit with 100,000 tons."[5] There are two incredible over-exaggerations in this statement which, seemingly, held enough authority for the prestigious *American Quarterly* to publish Franklin's essay. First, between "eight to fifteen million tons" represents a large disparity of range for scholarly writing. Imagine the reception awaiting any scholar of Southern History if he or she published an article stating that there were between three and six million slaves in the American South in 1861. In the case of bomb tonnages dropped during the Vietnam War, there are plenty of sources that place the figure at about eight million tons, including Raphael Littauer and Norman Uphoff's *The Air War in Indochina*, cited by Franklin in referencing this statement.

Second, Franklin's source for the fixture of 100,000 tons of bombs with which "Hanoi alone was hit" during Linebacker II is journalist Gloria Emerson's 1976 book, *Winners and Losers: Battles, Retreats, Gains, Losses and Ruins from a Long War*.[6] Following the footnote trail, one finds that Emerson's information came from an unnamed official in Hanoi. Thus a statement by "somebody in Hanoi" evolves into scholarship acceptable for publication in a journal as respectable as the *American Quarterly*.

Unfortunately, rather than being isolated examples of poor scholarship, Franklin's statements and Emerson's faulty reference are typical of much of the discussion about the air war. The figure of 100,000 tons need not be accepted at face value, at least by those with a modicum of historical training and a minimum knowledge of military hardware. One can accept with prudent caution official air force figures that held that during

Linebacker II, B-52s dropped 15,237 tons of bombs north of the 20th parallel in some 729 sorties and still refute the 100,000 ton figure.[7]

The willingness of many to accept statements on the air war so uncritically is indicative of some of the problems to be overcome in understanding and teaching the air war. There are few good books covering the entire aerial conflict. Understanding the air war requires some knowledge of technical matters such as weapons and aircraft capabilities. And because the air war is a subset of military history, like its parent field it cannot be fully comprehended outside the context of cultural, political, economic, and diplomatic factors.

APPROACHES

There are two approaches that can be used to teach the air war: episodical or chronological. If taught episodically, that is, by focusing on specific aerial operations or issues attendant to the air war, the teacher can integrate individual episodes into whatever approach may be used. With the episodic approach, Rolling Thunder, the bombing of North Vietnam from 2 March 1965 to 31 October 1968, can be taught as an entity. It may be discussed during a consideration of the massive build-up of American forces that began in 1965, or it can be dissected as a part of a study in policy formulation. The secret bombing of Cambodia in 1969 or Ranch Hand defoliation operations might also be taught as individual episodes.

The advantage to using an episodic approach is that it allows for a more detailed consideration of the issues. In considering the secret bombing of Cambodia, for instance, one can also address the proper roles of secrecy in the conduct of warfare and diplomacy. There are, however, at least two dangers in the episodic approach, both of them contextual. First, it is sometimes tempting to use various episodes to present political and ideologically biased arguments. As such, Ranch Hand defoliation operations might be interpreted as either ecological genocide on the one hand, or as a bold attempt to use technology to limit American casualties by removing the cover from which Viet Cong and North Vietnamese troops mounted attacks. The second danger is that individual episodes may not be placed within the larger context of the war. To understand the secret bombing of Cambodia, one has to consider the political and diplomatic factors that compelled Richard M. Nixon and Henry Kissinger to undertake these operations.[8]

The perhaps better approach is to teach the air war chronologically. The war developed through distinct periods. The period from 1961 to 1965 is the advisory phase. From 1965 to 1968, while Rolling Thunder strikes hit North Vietnam, the war in the South was Americanized as the troop deployments took place. Between 1969 and the end of 1971, during

Vietnamization, air power covered the American withdrawal and the bombing focused on the Ho Chi Minh Trail in neighboring Laos. In 1972, the American war in South Vietnam came to a climax first with the spring invasion of South Vietnam by 12 to 14 divisions of North Vietnamese troops and the air power response to that invasion, Linebacker I, and then second with Linebacker II, the bombing of North Vietnam for 11 days in December.

The chronological approach can be used in two ways. The teacher can integrate what is going on in the air war with military action in South Vietnam, Laos and Cambodia as well as with political and diplomatic events as they unfolded between 1961 and 1975. If one chooses this approach, there is still a need for some understanding about the history of air power doctrine and the development of deterrence theory. One way to handle these subjects is to teach an entire lesson on the American military in the post-World War II era.

Another chronological approach is to deal with the air war as an entity. This is, however, difficult to do in a single lesson. One must consider post-World War II developments in the American military. Students need to know that the air force dominated the budget battles of the 1950s, receiving, between 1954 and 1961, an average of 47 percent of the allocations against 29 percent for the navy and marine corps and 24 percent for the army.[9] An understanding of how budgetary competition exacerbated interservice rivalries in the 1950s is needed to comprehend the fight between the army and the air force over roles and missions in Vietnam in the early 1960s. The air war from 1961 through 1968 can be taught in a single session. This involves covering the advisory effort, secret Yankee Team reconnaissance and bombing missions in Laos, along with Rolling Thunder. After 1968, however, the nature of the war changed from an offensive strategy tied to Americanization to a defensive strategy with air power covering the American withdrawal during Vietnamization. The big aerial operations from late 1968 to 1972 were part of Commando Hunt, the bombing of the Ho Chi Minh Trail in Laos between 15 November 1968 and 31 March 1972; Linebacker I, the aerial response to the 1972 invasion of South Vietnam; and Linebacker II, the Christmas bombing.

THEMES

Regardless of approach, instructors examining the air war may wish to explore or inform their lectures with one or more of the following themes: United States Air Force history, doctrine, technology and management, the decline in institutional intellectual acumen, attributes of air power and the already alluded to mythology that surrounds the air war.

HISTORY

As all professional historians are aware, more than the study of the past, history is part of a dynamic linking yesterday to today as it defines the future. From the 1920s, air power enthusiasts within the Army, however well intended, engaged in subterfuge and intrigue to promote their case for a separate air force. Like an illegitimate child at a family reunion, the United States Air Force felt less than completely comfortable with its origins, and all the more so since its primary reason for being was based on faith in the unrealized promise of strategic bombing. With its force structure and major weapons acquisitions programs wedded to strategic bombing, the air force neglected other missions, particularly close air support, which tended to tie air assets to the needs of ground commanders. This aggravated interservice rivalries because, while the air force did not especially want the close air support mission, neither did it want the U. S. Army to have it and thereby procure combat airplanes. Interservice squabbling, which dominated and poisoned relationships between the armed services in the 1950s, were transplanted to Vietnam, where they had an adverse effect on operations, especially during the period 1962-1965.[10] Instructors should insure that students understand the context of this squabbling, so that it does not appear unique to the Vietnam conflict.

DOCTRINE

Strategic bombing involves flying to the enemy's heartland to destroy industrial vital centers. This concept has dominated Air Force doctrine from the first United States Air Force Manual (AFM) 1-series in 1953 to its latest published edition of AFM 1-1. Faith in strategic bombing led air force leaders to believe that North Vietnam, a pre-industrial, agricultural nation, could be subdued by the same kind of bombing that helped to defeat industrialized countries like Nazi Germany and Imperial Japan. Their faith in strategic bombing doctrine had the effect of blinding them to the point that they were incapable of seeing an alternative aspect of the war, which may have been at its essence, namely, that the war—especially until 1969—was a revolutionary civil conflict and a guerilla war, not a struggle between industrialized powers. Consequently, the generals and admirals in charge of air operations were unable to devise a plan applicable to the war at hand, forcing Presidents John F. Kennedy and Lyndon B. Johnson to turn to their civilian advisers for military strategy.

TECHNOLOGY

The strategic bombing doctrine espoused by the air force coincided with the Eisenhower administration's policy of massive retaliation, itself driven more by economic than military considerations. Thus, the air force was able to gobble up the largest slice of the budget pie in the 1950s to acquire B-52s, B-58s, and the century series fighters and to develop the tri-sonic XB-70, all of which were at the leading edge of technology. This fascination with technology in the 1950s transferred to Vietnam in the 1960s, where the air force was ever in search of a technologically inspired "silver bullet" to end the war quickly. Cluster bombs, napalm, herbicide defoliants, sensors dropped along the Ho Chi Minh Trail to monitor truck traffic and aid in targeting, gunships, electro-optically guided and laser-guided bombs—all promised much. While some of these weapons delivered a great deal of destruction, in the end technologically sophisticated weapons proved no substitute for strategy. What technology may have done, however, was to help foster a managerial mind-set. Instructors employing a decision-making approach to the war as outlined in chapter 4 by John James MacDougall, will wish to reference this factor and that which follows: the managerial ethos.

MANAGEMENT

The managerial ethos, used effectively in marshalling forces during World War II, institutionalized in the 1950s, took hold in the 1960s, and turned the air war into a production line affair. High tech weapons demand effective and efficient management from initial research and development through procurement and deployment. In seeking efficiency, the tendency is to look for definable and objective criteria for assessing effectiveness in terms of productivity. The managerial ethos, implemented during the massive build-up of the air force in the 1950s, dominated the service in the 1960s. It promoted the objectivity of the quantifiable at the expense of the subjectivity of the creative but predictable. War, however, being inherently more subjective than objective, proved both unpredictable and, in its larger aspects, not amenable to a process-oriented approach. The Vietnam War was especially "unmanageable" because the art of unconventional warfare practiced by the Viet Cong and to a lesser extent the North Vietnamese was not susceptible to the rigid approaches fostered by the air force's managerial elite. For the air force, the Vietnam War came to resemble production line warfare, where success was assessed on statistical compilations that became an end unto themselves. Statistics, however, proved a poor substitute for strategy and the perceived successes fostered by the numbers game succeeded in providing only the illusion of victory. What it may have done was to fool many into thinking that air power was winning the war.

DECREASED INTELLECTUAL ACUMEN

The intellectual acumen of the air force was stifled in an atmosphere of conformity created by managers intent on instituting methods to insure efficiency and productivity. The quality of articles appearing in the *Air University Quarterly Review*, which along with its bimonthly successor the *Air University Review*, served as the air force's professional journal, steadily declined during the 1950s and the 1960s. The decline in sophistication of articles signed by higher-ranking officers, particularly general officers, was especially obvious. A factor in this decline was Secretary of Defense Louis Johnson's Consolidation Directive Number 1, issued in 1949. It required that all information from the Pentagon be screened not only for security but also for policy and propriety. The decline in the quality of articles continued until the *Air University Review* was compelled to seek articles written by civilian scholars who were not subject to censorship by public affairs officers.

General Curtis E. LeMay's statement before Congress in 1961 that doctrine written in 1935 was still appropriate typified thinking before and during the Vietnam War.[11] One result was that air power leaders transferred strategic thinking to civilian think tanks like the air force-sponsored Rand Corporation. Consequently, when Presidents Kennedy and Johnson turned to their military leaders for a strategy to follow in Vietnam, the generals could not devise one appropriate to the war as perceived by the civilian leaders. Instead of understanding the dynamics of a limited war, air power leaders tried to refight World War II, a conflict for which the doctrine of strategic bombing was better suited. In Vietnam, the United States Air Force, along with other services, was rarely outfought, but like the other services, it was often *out thought*. Military historians and intellectual historians may wish to examine this aspect of the war.

ATTRIBUTES OF AIR POWER

There were two attributes of air power which are generic and beyond the control of the air force. First, air power is awesome in its destructive potential, and that is intimidating. Bombs and missiles, like bolts from Zeus, come from above. Since most Americans know little about air power, aerial warfare inherits many of the awe-inspiring attributes of the gods. When the Vietnam War dragged on, many Americans looked to air power for a quick way to end the conflict. However, when they were disappointed, they turned rather quickly to an almost opposite point of view; that their air force was unleashing its cruel technology on a peaceful and peace-loving people. Hanoi's propaganda apparatus found it easy to promote images of pagodas, churches, schools, hospitals and dikes obliterated by bombs.[12] When the public's perceptions about air power were skewed, an American strength was—jujitsu like—turned against itself.

Second, aerial warfare is inherently technical and difficult for most people to understand. While air power leaders, especially those in the air force, had little understanding of the unconventional aspects and political subtleties of the war, civilian leaders at the highest levels of the United States government had little grasp of the more technical aspects of aerial warfare, especially bombing. Presidents Kennedy and Johnson, for a number of different reasons, were more inclined to seek advice from their civilian staffs than from their generals even when it came to operational issues like whether or not to bomb surface-to-air missile (SAM) sites.[13] Although these civilians were more politically astute than the generals, men such as Robert S. McNamara, McGeorge Bundy and George Ball were as ignorant of the technical aspects of bombing as air force generals seemed to be of its political implications. "The best and the brightest" generally believed air power could work miracles far beyond those attributed to it by the most ardent air power enthusiasts. To the unschooled, it seemed that if X number of bombs could accomplish Y result, one-tenth X would achieve a correspondingly smaller objective. Therefore, limited bombing could achieve limited objectives.

Historians, political scientists, economists and lawyers are not expected to be masters of the art of war. It is understandable that they would not comprehend the factors affecting circular error probable CEP—the percentage of any number of bombs falling within a certain distance of the aiming point—and its relationship to force packaging. Most air force generals grasped CEP and force packaging, but they were not masters of the art of war because they could not integrate the social, cultural and political dimensions of the conflict with its military aspects. That was a key factor in structuring the setup that resulted in America's defeat.

MYTHOLOGY

Myths often serve to delude or excuse. For example, the stab-in-the-back thesis that emerged in Germany after the First World War held that a combination of Jews, democrats, and communists betrayed the cause, selling out the German nation and its army by forcing a surrender while the military was holding its own in the field. This myth, devised to cover the shortcomings of Kaiser Wilhelm II and Generals Hindenburg and

Ludendorff—commanders who lost the war—also deluded the nation and was a factor contributing to the failure of the Weimar Republic and the subsequent rise of Adolf Hitler and the National Socialists. Likewise, in the post-Vietnam War air force, a number of unhealthy myths, including a version of the stab-in-the-back thesis, may have enforced a kind of institutional self-delusion.

The most popular and most widely accepted air force Vietnam myth, referenced above, was that Linebacker II, the so-called "Christmas Bombing" of December 1972, "won" the war. A corollary to the myth holds that if air power had been used with equal resolve earlier, any time between 1965 and 1969, the war could have been concluded sooner and on more favorable terms. This line of reasoning engendered a our-hands-were-tied-behind-our-back thesis similar to the German stab-in-the-back thesis that held sway in the German officer corps after the First World War. The our-hands-were-tied thesis had dominated thinking about Vietnam in the air force because it blames the final outcome on a host of convenient villains: a pernicious press, anti-war activists, and, perhaps most disturbingly, on "interference" by politicians who "restrained" the military.

As with most myths, there are elements of truth to those that surround Linebacker II. Certainly the December 1972 bombing paved the way for a final agreement that allowed the United States to complete its withdrawal from South Vietnam. It also compelled Hanoi to release American prisoners of war. In the euphoria surrounding the signing of the Paris Accords, the withdrawal of the last American troops from the South, and the return of American prisoners of war, there was an illusion of victory. The conclusion that air power delivered that victory appealed to the air force, which not only saw Linebacker II as a vindication of the traditional tenets of strategic bombing, but also stated that this bombing proved the enduring worth of the manned bomber, a weapon considered by many air force officers as absolutely fundamental to its continued existence as a separate service.[14]

Bolstered by official policy pronouncements and by remarks of high-ranking officers, the myth of Linebacker II gained in prominence. Retired United States Air Force General T. R. Milton, lamenting the fall of Saigon in the June 1975 edition of *Air Force Magazine*, stated that the December 1972 bombing of North Vietnam was "an object lesson in how the war might have been won, and won long ago, if only there had not been such political inhibition."[15] In his book *Air Power in Three Wars*, former 7th Air Force commander, General William W. Momyer, prognosticating about the future of aerial warfare, wrote, "An early Linebacker II campaign (with the enforcing threat of subsequent Linebackers) can be strategically decisive if its application is intense, continuous and focused on the enemy's vital systems."[16] A decade after the end of the American involvement in

Vietnam, Milton wrote, "The Christmas bombings of 1972 should have taken place in 1965."[17]

Although appealing, there are many problems with this position. In 1965, the North Vietnamese would have had much to lose by ending the fighting. Their goals had not been realized, and Washington's demand that Hanoi stop supporting the National Liberation Front and remove its increasingly larger number of troops from South Vietnam was unacceptable. Furthermore, the guerrilla war in the South probably would have continued, because the Viet Cong, despite claims by Hanoi, was not yet controlled by the North Vietnamese. Additionally, what many hands-tied theorists tend to forget is that by December 1972 America's goals had changed and American troops were headed home. Hanoi, on the other hand, had secured the right to maintain a large army in South Vietnam. With time as their ally, the North Vietnamese figured that after the American withdrawal they would eventually win. In December 1972, with most of their military and political objectives won—or at least achievable—it made good sense for Hanoi to sign a peace agreement . . . one which President Nguyen Van Thieu of South Vietnam found absolutely abhorrent.[18] Finally, Linebacker II served very little tactical military purpose other than bouncing the rubble produced by the May through October bombings dubbed Linebacker I. It is noteworthy that the fighting inside South Vietnam did not subside after Linebacker II, nor did it decrease with the signing of the Paris accords.

The United States Air Force has no monopoly on Vietnam myths. There were myths about air power held by people outside the air force that have been perpetuated by those intent on criticizing America's role in Vietnam. Again, Linebacker II holds a prominent position in the ichnography.

At the time, the press dubbed Linebacker II "the Christmas bombing" and some journalists compared it to fire bomb raids on German and Japanese cities during the Second World War. When one wing of the Bach Mai Hospital was damaged, a cry went up not only from Hanoi but from many quarters of the world press. No one mentioned that the hospital was located close to Bach Mai airfield, a primary MiG base. No one raised the possibility that the damage might have been caused by a stray bomb aimed at the base or suggested that a spent North Vietnamese surface-to-air missile might have fallen on it. Certainly, no one made the point that the Air Force could have targeted the hospital legitimately since the roof and grounds had been used by anti-aircraft guns during Linebacker I.[19]

Indeed, Linebacker II has become as important to the mythology of those who were in the anti-war movement as it has to many within the air force. It was in reference to Linebacker II that H. Bruce Franklin made the suspect assertions regarding bomb tonnage referenced in the introduction to this essay. Professor Franklin is a self-declared Marxist and Maoist, but even mainstream scholars have occasionally accepted some of the more facile pronouncements concerning Linebacker II. Professor George C. Herring, a highly respected historian and author of *America's Longest War*, used Hanoi's figure of 34 B-52s shot down during Linebacker II rather than the figure of 15 released by the air force.[20]

There are other air power-associated myths precious to the anti-war viewpoint. Nancy Zaroulis and Gerald Sullivan's monumental study of the peace movement, *Who Spoke Up? American Protest Against the War in Vietnam, 1962-1975*, published in 1985, stated that "U. S. and South Vietnamese planes dropped 220 *million* tons of bombs in the area [around Khe Sanh] during the seventy-seven day siege."[21] No source is cited. In fact the United States dropped eight million tons of bombs in Indochina between 1962 and 1973. Instructors must use particular care in utilizing the sources, particularly secondary sources, when studying and teaching the air war in Vietnam.

SOURCES

Aerial warfare is rooted in sophisticated machinery. Beyond knowing what these weapons can and cannot do, the teacher needs to understand the United States Air Force's fascination with technology in order to appreciate why it fought the war as it did.

Institutions are complex entities and understanding them is not easy. Keep in mind that after the U. S. Air Force gained its independence from the U. S. Army shortly after World War II, it evolved into what can best be described as a bureaucratic technocracy. The best book on the development of U. S. Air Force doctrine, such as it has been, is Robert F. Futrell's *Ideas, Concepts, Doctrine: A History of Basic Thinking in the United States Air Force, 1907-1964*. Futrell explores the development of the Air Force doctrine of strategic bombing as well as its fascination with technology and its commitment to the manned bomber. To understand why Lyndon Johnson's civilian and military advisers devised the Rolling Thunder campaign as they did, one needs to understand both deterrence theory and the concepts of coercive diplomacy. Although related, they are different in that deterrence theory is rooted in preventing the initiation of specific actions, while coercive diplomacy involves modification of existing behavior. Henry Kissinger's *Nuclear Weapons and Foreign Policy*, Bernard Brodie's *Strategy in the Missile Age* and Robert E. Osgood's *Limited War: The Challenge to American Strategy* are important books on deterrence. The best book on power and coercion is Alexander George, David Hall and William Simon's *The Limits of Coercive Diplomacy*.

Next, the teacher might want a general overview of the air war. Four books provide a good starting point. John Morocco's *Thunder from Above* and *Rain of Fire*, two volumes in the Boston Publishing Company's *The Vietnam Experience*, are perhaps the best available sources for an overview. The second edition of the Office of Air Force History's *The United States Air Force in Southeast Asia, 1962-1973: An Illustrated Account*, edited by Carl Berger, and Phil Chinnery's *Air War in Vietnam* are less substantive, but still useful. All of these volumes are lavishly illustrated with photographs, maps and diagrams. For the teacher who is willing to make slides, these works are a treasure trove of pictures as well as a source of material that translates nicely into four or five 50-minute lectures.

General William W. Momyer's *Air Power in Three Wars* contains detailed information on weapons capabilities and tactics. His comments as to how the war was conducted are indicative of the thinking of most of the senior leadership during the conflict. Momyer feels strongly that if the military had been unimpeded by political constraints, air power could have ended the war quickly and on terms favorable to the United States and its South Vietnamese ally. Continuing along this line, the most forceful articulation of this "our hands were tied" thesis is found in U. S. Grant Sharp's *Strategy for Defeat*. These works need to be balanced by reading Raphael Littauer and Norman Uphoff's edited work, *The Air War in Indochina*, published by the Air War Study Group of Cornell University in 1972, or perhaps my own recent work, *Set-Up: What the Air Force Did in Vietnam and Why*.

There are five excellent books on bombing policy. Leslie H. Gelb and Richard K. Betts's *The Irony of Vietnam: The System Worked* and James Clay Thompson's *Rolling Thunder: Understanding Policy and Program Failure* need to be read in conjunction. I also recommend former Under Secretary of the Air Force Townsend Hoope's *The Limits of Intervention: An Inside Account of How the Johnson Policy of Escalation in Vietnam Was Reversed*. Two recently published volumes cover the air war in both South and North Vietnam. John C. Schlight's *The United States Air Force in Southeast Asia, The War in South Vietnam: The Years of the Offensive, 1965-1968*, part of the Air Force's official history series on Vietnam, covers the war over South Vietnam (where approximately four million tons of bombs fell). Probably the best book yet to appear on the air war against North Vietnam is USAF Major Mark Clodfelter's *The Limits of Air Power: The American Bombing of North Vietnam*.

The air war was dramatic, and four narratives are useful in getting a feel for what it was like to fly and fight in Southeast Asia. Retired Air Force Colonel Jack Broughton's *Thud Ridge*, written in 1969, reeks of bitterness directed not only at civilian policy-makers in the Johnson administration but also at the Air Force brass for not speaking out forcefully enough to ameliorate the constraints that, in his opinion, cost lives and denied aircrews the tactical latitude needed to bomb North Vietnam effectively. Broughton's second book, *Going Downtown: The War Against Hanoi and Washington*, written nearly two decades after the author's court martial and subsequent "forced" retirement, is less bitter and more balanced. In *Going Downtown*, Broughton focuses his anger on individual high ranking officers, branding many as self-serving careerists who never understood the nature of the war and who cared too little for the airmen flying against North Vietnam.

Broughton's is the perspective of the wing commander, the old warhorse who had flown and fought in three wars. G. I. Basel's *Pak Six* and Richard S. Drury's *My Secret War*, both narratives by junior, non-career officers, look at the war through the mil settings in their gunsights and in the shadow of the empty bunks in the squadron dormitories. These are exciting, but also poignant accounts.

Beginning in 1973, the Office of Air Force History undertook a multi-volume study of the air war. Most of the volumes, which tend to be specialized or focused on specific periods, are readily available to the public. Robert F. Futrell's *The United States Air Force in Southeast Asia: The Advisory Years to 1965*, along with Schlight's above-mentioned contribution to the same series, *The United States Air Force in Southeast Asia, The War in South Vietnam: The Years of the Offensive, 1965-1968*, cover the air war in South Vietnam, where most of the sorties were flown and half the bomb tonnages fell. Other excellent, albeit more specialized accounts, include Jack Ballard's *The Development and Deployment of Fixed-Wing Gunships*, William A. Buckingham, Jr.'s *Operation Ranch Hand: The Air Force and Herbicides in Southeast Asia, 1961-1971*, and Ray L. Bowers' *Tactical Airlift*. There are also volumes on air base defense and search and rescue operations.

For the teacher who becomes a student of the air war, or for the serious students in upper level undergraduate and graduate courses or seminars, the four-volume *The Pentagon Papers: The Defense Department History of Decision-making on Vietnam* edited by Senator Mike Gravel, and the five volumes of the *Hearings Before the Preparedness Investigation Subcommittee of the Committee on the Armed Services*, conducted in August 1967, and commonly referred to as "The Stennis Committee Hearings," are all valuable sources.

A significant problem in writing the history of the Vietnam War is that scholars are limited to one side of the story. At the end of the war there were no captured enemy archives to exploit nor interned officials to interview. Only a few books by North Vietnamese officials, such as Tran Van Tra's *Vietnam: A History of the Bulwark B-2 Theater: Concluding the Thirty Years War*, have appeared and none of these cover the air war. As yet, only a handful of American scholars have visited Vietnam and fewer have conducted research there. As for the air war, we are forced to rely on accounts by Americans and third-country nationals who were in Vietnam during the bombing. Because the only Americans who were in North Vietnam at the time were either anti-war activists or prisoners of war, there are problems with biases in their interpretations. Among the accounts by third country nationals, British diplomat John Colvin's "Hanoi in My Time," published in the spring 1981 edition of the *Washington Quarterly*, is probably the most useful.

Among books by Americans who traveled to North Vietnam during the bombing, Susan Sontag's *Trip to Hanoi*, Mary MacCarthy's *Hanoi* and Harrison E. Salisbury's *Behind the Lines - Hanoi* are worth reading, not so much for what is said about the bombing—which is predictable and wrong—but for the picture one gets of an embattled society coping with a form of warfare far beyond its technological capacity. Ideological biases, however, detract from the value of these books.

The other Americans in Hanoi during the bombing were prisoners of war. Their views of the air war are colored by individual ideological predilections that were, in many cases, intensified by years of torture and abuse at the hands of their captors. Generally the POW accounts credit the December 1972 bombing with bringing about their release.

Air power in "other wars" is more difficult to assess. Because of the sensitivity of operations in Laos and Cambodia, much of the information necessary to historical investigation remains classified. Works such as Arthur Dommen's *Laos: Keystone of Indochina* have little to do with air power. Norman B. Hannah's *The Key to Failure: Laos and the Vietnam War* is more enlightening, but it is not a history of aerial operations. John Clark Pratt's *The Laotian Fragments: The Chief Raven's Story*, while a historical novel, is a fine account of the role of the forward air controllers in the war over northern Laos. Christopher Robbins's, *Air America*, published in 1979, and his more recent book, *The Ravens: The Men Who Flew in America's Secret War in Laos*, are useful beginnings to understanding something of the nature of that covert war.

Cambodia presents a more difficult problem. William Shawcross's *Sideshow: Kissinger, Nixon and the Destruction of Cambodia*, remains a standard, if controversial, work in this field. Balance it with *Bombing in Cambodia: Hearings Before the Committee on Armed Services of the United States Senate's 93rd Congress*, and try to keep in mind that the Khmer Rouge, the Viet Cong and the North Vietnamese had as much to do with the fate of Cambodia as Richard Nixon and Henry Kissinger.

CONCLUSION

The air war is an intriguing topic, albeit a complicated and controversial one. The subject is as exciting to research as it is to teach. What is needed is twofold: scholarship that seeks to understand rather than to condemn or defend, and teachers who are dedicated to bringing knowledge to a generation too young to remember what went on—and what went wrong—in those turbulent years. To assist in the latter effort, an outline and bibliography of the air war is appended to this essay.

NOTES

1. Thomas C. Thayer, *War Without Fronts: The American Experience in Vietnam* (Boulder, Co.: Westview, 1985), pp. 25-26.

2. Ibid., p. 25.

3. See: Carl Berger, editor, *The United States Air Force in Southeast Asia, 1961-1973: An Illustrated Account* (Washington, D. C.: Office of Air Force History, 1984 edition), p. 369; and Phil Chinnery, *Air War in Vietnam* (New York: Exeter Books, 1987), p. 189.

4. See Gen. T. R. Milton, (USAF, retired), "The Lessons of Vietnam," *Air Force Magazine* (March 1983), p. 109. Writing in the January-February edition of *Air University Review*, p. 53, Lieutenant Colonel John F. Piowwaty, in "Reflections of a Thud Driver," expressed a similar viewpoint, "By the time President Nixon got serious and won in two weeks [referencing Linebacker II] what we could have done in any two weeks for nearly a decade, it was too late to hold the victory."

5. H. Bruce Franklin, "How American Management Won the War in Vietnam," *American Quarterly* (September 1988), p. 423.

6. Gloria Emerson, *Winners and Losers: Battles, Retreats, Gains, Losses and Ruins from a Long War* (New York: Random House, 1976), p. 42.

7. See: Testimony of Admiral Thomas Moorer, Chairman of the Joint Chiefs of Staff, 93rd Congress, 1st Session, 9-18 January 1973, House Committee on Appropriations, Subcommittee on Defense, p. 6; General William W. Momyer, *Air Power in Three Wars: World War II, Korea, and Vietnam* (Washington, D. C.: U. S. Government Printing Office, 1978), pp. 240-42; and Berger, *United States Air Force in Southeast Asia: An Illustrated Account*, pp. 95-96. Some scholars may be reluctant to accept government figures as documentation, at least without some degree of criticality. Mathematics coupled with an understanding of the capabilities of military hardware can be used to confirm the reliability of the U. S. government figures. There are 200 million pounds in 100,000 tons. That equates to 400,000 500-pound bombs, the standard munition used by B-52s for conventional bombing. There were about 450 B-52s in the Air Force inventory in late 1972, with approximately 200 of these deployed to Andersen Air Force Base, Guam and U-Tapao Royal Thai Air Force Base, Thailand, the only two installations from which B-52 missions were flown in Southeast Asia. The maximum bomb load for a B-52D, the version

modified to carry large conventional loads, was 84 500-pound bombs carried internally and either 21 five-hundred bombs or 18 750-pound bombs carried on underwing pylons. For the sake of argument, assume that each of the B-52s that struck north of the 20th parallel—and the ten sorties that bombed south of it—carried the maximum bomb loads of 105 500-pound bombs. The total bomb tonnage dropped by B-52s could not have exceeded 19,399 tons. Additionally, according to Admiral Moorer's congressional testimony, another 5,000 tons of bombs were dropped in 1,216 fighter-bomber sorties flown by the air force, navy, and marine corps. At the maximum capacity of 105 500-pound bombs it would require 3,810 B-52 sorties to drop 100,000 tons of bombs. The approximately 200 B-52s available for Linebacker II could not have performed such a feat in eleven days, especially since 155 of those bombers were based on Guam, requiring a 12-hour round trip to bomb North Vietnam and return.

8.   Henry Kissinger, *The White House Years* (Boston: Little, Brown, and Company, 1979), pp. 239-40.

9.   Alain C. Enthoven and K. Wayne Smith, *How Much Is Enough? Shaping the Defense Program, 1961-1969* (New York: Harper and Row, 1971), p. 14.

10.   Over the years, articles written by higher-ranking officers, especially general officers, became increasingly insipid. The problem did not resolve itself in the post-Vietnam era United States Air Force. See: Gen. Charles A. Gabriel, "The Air Force: Where We Are and Where We Are Going," *Air University Review* (January-February 1984), pp. 2-10; and Lt. Gen. James P. McCarthy, "SAC Looks to the Future," *Air University Review* (January-March 1986), pp. 13-23.

11.   LeMay quoted in Robert F. Futrell, *Ideas, Concepts, Doctrine: A History of Basic Thinking in the United States Air Force, 1907-1964* (Maxwell Air Force Base, Ala: Air University Press, 1974), p. 405.

12.   Many American scholars and journalists were duped by Hanoi's propaganda. For an excellent example, read Harrison E. Salisbury, *Behind Enemy Lines—Hanoi: December 23, 1966-January 7, 1967* (New York: Harper and Row, 1967), almost any page will do.

13.   See: *The Pentagon Papers: The Defense Department History of United States Decision-Making on Vietnam*, Senator Mike Gravel edition, volume 4, (Boston: Beacon Press, 1975), p. 24; and John Morocco, *The Vietnam Experience, Thunder from Above: The Air War, 1941-1968* (Boston: Boston Publishing Company, 1984), p. 107.

14.   See John L. Frisbee, "The Phoenix That Never Was," *Air Force Magazine* (February 1973), p. 4; John L. Frisbee, "Not with a Whimper but a Bang," *Air Force Magazine* (March 1973), pp. 5-6; and Martin W. Ostrow, "The B-52's Message to Moscow," *Air Force Magazine* (April 1973), p. 2.

15.   Gen. T. R. Milton (USAF, retired), "USAF and the Vietnam Experience," *Air Force Magazine* (June 1975), p. 56.

16. Gen. William W. Momyer (USAF, retired), *Air Power in Three Wars* (Washington: U. S. Government Printing Office, 1978), p. 339.

17. Gen. T. R. Milton, (USAF, retired), "The Lessons of Vietnam," *Air Force Magazine* (March 1983), p. 110.

18. Nguyen Tien Hung and Jerrold L. Schecter, *The Palace File* (New York: Harper and Row, 1986), pp. 196-204.

19. Hays Parks, "Linebacker and the Law of War," *Air University Review* (January-February 1983), p. 25.

20. George C. Herring, *America's Longest War: The United States in Vietnam, 1950-1975* (New York: Random House, 1979), p. 248.

21. Nancy Zaroulis and Gerald Sullivan, *Who Spoke Up: American Protest Against the War in Vietnam, 1962-1975* (New York: Holt, Rinehart, and Winston, 1985), p. 151.

AN OUTLINE OF THE AIR WAR

I.   The Advisory Phase (1961-1965)
     A. Farmgate
     B. Mule Train
     C. Ranch Hand

II. Rolling Thunder (1965-1968)
     A. Toward Bombing the North
     B. Operations
         1. Pressure Phase (March-July, 1965)
         2. Interdiction (August 1965-June 1966)
         3. Attack on Petroleum (June-September 1966)
         4. Isolating Hanoi (October 1966-1967)

III. Air Power and Vietnamization
     A. Tet Offensive and the Post-Tet Reaction
         1. Supporting the Ground Forces
         2. Air Power and the Siege at Khe Sanh
     B. Commando Hunt Operations
     C. Other Out-Country Operations
         1. Northern Laos
         2. Secret Bombing of Cambodia
         3. The Lavalle Affair

IV. 1972
     A. Linebacker I
     B. Linebacker II

V. 1973-1975
    A. Cambodia
    B. Fall of the South
    C. Final Considerations

SELECT BIBLIOGRAPHY OF THE AIR WAR

GENERAL

Berger, Carl, editor. *The United States Air Force in Southeast Asia: An Illustrated Account*. Washington, D. C.: Office of Air Force History, 1984 edition.

Chinnery, Phil. *Air War in Vietnam*. New York: Exeter Books, 1987.

Littauer, Raphael, and Uphoff, Norman, editors. *The Air War in Indochina*. Boston: Beacon Press, 1972.

Momyer, Gen. William W. *Air Power in Three Wars: World War II, Korea and Vietnam*. Washington, D. C.: Office of Air Force History, 1978.

Morocco, John. *The Vietnam Experience, Rain of Fire: The Air War, 1969-1973*. Boston: Boston Publishing Company, 1985.

———. *The Vietnam Experience, Thunder From Above: The Air War, 1941-1968*. Boston: Boston Publishing Company, 1984.

Tilford, Earl H., Jr. *Setup: What the Air Force did in Vietnam, and Why*. Maxwell Air Force Base, Ala.: Air University, 1991.

PRE-VIETNAM ERA AIR FORCE

Arnold, Henry. *Global Mission*. New York: Harper, 1949.

Brodie, Bernard. *Strategy in the Missile Age*. Princeton, N. J.: Princeton University Press, 1959.

Futrell, Robert F. *Ideas, Concepts, Doctrine: A History of Basic Thinking in the United States Air Force, 1907-1964*. Maxwell, Air Force Base, Ala.: Air University Press, 1971.

Kahn, Herman. *On Thermonuclear War*. Princeton, N. J.: Princeton, University Press, 1967.

Kissinger, Henry A. *Nuclear Weapons and Foreign Policy*. New York: Council on Foreign Relations, 1957.

Overy, R. J. *The Air War: 1939-1945*. New York: Stein and Day, 1980.

AIR POWER IN THE FRENCH INDOCHINA WAR

Christienne, Charles, and Lissarrague, Pierre. *A History of French Military Aviation*. Washington, D. C.: Smithsonian Institution, 1986.

Fall, Bernard B. *Hell in a Very Small Place: The Siege at Dien Bien Phu*. New York: Harper and Row, 1967.

"The Korean War Speaks to the Indo-China War," A Quarterly Review Staff Study, *Air University Quarterly Review*, Spring 1954.

Leary, William M. *Perilous Missions: Civil Air Transport and Central Intelligence Agency (CIA) Cover Operations in Asia*. Tuscaloosa: University of Alabama Press, 1984.

Prados, John. *The Sky Would Fall: Operation Vulture: The U. S. Bombing Mission in Indochina, 1954*. New York: Morrow, 1984.

THE ADVISORY YEARS

Futrell, Robert F. *The United States Air Force in Southeast Asia, The Advisory Years to 1965*. Washington, D. C.: Office of Air Force History, 1981.

ROLLING THUNDER

Basel, G. I. *Pak Six*. La Mesa, Calif.: Associated Creative Writers, 1982.

Broughton, Jack. *Going Downtown: The War Against Hanoi and Washington*. New York: Orion Books, 1988.

Broughton, Jack. *Thud Ridge*. Philadelphia: Lippincott, 1969.

Clodfelter, Mark. *The Limits of Air Power: The American Bombing of North Vietnam*. New York: Free Press, 1989.

Gelb, Leslie H. and Betts, Richard K. *The Irony of Vietnam: The System Worked*. Washington, D. C.: Brookings, 1979.

Gravel, Senator Mike, editor. *The Pentagon Papers: The Defense Department History of Decision-making on Vietnam*, 4 volumes. Boston: Beacon Press, 1971.

Gropman, Col. Alan C. "Lost Opportunities: The Air War in Vietnam, 1961-1973," in Grinter, Lawrence E., editor. *The American War in Vietnam: Lessons, Legacies, and Implications for Future Conflicts*. Westport, Conn.: Greenwood, 1988.

Hoope, Townsend. *The Limits of Intervention: An Inside Account of How the Johnson Policy of Escalation in Vietnam was Reversed*. New York: David McKay, 1969.

Sharp, U. S. *Strategy for Defeat: Vietnam in Retrospect*. San Raphael, Calif.: Presidio, 1978.

Thompson, James Clay. *Rolling Thunder: Understanding Policy and Program Failure.* Chapel Hill: University of North Carolina Press, 1980.

Tilford, Earl H., Jr. "Air Power in Vietnam: The Hubris of Power," in Grinter, Lawrence E., editor. *The American War in Vietnam: Lessons, Legacies, and Implications for Future Conflicts.* Westport, Conn.: Greenwood, 1988.

AIR POWER IN SOUTH VIETNAM, LAOS AND CAMBODIA

Drury, Richard S. *My Secret War.* New York: St. Martin's, 1979.

Gibson, James William. *The Perfect War: Technowar in Vietnam.* Boston: Atlantic Monthly Press, 1986. chapters 11-13.

Mickish, Robert C. *Flying Dragons: The South Vietnamese Air Force.* London: Osprey Publishers, Ltd. 1988.

Nalty, Bernard C. *Air Power and the Fight for Khe Sanh.* Washington, D. C.: Office of Air Force History, 1974.

Pratt, John Clark. *The Laotian Fragments: The Chief Raven's Story.* New York: Viking, 1974 (historical novel).

Robbins, Christopher. *Air America.* New York: G.P. Putnam, 1979.

———. *The Ravens: The Men Who Flew in America's Secret War in Laos.* New York: Crown Publishers, 1987.

Schlight, John. *The United States Air Force in Southeast Asia, The War in South Vietnam: The Years of the Offensive, 1965-1968.* Washington, D. C.: Office of Air Force History, 1989.

Shawcross, William. *Sideshow: Kissinger, Nixon, and the Destruction of Cambodia.* New York: Simon and Schuster, 1979.

SPECIALTY BOOKS

Ballard, Jack S. *The Development and Deployment of Fixed-Wing Gunships, 1962-1972.* Washington, D. C.: Office of Air Force History, 1982.

Bowers, Ray L. *The United States Air Force in Southeast Asia: Tactical Airlift.* Washington, D. C.: Office of Air Force History, 1983.

Buckingham, William A., Jr. *Operation Ranch Hand: The Air Force and Herbicides in Southeast Asia, 1961-1971.* Washington, D. C.: Office of Air Force History, 1982.

Dramesi, John A. *A Code of Honor.* New York: Norton, 1975.

McCarthy, James R., et al. *Linebacker II: A View from the Rock.* Maxwell Air Force Base, Ala.: Airpower Research Institute, 1979.

Risner, Robinson. *The Passing of the Night: My Seven Years as a Prisoner of the North Vietnamese.* New York: Random House, 1974.

Schemmer, Benjamin F. *The Raid.* New York: Harper and Row, 1976.

Tilford, Earl H., Jr. *A History of U. S. Air Force Search and Rescue Operations in Southeast Asia, 1961-1975*. Washington, D. C.: Office of Air Force History, 1982.

3

Teaching "People's Wars of National Liberation"
CECIL B. CURREY

During and since the Vietnam War, American military analysts have debated whether this conflict should be regarded as a guerilla war or a conventional war. This debate may have been, and may remain, misplaced due to America's inability then and now to understand the nature of what its opponents called "people's wars of national liberation," a theory of revolutionary action that at once transcended and allowed for the exploitation of both irregular and regular modes of combat operations.

In the early years of America's involvement in Southeast Asia, Edward Lansdale, voiced an understanding of the power and complexity of people's wars, but few heeded his warnings. This essay utilizes Lansdale's writings on the subject to illuminate the nature of people's wars, and explore its appeal and ideological roots. It will also describe a means of bringing this subject alive in the classroom, suggest sources for its study and identify the place of people's wars in the current debate over the lessons of the Vietnam War.

AN AMERICAN LOOKS AT PEOPLE'S WARS

In the early years of America's struggle in Vietnam, the Central Intelligence Agency sent one of the military's most insightful intelligence analysts, Edward G. Lansdale, to Saigon. His assignment was to disrupt the onward march of the government of Ho Chi Minh and to establish a noncommunist nation south of the temporary line along the 17th parallel that had been drawn across the land by the nations meeting in Geneva. An expert on unconventional and guerilla warfare, Lansdale was one of the first to realize that the conflict in Vietnam was different from other wars the United States had fought.

At that time and through all the years since, military training received by officers in America's armed forces concentrated on preventing a penetration by mechanized and motorized Soviet armies in case they struck west across the Iron Curtain in a surprise attack toward the Rhine River along the Hof Corridor or through the Fulda Gap. Such an assault, Lansdale would later lecture, was "a future war which may or may not happen." It made more sense, he believed, to focus "on the dirty, half-hidden war that is going on now—not on a future possibility. This [presently existing] war has [new] combat rules of its own [and] offers us a chance to learn these rules."[1]

Speaking some years later to a class of U. S. Air Force Academy cadets, Lansdale reminded his listeners of the hoary old military precept: "Take the high ground." Throughout history, he said, the terrain of a battlefield has been of crucial importance to warring parties. Armies attacked dominant terrain features so that those who held them could control avenues of approach and canalization. Terrain held the key both in the attack and in the defense. Lansdale pointed out that this was no longer true. Hills, cities, rivers, valleys and forests, even fortresses and bunkers, no longer counted. The paramount object of America's enemies, he warned, was to gain the loyalty of people who inhabited the land in the areas they sought to control.

The sole purpose of such enemies, Lansdale said, was "to win these people. When they are won, along with them go the terrain, the wealth of the land, the whole existence of the nation."[2] He put the matter in similar terms when he spoke to men training at the United States Army's Special Warfare School at Ft. Bragg: the goal of such enemies "is to win control of the people. Along with them go the land, its bounty, the independent life of the nation."[3]

If America's enemies obtained popular loyalty and the governmental army they opposed secured for itself an overwhelming superiority in fortified defensive positions, in tanks, planes, artillery and numbers of soldiers, that government would still ultimately fall. If Americans—civilian leaders and military generals alike—would only understand this basic fact, they "might awaken to how important a factor is their consideration of human behavior in the decisions they made. Always they ought to ask themselves, 'What will the people's reaction [be] to this proposed action?'"[4]

Lansdale insisted that of all the names given to those armed struggles around the world that seemed constantly to draw the attention and sometimes the intervention of the United States—insurgency, revolution, rebellion, guerrilla warfare, brushfire wars, wars of national liberation, low-intensity conflicts, foreign internal defense—"probably the name 'people's wars' is the one most useful."[5] This assessment made Lansdale one of the very few active serving military officers to hold a proper understanding of the basic nature of such conflicts.

THE ORIGINS OF PEOPLE'S WARS

Today, more than twenty years after Lansdale served his last tour of duty in Vietnam, Americans still have a difficult time understanding people's wars. We fail to see that they begin in the minds of those who have been rejected by their own governments, who know hopelessness and frustration and unchanging, grinding repression. There has always arisen a leader, a prophet, willing to lead such *misérables* in a quest to overthrow the existing power structure.

Despite the fact that no one should ever confuse the social and political conditions of the English Atlantic colonies of the eighteenth century with those that exist today in many third- and fourth-world nations, even the people of America once fought in such a cause. Our own Declaration of Independence sounds Jefferson's clarion call: "whenever any form of government becomes destructive of these ends, it is the right of the people to alter or to abolish it, and to institute new government, laying its foundation on such principles, and organizing its powers in such form, as to them shall seem most likely to effect their safety and happiness." British Colonists in America—our forebears—*believed* that their government in London had become destructive of their rights, and they rebelled. That action set an example to which many later revolutions have appealed, even when circumstances have been far different.

Those Americans who forget their revolutionary past might ask themselves the following questions. How would you react if soldiers stole your chickens or pigs or personal belongings—maybe roughing you up and having sport with your wife or daughter in the process? How would you feel if you faced a debt incurred by your grandfather from some greedy moneylender and you knew your own grandchildren would still be paying away at its grossly inflated amount with no hope of ever reducing the sum? What would you think if political leaders posed as men of integrity, but you saw them living "high on the hog," buying property and jewelry and expensive cars—all on a low government salary—and thus obviously, hoggishly corrupt? No amount of official rhetoric and propaganda can overcome a stolen chicken, debilitating taxes, or a carelessly driven jeep. What would you do if *every* act of your government, your police, your army, was a repressive one aimed at you and your family and others like you? What might be your attitude if you realized that *any* word of criticism might bring disappearance, torture and death not only to yourself but to those you loved? It is out of such circumstances that people's wars arise.

Former President of the Philippines Ramon Magsaysay was one of the few to realize how desperate must be those who rise in rebellion against their own government. "When a man is prepared to give up his life to overthrow [it]," he said, "he must first have suffered greatly." Magsaysay realized that "those who have less in life must have more in law."[6] In the few short years of his presidency, he tried manfully to raise Filipino standards of living, but he died in a plane crash before he could accomplish much. His successors reverted to more repressive ways.

In the decades since World War II, most of those who hoped to challenge their own governments have taken Marxism to heart and espoused communism in one form or another. They have also looked for ideological direction to Mao Zedong of China, often (and incorrectly) thought of as the "father" of people's wars. They cite Mao's deeply held beliefs about the correct way to treat civilians in combat areas. The Chinese revolutionary taught his soldiers three cardinal measures: act in accordance with others, do not take anything from people, do not allow self-interest to injure public interest.

Mao also insisted on "eight noteworthy points" to be used in order to retain the support of people in areas he was contesting. Put back the door [after using it as a bed]. Tie up straws [after using them for a mattress]. Talk pleasantly. Buy and sell fairly. Return everything borrowed. Indemnify everything damaged. Do not bathe in view of women. Do not rob personal belongings of captives. Mao knew that only by such behavior could revolutionary armies create an appropriate relationship between themselves and the people of a countryside. "There are those who cannot imagine how guerrillas could survive for long," Mao taught, "but they do not understand the relationship between the people and the army. The people are like the water and the army is like the fish. How can it be difficult for the fish to survive when there is water?"[7]

A more apt individual to look to who has headed a people's war might well be the Vietnamese general Vo Nguyen Giap. He took the revolutionary ideas of Mao and developed them into a systematic form of struggle. The system he developed will be the one America may face on the field of battle for many decades to come. He is worth knowing.

His "army" began as a collection of rag-tag, ill-armed, barefoot peasants. Yet Giap provided Ho Chi Minh with military victory over both the French empire and the armed forces of the United States. Starting with only 34 men, he could later boast of divisions. His approach emphasized the tri-partite nature of people's wars. First came guerrilla warfare, then mobile warfare, then counterattack and final confrontation. The French did their best, but it was not enough. At Dien Bien Phu in 1954 they finally realized that victory was beyond their grasp and they made preparations to depart.

America's response to the French withdrawal was to send hundreds, then thousands, then hundreds of thousands of troops to fight against

Vietnamese enemies. Lansdale had known better. He was firmly convinced of the aphorism that "the best weapon to use against a guerrilla is a knife; the worst is a bomber. The second best is a rifle; the second worst is artillery."[8] America chose to rely on air power and artillery when it fought in Vietnam. It also saw fit to create a massive collection of governmental alphabet agencies there: among them were CORDS, CIA, USIA, USIS, MAAGs and MACVs. The agencies overwhelmed recipients with large headquarters complexes and warehouses, hordes of staff personnel, fleets of vehicles and extensive housing and recreation sites. A surge of hard-charging can-do American advisers and field representatives spread across the military zones. They stifled Vietnamese initiative. American leaders relied heavily on military solutions in a war that begged for political answers. One observer has written that "we mostly sought to destroy enemy forces. The enemy sought to gain control of the people."[9] Each side pursued its goal until America left Vietnam in frustration and anger over its inability to bring the war to a successful conclusion.

As early as 1964, Lansdale had warned of the possibility of such an outcome. "The harsh fact," he wrote, "is that, despite the use of overwhelming amounts of men, money and material, despite the quantity of well-meant American advice and despite the impressive statistics of casualties inflicted on the Vietcong, the Communist subversive insurgents . . . still retain the initiative to act at their will in the very areas of Vietnam where Vietnamese and American efforts have been most concentrated."[10] What he observed in 1964 became increasingly apparent in the nine years that followed.

One of this century's most insightful theoreticians of guerrilla warfare explained what happened. Robert Taber wrote *The War of the Flea* in 1965, just as President Lyndon B. Johnson was beginning to send massive numbers of American troops to Vietnam. The United States Army purchased large quantities of this book for internal distribution, yet its leaders paid scant heed to the text. Guerrilla warfare, Taber said, is "the single sure method by which an unarmed population can overcome mechanized armies, or, failing to overcome them, can stalemate them and make them irrelevant." He insisted that there "is only one means of defeating an insurgent people who will not surrender, and that is extermination. There is only one way to control a territory that harbors resistance, and this is to turn it into a desert. Where these means cannot, for whatever reason, be used, the war is lost."[11]

Sir Robert Thompson agreed. This British expert on counter-guerrilla warfare in Malaya wrote that "where a guerrilla force enjoys support from the people, whether willing or forced, it can never be defeated by military means, however much it is harassed and attacked, shelled, mortared, and bombed by superior forces of infantry and artillery, air and sea power."[12] It was a difficult lesson for America to learn and consequently we withdrew from Vietnam in early 1973. Two years later, armies of the North swept into Saigon, and the southern government fell. Vietnam was unified at last.

CLASSROOM APPROACHES

After a general orientation covering theory and practice of guerrilla warfare, I play a game with my class. I state that if they were launching forth on a real-life endeavor, everyone in a 60-person class would be dead within five years. I then have them organize themselves into guerrilla cells, with only one person in each cell knowing the name of someone in another cell. After organizing, I act as a police authority and try to trace through the cells to locate the leader of the entire group. They can see in a practical way how difficult it is to eradicate guerrillas.

Each cell then makes plans to disrupt and ultimately destroy the civilian government in the county in which we live: usual offerings include assassination, kidnapping and arson. I suggest to them at this point that the one thing that keeps an American government in power is faith on the part of the people that tomorrow will be much the same as today: trust in continuity. If that is lost, then so will be the ability of the government to retain authority and power.

I then suggest other things guerrillas might do: seek jobs in crucial businesses such as radio, television and newspapers, in computer-dependent services such as power and telephone companies, and in police and fire departments. Guerrillas in such positions can wreak quiet havoc in community life. By this point, students are ready to become more imaginative. They talk of black propaganda and psychological warfare, of securing the allegiance of the populace around them. They learn that acts of terror against others can be redirected to reflect badly upon the government and bring popularity upon themselves. They talk of meeting places, messages, ways to secure weaponry, safe houses, and base camps. In a two-hour setting, students begin to perceive the complexities of organization and life as a partisan of people's wars.

SOURCES

There are a great number of available sources that can be extremely valuable in teaching this aspect of the Vietnam conflict. The oldest and still the best is that by Sun Tzu, who wrote *The Art of War* some six hundred years before the common era. It is available in several editions. There is a paperback version by Samuel B. Griffiths, who served as translator and who wrote an introduction to the edition published in 1963 by Oxford University Press. Another effort is that by James Clavell, who served as editor and wrote a foreword, published by Delacorte Press in 1983 and 1988. Lastly, Leon Cyens served as editor and wrote an introduction to a translation by Lionel Ciles that was published in 1988 by Chelonia Press. The aphorisms of Sun Tzu, while they relate directly to organized armies, also provide much wisdom for those who would wage people's wars. The second oldest source is probably unavailable in all save specialized libraries. This source is Roger Stevenson, *Military Instructions for Officers Detached in the Field: Containing a Scheme for Forming a Corps of a Partisan, Illustrated with Plans of the Maneuvers Necessary in Carrying on the Petite Guerre* (Philadelphia: Aitken Publishers, 1775). This 232-page book includes 12 plates and was the first book carrying a dedication to George Washington. Very rare, it was probably the first book on partisan warfare published in America. (A copy was recently advertised for sale at $2950!)

Modern works abound. The best include two by Mao Zedong: *Selected Military Writings* (Beijing: Foreign Language Press, 1963) and *Basic Tactics* (translated by S. R. Schram; New York: Praeger, 1966). Also study Vo Nguyen Giap, *Initial Failure of the U. S. Limited War* (1967); *Once Again We will Win* (1966) and *South Vietnam: A Great Victory* (1967), all by Foreign Languages Publication House of Hanoi. Instructors should be certain to read as well his *People's Wars, People's Army* (New York: Praeger, 1962). Although full of propaganda and poorly organized, these books provide insight into the mind of this tactician. Helpful also is Ho Chi Minh, *On Revolution* (New York: Praeger, 1967). Other books that should be studied include Regis Debray, *Revolution in the Revolution?* (New York: Monthly Review Press, 1967) and Che Guevara, *Guerrilla Warfare* (New York: 1961).

Familiarity with the works of Bernard Fall are basic for an understanding of the errors made by the French in Indochina when they found themselves faced with a people's war. See *The Two Viet-Nams* (New York: Praeger, 1964), *Street Without Joy* (Harrisburg, Penn.: Stackpole Press, 1964) and any other of his works that may come to hand.

Four books that describe much that went wrong in Vietnam due to ignorance on the part of the American military include Loren Baritz, *Backfire: A History of How American Culture Led Us into Vietnam and Made Us Fight the Way We Did* (New York: Morrow, 1985); James William Gibson, *The Perfect War: Technowar in Vietnam* (Boston: Atlantic Monthly Press, 1986), Andrew F. Krepinevich, Jr., *The Army and Vietnam* (Baltimore: Johns Hopkins Press, 1986) and my own *Self-Destruction: The Disintegration and Decay of the United States Army During the Vietnam Era* (New York: Norton, 1981), written under the pseudonym of "Cincinnatus."

Robert Taber, *The War of the Flea: A Study of Guerrilla Warfare, Theory and Practice* (New York: Citadel Press, 1965) is the single best work on people's war in action. Two books show how endemic people's wars have been in the last four decades: Douglas S. Blaufarb, *The Counterinsurgency Era: U. S. Doctrine and Performance, 1950 to the Present* (New York: Glencoe Free Press, 1977) and Robert B. Asprey, *War in the Shadows,* 2 volumes (Garden City, N. Y.: Doubleday, 1975). William J. Lederer, *Our Own Worst Enemy* (New York: Norton, 1968) shows in real detail and with deeply felt concern how we supplied the Vietnamese enemy forces with most of their needs during the period of American intervention there. My own *Edward Lansdale: The Unquiet American* (Boston: Houghton Mifflin, 1989) tells the story of Lansdale's life and his vision for America in Asia and covers in detail his understanding of people's wars and how he would address them.

THE DEBATE GOES ON

In recent years, an influential commentator on military affairs, Colonel Harry Summers, has argued that Americans in Vietnam were misled by "the fashionable new model of Communist revolutionary war" into fighting against guerrillas, who were a secondary enemy, leaving untouched the enemy's real power, its conventional forces.[13] We thus paved the road that their tanks eventually travelled into Saigon in 1975. The concept of people's wars, in Summers's view, is a mere canard, for the guerrilla force in Vietnam, the Viet Cong, "did not achieve any results on its own."[14]

Summer's assertions are fiercely contested by several respected military historians, including John M. Gates.[15] Gates contends that Summers's argument betrays a lack of understanding of people's wars. Gates explains that the chief architects of people's wars, Mao Tse-Tung, Vo Nguyen Giap and Troung Chinh "all commented upon the need for revolutionaries to move from guerrilla to mobile warfare, and they also identified mobile or conventional warfare as the more important and necessary for success."[16] "Mao," Gates notes, called guerrilla forces supplementary because it could "not shoulder the main responsibility in deciding the outcome."[17] According to Giap and others, the decisive role was to be played by regular forces, as indeed they did in 1975. Gates reminds us that "according to [counter-insurgency expert Sir Robert Thompson], the defeat of the government forces *'by the regular forces of the insurgents . . . in conventional battle' constituted a 'classical ending in accordance with the orthodox theory.'*" Thus, Summers clearly errs in thinking that revolutionary war theory "implied that the Viet Cong would achieve decisive results on its own."[18]

Gates also challenges Summers's contention that America focused on the "wrong war: counter-insurgency." It is clear from Lansdale's failure to mold American policy in Vietnam, a failure evidenced by General Westmoreland's relegation of the "other war" (pacification) to secondary status, that American forces were not "overly involved in a campaign of counter-insurgency."[19]

In words that could have been Lansdale's own, Gates states that the "real key" to the Vietnam War or any war is "not the analysis in the way in which the war was fought, but a study of the people involved and their reasons for fighting."[20] The goal of the communists in Vietnam was revolution, and the fire provided by revolutionary goals was what made their forces formidable, not its tactics or form of content. Summers's inability to perceive what Gates holds to be the true nature of people's wars may be of considerable import. Noting that Summers's work is used as a text for the training of American military officers, Gates expresses a concern that "instead of forcing the military to come to grips with the problem of revolutionary warfare that now exists in Guatemala or El Salvador, Summers's analysis leads officers back to the conventional war model that provided so little preparation for solving the problems forced in Indochina by the French, the Americans, and their Vietnamese allies."[21]

CONCLUSION

It is clear from the Summers-Gates debate that revolutionary warfare is a fascinating and complex issue, challenging to students and essential if they are to understand not only what went wrong for France and the United States in Southeast Asia but what the major challenge will be for American armed forces in the coming decades.

NOTES

1. Edward G. Lansdale's work with Ramon Magsaysay in the Philippines against the communist-backed Huk rebellion there was well known in and had been fully supported by top governmental circles in Washington. He returned to Washington from that assignment early in January 1954, but did not remain long in the United States. On the eighth of that month President Dwight Eisenhower called to order a meeting of the National Security Council (NSC), on the agenda of which was the issue of French problems in Indochina. During that meeting, Eisenhower warned that "this war in Indochina would absorb our troops by divisions." (This remark is recorded in the "Foreign Relations of the United States," quoted in L. Fletcher Prouty, "The CIA's Saigon Military Mission," *Freedom*, December 1965, p. 20). Still, the president believed that he should do something. Both he and his secretary of state, John Foster Dulles, were impressed by Lansdale's work in the Philippines and thought similar tactics might effectively change the situation in Vietnam.

At a second meeting of the NSC on 14 January, those present agreed with the president that Allen Dulles, director of the Central Intelligence Agency, in cooperation with his brother, John Foster Dulles, who served as secretary of state, should develop contingency plans for American action in Indochina. The Dulles brothers talked further about Edward Lansdale. On 29 January, the President's Special Committee on Indochina met to talk over plans for helping the French. Lansdale was present, as were both Dulles brothers and Admiral Arthur S. Radford, Chairman of the Joint Chiefs of Staff. During that meeting, John Foster Dulles turned to Lansdale and said, "We're going to send you over there. . . . I want you to do [there] what you did in the Philippines." "So," Lansdale recounted to this writer in an interview on May 16, 1984, "I went and actually tried to do my best to do what I thought I had done in the Philippines to help the Filipinos." See also David Wise and Thomas B. Ross, *The Invisible Government* (New York: Random House, 1964), p. 156; Edward G. Lansdale, *In the Midst of Wars: An American's Mission to Southeast Asia* (New York: Harper and Row, 1972), p. 127; John Prados, *The Sky Would Fall: Operation Vulture—The U. S. Bombing Mission in Indochina, 1954* (New York: Dial, 1983), pp. 471ff. For Lansdale's views on the nature of people's wars, see his speech entitled "Southeast Asia," 3 December 1958, Army War College, Carlisle Barracks, Pennsylvania, Mimeographed, 8 pp., in The Lansdale Papers, Hoover Institution for War, Revolution and Peace, Stanford University, Palo Alto, California. Hereafter cited as LP, THIWRP.

2. For his address to cadets at the USAF Academy, see "The Insurgent Battlefield," 25 May 1962, Air Force Academy, Colorado Springs, Colorado. Mimeographed, 9 pp., LP, THIWRP.

3. Memorandum for Secretary [Robert] McNamara/Deputy Secretary [Roswell] Gilpatric, 16 April 1962, Correspondence, United States Department of Defense, Office of the Secretary of Defense, Box 40, LP, THIWRP.

4. A copy of this speech, entitled "People's Wars: Three Primary Lessons," was given to students at the Air War College at Maxwell Air Force Base, Montgomery, Alabama on 15 January 1973. A mimeographed copy may be consulted in LP, THIWRP.

5. Ibid.

6. Interview, Senator Manuel Manahan with Cecil B. Currey, 24 July 1985, Manila, Republic of the Philippines. Manahan was one of Magasaysay's closest friends and supporters.

7. I have derived Mao's Three Cardinal Measures and Eight Noteworthy Points, as well as his analogy about fish and water from Lansdale, "Southeast Asia."

8. Quoted in Roger Hilsman, *To Move a Nation: The Politics of Foreign Policy in the Administration of John F. Kennedy* (Garden City, NY: Doubleday, 1967), p. 453. In several of my personal discussions with Lansdale this phrase came up, and he inevitably concurred that it summarized much wisdom. See Cecil B. Currey, *Edward Lansdale: The Unquiet American* (Boston: Houghton Mifflin, 1988), *passim.*

9. Carl F. Bernard, "The War in Vietnam: Observations and Reflections of a Province Senior Advisor," U. S. Army Command and General Staff College Student Paper, 1969.

10. In a 1964 foray into public print, Lansdale wrote this jaundiced view of the progress of the war in Vietnam. He admitted that his choice of outlet was an unusual one in which to air his views, describing the magazine as one for "stuffed shirts and intellectuals—strange company for me—but the group that has a lot to do in shaping opinion towards our policies abroad." Consequently, he chose *Foreign Affairs* as a way to "strike at their thinking through one of their own bibles." For these quotes, see letter, Edward Lansdale to Peter C. Richards, 17 October 1964, private collection of Lansdale correspondence, Manila, Republic of the Philippines, and Letter, Edward Lansdale to Samuel T. Williams,, 10 October, 1964, William Papers, Box 10, LP, THIWRP. For the quote from the article, see Edward G. Lansdale, "Viet Nam: Do We Understand Revolution?" *Foreign Affairs*, XLIII (October 1964), p. 76.

11. Robert Taber, *The War of the Flea: A Study of Guerrilla Warfare, Theory and Practice* (New York: Citadel Press, 1965), p. 11.

12. Cited in Hilsman, *To Move a Nation*, p. 430.

13. Harry G. Summers, Jr., "A Strategic Perception of the Vietnam War," *Parameters*, 13 (June 1983), pp. 41-46, summarizes Summers' argument, as does "Vietnam Reconsidered." *The New Republic*, 12 July 1982, pp. 25-31. A more extensive presentation is contained in Summers' book, *On Strategy: A Critical Analysis of the Vietnam War* (Novato, Calif.: Presidio, 1982).

14. Summers, "A Strategic Perception of the Vietnam War," p. 42.

15. John M. Gates, "Vietnam: The Debate Goes On," Parameters 15 (Spring 1985), pp. 77-83; Peter M. Dunn, "On Strategy Revisited: Clausewitz and Revolutionary War," and Noel C. Eggleston, "On Lessons: A Critique of the Summers Thesis," in Lawrence Grinter and Peter Dunn, editors, *The American War in Vietnam: Lessons, Legacies and Implications for Future Conflicts* (Westport, Conn.: Greenwood, 1987) pp. 95-109, and 109-126.

16. Gates, "Vietnam: The Debate Goes On," p. 16.

17. Ibid.

18. Ibid.

19. Ibid., p. 21. Gates notes that Richard A. Hunt and Richard H. Schultz, Jr., editors, *Lessons from an Unconventional War: Reasoning U. S. Strategies for Future Conflicts* (New York: Pergamon, 1982) and Douglas S. Blaufarb, The Counterinsurgency Era: U. S. Doctrine and Performance 1950 to the present (New York: The Free Press, 1977) "make it clear that the American approach in Vietnam was not in harmony with counter-insurgency theory."

20. Ibid., p. 17

21. Ibid.

4

A Decision-Making Approach to Understanding American Policy-Makers

JOHN JAMES MacDOUGALL

From 1976 on I have intermittently taught or prepared an introductory course for undergraduates that focussed partly on the causes of America's failure in Vietnam. As a result of my experiences as a soldier in post-war Korea, as a Foreign Service officer in Cambodia, as an academic specialist in Southeast Asian politics, and as a former researcher for the U. S. Department of Defense who had conducted contract research on the Vietnam War from 1970 to 1973, I became persuaded that America failed in Vietnam in large part because our "best and brightest" decision-makers were incapable—for a host of reasons beyond their control—of understanding and coping with their Vietnamese enemy. When I sought to create a class on the Vietnam era, I found that a course which took the failure of American foreign policy-making on the Vietnam War as its theme would allow me to distill a mass of information on this complex subject without grossly oversimplifying it in a course for undergraduates ignorant of the war itself.

After reviewing the available literature, I concluded that American policy-makers in the 1960-1968 period of the war against Vietnam failed because they demonstrated salient behavioral characteristics that defined them as "technocrats." As highly rational, economically calculating, politically obedient and dependent technocrats, such policy-makers, as described by Theodore Roszak,[1] Michael Macoby[2] and Robert Presthus,[3] seemed, in my view, extremely unlikely to diagnose and to control successfully the motivations of Vietnamese opponents who differed from them in so many ways. In the 1960s, successful and calculating American policy-makers, from the highest ramparts of a secure global military and economic power, were ill-equipped to understand the remote motivations of obscure, lifelong revolutionaries who had sacrificed whatever they possessed for a political crusade. In the period 1960-1968, America's "best and brightest" despite brilliant achievements in their own high tech, economically ordered, rational world seemed to have been virtually predestined to fail to control determined revolutionaries and irrational events that were so remote from their mode of understanding.

Several American writers including David Halberstam,[4] Irving L. Janis,[5] Larry Berman,[6] Charles W. Kegley and Eugene R. Wittkopf[7] and James C. Thomson[8] have explicitly or otherwise described America's policy-makers as technocrats in order to explain how they failed. I decided to make their works the basis of my course. I relied most heavily on Halberstam. I also relied upon audio-visual materials mentioned below.

AN OVERVIEW OF THE COURSE

The first two weeks of the course are devoted to the study of a theoretical explanation of technocrats and the technocratic mind-set. According to Theodore Roszak, the world has changed over time and created two very different kinds of elites.[9] In contrast to the elites of the traditional or pre-industrial, natural world, there have emerged new, modern, technocratic elites who are extremely successful in solving technical-economic problems amenable to the practical, material solutions of science. Despite their excellent educations and their diligence, these ultra-rational technocrats have not been successful in coping with eternal political-value problems that involve irrational, passionate emotions, total moral or ideological commitment and profound questions of justice and fairness.[10] In the imprecise world of politics where factual data is inadequate, where issues are ambiguous and where commitments are open-ended, a technocratic policy-maker relying almost entirely on facts, hard data, and logical analysis can dangerously misdiagnose problems and fatally misprescribe solutions. Roszak's work contains a stern warning to technocratic decision-makers to be extremely cautious in approaching political-value problems of which they are profoundly ignorant or for which they have very poor data; he warns them against acting with their usual confidence or hubris and speed in prescribing well-intentioned solutions based on their drives to act and to control events.

In his rich portrait of the ideal technocrat, Roszak describes a peculiar behavioral type of managerial personality in terms that are strikingly similar to those attributed to American policy-makers for Vietnam by Halberstam and by Kegley and Wittkopf. Roszak's abstract technocrat has many admirable traits: he is a highly disciplined, well-educated man, but he places his faith in technological solutions to all problems and understands reality as something to be controlled and improved. Toughminded, cool and realistic, a technocrat is a hard man who approaches reality unemotionally, impersonally and amorally or without direct reference to ordinary ethical concerns. Uninterested in profound questions of justice or morality, he is unmotivated and indifferent to the power of such concerns over others.

Incurious about the most deeply held subjective religious and emotional values of others, he relies for understanding on such objective analytic tools as statistics and systems analysis.[11]

Technocrats are new men who are ruled not by turbulent political or moral passions or emotions, but by carefully calculated judgments based on hard factual evidence linked to logical theoretical assumptions. Uncaptured by any explicit religious or ideological formulas, technocrats are free to adapt whatever ideological or other propositions are forced on them by the political authorities who rule and employ them.[12] In the age of management and science, technocrats successfully apply abundant hard-headed solutions to many material-technical problems.

Unfortunately, they are also eager to apply their hard-won, impersonal analytical skills and solutions in moral-ethical-political arenas of understanding that are still incomprehensible to personalities who wrestle deeply and daily with them. Unlike ordinary individuals who are made prudent and cautious by their daily efforts to resolve puzzling age-old political problems of justice and value, technocrats intervene boldly with relatively unfeeling or deadening managerial hands to apply their technical solutions with supreme confidence.[13]

As relatively detached, analytical, unconstrained and capable problem-solvers, technocrats dare to make mistakes; they work hard and produce much; they work with like-minded teams of peers and subordinates and avoid, isolate or exclude individuals bearing contrary values, assumptions or priorities. Technocrats, lacking much personal charisma and any independent political base, are and must be loyal to whatever authorities employ them; they are impatient with unrealistic or soft-hearted dissenters who are unwilling to recognize and accept the real political, ideological, material and other constraints that bind them and shape their decisions. As active managers and innovative members of a closed and constrained community, technocrats speak their own shorthand jargons and communicate with discretion. Busy, energetic and projecting an air of certainty, these bureaucrats-fixers are invariably optimistic about their latest decisions. Despite their optimism, the willingness of technocrat-bureaucrats to prescribe solutions impetuously in uncertain and puzzling value-laden areas (politics, justice, education, ethics, allocation of available resources) makes them dangerous.[14]

I encountered the description of technocrats provided in the works of Roszak and some other scholars before reading David Halberstam's *Best and the Brightest*. Although Halberstam writes as a journalist and although he makes no reference to the existing literature on technocratic decision-makers, he describes American decision-makers (McNamara, Bundy, Rostow, and others) so richly that they are clearly identifiable as technocrats who made policy in a political problem area (Vietnam) where their technocratic traits operated to destructive effect. Halberstam's work appears based on extensive interviews with insightful individuals who worked closely over the years with key American decision-makers for Vietnam. His work is partly supported by observer-analysts such as Thomson, Janis and Berman (whose works are also assigned in this course), who also attribute much responsibility for bad policy-making on Vietnam to the technocratic traits of decision-makers.

To assist students in reading the assigned texts, a detailed outline of reading assignments, based on the citations contained in this description, is distributed. As described below, students who were presented in the first two weeks of the course with Roszak's model of the technocrat and an explanation of a typical technocrat's strengths and weaknesses are subsequently presented with the case of American policy-making for Vietnam as the particular stage on which teams of American decision-makers bearing dangerously technocratic traits seemingly acted according to a tragic, preordained fate. The students' reading (primarily in Halberstam) and other assignments allow them to focus sequentially on how America's "best and brightest" technocrats dealt with such policy matters as: the complex historical and political background of the Vietnamese national revolution; the heavy domestic pressures that influenced them to intervene quickly to stifle a nationalist-communist revolution; American technocratic decision-makers' ignorance of Vietnamese history, geography, political values and goals; the technocrats' invention of or reliance on false political premises and analogies to compensate for their ignorance of the actual forces at work in Vietnamese history; the technocrats' diagnosis of Vietnam's ancient political revolution as amenable to technical-military controls; the counterproductive, technocratic behavioral traits of key decision-makers; the technological solutions applied by technocrats unsuccessfully to win a political war; and the lessons of Vietnam for future policy-makers.

The lectures on these topics are supplemented by audio-visual materials from such sources as The Public Broadcasting System's series *Vietnam: A Television History*. These were employed to help students obtain a sense of the peculiar physical terrain of Vietnam, the difficulties encountered in trying to identify, contain and control an elusive enemy operating according to rules of war foreign to Americans, the implacable character of the nationalist and communist opposition, the weakness of the anti-communist Vietnamese government leaders and so forth.

VALIDITY OF FOCUS

The focus of this course on the technocratic traits of American policy-makers is explicitly supported by reliable sources. According to a reliable policy-making insider, American policy failed because "a group of able, dedicated men were regularly and repeatedly wrong."[15] Thomson explicitly described these men as "technocracy's own Maoists" who brought a "new missionary impulse to America's foreign relations based on their confidence in our unsurpassed military might, our clear technological supremacy, and our invincible benevolence."[16] These technocrats were so convinced of our superior technology and rectitude that they saw their duty as easing the nations of the earth toward a "full-fledged Pax America Technocratica."[17]

The narrow explanatory focus of this course on the personal behavioral traits of particular foreign policy-makers is also justified by the theoretical literature. Although American foreign policy decisions are often made by a remarkably small number of individuals, most conspicuous of whom is the President of the United States and although the images of foreign policy situations by these decision-makers have long been deemed important, the fact that the same sort of individuals over time usually frequent the top layer decision positions by a "revolving door principle" has tended to discourage investigation of their personal characteristics to explain policy variations.[18] Most foreign policy decision-makers are from the same socio-political background.[19] In a crisis situation, however, several conditions arise that make the individual characteristics of decision-makers particularly influential. In crises, decision-making power gravitates to the very highest level of government; such power is organized and exercised by informal teams who are relatively freed from formal bureaucratic constraints to make decisions independently; decision-makers rely on their own preferred type of information in an atmosphere where generally reliable information is at a premium; decision-makers working in teams tend to adapt their views to team needs; and the scarcity of adequate information about the crisis situation encourages decision-makers to rely on inherited assumptions and analogies. In crises where the use of force is involved, such as Vietnam, the influence of personality on the decisions of American foreign policy-makers has been found to be so especially strong that it may well be the most potent explanation of these decisions.[20] Consequently, the narrowly focused decision-making approach to explaining the war is deemed useful.

APPLICATION OF FOCUS

At the conclusion of the two-week introduction to the technocratic mind-set, the course turns to an introduction to the historical background of Vietnam's national revolution, and then to the study of six key policy-making propositions, which are addressed through lectures, films and readings.

The introduction to the historical background of Vietnam's national revolution focuses on its irrational, uncompromising, open-ended, emotional character. Six lectures are devoted to helping students to understand the absolute commitment of many national revolutionaries to the cause of national independence. Attention is drawn to the ancient, centuries-long struggle of Vietnam for unification, the geography that made Vietnam so different from Korea or the Middle East, and the economy that made Vietnam less vulnerable to air power. A description is given of America's erroneous perception of the character of Vietnam's political ties to Communist China and the Soviet Union and Vietnam's wars against colonialist Chinese, Japanese and French invaders. These lectures attempt to reveal the local and national character of Vietnam's fight for independence as it existed prior to the arrival of international communism or the Cold War. Two episodes of the Public Broadcasting System's *Vietnam: A Television History* (Episode 1, "The Roots of War"; and Episode 2, "The First Vietnam War 1946-1954") are assigned, with appropriate reading assignments from Halberstam and others. An outline of important dates, events and statistics tracing America's escalating economic, military and political investment in this war is also distributed. From these experiences, students are expected to place America's intervention in Vietnam in historical perspective, that is, as following other foreign interventions. They are expected to appreciate the stubbornly anti-colonial, xenophobic character of Vietnam's struggle for national, cultural independence; the ambiguous character of communist influence on the national revolution; the emergence of an alien Cold War rationale for intervention by the superpowers in the 1950s; the Cold War perceptions of Vietnam by American policy-makers in the 1950s and 1960s; and the annihilation of Vietnam's land and society by military might during twenty years of war. Students are expected to appreciate how the Vietnamese, after wars for liberation against the Chinese and Japanese, learned patience and conceived a military-political strategy for fighting a patient or protracted, people's war that capitalized on the unique geographical characteristics of their land. They should be able to grasp that after a victorious war against the French, the Vietnamese also learned how to exploit the impatience of Western policy-makers anxious to win as swiftly as possible. They should also be aware that by the time American policy-makers discovered Vietnam, the Vietnamese communists had a charismatic, unified and talented leadership, pervasive and concealed civilian political organizations, a protracted-war strategy designed to exploit the impatience of the Americans, and an emotional and psychological commitment to national independence forged by decades of total sacrifice. Finally, students should be able to perceive that American technocratic policy-makers seemed ignorant of critical elements of Vietnamese culture. Upon completion of their introduction to the Vietnamese context of American policy-making for Vietnam, students begin an exploration of the six policy-making propositions which may account for our policy-makers' lack of knowledge of and their overall inability to successfully address the cultural and historical context of American intervention in Southeast Asian affairs.

Proposition One: Heavy domestic political pressures on U. S. policy-makers-technocrats may have influenced them to intervene in Vietnam quickly in order to halt world-wide communist expansion by uprooting an indigenous nationalist movement led by communists. The Korean War was fought on a peninsula on relatively open terrain that was relatively accessible to oversight by American air power and to containment by conventional hi tech American military forces. Vietnam however, had, amorphous, ill-defined and open land borders on three sides, was often covered by heavy cloud-cover or heavy foliage, and was riddled by miles of underground tunnels and swamps capable of providing daytime refuge for thousands of soldiers. Benefiting by such natural defenses, communist forces could "hit and run" and maintain the initiative and pace of the war as it chose and could neutralize the superior weight of American technological power at its discretion. Patient, flexible and committed to a long war to win independence, Vietnamese communist leaders confronted impatient, technology-minded and confident technocrats determined to achieve immediate and dramatic results.

The domestic American political setting in the 1960s described by analysts was a crisis-ridden environment that greatly stimulated impatient, eager, action-oriented, ill-informed and inexperienced technocrats to commit American resources promptly to halt global communist expansion. The Kennedy Administration, in office by virtue of only a slim margin of electoral victory, was expected to strengthen national defense, was under strong pressure by a conservative congress and was motivated to take an assertive, anti-communist stand in Vietnam following a recent setback at the Bay of Pigs and Kruschev's challenge in Vienna.[21] Further, when faced with simultaneous, successive crises in Cuba, Laos, Congo, and Berlin, Kennedy's inexperienced decision-makers had little time to re-evaluate old or inherited policy assumptions or to deliberate or plan new policies.[22] Such factors pressed these technocrats to act swiftly and forcefully in Southeast Asia. Yet, they had to act in ignorance of Vietnamese history, economics, politics and geography and were without the advice of the experienced American diplomats who had been expelled from key State Department posts by Senator McCarthy following the communist takeover of China.[23]

The decision-making atmosphere was also pressurized by a fear of failing to defend the containment policy aimed at the Soviet Union which earlier administrations had extended from Western Europe to Vietnam. A communist gain of territory anywhere in the world was forbidden. Communists everywhere were perceived as part of an homogenous, uniform diabolic force or as a political tide to be contained wherever it surged.[24] Leading technocrats, with little time to re-examine old ideological slogans or understand complicated Vietnamese politics, readily accepted this perception of communist insurgencies and perceived Vietnam as a site where the geo-political will of the free West would be tested in battle against the evil East and where the prestige of America as guardian of freedom would be challenged by the Anti-Christ. Presidents Kennedy and Johnson, fearful of being judged weak doves by domestic hawks, were inclined to contain the expansion of the "red tide" by force in Vietnam.[25]

Proposition Two: The technocrats were so ignorant of Vietnamese history, politics and resources that they made momentous political decisions "in the dark." As indicated above, technocrats lacked time for an exhaustive search for complete information on Vietnam. Profoundly ignorant of the peoples and history of Vietnam and confused regarding the type of war waged there, decision-makers made daringly momentous decisions without adequate information. Crippled by the timid reporting of State Department experts following their punishment for the so-called loss of China and misinformed by substitute personnel who were ignorant of the situation, the "brightest" decision-makers operated "in the dark."[26] These highly enlightened rational and brilliant technocrats lacked personal knowledge of Vietnam or of guerrilla war.[27]

Proposition Three: Lacking reliable political knowledge of their enemy, technocrats based their erroneous policies on false assumptions. Lacking the advice of informed, experienced counselors, the cerebral technocrats— under keen pressure and eager to act decisively—reasoned by analogy or on the basis of unexamined inherited premises. The initial acceptance of false premises for policy-making by ignorant, inexperienced, hard-pressed, and ideologically accommodating functionaries is understandable. In the crisis of Vietnam, however, the technocrats lacked personal practical experience of Asia and failed to find the time needed to test their false assumptions about Vietnam early or adequately. Instead, these brilliant theoreticians, who were renowned for their rational-analytic capacities, made policy on the basis of six false theoretical assumptions and bungled the policy-making process.[28]

The first of these assumptions was that Communism was a monolith. This assumption discouraged political efforts to create a "Titoist" type of communism and discouraged strategic efforts to wage total military war against Hanoi lest it trigger a global war with Soviet and Chinese communists.[29]

The second of these assumptions was that Vietnamese political revolutionaries, after twenty years of total political war, would surrender their cause after the limited application of American military might. Ignorant of the motivations of Vietnamese revolutionaries and basing their judgments on the American experience of communist leaders in the Korean War decision-makers failed to see that while the United States fought a strategic, limited war for geo-political, theoretical (containment) reasons, the enemy fought an unlimited, open-ended, total war for revolutionary, national survival. With specific limited goals, the United States sought to end the war in a particular timeframe. With total, holistic goals, the Vietnamese sought to prolong the war. Technocrats assumed that the war was a contest between Asian and Anglo-Saxon wills, in which their superior might would prevail. They failed to understand that Hanoi had made an unlimited final commitment to the cause of unification.[30]

The third of these assumptions was that Vietnam was the pivotal free world domino in a theory in which any nation labelled such a domino automatically becomes one. For technocrats profoundly ignorant of the radical differences among Asian states, the domino theory—stemming from containment theory—was used to define the territory of Vietnam as vital to American global security interests. As an ill-conceived legacy of previous American presidents, the domino theory was accepted by the technocrats as the rationale used to justify an inflated commitment to a jungle war against an elusive, skilled and dedicated enemy. By labelling Vietnam the pivotal domino, the technocrats justified the commitment of American strategic resources to war in a most inappropriate social, political and geographical terrain.[31]

The fourth of these assumptions was that the Government of South Vietnam was politically viable. Based on their invariable optimism and their ignorance of different societies technocrats assumed that this government would survive.[32] When it was apparent to all that this government was nonviable, it was too late. By then, American complicity in the killing of Diem "morally locked" the technocrats into Vietnam and the enormous investment of American prestige and resources was too great to be written off.[33] This process is traced in Episode 3 of *Vietnam: A Television History*, "America's Mandarin 1954-1963".

The fifth of these assumptions was that the enemy would fight an American-style conventional war. In their ignorance of Vietnamese terrain and strategies and in their supreme confidence in the preponderant volume and sophistication of American technology, technocrats assumed that Hanoi would fight a Korean-style conventional war most suitable for America's superior firepower and technology. Acting boldly on this false assumption in 1965, technocrats committed conventional combat battalions to fight against an elusive enemy,[34] a fact made clear in Episode 5 of *Vietnam: A Television History*, "America Takes Charge, 1965-1976," Episode 6, "With America's Enemy, 1954-1967" and Episode 7, "Tet 4 1968." While American troops employed conventional forces to search out and destroy the enemy, the guerrillas generally fought in small units, selected the targets and times for battle and, by using tactics of avoidance and concealment, found shelter in nature as American forces attacked nature and destroyed rural Vietnamese society in an effort to destroy the enemy.

The sixth and last of these assumptions was that American air power would decide the war. The technocrats, excessively confident of and optimistic regarding the superiority of American technology and having a rich store of combat aircraft assumed that technological superiority would triumph and that Hanoi revolutionaries could be bombed into halting their infiltration of South Vietnam and negotiating an end to their crusade. Instead, the bombing worked to opposite political effect.[35] It failed to stiffen the will of the South Vietnamese government and increased Hanoi's infiltration of the South.

Proposition Four: The technocrats diagnosed the political struggle in Vietnam on the basis of false assumptions that defined it as amenable to technical-military controls. In light of their ignorance of the political history of Vietnam, of the falseness of the fundamental conceptions of the struggle and of their misplaced confidence in the superiority of American technology in a non-technological war, decision-makers tended to think about Vietnam's national political problem in such global, strategic military terms that they eventually treated it as a military problem. With an abundance of military technology available for use in Vietnam, with great faith in technological-military might, with their fears of being seen as "soft on communism," with their confusion regarding the objectives of the war, and with their determination to defeat the first of many expected wars of communist-style national liberation, technocrats perceived Vietnam as one key part of a global geo-political problem—the expansion of communism—to be contained by military means.[36] Unable or unwilling to comprehend the "wild irrationality" and general "messiness" of third world politics,[37] the rational-logical technocrats relied upon their vastly superior military technology which they comprehended and controlled to "tighten the noose" on the enemy.[38] Avoiding superior American military firepower whenever and wherever possible, the enemy survived to wage a political war in Vietnam and overseas.[39]

Proposition Five: The counterproductive behavioral traits of technocratic policy-makers led them to accommodate to the false assumptions and analogies of their political chiefs, to exclude serious examinations of alternate policies, to surround themselves with like-minded colleagues and to exhibit behavior that limited their flexibility. The personal characteristics attributed to such key decision-makers as McNamara, Bundy, Rostow, Harkins, Taylor, Johnson and Kennedy are similar to those attributed to Roszak's technocrats and associated "pragmatists."[40] The technocrats behaved as technocrats usually do. The class examines each of these characteristics in turn.

Technocrats worked in like-minded teams. To act promptly in crisis, decision-makers were organized in informal, tightly knit teams under Presidents Kennedy and Johnson. Working in teams, there was such pressure to be loyal to the team that members tended to restrict debate on and information about policies to their own numbers and to focus on short-run problems. Individualistic characters who were not willing to conform to team discipline or to respect the team consensus were excluded. Individualists who recommended policies that challenged the team consensus were not heeded.[41]

Technocrats adapted to the prevailing Cold War ideological view of Vietnam. While all American decision-makers were anti-communists, decision-makers who were insiders, such as Johnson, Rusk and Rostow, tended to see all communists as alike. Outsiders or non-technocrats such as Stevenson and Harriman tended to perceive the communist world as more pluralistic or heterogeneous. Given the technocrats' perceptions of the communists as united solidly in one block, they failed to perceive Vietnam as potentially separable from other communist states as China toward whom Vietnamese felt historic antagonisms.[42]

Technocrats lacked practical knowledge of Vietnam. As indoor men who lacked direct personal experience of the political life of Asia, as men who had been clerks rather than political activists, most advisers had little basis for understanding the violent revolutionary forces of Vietnam Opponents of America's Vietnam policy, such as George Ball, who had deep personal knowledge of the French experience in Indochina, were able to see the situation more accurately.[43]

Technocrats were adaptable to the views of their leaders. Lacking any independent political or ideological base and any body of contradictory information and pressured to produce promptly a coherent Vietnam policy, technocrats tended to adapt their views to those of their leaders. Presidents Kennedy and Johnson also adapted to political pressures from hard-line anti-communists. Some advisers who did not adapt to the views of their leaders were excluded from power.[44]

Technocrats were active. In an extremely uncertain and ambiguous policy situation, technocrats were regularly described as eager to act boldly and decisively to achieve results. Individual policy-makers who were described as cautious or hesitant to plunge boldly into the murky policy waters of Vietnam were excluded from the inner power circles.[45]

Technocrats were diligent. Acting productively in crisis, the top technocrats and their teams were famed for their hard work. Policy critics who failed to work as hard had their criticisms rejected as the products of lazy dilettantes.[46]

Technocrats were loyal and discreet. Insiders without loyalties to any independent political base or code, they committed their loyalties to their jobs and to the Presidents who employed them. Presidents confused dissent with disloyalty and discouraged technocrats from raising critical questions about false assumptions. Technocrats turned away from Outsiders and communicated less and less with individuals possessing different views.[47]

Technocrats were amoral, realistic, practical and confident. Technocrats were action-oriented in a climate of extreme uncertainty. Individuals who expressed moral reservations or raised moral questions regarding certain policy proposals were considered soft-headed and effete and were excluded from the inner circles. Technocrats were confident. The high confidence or even hubris of decision-makers regarding the power of America made any serious thought of a Hanoi victory very unlikely.[48] President Johnson's personal insecurity in the field of foreign policy led him to be overconfident of his advisers.[49]

Technocrats were optimistic. Technocrats were described as "can do" fixers and "wishful thinkers" who were so unconstrained by any personal knowledge of the complexities of Vietnam, so deaf to contradictory counsel from outsiders, and so confident in the superiority of American technological power that they were investing in Vietnam that they dared boldly to invest more and more military resources in their confidence of success.[50] Key leaders were relentlessly and excessively optimistic.[51] Optimistic subordinates misled presidents. Pessimistic counselors, such as Ball and Clifford, went unheeded.

Technocrats pursued a scientific approach. Lacking personal knowledge of Vietnam, key technocrats, especially McNamara, generated quantitative, empirical data on the war that they brilliantly employed to support their policies. Critics of the war, such as Ball and Clifford, who lacked such "scientific" data to bolster their critiques, were relatively ineffective. When this new data base eventually proved false, this added to the confusion of decision-makers. As a reliable measure of the all-important, qualitative (motivational) capabilities of hostile combat forces, the database was useless.[52]

Proposition Six: The technocrats mistakenly applied brilliant technological solutions to a non-technical political problem, producing counterproductive effects. Under domestic political pressure to act militarily and having diagnosed Vietnam as a site for the firm containment of a world communist tide, decision-makers who were unaware of the local, national and political character of the Vietnam War and ignorant of the capacities or intentions of its revolutionary leaders recommended solutions based on their confidence in America's military and industrial might.[53]

Among the solutions advanced were counterinsurgency forces (Green Berets), which were created early in the war in order to use unconventional, guerrilla forces to fight similar enemy forces. Unfortunately, the American military bureaucracy was geared to fight a high tech, conventional Russian war machine, and it was unwilling to restructure its forces significantly to develop an effective counterinsurgency force capable of fighting an unconventional war.[54] Another solution advanced was air mobility, but helicopters failed to live up to their promise as a decisive weapon.[55] The strategic hamlet program and the use of strategic bombing were brought forward as war-winning initiatives, but the former was mis-managed by the Vietnamese government and the escalation of the later failed to halt Hanoi's infiltration and stiffened the enemy's will to fight.[56] The use of modern conventional forces, systematic progress reporting, and waging a war of attrition also appealed to the technocrat as war-winning strategies. Yet, the efforts of conventional forces to root the communists out of the countryside by napalm, defoliation, free-fire zones and search and destroy tactics managed to destroy much of rural society but were unable to locate or eliminate the elusive enemy forces (Francis Ford Coppola's *Apocalypse Now* may be employed as a means of demonstrating the tactics of American forces versus the enemy).[57] Further, the Pentagon's effort to create systematic progress reporting led to the collection of data that often proved false or misleading and was ineffective in neutralizing the enemy's capacity for surprise (a point that can be illustrated by showing students the color chart scene in the film *Go Tell the Spartans*).[58] Finally, superior American firepower caused great quantities of casualties among enemy forces but the pursuit of a war of attrition failed to break their will and had serious domestic political consequences (see *Vietnam: A Television History*, Episode 6, "With America's Enemy, 1945-1967" and Episode 11, "Homefront U.S.A.").[59]

STUDENT DISCUSSION AND EVALUATION

After completing their examination of the war's historical background and the six key policy-making propositions discussed above, students are directed to explore the lessons of the Vietnam War. Students are expected to raise and address their own individual questions about the failure of policy-making in Vietnam. Among those questions most often raised are: is it possible to define a profile of technocrats so carefully that one can identify teams of policy-makers bearing such characteristics in similar American policy-making areas? Were the "best and brightest" technocrats, or were they simply victims, as Janis has observed, of group think? Can one use other sources to conduct in-depth research in order to determine more clearly the characteristics that differentiate technocrats such as McNamara, Bundy and Rostow from non-technocrats such as Bowles, Ball and Clifford? Can one use interviews or the memoirs of veterans of American decision-making crises in order to measure the weight of pressures on them to conform?

Given the vast literature on the validity of the Domino Theory, can one write a paper clearly demonstrating its value for explanation and analysis? How can the hi-tech leaders of our hi-tech society hope to understand and deal effectively with third world societies whose passionate attachment to broad political ideologies and charismatic leaders mirrors that of the

Vietnamese, such as the Iraqi, Iranian, Libyan and Palestinian people? If so many of our leaders must have the virtues of technocrats in order to get access to policy-making power, how can one insure that they are not ruled by the vices of technocrats-in-crisis acting in policy areas outside their sphere of knowledge? Is Roszak's critical analysis of our society valid and, if not, what are its major weaknesses? Can students debate the merits of our current policy toward Central America or Iraq, with different teams arguing for a technocratic versus a non-technocratic approach to policy?

Students course grades are based on research papers that apply course content to topics to specific issues, such as Vietnam's Protracted War Strategy; The Domino Theory: Pros and Cons; The Non-technocratic Character of the North Vietnamese Politburo; The Achievements and Failures of America's Bombing Strategy; and The Reasons for America's Failure to Annihilate North Vietnamese Society.

CONCLUSION

It is to be expected that political scientists will find the course described above more suitable than instructors in other fields. It is hoped, however, that teachers of all disciplines will find it useful when designing that unit or section of their course that explores the reasons that America's leaders became involved in Vietnam affairs and, once involved, performed as they did.

NOTES

1. Theodore Roszak, *Where the Wasteland Ends: Politics and Transcendence in Post-Industrial Society* (Garden City, N. Y.: Doubleday, 1972).

2. Michael Macoby, *The Gamesman: The New Corporate Leaders* (New York: Simon and Schuster, 1978).

3. Robert Presthus, *Organizational Society* (New York: Martin's, 1978).

4. David Halberstam, *The Best and the Brightest* (Greenwich, Conn.: Fawcett Publications, 1972).

5. Irving L. Janis, *Group Think* (Boston: Houghton Mifflin, 1982).

6. Larry Berman, *Planning a Tragedy: The Americanization of the War in Vietnam* (New York: Norton, 1982).

7. Charles W. Kegley and Eugene R. Wittkopf, *American Foreign Policy Pattern and Process* (New York: St. Martin's, 1982).

8. James C. Thomson, "How Could Vietnam Happen? An Autopsy," in Charles W. Kegley and Eugene R. Wittkopf, editors, *Perspectives on American Foreign Policy: Selected Readings*, (New York: St. Martin's, 1983), pp. 379-89. Also available in Grace Sevy, editor, *The American Experience in Vietnam: a Reader* (Norman, Okla.: University of Oklahoma, 1989), pp. 37-50.

9. Roszak, *Making of a Wasteland*, chs. 1-8.

10. Ibid., ch. 7.

11. Ibid., pp. 28-31, 32-34, 59, 502-5.

12. Ibid., pp. 36-38, 218-21.

13. Ibid., pp. 8-10, 18.

14. Ibid., pp. 33, 38, 49, 57-63, 215-16, 350-52.

15. Thomson, "How Could Vietnam Happen," p. 387.

16. Ibid., p. 389.

17. Ibid.

18. Charles W. Kegley and Eugene R. Wittkopf, *American Foreign Policy, Pattern and Process*, pp. 492-94, 530.

19. Ibid., pp. 249-54.

20. Ibid., pp. 516, 541, 546.

21. Halberstam, *The Best and the Brightest*, p. 97.

22. Ibid., pp. 82-87, 92, 97, 128, 391; Thomson, "How Could Vietnam Happen," p. 381.

23. Halberstam, *The Best and the Brightest*, pp. 104-7, 128-35, 139-40.

24. Ibid., pp. 130-34, 372, 395-403.

25. Berman, *Planning a Tragedy*, pp. 22-27, 43-44, 130-31, 145; Kegley and Wittkopf, *American Foreign Policy Pattern and Process*, p. 367.

26. Kegley and Wittkopf, *American Foreign Policy-Planning and Process*, pp. 357-62, 544. See also, Berman, *Planning a Tragedy*, p. 142; Thomson, "How Could Vietnam Happen," pp. 379-81.

27. Halberstam, *The Best and The Brightest*, pp. 84, 106-7, 222-29, 397-99, 407-8.

28. Ibid., pp. 187, 371; Kegley and Wittkopf, p. 544.

29. Berman, *Planning A Tragedy*, pp. 74, 93, 131, 142-3; Halberstam, *The Best and the Brightest*, pp. 187, 637.

30. Berman, *Planning A Tragedy*, pp. 93, 141-44; Halberstam, *The Best and The Brightest*, pp. 211, 501, 533, 587, 607-8, 621, 702, 744, 752; Thomson, "How Could Vietnam Happen," p. 386.

31. Berman, *Planning A Tragedy*, pp. 8, 9, 16, 30, 91-93, 110, 116, 131, 134; Halberstam, *The Best and The Brightest*, pp. 152, 433, 791.

32. Berman, *Planning A Tragedy*, p. 26; Halberstam, pp. 152, 245, 254, 372, 415; Thomson, "How Could Vietnam Happen," p. 385.

33. Berman, *Planning A Tragedy*, pp. 28-29, 49, 68, 77, 108.

34. Ibid, pp. 67, 71-73, 102-11, 135-37; Halberstam, *The Best and The Brightest*, pp. 212, 589.

35. Berman, *Planning A Tragedy*, pp. 51-52, 56-66, 82; Halberstam, *The Best and The Brightest*, p. 213; Kegley and Wittkopf, *American Foreign Policy-Pattern and Process*, p. 368; Thomson, "How Could Vietnam Happen," p. 385.

36. Berman, *Planning A Tragedy*, pp. 27, 59-60; Halberstam, *The Best and The Brightest*, pp. 97, 225, 261, 297-9, 367, 424-28; Kegley and Wittkopf, *American Foreign Policy Pattern and Process*, pp. 368-70.

37. Halberstam, *The Best and The Brightest*, pp. 120, 428-31, 585-87, 756-59, 618, 627, 663, 759.

38. Berman, *Planning A Tragedy*, pp. 22, 59-60.

39. Halberstam, *The Best and The Brightest*, p. 667.

40. Kegley and Wittkopf, *American Foreign Policy Patterns and Process*, pp. 503-5.

41. Ibid., pp. 332-33, 340; and Halberstam, *The Best and The Brightest*, pp. 78, 275-76, 367, 599-600.

42. Halberstam, *The Best and the Brightest*, pp. 32, 114, 198, 397-403, 455, 549.

43. Ibid., pp. 71-72, 162-64, 215, 222-31, 395-99, 407-8, 483, 599.

44. Berman, *Planning A Tragedy*, pp. 5, 22, 42-43, 45; Halberstam, *The Best and The Brightest*, pp. 42-43, 91-92, 187-88, 628; Kegley and Wittkopf, *American Foreign Policy Patterns and Process*, pp. 519-20.

45. Halberstam, *The Best and The Brightest*, pp. 23, 32, 50-52, 92-97, 105, 114-17, 200-06, 644-45.

46. Ibid., pp. 40, 43, 58, 193-95, 207, 264-65, 280, 302, 380-83, 666.

47. Ibid., pp. 4-6, 219, 234, 270, 300, 344, 525-27, 554-55; Berman, *Planning A Tragedy*, p. 131; Kegley and Wittkopf, *American Foreign Policy Patterns and Process*, pp. 333-34.

48. Halberstam, *The Best and The Brightest*, pp. 10, 25, 30-32, 37, 50-55, 74-75, 152, 197, 213, 256, 265, 296, 371, 398, 584, 598-99, 645, 796.

49. Berman, *Planning A Tragedy*, pp. 145-49.

50. Ibid., pp. 89, 112-17; Thomson, "How Could Vietnam Happen," pp. 381, 385-87.

51. Halberstam, *The Best and The Brightest*, pp. 223-63, 312, 773, 784-85.

52. Ibid., pp. 226-52, 263, 304, 306, 336-43, 346-47, 371-72, 563; Berman, *Planning A Tragedy*, pp. 144-45.

53. Halberstam, *The Best and The Brightest*, pp. 562-82.

54. Ibid., pp. 55, 153-54, 188, 199, 205, 212, 223, 227, 256, 335, 426, 586, 658.

55. Ibid., p. 248.

56. Ibid., pp. 170-71, 199-200, 225, 258-59, 331, 337, 363, 426-36, 580-88, 651-53, 697-98, 745-48.

57. Ibid, pp. 201-6, 223-28, 569, 657, 703, 743-45, 751-52.

58. Ibid., pp. 345, 374, 493, 593.

59. Ibid., pp. 658, 750, 787.

5

Teaching the Dynamics of the Conflict

MELFORD WILSON, JR.

Teaching today's generation of college students about the Vietnam War presents the dual problems of too little classroom time to invest in the subject and student disinterest in a conflict some consider a "loser." First, Vietnam was a long and complicated war. The history of the conflict has been captured fairly well in works like George C. Herring's appropriately named book, *America's Longest War: The United States and Vietnam, 1950-1975* (New York: Knopf, 1979, 2nd ed., 1986) and also in the several television documentaries on the war. While these are very well done, students do not seem to capture the dynamics of the conflict from these sources. Perhaps these sources would work in a less hurried format, but unfortunately, few of us in political science are allowed the luxury of having courses on the undergraduate level where one can spend a whole semester on the war.

The second problem stems from basic differences in subjective perception between ourselves and our students. Our professional lives as instructors parallel the war. We have formed our opinions from firsthand experiences and long study. We feel very keenly about how this war has changed America and the international system. Some of our students, on the other hand, like much of America, have "tuned out" this unpopular war.

I was awakened to this reality when a student wrote on my course evaluation for American Foreign Policy, "Don't get so bogged down in Vietnam." I remembered in my college days how bored I got with my professors who went on and on about the Great Depression. In memory, I can still hear one professor saying, "You had to live through it to truly understand it." It is often hard for us to remember that the United States had withdrawn from Vietnam before today's freshmen class entered first grade.

In recent years, movies about Vietnam seem to be the students' major source of information and opinions. The better of these are designed to make an artistic statement, while the rest of them are typical war movies set in this unique location. In both cases, they emote more than they educate. These movies say little about the political dynamics of the policy debate in the United States and do not leave the student with an objective understanding of Vietnam.

I would like to share my solution to the problem of teaching about the war. Variations of this technique in several of my classes have been used with considerable success. The approach was tried first in an interdisciplinary course, International Area Studies, in 1981, with fourteen students enrolled. Since then I have used it in my regular American Foreign Policy course with 20 to 30 students. Each course met twice a week for 16 weeks, with two weeks set aside for study of Vietnam.

The object of the exercise was to help the student break down any barriers he or she might have to learning about Vietnam, gain an understanding of the many dimensions of this conflict in particular and of conflicts in the third world in general, gain a better understanding of the dynamics of the policy debate in the United States between the articulate and policy elites (stated as an objective only in the American Foreign Policy course), and come to a better understanding of how the Vietnamese conflict has changed our world.

A list was prepared to present to students critics (and critical sources) with different views on the conflict and on our policy toward Vietnam. The focus of their study was on the period from 1965-1968. More specifically, it began with America's forces taking over the major responsibilities for fighting and ended with President Johnson's decision not to run for re-election.

All of the students were given questions to direct them to read more analytically. The questions were divided into four groups that were intended to apply to the four class periods. In practice, the first set took nearly all of the first two class meetings. The reading assignments and questions were assigned two weeks prior to the first class discussion period to give the students ample time to prepare. Most of the students in each class were juniors, and about half of each group were political science majors.

THE ASSIGNMENT

Students were given the questions outlined below and asked to briefly answer and be ready to discuss each according to a specific author or source's point of view.

I.   Dimensions of Asian Conflict

   A.   *Great Power*. What patterns of great power interaction exist?
        How and why are the United States, the Soviet Union and China
        involved? How are their interests at stake?
   B.   *Regional*. How and why are North Vietnam and South Vietnam
        involved?
   C.   *Sub-national*. Who are the significant sub-national actors? How
        and why are they involved?

II.   Analysis of Conflict

   What is the real nature of the conflict? How is the conflict defined?
   A.   What are the relative capabilities of the participants?
   B.   How and why was the conflict started?
   C.   How and why did the United States get involved?

III. Conflict in United States

   A.   What major perceptual mistakes did the United States (i.e.,
        definition of conflict, interest, capabilities)
   B.   What policy alternatives and strategies were recommended for
        United States.
   C.   What was the nature of the conflict between the policy elite and
        the critics?

IV.   General Discussion

   What are your own views (not those of your source) on the conflict and
how the Vietnam War has changed our world?

SOURCES

   The following is the list of sources used in my American Foreign Policy
course. Each student picked one as his or her source for answering the
questions and participating in class discussion. No two students could
choose the same source. Unless otherwise specified, the students were to
select from the following writings between 1965-1968:

   1. I. F. Stone, edition of *I. F. Stone's Weekly*. Read six articles to
       include "A Reply to the White Paper," March 8, 1965.
   2. Jean Lacouture, *Vietnam: Between Two Truces* (New York:
       Random House, 1966).

3. *The New Leader*. Read eight articles to include: Reinhold Niebuhr, "Pretense and Power," 48 (March 1, 1965), p. 6, and Robert Elegant, "South Vietnam: The Theory" 45 (April 16, 1962), p. 8.

4. Jonathan Schell, *The Village of Ben Suc* (New York, Knopf 1967).

5. Hans J. Morganthau. Read six articles or chapters in books, to include: "We are Deluding Ourselves in Vietnam," *The New York Times Magazine*, 1 (April 18, 1965), p. 25.

6. *The New Republic*. Read eight articles, to include Edgar Snow's "Deeper into the Trap: A Christmas Message on Vietnam;" 153 (December 25, 1965), pp. 15-18.

7. *National Review*. Read eight articles, to include W. H. von Dreele, "Bombing North with L.B.J." 17 (July 13, 1965), p. 191.

8. *The Nation*. Read eight articles.

9. *Commonweal*. Read eight articles.

10. *Commentary*. Read eight articles.

11. *The Christian Century*. Read eight articles.

12. David Halberstam, *The Making of a Quagmire* (New York: Random House, 1965). You may also want to read some of his later articles in *The New York Times*.

13. Bernard B. Fall. Read six articles or chapters from Fall's books to include: "Viet Cong—The Unseen Enemy in Viet-Nam," *New Society*, April 22, 1965, reprinted in Marcus G. Raskin and Bernard B. Hall, editors, *The Viet-Nam Reader*, (New York: Vintage, 1965). May include chapters from *Viet-Nam Witness* (New York: Praeger, 1966).

14. *The Great Speckled Bird*. Read eight articles.

15. Walter Lippman. Read chapters in his books or six articles, which may be found in the *Washington Post*.

16. Howard Zinn, *Vietnam: The Logic of Withdrawal* (Boston: Beacon Press, 1967).

17. U. S. Congress, Senate Committee on Foreign Relations, *Supplement Foreign Assistance Fiscal Year 1966—Vietnam* (Washington, D. C.: U. S. Government Printing Office, 1966). Read statements and questions of Lt. General James M. Gavin and George F. Kennan.

18. Same source as no. 17. Read statements and questioning of General Maxwell Taylor and Secretary of State Dean Rusk.

19. Wolfgang Friedmann, "U. S. Policy and the Crisis of International Law," *The American Journal of International Law*, 59 (1965), p. 857, and Quincey Wright, "Legal Aspects of the Viet Nam Situation," *The American Journal of International Law*, 63 (1969), p. 185.

20. James Reston. Read eight articles found in *The New York Times*.

21. J. William Fulbright. Read six articles of chapters in books, to include "The War in Viet-Nam," *Congressional Record*, June 15, 1965, p. 13656-8, reprinted in Marcus G. Raskin and Bernard Fall, editors, *The Viet-Nam Reader* (New York: Vintage, 1965).
22. Robert Scalopino. Read six articles or chapters from books.

Read ten major articles or editorials (not short news reports or wire service reports) from the following sources. Read at least two from each year, 1965-68.

23. *U. S. News and World Report.*
24. *Time.*
25. *Newsweek.*
26. *The New York Times.*
27. *Washington Post.*
28. *The Christian Science Monitor.*

EVALUATION AND CONCLUSION

As mentioned above, the questions and list of sources included in this paper were selected from the American Foreign Policy course. The primary change from the earlier offering was in the presentation of the administration's view. In the International Area Studies course, one of the students used speeches by President Lyndon Johnson and another used speeches and articles by Secretary of State Dean Rusk as their sources. This did not work well because these students felt the other students were ganging up on them. In the American Foreign Policy class, all of the students were assigned sections from the second white paper on Vietnam issued by the Department of State, *Aggression from the North, the Record of North Viet Nam's Campaign to Conquer South Viet Nam*, U. S. Department of State Publication 7839, Feb. 27, 1965, excerpts from Secretary of State Dean Rusk's address before the American Society of International Law, April 23, 1965, reprinted in the *Department of State Bulletin*, 7 (May 10, 1965), p. 94, and President Johnson's Johns Hopkins speech reprinted in the *Department of State Bulletin*, 7 (April 26, 1965), p. 606.

Assigning each student responsibility for an individual source had several advantages. In the first place, the student felt an individual responsibility to report on his portion to the class. Therefore, the exercise had the advantages of any individually directed learning experience. In the second place, since each student had a different source, each was the expert on that particular critic and engaged in the discussion much more readily. One of the pleasant surprises was that several students who had only spoken when spoken to voluntarily entered the discussion. In the third place, it was harder for the student not to prepare for the class. I have often found that when all of the students are assigned the same readings, some students are likely to hide behind the perennial class discussion leaders. Finally, since the professor knew which sources stressed specific aspects of the conflict, it was easier to call on the students who should be better versed on that particular point.

Overall, this experiment was very successful. The students reacted in a very positive manner, and class discussion was very lively. The technique worked best for stimulating interest in Vietnam and getting the students to understand the scope of policy criticism concerning America's role in the conflict. If there is a weakness, it is that the students may not have acquired a very balanced view of the war. Most of the students accepted the views of their source as the gospel for the first two to three class periods. Perhaps for this reason, the students who had a single author liked the exercise better. By the final class period, however, most of the students realized the complexity of the conflict and were critical of their source as well as the administration.

Unfortunately, average students had difficulty finding answers to the questions because of their lack of sophistication in source selection. It is likely that they read the first six or so articles on Vietnam they came across. The professor might be able to assist those students with source selection if he has had ample opportunity to evaluate ability prior to this unit of study.

6

Broadening the Horizons of a Course on the American War in Vietnam
MARC JASON GILBERT

In the aftermath of what Americans call the Vietnam War, a conflict that Asian historians prefer to term the Second Indochina War, a number of scholars came to the conclusion that America's ignorance of the Vietnamese, its ethnocentric view of the wider world, and its lack of self-knowledge contributed to the failure of American policy in Southeast Asia and its painful aftermath at home. This realization has prompted some instructors to set much of their discussion of America's Vietnam War in the broader context of Southeast Asian, global and American history. Most of those educators who are responsible for courses on the war endorse this strategy, but many are reluctant to pursue it themselves. They argue, with some justice, that they are too hard-pressed by the limits of a one-quarter or one-semester course to devote any time to examining material drawn from areas of knowledge with which many are unfamiliar. Further, the subject they wish to teach and about which they believe their students come to their classes to learn is America's Vietnam War, not about Vietnam, Southeast Asia, world history or the place of the war in the greater pageant of American history. Yet, the most widely respected teachers of America's Vietnam War have long believed that a broader approach is not only vital to our understanding of the nature of the war but can be mastered through creativity and imagination rather than extensive training and will provide students with information that will arrest and repay their attention.

VIETNAM AND THE VIETNAMESE WARS

When the United States first took serious notice of Southeast Asian affairs in the mid-twentieth century, its interest was drawn to the region by war—a global war that evolved locally into an anti-colonial revolutionary war in a Cold War setting. Yet, it is clear that Vietnamese society was shaped by earlier wars of longer duration and possibly greater impact than the modern conflicts that so greatly contributed to its final form. War attended the birth of the Vietnamese people who, alone among the many peoples of southern China, were able to sustain an identity distinct from Han civilization. Centuries of wars of liberation waged against the imperialists of the Greater Dragon to the north set the pattern not only of Vietnamese national identity and political culture, but of the martial strategy that the Vietnamese would later employ against Western adversaries. Vietnam's own wars of expansion against the non-Viet peoples to the south provided the vehicle for the spread of a Vietnamese settler society that was to help give the modern Vietnamese village its cohesion and strength. Armed conflict also shaped Vietnam's relations with its Cambodian and Laotian neighbors, and another kind of war, civil war, provided an opening for French imperialism, itself threatened and later sustained by hot and cold global warfare between 1940 and 1954. Finally, Vietnam's violent resistance to French colonialism, Japanese occupation and Western efforts to block national redemption following the Second World War both insured that Vietnam's drive to recover its independence would be revolutionary in nature and enhanced the communist leadership's ability to identify themselves with that cause.

The inability of the French to successfully cope with the legacies of Vietnam's martial past in the decade after the Second World War (The First Indochina War) should have signalled American policy-planners that the successful prosecution of warfare in Southeast Asia was dependent upon an understanding of indigenous social structures, behavior patterns, cultural loyalties and military traditions forged by 2,000 years of almost continuous struggle. Yet, as South Vietnam's wartime Ambassador to the United States observed, his people and, by extension, the people of Cambodia and Laos, were negligible factors in America's wartime calculations: they were little more than "a geo-political abstraction, a factor in the play of global American interests."[1] John James MacDougall has outlined some of the possible reasons why American policy-makers during the First and Second Indochina conflicts regarded the people of Southeast Asia as a people without history, or rather, as a people whose history did not count.[2] While these "reasons why" will be the subject of debate for a long time to come, few scholars doubt that, at the policy-making level, American interest in and knowledge of Vietnamese society was never great.[3]

America's disinterest in the battle-tempered political and social heritage of Southeast Asia pervaded not only the American way of war in Southeast Asia, but also imposed itself on early Vietnam War course materials. There were clear reasons for this development.

America's defeat in Vietnam reinforced America's wartime cultural myopia. It is axiomatic that failed allies and the enemy have little place in the study of a nation's military defeats, for that effort is primarily an exercise in self-analysis. One of the first and most influential post-mortems of the war, Harry Summers' *On Strategy: The Vietnam War in Context* (Novato, Calif.: Presidio, 1982) contained virtually nothing about communist strategy. As late as 1989, there was only one detailed scholarly analysis of the Viet Cong and of the People's Army of Vietnam (PAVN).[4]

The ideological allegiances of many American educators also helped blind Americans to the war's Asian setting. Teachers with allegiance to the American Left regarded our non-communist allies much as those with allegiance to the Right viewed our opponents—in negative stereotyped terms. Further, few of those American historians who initially bore the greater part of the burden of teaching the war were prepared to examine the Vietnamese psyche or history. The students enrolled in their classes were understandably more concerned with American foreign policy, which might someday require that they fight in a foreign land, than with an ally or enemy portrayed in American film and literature as an undifferentiated Yellow Man (the Vietnamese characters in the 1957 Vietnam War film *China Gate* were portrayed by Chinese actors wearing Mao jackets).[5] It is not surprising, then, that the first post-war generation of Vietnam War texts, such as George Herring's otherwise excellent *America's Longest War: The United States and Vietnam, 1950-1975* (New York: Knopf, 1979), did not delve deeply into the complexities of Vietnamese culture and society.

The state of immediate post-war historiography may have been understandable, but it was not acceptable to American specialists in Southeast Asian studies. Many of these scholars had served in Vietnam in the capacity of political analysts and had learned the hard way about the cost of ignoring the local political dimensions of America's intervention. They did not challenge the propriety of an American focus for courses on the war, for they considered it essential to America's own search for meaning and lessons to be learned. They did, however, strive to inform their colleagues in American studies of the best means of integrating Vietnamese history and society into existing courses on the war.

The first fruits of this effort were, like all first fruits, welcome but bittersweet: Stanley Karnow's *Vietnam: A History* (New York: Viking, 1983) and Richard Ellison's *Vietnam: A Television History* (Boston: WGBH Television, 1984), a 13-part series related to the Karnow text that was produced for the Public Broadcasting System. These works featured a treatment of Vietnamese history based upon the assessments of leading specialists. Yet, despite his considerable skill and deep sympathy for the Vietnamese, Karnow deliberately constructed his work as a history of Vietnam's encounter with the French and the Americans in the First and Second Indochina Wars, not as a history of the Vietnamese people, as the title of his work might suggest. As a result, his treatment of early Vietnamese history and Vietnamese political culture is limited, though still more extensive than most other Vietnam War texts. Further, while the makers of *Vietnam: A Television History* made a laudable attempt to humanize "America's enemy" and illuminate the darker side of American interventionism, they were less circumspect in their effort than they might have been. Their lack of a clear analytical focus, the short shrift given to non-communist South Vietnamese, and the series' mildly dovish subtext provoked a heated response. As George Herring has noted, the Left discounted the 13-part series "as an apologia for American imperialism, [while] the South Vietnamese refugees . . . felt victimized," and the Right produced a rebuttal that, in Herring's view, repeated in exaggerated form each of the PBS series' alleged errors of judgment in an effort to keep Americans under the white hats and the communists under the black hats.[6]

Yet, historiographically speaking, the Karnow-Ellison project was an unqualified success. Testimony advanced at most Vietnam workshops since the debut of *Vietnam: A History* and *Vietnam: A Television History* indicates that whatever their alleged shortcomings, they have helped convince many teachers that the American struggle in Vietnam was but one of three, or perhaps four, wars that have altered Vietnamese history in this century and that America's involvement in these wars must be studied in this context.[7] The contents of most recent Vietnam War texts and readers reflect these concerns, leaving little doubt that the time has come to bring the Vietnamese into American courses on the Vietnam War.[8]

THE PACIFIC RIM, CAMBODIA, LAOS, THE HMONG, NATO AND ASEAN

Asianists, together with an increasing number of Vietnam War specialists, have not confined their efforts to put the war in a broader perspective to the study of Vietnam. The horizons of teaching and scholarship on the war have been greatly extended by their work in the field of diplomatic and regional history. They have traced Vietnam's relationship with China and the Soviet Union and established how North Vietnam's communist allies attempted to manipulate its policies and goals.[9] They have also shown that the war marked a turning point for the Japanese economy, strained America's relations with its European allies, occasioned a bitter period in Australian social and diplomatic history and constituted both a hypocritical episode in Canadian international relations and a challenge to well-established precedents in international law.[10] Thanks to their efforts, moreover, we are better able to grasp the central role of Laos and Cambodia in the war and the tragic fate of ethnic minorities in Vietnam and Laos.

It was not easy to begin to remove the wartime "sideshow" sobriquet that followed Cambodia, Laos and the Hmong people from the Vietnam War into the classroom. Instructors who were inclined to explore the Indochinese context of American intervention were naturally drawn to the central role of Vietnam in colonial and post-colonial Indochina and Vietnam's place as the scene of the bulk of American military operations. As specialists have reminded us, however, the security of Laos was one of Eisenhower's and Kennedy's main preoccupations, and Laos "could easily have become the big war that Vietnam did, had a Tonkin Gulf incident happened there in 1964."[11] They argue that Cambodia also deserves close attention. There is a Cambodian dimension to every aspect of American military operations in Vietnam and to the course of the anti-war movement at home. For example, the incursion into Cambodia that led to tragedy at Kent and Jackson State Universities was deemed necessary to facilitate Vietnamization and the attendant American withdrawal of its ground forces from Vietnam. At the very least, the rise and persistent strength of the Khmer Rouge not only has insured continuing American interest in Cambodian politics, but, at the time of this writing, has brought Vietnam and the United States into closer relations than at any time since 1975.[12] It has been further argued that the fate of the Hmong and other non-Viet peoples of the Laotian-Vietnamese highlands also demands our attention by virtue not only of their status as abandoned wartime allies, but as the latest addition to the American melting pot.[13]

Finally, if, as some revisionist historians point out, America succeeded in Vietnam because American blood and treasure created a valuable breathing space for the growth of the member states of the Association of Southeast Asian Nations (ASEAN), it would seem only proper that a course on the American War examine the impact of the war on Southeast Asia as a whole.[14]

THE PLACE OF THE VIETNAM WARS IN WORLD HISTORY

The global reach of the wars that attended Vietnam's passage from Han satrap to a modern nation state unquestionably poses a problem for those instructors who are responsive to arguments that their course horizons must be extended, but remain puzzled as to how it can be done. This problem was recognized from the outset by Asianists and Vietnam specialists. They found the solution in the very methodology that enabled them to examine and understand the local dimensions of the American War. In order to explain to students the unique Vietnamese political and social heritage and the place of liberalism, revolutionary anti-colonialism and socialism in that heritage, scholars like William J. Duiker, Samuel Popkin and William S. Turley had to draw on the methodology of comparative civilization subsumed under the broad mantle of world history.[15]   They soon found that there were a variety of reasons for believing that a global or world history approach was an excellent means of organizing their course material.

The perspective of world history enables scholars to demonstrate to students how and why Vietnam became a factor in European colonialism; how Vietnam's response to colonialism was similar to or differed from the responses of other colonized people and how Western currents of liberalism, nationalism and socialism influenced that response.   It can, moreover, be used to show how the coming of global war, which ushered in a new age of revolution at the beginning of the twentieth century, later acted in Southeast Asia to undermine the established order and create an opening for dissident elements.   Further, it constitutes an essential tool in our effort to understand why armed struggle and social revolution on the Vietnamese pattern has taken so different a course in Cambodia, Laos, the Philippines and Indonesia,[16] and provides the only means by which we can evaluate the "killing fields" of Cambodia, the Vietnam War's chief contribution to the science and practice of genocide.[17]   Additionally, the perspective of world history may facilitate analysis of the many parallels that are often drawn, rightly or wrongly, between the Soviet experience in Afghanistan and the American experience in Vietnam.   Iraq did not prove to be Arabic for Vietnam, but the Soviet debacle in Afghanistan indicates that the beckoning sirens of the quagmire can call out from desert sand and rocky slopes as well as from jungle mud.[18]   Whether they will continue to do so, and, if so, under what circumstances, are issues that are germane to the field of world history.

The place of Vietnam in the communist world and in the West's effort to restrict the spread of communism can best be understood when it is examined from a global perspective.   Such a perspective can alone permit students to fully investigate how the communists were able to gain control of the Vietnamese independence movement; how and to what degree indigenous and Chinese models of a people's war of national liberation influenced the strategy of Vo Nguyen Giap; and how the former North Vietnam's land reform policy, its institutions of government, and its foreign policy were influenced by the Soviet Union and China's policy in Southeast Asia.   It is the only vehicle for understanding Vietnam's place in the Cold War and its seeming aftermath in Southeast Asia: the coming of *peristroika*, or *doi moi*, to Vietnam.   The recent calls from Bui Tinh, editor of the Vietnamese communist party organ *Nhan Dan*, and Nguyen Khac Vien, one of Vietnam's best-known historians, for the removal from power of Vietnam's current leaders must be studied against the background of the decline of the communist parties in Europe.[19]

The perspective of world history also possesses value as a focus for course organization. It can help integrate the many elements, foreign and indigenous, of the various Vietnamese Wars and thereby so streamline the discussion of Indochinese society and history as to increase the likelihood of its inclusion in a course that addresses the Vietnam War chiefly as an episode in modern American foreign policy. By employing a world history approach, instructors can also avoid asking those students drawn from the general student body into courses on the war to be responsible for the in-depth discussion of Southeast Asian and American history better suited to upper-division students majoring in these fields. Instead, by focusing on the sweep of historical and socio-political processes rather than their local products—a characteristic of world history—undergraduate surveys of world and Asian history, courses on modern American history and other courses that only briefly address the Vietnam War can convey the essence of this conflict without overwhelming students with detail. Such detail as is necessary can be conveyed in reading assignments or via critical-thinking exercises described in chapter 11 of this volume.

It can be argued that lectures, reading assignments and examinations stressing thematic and comparative topics—which are the workhorses of global studies—are more likely to hold the attention of students than a more conventional approach. Instructors who are not Southeast Asian area specialists will, moreover, quickly come to appreciate an approach which would exchange an entire detailed lecture on the composition of the various early incarnations of the Vietnamese Communist Party, the Vietnamese Nationalist Party (VNQDD), the Dai Viet and other Vietnamese political organizations for a brief discussion of the process by which the various strains of Western liberalism and socialism mixed with Vietnamese nationalist aspirations to produce a wide range of parties and political platforms. Such a lecture is not only well within the abilities and knowledge of most instructors, but essential to their students' understanding of the politics of the third world.

The methodology of world history can be employed to serve a variety of additional classroom needs. It can provide much needed criteria for the discussion of the many parallels between the Vietnamese anti-colonialist struggle and America's own war for independence that often arise during the study of the Vietnam War. Without such criteria, these parallels can be badly misconstrued. The Viet Minh can easily be identified as "the moral equivalent of our founding fathers," or conversely, any parallel between America's "freedom fighters" and the Viet Minh and Viet Cong can be rejected out of hand, thereby potentially relegating the victors of the Vietnam War to the status of communist mercenaries knowingly bent on the oppression of their own people for the greater glory of Moscow and Beijing.

The methodology of world history can also help instructors address one of the great weaknesses of current course offerings: their failure to examine conditions in post-1975 Vietnam. To the world historian, the last fifteen years witnessed a crisis in command economies throughout the world as they grappled with an internal economic structure incapable of sustaining the high technology service and consumer products industries that have come to dominate the global economy. Vietnam has its own place in this pattern. During the First and Second Indochina Wars, necessity had often been the mother of experiments in economic liberalization in North Vietnam. However, in the closing years of the latter struggle, the demands of total war had led to a great degree of centralization. Victory reenforced the communist leadership's faith in both the value of a command economy and the maintenance of democratic centralism within the party. In the 1980s, these leaders were ultimately hoisted on their own petard as their political and economic programs often impeded the course of recovery already threatened by continued Western hostility. As in the 1950s, hardliners in Hanoi then looked to China for their model: economic and political reform was to be conducted only within the framework of the Communist Party. The future is uncertain, but it may be that, as in the Soviet Union, consumer demand in Vietnam is accomplishing what American might could not. As Stanley Karnow remarked after a recent visit to Hanoi, "To coin a phrase, the V.C. is being defeated by the VCR."[20]

Such an analysis, while open to question, indicates that much of Vietnam's recent history can be presented to a class on the war with a minimum amount of preparation and in a minimum of time so long as the perspective of the instructor is a global one. The interpretation of recent Vietnamese history that appears above is based on material drawn from readily available sources and would not take more than fifteen minutes to present to students.[21] Yet, for all its brevity and reliance on inspiration rather than perspiration, it can not only conveniently supply a legitimate cap to a course on the war, but introduce students to the multi-faceted nature of the emerging global civilization in which they live and the Vietnam War helped create.

THE LAST DOMINO: AMERICA AND THE VIETNAMESE WARS

To be sure, the perspective of world history can help illuminate many facets of the American experience in Vietnam. It can assist in the examination of the impact of the First and Second Indochina Wars on America and help set American participation in these wars in the context of its role as a global power. It can facilitate the comparison of American intervention in the Philippines and in Vietnam and allows similarities and differences to be drawn between these interventions and contemporary European imperial expansion. It may also help illuminate any relationships that may exist between the Vietnam War and the Korean War, the Malayan Emergency, the Indonesian crisis and American intervention in the Dominican Republic.[22] A comparative perspective can also lend insight into any parallels that may be said to exist between American policy in Vietnam and in present day Central America or the Persian Gulf, but the drawing of analogies between historical events as separated in time as the Vietnam and Gulf Wars requires the kind of special scholarly care this subject is not likely to receive now or in the near future.[23]

Fortunately, most instructors are aware of the value of and the possible dangers inherent in employing a global or comparative perspective when dealing with American foreign policy, both past and present. The most serious error in perspective in regard to the role of the wars in Vietnam in American history, however, lies not here but in the failure of American courses on the war to discuss the impact of the war on America. Just as these courses often end their discussion of Vietnamese history with the communist victory in 1975, they also frequently end their discussion of America's involvement in Southeast Asia with the image of an American helicopter picking evacuees off a rooftop and flying into the skies above what would soon be renamed Ho Chi Minh City.

As Allan Goodman has recently remarked in an influential article on the teaching of the war, American instructors too often fail to identify the war's legacy beyond the common nostrums of post-Vietnam foreign policy (the so-called Vietnam syndrome). Yet, the war divided generations, deepened the national debt, negatively altered the relationship between the legislative and executive branches of the national government and gave rise to a credibility gap that poisoned relations between the American people and their government. Goodman further reminds us that the Vietnam War, like all past wars, has led to widespread changes in the political process:

> After a war, most governments find themselves in debt, and politicians run for election based on pledges to cut spending. This reduces substantially—if it does not eliminate altogether—the chance for the poor to escape poverty and for the middle class to assure that their children will have a higher quality of life than they did. Historians must ask, and help students consider, whether wars are worth the social polarization and economic problems they often produce. If they do not ask these questions, what is there to prevent my daughter's generation from thinking that it can control and limit the effects of war better than my generation did?[24]

The poignancy of this observation grows with the realization that it was recorded only days before the Iraqi invasion of Kuwait that ultimately spawned Operation Desert Storm. It can be argued that some wars are worth their long-term social costs. It is, however, to be regretted that, despite the benefit of more than a fifteen year interval in which to ponder the question, the United States again went to war without having adequately evaluated the impact of its last major conflict on its economy and social structure, let alone having introduced the problem to students who will likely bear a good part of the financial and social burdens that will be imposed by the Gulf War.[25] Those who would argue that such an evaluation might inhibit the taking of necessary martial action may recall that to forewarn is to forearm, not to paralyze. Men and women have shown throughout history that they can bear the inevitable, even if it be utter defeat: it is the shock of the new to which the morale of a nation succumbs, as any student of the American reaction to the Tet Offensive can tell us.

SOURCES, CLASSROOM APPROACHES AND EXERCISES

There are a variety of resources in addition to those referenced above that can assist teachers to address the Vietnam War or Wars in a broader perspective.

Teaching About Southeast Asia

Instructors seeking guidance in addressing the war's Southeast Asian cultural setting may wish to begin with John Whitmore, editor, *Introduction to Indochinese History, Culture, Language and Life* (Ann Arbor, Mich.: University of Michigan Center for South and Southeast Asian Studies, 1979), or with the first of a projected series of teaching guides prepared by the California Department of Education: Huynh Dinh Te, *The Indochinese and Their Culture* (1989). Forthcoming titles include Te's *Introduction to Vietnamese Culture*, Khamchong Luangpraseut's *Introduction to Cambodian Culture* and Sun Him Chhim's *Introduction to Laotian Culture*. *The Indochinese and Their Culture* is a useful resource and possible text that can be obtained, along with the other titles in the series as they become available, from Van Le, Consultant, TPRC Coordinator, Bilingual Education Office, California State Department of Education, P.O. Box 94272, Sacramento, California 94244-2720. Less useful but valuable for the light it can shed on the manner in which the Vietnamese examine their own traditions is Pham Kim Vinh, *The Vietnamese and Their Culture* (Costa Mesa, Calif.: Pham Kim Vinh Research Institute, 1990). This slim volume can be purchased by writing to the author at 3021-B Harbor Boulevard, Suite 187, Costa Mesa, California 92626.

Instructors seeking an introduction to the region may wish to consult one of the more recent general histories of Southeast Asia, such as Milton

Osborne, *Southeast Asia: An Illustrated Introductory History* (Winchester, Mass.: Allen and Unwin, 3rd ed., 1985), Damodar R. SarDesai, *Southeast Asia: Past and Present* (Boulder, Col.: Westview, 1983), David J. Steinberg, *In Search of Southeast Asia: A Modern History* (Honolulu: University of Hawaii, 2nd rev. ed., 1987), or John Coedes's still valuable *The Making of Southeast Asia* (Berkeley, Calif.: University of California, 1966). Another survey text, John H. Esterline and Mae H. Esterline, *How the Dominoes Fell: Southeast Asia in Perspective* (Lanham, Md.: University Press of America, 2nd. rev. ed., 1990) focuses on indigenous and colonial political culture, the rise of nationalism and the regional impact of Vietnam War.

Teachers in search of model course outlines and syllabi on Southeast Asia and Vietnam will find a useful sample of these materials in Grant Goodman, editor, *Asian History* (New York: Markus Weiner, 1986).[26] Those seeking a guide to teaching the war through Vietnamese eyes will wish to consult two articles by David M. Berman, including "Vietnam Through Vietnamese Eyes: A Review of the Literature," *Asia Pacific Community* 28 (Spring 1985), pp. 88-104, and "'Every Vietnamese Was a Gook:' My Lai, Vietnam, and American Education," *Theory and Research in Social Education* 16 (Spring 1988), pp. 141-59.

Teaching About Vietnam

Joseph Buttinger's *Vietnam: A Political History* (New York: Praeger, 1968) and his *Dragon Defiant* (New York: Praeger, 1972) are good starting points for the non-specialist attempting to introduce him or herself to that nation's past. Alexander B. Woodside's *Community and Revolution in Modern Vietnam* (Boston: Houghton Mifflin, 1976) is an indispensible source-work for Vietnamese social and political history. Instructors seeking very brief introductions to Vietnamese history, society and culture, both for themselves and for their students, will find them in essays by David Elliot, Alexander B. Woodside and others in *The Bulletin of Concerned Asian Scholars* 21, nos. 2-4 (April-December 1989) and in David Elliot et al., *Vietnam: Essays on History, Culture and Society* (New York: The Asia Society, 1985). William J. Duiker's *Vietnam: A Nation in Revolution* (Boulder, Colo.: Westview, 1983) and Damodar R. SarDesai's *Vietnam: Struggle for National Identity* (Boulder, Colo.: Westview, 1991) are invaluable brief surveys of Vietnam's history that differ chiefly in that SarDesai's work contains more material on the pre-modern period.

Pre-modern Vietnam is well-served by several monographs, including Keith Weller Taylor, *The Birth of Vietnam* (Berkeley, Calif.: University of California, 1983), to be released in a paperback edition in 1991; Alexander Woodside, *Vietnam and the Chinese Model* (Cambridge, Mass.: Harvard, 1971); Edgar Wickberg, editor, *Historical Interaction Between China and Vietnam: Institutional and Cultural Themes* (Lawrence, Kan.: Center for

East Asian Studies, University of Kansas, 1969); Nguyen Khac Vien, editor, *Traditional Vietnam: Some Historical Stages* (Hanoi: Xunhasaba, 1965), which offers a patriotic and Marxist interpretation of pre-modern and early modern Vietnam; and Joseph Buttinger, *The Smaller Dragon: A Political History of Vietnam* (New York: Praeger, 1958), the best-known introduction to this subject. Pre-modern Vietnam can be brought into a course on the war with less difficulty than some instructors may think. For example, a map quiz item asking students to locate the ancestral homeland of the Vietnamese in the north of what today is Vietnam can help focus their attention on the regional differences and national loyalties of the Vietnamese people that are crucial to an understanding of the war.

The culture of pre-colonial Vietnam is an excellent vehicle through which students can gain an understanding of the roots of modern Vietnam. It can certainly provide them with a grasp of the essential unity of the Vietnamese people and hence an appreciation of the tragedy of their internecine conflicts. Nguyen Ngoc Bich's *The Original Myths of Vietnam* (Fairfax, Virginia: The Indochina Institute, George Mason University, 1985) is an inexpensive collection of Vietnamese legends that illustrate this facet of Vietnamese life. When these legends and other literary sources, such as Nguyen Ngoc Bich, Burton Raffel and W. S. Mervin's *A Thousand Years of Vietnamese Poetry* (New York: Knopf, 1975), are used in conjunction with a selection of modern Vietnamese war art and poetry, the magnitude of that tragedy can be easily grasped by students. Such a selection can be found in Thich Nhat Hanh and Vo-Dinh, *The Cry of Vietnam* (Santa Barbara, Calif.: Unicorn, 1968), whose deeply moving verses and disturbing drawings are accessible to any high school student. Also useful in this regard is *Under the Starfruit Tree: Folktales from Vietnam* (Honolulu: University of Hawaii, 1989) edited by Alice M. Terada and illustrated by Janet Larsen.

The manner in which individuals made their own separate peace during Vietnam's turbulent past is one of the subjects treated in Nguyen Du's *Tale of Kieu* (New Haven, Conn.: Yale University, 1987), translated by Huynh Sanh Thong. This early modern work, one of the treasures of world literature, also lends insight into the penetration of Chinese culture and political institutions into Vietnam. Those instructors who are reluctant to assign it to students due to the limits imposed by time or the length of other supplemental readings should note that Lynne H. Nelson, editor of *A Global Perspective: Sources Readings from World Civilization* (New York: Harcourt Brace Jovanovich, 1989) has included in the second volume of this two-volume anthology a descriptive essay on the *Tale of Kieu* and a brief, but very fine excerpt from the work ideal for classroom use.

The Vietnamese encounter with the French and the rise of modern Vietnamese nationalism to 1954 is treated in Joseph Buttinger's *A Dragon Embattled: A History of Colonial and Post-Colonial Vietnam,* 2 volumes

(New York: Praeger, 1967); William Duiker's *The Rise of Nationalism in Vietnam* (Ithaca, N. Y.: Cornell University, 1976) and *The Communist Road to Power* (Boulder, Colo.: Westview, 1981); Huynh Kim Khanh, *Vietnamese Communism 1925-1945* (Ithaca, N. Y.: Cornell University, 1982); and David G. Marr's *Vietnamese Anti-Colonialism, 1885-1925* (Berkeley, Calif.: University of California, 1971) and *Vietnamese Nationalism on Trial: 1920-1945* (Berkeley, Calif.: 1981). A Marxist perspective on these developments can be found in Thomas Hodgkin's *Vietnam: The Revolutionary Path* (New York: St. Martin's, 1981) and Nguyen Khac Vien's *Tradition and Revolution in Vietnam* (Berkeley, Calif.: Indochina Resource Center, 1974). John T. McAlister and Paul Mus, *The Vietnamese and Their Revolution* (New York: Harper and Row, 1970) blends Vietnamese social history into an account of the origins of the First Indochina War. Students will derive great benefit from readings drawn from any of these sources.

Other valuable works on the impact of colonialism include: Milton E. Osborne, *The French Presence in Cochin China and Cambodia: Rule and Response, 1859-1905* (Ithaca, N. Y.: Cornell University, 1969); Martin J. Murray, *The Development of Capitalism in Colonial Indochina* (Berkeley, Calif.: University of California, 1980); Ngo Vinh Long, *Before the Revolution: The Vietnamese Peasants under the French* (Cambridge, Mass.: Harvard, 1973); Pam Cao Dung, *Vietnamese Peasants under French Domination, 1861-1945* (Berkeley, Calif.: Center for South and Southeast Asian Studies, University of California, 1985); Charles Robequain, *The Economic Development of French Indochina* (London: Oxford, 1964); Troung Buu Lam, *Patterns of Vietnamese Response to Foreign Intervention, 1858-1900* (New Haven, Conn.: Southeast Asia Studies, Yale University, 1967); and Alfred W. McCoy, *The Politics of Heroin in Southeast Asia* (New York: Harper and Row, 1972). John Cady, *The Roots of French Imperialism in Eastern Asia* (Ithaca, N. Y.: Cornell University, 1954) remains the best introduction to French imperial policy in the region. Perhaps the most useful source in a classroom setting is Tran Tu Binh, *The Red Earth: A Vietnamese Memoir of Life in a Colonial Rubber Plantation* (Athens, Ohio: Ohio University Center for Southeast Asian Studies, 1985), a work edited by David G. Marr.

There are numerous autobiographies, biographies, memoirs and collected writings of major Vietnamese leaders that can be effectively employed to introduce Vietnamese political currents in Vietnam from the 1930s to the Geneva Accords and in the two Vietnams after 1954. The life and work of Ho Chi Minh,[27] Ho Dinh Diem,[28] Vo Nguyen Giap,[29] Nguyen Cao Ky[30] and Troung Chinh[31] are adequately represented in the literature of the war. While these sources generally fail to reveal the complexities of the characters of these men, they accurately convey the passionate commitment of each to their vision of Vietnam's history and destiny.

The most accessible biographical studies of any Vietnamese leader are David Halberstam, Charles Fenn and Jean Lacoutre's biographies of Ho Chi Minh.[32] Some instructors will find the approach employed by these authors to be too sympathetic, but these studies clearly indicate why the image of Ho Chi Minh commanded respect among so many Vietnamese.

Scholarly balance and detachment is the watchword of Bui Diem's *The Jaws of History* (Boston: Houghton Mifflin, 1987), the autobiography of South Vietnam's former Ambassador to the United States. In his youth, Diem was invited to join the communists by his history professor, Vo Nguyen Giap. Giap knew a good student of history when he saw one: Diem's account of Vietnamese nationalism after the Second World War and the failings of the regime he served is deeply humane, and the work itself possesses a historical sweep and sensitivity that renders it useful as supplementary text or reading.

While no work has yet appeared on the life of the now reclusive Nguyen Van Thieu, his state of mind as the war came to a close is described by Bui Diem in *The Jaws of History* and by Nguyen Tien Hung and Jerold Schecter in *The Palace File* (New York: Harper and Row, 1986). Tran Van Don's *Our Endless War* (San Rafael, Calif.: Presidio, 1978) is the most clear-sighted of the memoirs published by former South Vietnamese military men.[33] General Van Tien Dung's account of the final Hanoi offensive, *Our Great Spring Victory* (New York: Monthly Review Press, 1977 [also available in two volumes from the Foreign Broadcast Information Service as FBIS-APA-76-110 and 131]), reflects the sense of destiny and certainty of victory that often, if not always, motivated Hanoi's army during thirty years of war. Those moments of doubt that did occur are partially illuminated in Tran Van Tra's *Vietnam: History of the B-2 Bulwark Theatre*, volume 5, *Concluding the Thirty-Years War* (Springfield, Vir.: Joint Publications Research Service, 1983).

Very good use can be made in the classroom of the small number of accounts of ordinary Vietnamese to illuminate modern Vietnamese society. Le Ly Haslip's *When Heaven and Earth Change Places* (New York: Doubleday, 1989) is one of the finest contributions to the literature of the Vietnam War. This work, written with Jay Wurts, describes Haslip's life as a country girl, a refugee, a Viet Cong courier, a black marketeer, a bar girl and a war bride. It is currently widely employed as an educational tool and should be on every supplementary reading list. Thich Nhat Hanh's *Lotus in a Sea of Fire* (New York: Hill and Wang, 1967) captures the Buddhist community's outlook on the war. As mentioned above, Thich Nhat Hanh and Vo-Dinh's *The Cry of Vietnam* (Santa Barbara, Calif.: Unicorn, 1968) is an extraordinary resource for gauging the feelings of the Vietnamese people at war. There are a few collected accounts of

Vietnamese voices in wartime, of which the best are the selections edited by James A. Freeman, *Hearts of Sorrow: Vietnamese American Lives* (Stanford, Calif.: Stanford University, 1989) and by Don Luce and John Summer, *Vietnam: The Unheard Voices* (Ithaca, N. Y.: Cornell University, 1969). Also useful are Ching Qui, editor, *Between Two Fires: The Unheard Voices of Vietnam* (New York: Preager, 1970) and Francois Sully, editor, *We the Vietnamese: Voices from Vietnam* (New York: Praeger, 1971). Nguyen Ngoc Bich has collected, translated, and edited a number of works by contemporary Vietnamese authors whose efforts are illustrated by Vo-Dinh. These appear in a volume entitled *War and Exile: A Vietnamese Anthology* that can be obtained at a cost of $12.00 by writing directly to Nguyen Ngoc Bich, 6433 Northanna Drive, Springfield, Virginia 22150.

The discussion of Vietnamese society at war between 1954 and 1975 can be enhanced by the employment of scholarly monographs. There is no better treatment of that society than that which has been given to the war in the villages. Several scholarly studies trace the war in the countryside from Hue to the Mekong Delta.[34] When used along side the rich literature of pacification and counterinsurgency,[35] a clear picture can be presented to students both of the spread of communist influence in the South and of the failure of early American and South Vietnamese pacification efforts. Two of these provincial studies are "must" readings for students of the war. Jeffrey Race's *War Comes To Long An: Revolutionary Conflict in a Vietnamese Province* (Berkeley, Calif.: University of California, 1972) reveals the building blocks of the revolutionary movement in South Vietnam's Mekong delta. Now available in paperback, this powerful and well-written book has long been considered required reading for courses on the war.[36] Eric Bergerud's just published tour de force, *The Dynamics of Defeat: The Vietnam War in Hau Nghia Province* (Boulder, Colo.: Westview, 1991) also focuses on the Mekong delta, but his target area is larger than Race's: it concludes with a powerful refutation of the views of William Colby, Anthony James Joes and others who have argued that South Vietnam could have been saved if the United States had used better tactics and not abandoned the war in the early 1970s, when, they contend, the war in the villages was being won.[37]

Students can also benefit from the vivid, though no longer authoritative, picture of insurgent warfare painted by Bernard B. Fall in *Street Without Joy* (New York: Schocken, 4th ed., 1967) and by Frances FitzGerald in *Fire in the Lake* (New York: Vintage, 1973). Instructors can further enliven their presentation of warfare in the South by drawing on two memoirs that have become a staple of courses on the war. *No Other Road to Take* (Ithaca, N. Y.: Cornell University Southeast Asia Studies Program, 1976) by Madame Nguyen Thi Dinh is the author's account of her service as a colonel in command of anti-government forces in the region studied by Race and Bergerud. *A Vietcong Memoir* (San Diego, Calif.: Harcourt,

Brace, Jovanovich, 1985) by Troung Nhu Tang is a very popular reading selection among students examining guerrilla war and is quite effective when used with care. It concludes with a description of what the author believes to be the betrayal of the ideals and goals of the Viet Cong by Hanoi in 1975.

The memoirs of Madame Nguyen Thi Dinh and Troung Nhu Tang can be used as a point of departure for the further study of the revolutionary aspects of the war in the South. Cecil B. Currey has discussed some of the major sources and techniques that can be used to teach about the nature of this struggle.[38] Its key elements are the subject of Douglas Pike's landmark works: *Viet Cong* (Cambridge, Mass.: Massachusetts Institute of Technology, 1966) and *PAVN: People's Army of Vietnam* (Novato, Calif.: Presidio, 1986). Carlyle A. Thayer's *War by Other Means: National Liberation and Revolution in Viet-Nam, 1954-1960* (Boston: Allen Unwin, 1989) takes a fresh and somewhat different view of these organizations, as does Greg Lockhart, *Nation in Arms: the Origins of the People's Army of Vietnam* (Sydney: Asian Studies Association of Australia, 1989). These works may be supplemented by William Darryl Henderson, *Why the Vietcong Fought: A Study in Motivation and Control of a Modern Army* (Westport, Conn.: Greenwood, 1979).

The politics and government of the North and South, and of the reunited state of Vietnam since 1975, has been closely examined by many scholars. Instructors can make good use of Bernard Fall's *The Two Viet-Nams: A Political and Military Analysis* (New York: Praeger, 2nd rev. ed., 1967), the famed French journalist's eyewitness account of the evolution of the Hanoi and Saigon regimes. Fall's *Viet-Minh Regime* (Ithaca, N. Y.: Southeast Asia Program, Cornell University, 1956) provides an interesting description of the North's leaders. The authoritative source on the North's political program is William J. Duiker, *The Communist Road to Power* (Boulder, Colo.: Westview, 1981). A short introduction to Vietnamese communism from its inception to the end of the war can be found in Douglas Pike, *History of Vietnamese Communism* (Stanford, Calif.: Hoover Institution, 1978). The war as seen from Hanoi is the subject of Nguyen Khac Vien, *The Long Resistance, 1958-1974* (Hanoi: Foreign Languages Press, 1975). Nguyen Khac Vien's *Tradition and Revolution in Vietnam* (Berkeley, Calif.: Indochina Resource Center, 1974) describes the process of collectivization in North Vietnam. Gerard Chaliand, a sympathetic observer of revolutionary movements in the third world, provides an account of wartime conditions in the North in *The Peasants of North Vietnam* (Harmondsworth: Penguin, 1969). John Van Dyke describes Hanoi's response to the American air war and strategy of attrition in *North Vietnam's Strategy for Survival* (Palo Alto, Calif.: Pacific, 1972). The development of socialism in North Vietnam described in Nguyen Tien Hung, *Economic Development of Socialist Vietnam* (New York: Praeger,

1977) can be further illustrated by employing the selection of writings to be found in Le Duan, *This Nation and Socialism Are One* (New York: Vanguard, 1976).

There are several old and new accounts of the Republic of Vietnam. Instructors will want to begin with the brief and fair-minded overview of the South's dilemmas provided by Lawrence Grinter's essay, "The Cost of Ignoring Political Requirements," in Lawrence Grinter and Peter Dunn, editors, *The American War in Vietnam: Lessons, Legacies, and Implications for Future Conflicts* (Westport, Conn.: Greenwood, 1987), pp. 30-48. The Diem government is the focus of Jean Lacoutre's *Vietnam: Between Two Truces* (New York: Random House, 1966) and Robert Scagliano's *South Vietnam: Nation under Stress* (Boston: Houghton Mifflin, 1964). Tran Van Don, *Our Endless War,* Denis Warner, *The Last Confucian* (New York: MacMillan, 1963), Roger Hilsman, *To Move A Nation* (Garden City: Doubleday, 1967), Nguyen Thai, *Is South Viet Nam Viable?* (Manila: Carmello and Bauerman, 1962) and Robert Shaplen, *Time Out of Hand: Revolution and Reaction in Southeast Asia* (New York: Harper and Row, 1969) are also useful for the period.

The four existing detailed treatments of the South's political institutions by Dennis J. Duncanson, Allan E. Goodman, Charles Joiner, and Nghiem Dang are products of their time: the late 1960s and early 1970s.[39] The South Vietnamese government is not the principle focus of Neil Sheehan's *A Bright and Shining Lie: John Paul Vann and Vietnam* (New York: Random House, 1988), but the portions of this work devoted to intra-governmental and inter-governmental relations in the South, has the virtue of being accessible to students. When used with care, it can provide a glimpse into how the South's political culture impeded the work of even those American advisors who tried to attune themselves to waging war and building peace in a Southeast Asian setting. As Vann was a member of the Hau Nghia advisory team, Sheehan's work can be employed by students engaged in a classroom debate to support Bergerud's conclusion that the American War in Vietnam was not winnable within its own historical context. Conversely, Goodman's optimistic assessment of the viability of the Saigon government, rendered two years before its collapse, can be cited by those students defending the position that the war was, indeed, winnable. If the truth lies somewhere in between these two arguments, students will probably find it in Bui Diem's *The Jaws of History*, perhaps the most accessible treatise on the high aspirations and harsh realities of the South Vietnamese government.

Three accounts of the final years of South Vietnam can be used to recreate the atmosphere of the period. Frank Snepp's *A Decent Interval* (New York: Random House, 1977) and Arnold Issac's *Without Honor: Defeat in Vietnam and Cambodia* (Baltimore, Md.: Johns Hopkins, 1983) offer highly critical assessments of American policy after the Paris Peace

Accords. In *The Palace File*, Jerold Schecter and Nguyen Tien Hung offer an analysis of the secret promises of support given by Nixon to Nguyen Van Thieu at the time of the signing of those agreements. The authors conclude that the manner in which Nixon and Kissinger conducted diplomatic relations with South Vietnam may have precluded the latter from retaining the support of members of Congress and the American people in 1975. They suggest also that if America lost the war because it was stabbed in the back, Nixon administered the fatal blow.

The Second Indochina War's last campaign is described in the words of South Vietnamese combatants and non-combatants in three works: Cao Van Vien, *The Final Collapse* (Washington, D. C.: Center for Military History, United States Army, 1982); Larry Engleman, *Tears Before Rain: An Oral History of the Fall of South Vietnam* (New York: Oxford University, 1990); and Stephen J. Hosmer, Konrad Kellen and Brian M. Jenkins, editors, *The Fall of South Vietnam: Statements by Vietnamese Military and Civilian Leaders* (New York: Crane Russak, 1980). The views of the victorious communist forces are recorded in Nguyen Khac Vien, editor, *Collapse of the Neo-Colonial Regimes in Indochina* (Hanoi: Vietnamese Studies no. 47, 1977) and in two previously mentioned works, Tran Vanh Tra's *History of the B-2 Bulwark Theatre*, volume 5, *Concluding the Thirty-Years War* and Van Tien Dung, *Our Great Spring Victory*. Tizano Terzani's *Gia Phong!* (New York: St. Martin's, 1976) is an account of the final communist offensive as seen through the eyes of an admiring Western journalist.

The best survey of Vietnam since 1975 is William J. Duiker, *Vietnam Since the Fall of Saigon* (Athens, Ohio: Ohio University, Center for International Studies, 1985). Nayan Chanda, *Brother Enemy: The War After the War* (New York: Harcourt Brace Jovanovich, 1986) and David Elliot, editor, *The Third Indochina Conflict* (Boulder, Colo.: Westview, 1981) are the authoritative sources for the study of the on-going Vietnam-China-Cambodia conflict. America's interest in that conflict is deftly described in Frederick Z. Brown, *Second Chance: The United States and Indochina in the 1990s* (Washington, D. C.: Council for Foreign Relations, 1989). Nguyen Van Khanh, *Vietnam Under Communism, 1975-1982* (Palo Alto, Calif.: Hoover Institution, 1982), Nguyen Long, *After Saigon Fell: Daily Life under the Vietnamese Communists* (Berkeley, Calif.: Institute of East Asian Studies, University of California, 1982) and the more recent, ambivalent and quite valuable Vo Nhan Tri, *Vietnam's Economic Policy Since 1975* (Singapore: Institute of Southeast Asian Studies, 1990) address the state of the Vietnamese economy since reunification. Nguyen Ngoc, *The Will of Heaven* (Ontario: Van Lan, 1982) may be used in conjunction with Doan Van Toai and David Chanoff, *The Vietnamese Gulag: A Revolution Betrayed* (New York: Simon and Schuster, 1986) and Tran Tri Vu, *My 1,632 Days in Vietnamese Reeducation Camps* (Berkeley, Calif.: Institute of East Asian

Studies, University of California, 1988) to assess the penalty paid by those on the losing side of a conflict possessing elements of civil war and revolutionary struggle. Bruce Grant, *The Boat People* (New York: Penguin, 1979) examines a phenomena no longer confined to Vietnam, but which will always be associated with it.

Teaching About Cambodia, Laos and the Hmong

Cambodia and Laos and the ethnic minorities of Vietnam are not as yet well represented in the literature of the war as Vietnam in terms of quantity, but the quality of the literature is good. Any study of Cambodia should begin with David Chandler's *History of Cambodia* (Boulder, Colo.: Westview Press, 1983). Instructors may also wish to consult three standard surveys of modern Cambodia: Milton Osborne, *Before Kampuchea* (Boston: Allen Unwin, 1979); Michael Leifer, *Cambodia: The Search for Identity* (New York: Praeger, 1967); and Michael Vickery, *Kampuchea: Politics, Economics and Society* (London: Pinter, 1986). Also useful are two autobiographical studies by Norodum Sihanouk, *My War with the CIA* (New York: Pantheon, 1973) and *War and Hope* (New York: Pantheon, 1980). Nayan Chanda provides an excellent survey of Vietnamese—Cambodian relations in "Vietnam and Cambodia: Domination and Security," which appears in Joseph J. Zasloff, editor, *Postwar Indochina: Old Enemies and New Allies* (Washington, D. C.: Foreign Service Institute, U. S. Department of State, 1988), pp. 63-76. The impact of American policy in Cambodia is traced in William Shawcross, *Sideshow: Kissinger, Nixon and the Destruction of Cambodia*, (New York: Simon and Schuster, 1979); Peter A. Poole, *The Expansion of the War Into Cambodia* (Athens: Ohio: Ohio University Center for International Studies, 1970); Malcolm Caldwell and Lek Tan, *Cambodia in the Southeast Asian War* (New York: Monthly Review, 1973); and Henry Kissinger, *White House Years* (Boston: Little Brown, 1979).

The rise to power of the communists in Cambodia is the focus of Timothy M. Carney, *Communist Party Power in Kampuchea* (Cambodia) (Ithaca, N. Y.: Cornell University Southeast Asia Studies Program 1977); Craig Etcheson, *The Rise and Demise of Democratic Kampuchea* (Boulder, Colo.: Westview, 1984); Ben Kiernan, *How Pol Pot Came to Power: The Rise and Demise of Democratic Kampuchea* (London: Verso, 1985); Ben Kiernan and Chanthou Boua, editors, *Peasants and Politics in Kampuchea, 1943-1982* (New York: M. E. Sharpe, 1982); and Michael Vickery, *Cambodia: 1975-82* (Boston: South End, 1984).

The genocidal policies of the Khmer Rouge are described in John Barron and Anthony Paul, *Murder of Gentle Land* (New York: Readers Digest, 1977); George Hildebrand and Gareth Porter, *Cambodia: Starvation and Revolution* (New York Monthly Review, 1976); and Francois Ponchaud, *Cambodia: Year Zero* (New York: Holt, Rinehart and Winston,

1978). Vietnam's subsequent intervention in Cambodian affairs is discussed in Nayan Chanda, *Brother Enemy: The War After the War* (New York: Harcourt, Brace, Jovanovich, 1986).

The events described in scholarly studies on Cambodia can be introduced to students through the use of the following popular accounts and memoirs: Elizabeth Becker, *When the War Was Over: The Voices of Cambodia's Revolution and Its People* (New York: Simon and Schuster, 1986); Timothy M. Carney, translator, *Regrets of the Khmer Soul* (Ithaca, N. Y.: Cornell, 1976); Joan Criddle and Teedabutt Man, *To Destroy You Is No Loss: The Odyssey of a Cambodian Family* (New York: The Atlantic Monthly Press, 1987); Someth May, *Cambodian Witness; The Autobiography of Someth May* (London: Faber and Faber, 1986); Hang S. Ngor, *A Cambodian Odyssey* (New York: MacMillian, 1987); and Molyda Szymusiak, *The Stones Cry Out: A Cambodian Childhood, 1975-1980* (New York: Hill and Wang, 1986).

The best overviews of American policy, Vietnamese influence and revolutionary action in Laos are Arthur J. Dommen, *Laos: Keystone of Indochina* (Boulder, Colo.: Westview, 1985); Charles Stevenson, *The End of Nowhere: America Policy Towards Laos Since 1954* (Boston: Beacon, 1972); Hugh Toye, *Laos: Buffer State or Battleground* (New York: Oxford, 1968); and Nina S. Adams and Alfred McCoy, editors, *Laos: War and Revolution* (New York: Harper and Row, 1970). Paul Langer and Joseph J. Zasloff, *North Vietnam and the Pathet Lao* (Cambridge, Mass.: Harvard, 1970); Martin Stuart-Fox, *Laos: Politics, Economics and Society* (London: Pinter, 1986); and Joseph J. Zasloff, *The Pathet Lao: Leadership and Organization* (Lexington, Mass.: D. C. Heath, 1973) provide a foundation for the study of communism in Laos and its relationship with Vietnam. The current authoritative source, MacAlister Brown and Joseph J. Zasloff, *Apprentice Revolutionaries: The Communist Movement in Laos, 1930-1985* (Palo Alto, Calif.: Stanford University, 1986), has been partially updated by Joseph J. Zasloff in "Vietnam and Laos: Master and Apprentice," in Joseph J. Zasloff, *Postwar Indochina: Old Enemies and New Allies*, pp. 37-62. The most recent work on Laos, Grant Evans's *Laotian Peasants Under Socialism* (New Haven, Conn.: Yale, 1990), is a critique of the moral economy of Laotian peasants and the failure of government policies designed to exploit it.

While the Laotian people are not as well represented in literature in English as the Vietnamese or Cambodians, three sources can be used to bring their voices to the attention of students: Fred Branfman, editor, *Voices From the Plain of Jars: Life Under an Air War* (New York: Harper and Row, 1972); Ben Kiernan, editor, *Peasants and Politics* (White Plains, N. Y.: M. E. Sharpe, 1982); and Marek Thee, *Notes of a Witness: Laos and the Second Indochinese War* (New York: Random House, 1973).

The non-Viet peoples of the Laotian-Vietnamese highlands, including the Hmong and the Montagnards, are described in Glenn L. Hendricks, et al., editors, *The Hmong in Transition* (Staten Island, New York: Center for Migration Studies, 1986); Gerald Hickey, *Sons of the Mountains: An Ethnohistory of the Vietnamese Central Highlands to 1954* (New Haven, Conn.: Yale University, 1982) and his *Free in the Forest: An Ethnohistory of the Vietnamese Central Highlands, 1954-1976* (New Haven, Conn.: Yale University, 1982); Peter Kunstadter, editor, *Southeast Asian Tribes, Minorities and Nations* (Princeton, N. J.: Princeton University, 1967); Ronald Provencher, *Mainland Southeast Asia: An Anthropological Perspective* (Pacific Palisades, Calif.: Goodyear, 1975); and Keith Quincy, *Hmong: History of a People* (Cheney, Wash.: East Washington University, 1988). The recruitment of the Hmong as America's ally is discussed in Norman B. Hannah, *The Key to Failure: Laos and the Vietnam War* (New York: Madison, 1987). The Public Broadcasting System has produced an excellent documentary on the Hmong, *No More Mountains: The Story of the Hmong* (Boston: WGBH Television, 1980), which explores their history, their involvement in the opium trade, their participation in the Vietnam War and the condition of their community in the United States.

Teaching About the War's Global Context

Edward L. Farmer, Gavin R.G. Hambly, David Kopf, Byron Marshall, and Romeyn Taylor's *Comparative History of Civilizations in Asia*, 2 volumes (Boulder, Colo.: Westview, 1977-1986) establishes the place of Southeast Asia in Asian and world history. The emergence of Southeast Asia in Asian and world history is traced in O. W. Wolters, *History Culture and Region in Southeast Asian Perspective* (Singapore: Institute of Southeast Asian Studies, 1982) and David G. Marr and A. C. Milner, editors, *Southeast Asia in the Ninth to Fourteenth Centuries*, (Canberra: Research School of Pacific Studies, the Australian National University, 1986). Anthony Reid, *Southeast Asia in the Age of Commerce*, volume 1, *The Lands Below the Winds*, (New Haven, Conn.: Yale University, 1988) and Donald F. Lach, *Asia in the Making of Europe* (Chicago: University of Chicago, 1965) describe the integration of Southeast Asia into an increasingly global economy. Vietnamese resistance to the European domination of that economy can be placed in global and regional perspective by employing Michael Adas, *Prophets of Rebellion: Millenarian Protest Movements Against the European Colonial Order* (Chapel Hill: University of North Carolina, 1979); Benedict Kirkvliet, *The Huk Rebellion: A Study of Peasant Revolt in the Philippines* (Berkeley, Calif.: University of California, 1977); John Lewis, editor, *Peasant Rebellion and Communist Revolution in Asia* (Stanford, Calif.: Stanford University, 1974); Samuel Popkin, *The Rational Peasant* (Berkeley: University of California, 1979);

J. M. Pluvier, *Southeast Asia From Colonialism to Independence* (New York: Oxford University, 1974); James Scott, *The Moral Economy of the Peasant: Rebellion and Subsistence in Southeast Asia* (New Haven: Yale University, 1976); and Eric Wolff, *Peasant Wars of the Twentieth Century* (New York: Harper and Row, 1969).

The place of modern Vietnam in world history is noted in Paul Kennedy, *The Rise and Fall of the Great Powers: Economic Change and Military Conflict, 1500-2000* (New York: Random House, 1987) and in Lloyd C. Gardner, *Approaching Vietnam: From World War II through Dein Bien Phu, 1941-1954* (New York: Norton, 1988). It is also the principal theme of two major works by Ralph B. Smith, *Vietnam and the West* (London: Heinemann Educational, 1971) and *An International History of the Vietnam War,* 4 volumes (London: MacMillan, 1983-1990). William S. Turley, editor, *Vietnamese Communism in Comparative Perspective* (Boulder, Colo.: Westview, 1980); and William Duiker, *The Rise of Nationalism in Vietnam* (Ithaca, N. Y.: Cornell University, 1976) and, by the same author, *The Communist Road to Power* (Boulder, Colo.: Westview, 1981) attempt to place Vietnamese politics and society in global perspective. Guides to the teaching the place of the Vietnam War in world history can be found in the world history course outlines collected by Kevin Reilly, editor, *World History* (New York: Markus Weiner, 3rd ed., 1991) and can also be derived from leading world history texts and anthologies. Among the latter are several works offering alternative approaches, primary source materials and discussion questions that are designed to focus student attention on the global dimension and impact of the war: Alfred J. Andrea and James H. Overfield, *The Human Record: Sources of Global History*, volume 2 (Boston: Houghton Mifflin, 1990), p. 504; Richard Goff, Walter Moss, Janice Terry and Jiu-Hwa Upshur, *The Twentieth Century: A Brief Global History* (New York: Knopf, 1986) pp. 340-54; Kevin Reilly, *The West and the World: A History of Civilization*, volume 2 (New York: Harper and Row: 2nd ed., 1989) pp. 402-407, 424;   Philip F. Riley, Frank A. Gerome, Henry A. Myers, and Chong K. Yoon, *The Global Experience: Readings in World History* volume 2 (Englewood Cliffs, New Jersey: Prentice-Hall, 1987), pp. 285-98.

Teaching About the Impact of the War on America

During a visit to Saigon, John Kenneth Galbraith sent a cable to John F. Kennedy that expressed concern about the future impact of American intervention in Southeast Asia. "It is those of us who . . . have committed our hearts most strongly to the New Frontier," the cable read, "who worry most about its bright promise being sunk under the rice fields."[40] While haunted by nightmares of Munich, Lyndon Johnson knew that "if I left the woman I really loved—the Great Society—in order to get involved with that bitch of a war on the other side of the world, I would lose everything at home."[41]   The examination of whether or to what degree Galbraith's and Johnson's fears were realized is no small task. Instructors who make the attempt, however, can draw upon a wide variety of materials that will challenge students to use the very skills of analysis that are employed by members of an educated electorate to assess the impact of any action taken by their government. These materials are adequate not only for the consideration of the socio-economic impact of the war, but for the study of its impact on American foreign policy and military traditions.

There are several general surveys of the socio-economic and cultural impact of the war. The best-known of these surveys are: Gloria Emerson, *Winners and Losers: Battles, Retreats, Gains, Losses and Ruins from a Long War* (New York: Random House, 1976); Robert Warren Stevens, *Vain Hopes, Grim Realities: The Economic Consequences of the Vietnam War* (New York: New Viewpoints, 1976); James Veninga and Harry A. Wilmer, editors, *Vietnam in Remission* (College Station, Tex.: Texas A&M, 1985); John Wheeler, *Touched With Fire: The Future of the Vietnam Generation* (New York: Avon, 1985); and Myra MacPherson, *Long Time Passing: Vietnam and the Haunted Generation* (New York: Doubleday, 1984), a volume which draws upon interviews with five hundred servicemen and war resisters to assess the human cost of the war. The most recent and the most detailed study of this subject is Anthony S. Campagna, *The Economic Consequences of the Vietnam War* (New York: Praeger, 1991).

The impact of the war on its veterans and their families is well documented. In *Legacy of a War* (Armon, New York: M. E. Sharpe, 1986), Ellen Frey-Wouters and Robert S. Lanter survey over a thousand veterans to assess the impact of the war on its American combatants.   William Broyles, Jr., *Brothers in Arms* (New York: Knopf, 1986); Allen Glick, *Winter's Coming, Winter's Gone: There Were Other Tragedies, Besides Dying in Vietnam* (New York: Pinnacle Books, 1984); Peter Goodman, *What Vietnam Did to Us* (New York: Ballantine, 1980); Bob Greene, *Homecoming* (New York: G. P. Putnam/Ballantine, 1969); Robert Jay Lifton, *Home from the War* (New York: Basic Books, 1973, 1985); Patience H. C. Mason, *Recovering From the War* (New York: Viking, 1990); and Michael Norman, *These Good Men* (Iowa City, Iowa: Crown Publishers, 1990) contain vivid descriptions of veterans' experiences upon their return to the United States. The impact of the war on American women veterans and American women is traced in three well-known works: Barthy Byrd, *Home Front: Women and Vietnam* (Berkeley, Calif.: Shameless Hussy Press, 1986); Lynda Van Devanter, *Home Before Morning: The Story of an Army Nurse in Vietnam* (New York: Beaufort Books, 1983); and Keith Walker, *A Piece of My Heart: The Stories of Twenty-Six American Women Who Served In Vietnam* (New York: Ballantine, 1985). Uwe Siemon-Netto, *The*

Acquittal of God (New York: Pilgrim Press, 1990), addresses the theological dilemmas of Vietnam veterans. William P. Mahedy, a chaplain during the war, examines the spiritual and theological implications of the war for veterans and nonveterans alike in *Out of the Night* (New York: Ballantine, 1986).

The medical needs of veterans and the treatment they have received are described in David Bonior, *The Vietnam Veteran: A History of Neglect* (New York: Praeger, 1984); Robert Klein, *Wounded Men, Broken Promises: How the Veterans Administration Betrays Yesterday's Heroes* (New York: MacMillan, 1981); Richard A. Kukla, *Trauma and the Vietnam War Generation: Report of the Findings from the National Veterans Readjustment Study* (New York: Brunner Mazel, 1990); Peter H. Shuck, *Agent Orange On Trial* (Cambridge, Mass.: Harvard, 1986); and Steven M. Sonneberg, Arthur S. Blank, Jr., and John A. Talbot, editors, *The Trauma of War: Stress and Recovery in Vietnam Veterans* (Washington, D. C.: American Psychiatric Press, 1985); and Fred D. Wilcox, *Waiting for an Army to Die* (New York: Random House, 1983). Those instructors who wish their students to examine the medical issue in depth may wish to acquire the excellent bibliographies on the subject compiled by Norman M. Camp, Robert H. Stretch and William C. Marshall, *Stress, Strain, and Vietnam: An Annotated Bibliography of Two Decades of Psychiatric and Social Science Literature Reflecting the Effect of the War on the American Soldier* (Westport, Conn.: Greenwood, 1988) and Caroline D. Harley, *Agent Orange and the Vietnam Veteran: An Annotated Bibliography* (Monticello, Ill.: Vance Bibliographies, 1985).

One of the most controversial aspects of the impact of the Vietnam War upon America is how that conflict came to define America itself. After exploring the origins and course of the war, many scholars and social commentators came to rather disturbing conclusions about the nature of American society, while others found only reason for pride.[42] Because some of these examinations were not conducted by experts in military history or foreign policy and often appear to be conducted along ideological lines, some instructors tend to dismiss them rather than discuss their place in the debate over the war's impact or allow students to develop their own critique. Yet, students who read them or become acquainted with them via extracts included in virtually all Vietnam War anthologies have no difficulty separating the wheat from the chaff and often turn their readings into a useful foundation for their further investigation of the war. Much the same can be said of the literature of anti-war movement, one of the few means of illuminating the place of the war in American history.

Instructors are rightly wary that any course that delves too deeply into the roots of the antiwar movement can become lost in the maze of modern American history. By assigning students an exercise that permits them to sample and report on one of the many facets of the movement, however, instructors can accomplish the necessary task of illuminating this vital aspect of the war and recent American history without risk to the integrity of a course on the war. Such an assignment will be greatly facilitated by the just published, *An American Ordeal: The Antiwar Movement of the Vietnam Era* (Syracuse, N. Y.: Syracuse University Press, 1990) written by Charles DeBeneditti and completed by Charles Chatfield after DeBeneditti's death in 1987. This work is already being touted as the best survey of the movement. It certainly is a useful guide to sources on the movement's roots in new left ideology,[43] the revolution and counter-revolutions of 1968;[44] the student revolts and intergenerational and counter-cultural conflicts of the 1960s,[45] the civil rights movement,[46] anti-war strategy,[47] resistance to the draft,[48] the impact of the movement on government policy, and the government's response to the movement;[49] and the reflections of former radicals on the 1960s.[50] Other useful surveys are: Dick Cluster, editor, *They Should Have Served That Cup of Coffee* (Boston: Beacon, 1979); Alexander Kendrick, *The Wound Within: America in the Vietnam Years, 1945-1975* (Boston: Little, Brown, 1974); Thomas Powers, *The War at Home: Vietnam and the American People, 1964-1968* (New York: Grossman, 1973); Sohnya Sayres, Anders Stephanson, Stanley Aronowitz, and Frederic Jameson, *The 60s Without Apology* (Minneapolis, Minn.: Beacon, 1984); Charles Tilly, *From Mobilization to Revolution* (Reading, Mass.: Addison-Wesley, 1978); Lawrence S. Wittner, *Rebels Against the War: The American Peace Movement* (Boston: Beacon, 1987); and Nancy Zaroulis and Gerald Sullivan, *Who Spoke Up? American Protest Against the War in Vietnam, 1963-75* (New York: Holt, Rinehart & Winston, 1984). Mark Kitchell's documentary on video, *Berkeley in the Sixties* (1990) evokes the period and its socio-political movements. It may be obtained for purchase or rent by writing to California Newsreel, 149 9th Street, #420, San Francisco, California 94103 or by calling (415) 621-6196.

Lawrence Grinter and Peter Dunn, editors, *The American War in Vietnam: Lessons, Legacies, and Implications for Future Conflicts* (Westport, Conn.: Greenwood Press, 1987) is an invaluable tool for assessing the impact of the war on American military policy. The essays contained in this remarkable book discuss or identify further readings on the lessons of the air war, the ground campaigns, the "Summers Thesis" and the application of the Vietnam experience to Latin America and other third world locales. The consideration of the "Summers Thesis" and the associated "new scholarship" on the war is the focus of Lloyd J. Mathews and Dale E. Brown, editors, *Assessing the Vietnam War* (McLean, Vir.: Pergamon-Brassey, 1987). This volume, composed of articles originally published in *Parameters*, the premier journal of American military history, includes an essay by Paul M. Kattenberg that provides an excellent

introduction to and wry refutation of the revisionist school that dominated
writing on the conduct of the war in the 1980s.[51]

Those instructors seeking to explore the impact of the war on political
institutions and American foreign policy may draw upon a number of
monographs and collected essays on these subjects. The impact of the war
on the conduct of American foreign policy in the years immediately after
the war can be gleaned from Ole R. Holsti and James N. Rosenau,
*American Leadership in World Affairs: Vietnam and the Breakdown of
Consensus* (Winchester, Mass.: Allen Unwin, 1984); Paul M. Kattenberg,
The Vietnam Trauma in American Foreign Policy, 1945-1975 (New
Brunswick, N. J.: Transaction, 1980); Anthony Lake, *The Legacy of
Vietnam: The War, American Society and the Future of American Foreign
Policy* (New York: Council on Foreign Relations, 1976); Richard N.
Pfeffer, editor, *No More Vietnams? The War and the Future of American
Foreign Policy* (New York: Adlai Stevenson Institute of International
Affairs, 1968); and Earl C. Ravenal, *Never Again: Learning from America's
Foreign Policy Failures* (Philadelphia, Penn.: Temple University, 1978).
Studies of the war's impact on American political institutions are few, but
four monographs can serve as sources and models: William Gibbons, *The
United States Government and the Vietnam War—Executive and Legislative
Roles and Relationships,* 2 volumes (Washington, D. C.: Superintendent of
Government of Printing, 1986, 1987); John E. Muller, *War, Presidents and
Public Opinion,* (Lanham, Md.: University Press of America, 1973);
Herbert Y. Schandler, *The Unmaking of a President: Lyndon Johnson and
Vietnam* (Princeton, N. J.: Princeton University, 1977): and Arthur
Schlesinger, Jr., *Bitter Heritage: Vietnam and American Democracy, 1941-
1966* (Boston: Houghton Mifflin, 1968).

The large number and controversial nature of studies of the impact of
the war on the United States make it possible for an instructor to expose
students to a wide range of opinions on the subject. Teachers seeking to
bring them into the classroom may wish to consider two options: choosing
some of the more central issues as topics for student debates or assigning
students the most controversial issues as topics for term papers or book
reviews. In this fashion, students can be made to feel the living pulse of
the continuing efforts of scholars to find meaning in the Vietnam
experience.

Guides to alternative thematic approaches and exercises can be found
in two familiar but easily overlooked resources: those textbooks and
readers for courses on American history that devote attention to the war.
Textbooks such as Alan Brinkley, et al., *American History: A Survey* (New
York: McGraw-Hill, 8th ed., 1991) should leave no doubt that it is not only
possible, but easy to discuss the domestic impact of the war in a relatively
small amount of class time. A reader such as Robert D. Marcus and David
Burner, editors, *American Since 1945* (New York: St. Martin's, 5th ed.,

1991), which features selections from the SDS manifesto and the writings of Myra McPherson and Michael Herr, can suggest the means of incorporating such materials in a course on the war. Such sources can also provide models for integrating the Vietnam War into American history survey courses, which often devote little time to the post-Second World War period.

CONCLUSION

The sources described above are intended to render the task of introducing students to Vietnam and the place of the Vietnam War in Vietnamese, Southeast Asian, global and American history a relatively easy one. They can, as has been suggested above, be used as background material for lectures, assigned as supplementary reading, or used as the basis for course book reviews and even objective examination questions. They can also serve as the raw material for research papers and classroom round table discussions described in detail in chapter 11 of this volume. The succeeding three chapters of this work, moreover, offer a wide variety of resources and means for employing the medium of the novel and film to illuminate the broader dimensions of the war. These sources will further indicate how an instructor may prepare a course that brings together the many cultures and societies drawn into the malestrom of the wars in Vietnam.

NOTES

1. Bui Diem with David Chanoff, *The Jaws of History* (Boston: Houghton Mifflin, 1987), p. 341.
2. See chapter four, pp. 61-69.
3. Leslie H. Gelb and Richard K. Betts, *The Irony of Vietnam: The System Worked* (Washington, D. C.: Brookings, 1979), p. 25.
4. Both works, now classics of the genre, are by the same author. See Douglas Pike, *Viet Cong* (Cambridge, Mass.: Massachusetts Institute of Technology, 1966) and *PAVN: People's Army of Vietnam* (Novato, Calif.: Presidio, 1986).
5. The author wishes to thank Kenneth Van Sibert, a Vietnam veteran, for this reference. Van Sibert maintains one of the finest collections of Vietnam War films in the country and is very generous in his support of teaching the war through film. Instructors seeking to avail themselves of his expertise in identifying or locating film resources can write to him at the Pullman Center for Journalism and Communication, Department of Communications, Room 301, Baker University, Baldwin City, Kansas 66006.

6. George Herring, review of Stanley Karnow, *Vietnam: A History* (New York: Viking, 1983); Richard Ellison, producer, *Vietnam: A Television History* (Boston: WGBH Television, 1984); and Peter Rollins, *Television's Vietnam: Part I: The Real Story; Part II: The Impact of the Media* (New York: Accuracy in Media, 1984-1985), in the *Journal of American History*, 74, (December 1987), pp. 1123-24.

7. Many Vietnamese add their war against Japanese occupation to the list of wars waged with the French, Americans and Chinese in the twentieth century.

8. See John Warren, *American Intervention in Vietnam* (New York: Longmans, 1987); William S. Turley, *The Second Indochina War: A Short Political and Military History, 1954-1975* (Boulder, Colo.: Westview Press, 1986); and James S. Olson and Randy Roberts, *Where the Domino Fell: American and Vietnam, 1945 to 1990* (New York: St. Martins's, 1990).

9. King C. Chen, *China and Vietnam, 1938-1954* (Princeton, N. J.: Princeton University Press, 1969); William Duiker, *China and Vietnam: The Roots of Conflict* (Berkeley, Calif.: Institute of East Asian Studies, University of California, 1986) and "China and Vietnam and the Struggle for Indochina" in Joseph Zasloff, editor, *Postwar Indochina: Old Enemies, New Allies* (Washington, D. C.: Foreign Service Institute, U. S. Department of State, 1988) pp. 147-91; Douglas Pike, *Vietnam and the Soviet Union: Anatomy of An Alliance* (Boulder, Colo.: Westview, 1987); Daniel Papp, *Vietnam: The View from Moscow, Peking and Washington* (Jefferson, N. C.: McFarland, 1981); Lief Rosenberger, *The Soviet Union and Vietnam* (Boulder, Colo.: Westview, 1986); R. B. Smith, *An International History of the Vietnam War*, 2 volumes (London: MacMillan, 1983-1990); W. R. Smyser, *The Independent Vietnamese: Vietnamese Communism Between Russia and China, 1956-1969* (Athens, Ohio: Ohio University Center for International Studies, 1980); and Donald S. Zagoria, *Vietnam Triangle* (New York: Pegasus, 1967).

10. See Thomas Havens, *Fire Across the Seas: the Vietnam War and Japan, 1965-1975* (Princeton, N. J.: Princeton University, 1987); Robert O'Neil, "The Vietnam War and the Western Alliance," in John Schlight, editor, *Second Indochina Symposium*: Papers and Commentary (Washington, D. C.: Center of Military History, United States Army, 1986), pp. 229-44; Glen St. John Barclay, *A Very Small Insurance Policy: The Politics of Australian Involvement in Vietnam* (New York: University of Queensland Press, 1988); Victor Levant, *Quiet Complicity* (Toronto: Between the Lines Press, 1986); Douglas A. Ross, "Canada, Peacemaking, and the Vietnam War: Where Did Ottowa Go Wrong?" in Elizabeth Jane Errington and B. J. C. Mckercher, editors, *The Vietnam War as History* (New York: Praeger, 1990); Charles Taylor, *Snow Job: Canada, the United States and Vietnam [1954-1973]* (Toronto: Anansi, 1974); Richard Falk, *The Vietnam War and International Law*, 4 volumes (Princeton. N. J.:

Princeton University, 1968-1976); Peter D. Trooboff, editor, *Law and Responsibility in Warfare: The Vietnam Experience* (Chapel Hill, N. C.: University of North Carolina, 1975); and Richard Lael, *The Yamashita Precedent* (New York: Columbia University, 1986).

11. Sandra C. Taylor, "Laos: The Escalation of a Secret War" in Elizabeth Jane Errington and B. J. C. McKercher, *The Vietnam War as History*, p. 86.

12. See Frederick Z. Brown, *Second Chance: the United States and Indochina in the 1990s* (New York: The Council of Foreign Relations, 1989).

13. Valerie O'Connor, *The Indochina Refugee Dilemma* (Baton Rouge, La.: Louisiana State University, 1990). Vietnam Generation 2, no. 3 (1990) contains several articles on the Hmong and other Southeast Asian refugee communities resettled in the United States. See also David Haines, editor, *Refugees As Immigrants: Cambodians, Laotians and Vietnamese in America* (Totowa, N. J.: Rowman and Littlefield, 1989).

14. See John H. Esterline and Mae H. Esterline, *How the Dominoes Fell: Southeast Asia and Perspective* (Lanham, Md.: University Press of America, 2nd rev. ed., 1990); James R. Rush, "ASEAN's Neighborhood," in Joseph J. Zasloff, editor, *Postwar Indochina: Old Enemies and New Allies,* pp. 193-223 and Robert O. Tilman, *Southeast Asia and the Enemy Beyond: ASEAN Perceptions of External Threats* (Boulder, Colo.: Westview, 1986).

15. See William J. Duiker, *The Rise of Nationalism in Vietnam, 1900-1941* (Ithaca, N. Y.: Cornell University, 1976) and *The Communist Road to Power* (Boulder, Colo.: Westview, 1981); and Samuel Popkin, *The Rational Peasant* (Berkeley, Calif.: University of California, 1979).

16. See Lawrence Grinter, *Realities of Revolutionary Violence in Southeast Asia: Challenges and Responses* (Maxwell Air Force Base, Ala.: CADRE Paper Series, Air University, 1990).

17. Ervin Staub, *The Roots of Evil: The Origins of Genocide and Other Group Violence* (New York: Cambridge University, 1989).

18. See Gennady Bocharov, *Russian Roulette: Afghanistan Through Russian Eyes* (New York: Harper Collins, 1990).

19. Steven Erlanger, " A Second Senior Vietnamese Criticizes Hanoi's Leadership," in *The New York Times* (March 5, 1991), International edition, sec. a, p. 4.

20. Remark made during a presentation at George Mason University on July 23, 1990. This presentation was recorded on an audio cassette which is on deposit at The Indochina Institute, George Mason University, Fairfax, Virginia, 22030-4444.

21. See the brief but effective treatment of this subject in James Olson and Randy Roberts, *Where the Domino Fell: American and Vietnam, 1945-1990* (New York: St. Martin's, 1990), pp. 274-8 and Stephan T. Johnson,

"Vietnam's Politics and Economy in Mid-1987," in Joseph J. Zasloff, editor, *Postwar Indochina: Old Enemies and New Allies*, pp. 3-36.

22. See Larry E. Cable, *Conflict of Myths: The Development of American Counterinsurgency Doctrine and the Vietnam War* (New York: New York University, 1966) and *Unholy Grail: The U. S. and the Wars in Vietnam, 1965-1968* (New York: Routledge, 1991); John M. Gates, *Schoolbooks and Krags* (Westport, Conn.: Greenwood, 1973); Robert Jackson, *The Malayan Emergency: The Commonwealth Wars, 1948-1966* (New York: Routledge, 1990); Brian Linn, *The U. S. Army and Counterinsurgency in the Philippine War, 1899-1902* (Chapel Hill, N. C.: University of North Carolina, 1989); and Richard Stubbs, *Hearts and Minds in Guerrilla Warfare: The Malayan Emergency, 1948-1960* (Singapore: Oxford, 1989).

23. "President Bush said the specter of Vietnam has been buried forever in the desert sands of the Arabian Peninsula. But amid such euphoria, there were warnings that a military victory, no matter how overwhelming, against a country with an economic output the size of Kentucky's and a population less than a third of the size of Vietnam's does not necessarily herald a new day." See Peter Applebome, "At Home, War Healed Several Wounds," in *The New York Times* (March 4, 1991), sec. a, p. 1. Those arguing that the Gulf War has buried the so-called lessons of the Vietnam War and created a new American military paradigm may benefit from David Petraeus' pre-Gulf War admonition that we should always beware of the "literal application of lessons extracted from Vietnam, or any other past event, to present or future problems without due regard for the specific circumstances that surround those problems." See David Petraeus, "Lessons of History and Lessons of Vietnam," in Lloyd Mathews and Dale E. Brown, editor, *Assessing the Vietnam War* (McLean, Vir.: Pergamon-Brassey, 1987), p. 181.

24. Allan Goodman, "Scholars Must Give More Serious Thought to How They Teach and Write About the War in Vietnam," in *The Chronicle of Higher Education* 36 (July 25, 1990), sec. a, p. 36.

25. See John Wheeler, "Toting Up the Cost of the Gulf War," in *The Atlanta Journal and Constitution* (February 23, 1991), sec. a, p. 19. Wheeler, the former director of the federal Vietnam Veterans Leadership Program, concluded that if American casualties in the Gulf War were high, those wounded would "suffer the same conditions in veterans hospitals that brought so much pain in the Vietnam era: underbugeting, too few nurses, overburdened doctors, red tape and a feeling of abandonment by their country."

26. Several other sources for Southeast Asian syllabi can be found in chapter 14, pp. 227-8 and in the appendix to this volume.

27. The most useful collections of the writings of Ho Chi Minh are Bernard Fall, editor, *Ho Chi Minh: Selected Articles and Speeches, 1920-1967* (London: Lawrence Wishart, 1969); Ho Chi Minh, *President Ho Chi Minh Answers President L. B. Johnson* (Hanoi: Foreign Languages Publishing House, 1967); and David G. Marr, editor, *Reflection From Captivity* (Athens, Ohio: Ohio University Press, 1978).

28. Anthony Bouscaren, *The Last of the Mandarins: Diem of Vietnam* (Pittsburgh, Penn.: Duquesne University, 1965); Joseph Buttinger, *Vietnam: The Unforgettable Tragedy* (New York: Horizon, 1977); Ellen J. Hammer, *A Death in November: America in Vietnam, 1963* (New York: E. P. Dutton, 1987); Edward G. Lansdale, *In the Midst of Wars* (New York: Harper and Row, 1972); Dennis Warner, *The Last Confucian* (New York: Macmillan, 1963); and Morris West, *The Ambassador* (New York: William Morrow, 1965).

29. Giap's writings offer insight into most aspects of the war. His *Unforgettable Months and Years* (Ithaca, N. Y.: Cornell, 1975) and *Unforgettable Days* (Hanoi: Foreign Languages Publishing House, 1978) throw light on the nationalist and communist struggle. His *People's War, People's Army* (New York: Praeger, 1962); *Big Victory, Great Task* (New York: Praeger, 1968); *Banner of People's War, the Party's Military Line* (New York: Praeger, 1970); *The Military Art of People's War: Selected Writings of Vo Nguyen Giap* (New York: Monthly Review, 1970); *How We Won The War* (Philadelphia: Recon, 1976); offer insights into Vietnamese military strategy. See also Robert O'Neill, *General Giap: Politician and Strategist* (New York: Praeger, 1969) and *The Strategy of General Giap Since 1964* (Canberra: Australian National University, 1969).

30. Nguyen Cao Ky, *Twenty Years and Twenty Days* (New York: Stein and Day, 1976) and *How We Lost the War* (New York: Stein and Day, 1978).

31. Troung Chinh, *Selected Writings* (Hanoi: Foreign Languages Publishing House, 1977).

32. David Halberstam *Ho* (New York: Knopf, 1987), Charles Fenn, *Ho Chi Minh: A Biographical Introduction* (New York: Scribner, 1973) and Jean Lacouture, *Ho Chi Minh: A Political Biography* (New York: Random House, 1968).

33. Instructors wishing to create a large sample of the observations by members of the South and North Vietnamese military for student reading assignments can make good use of Cao Van Vien and Dong Van Khuyen, *Reflections on the Vietnam War* (Washington, D. C.: Center for Military History, United States Army, 1980); Hoang Ngoc Lung, *The General Offensives of 1968-1969* (Washington, D. C.: Center for Military History, United States Army, 1981); and Patrick J. McGarvey, editor, *Visions of Victory* (Stanford, Calif.: Hoover Institution, 1969). Several works containing the testimony of captured North Vietnamese officers and

defeated South Vietnamese generals are referenced in *Vietnam, 1964-1973: An American Dilemma* (Colorado Springs, Colo.: Special Bibliography Series no. 80, United States Air Force Academy Library, 1990). While by no means complete, this 66-page pamphlet has the virtue of citing the Library of Congress call numbers as well as standard citations for scores of works on the war, including hard to locate "think-tank" papers and reports.

34. See Gerald Cannon Hickey, *Village in Vietnam* (New Haven, Conn.: Yale University, 1964); Harvey Meyerson, *Vinh Long* (Boston: Houghton Mifflin, 1970); Samuel Popkin, *The Rational Peasant*, mentioned above; Robert L. Sansom, *The Economics of Insurgency in the Mekong Delta of Vietnam* (Cambridge, Mass.: Massachusetts Institute of Technology, 1970); James Walker Trullinger, *Village at War* (New York: Longman, 1980); the recently reprinted F. J. West, *The Village* (Madison, Wis.: University of Wisconsin, 1985); and Alexander B. Woodside, *Community and Revolution in Modern Vietnam* (Boston: Houghton Mifflin, 1976).

35. The best of these works are Douglas S. Blaufarb, *The Counter Insurgency Era: U. S. Doctrine and Performance; 1950 to the Present* (New York: Glencoe Free Press, 1977) and Stuart Herrington, *Silence Was a Weapon: The Vietnam War in the Villages* (Novato, Calif.: Presidio, 1982).

36. A useful excerpt from this work appears in John C. Warren, *America's Intervention in Vietnam: An Anthology* (New York: Longman, 1987), pp. 53-66.

37. See William Colby and James McCargar, *Lost Victory: A Firsthand Account of America's Sixteen Year Involvement in Vietnam* (Chicago: Contemporary Books, 1989) and Anthony James Joes, *The War for South Vietnam* (New York: Praeger, 1989).

38. See chapter three, pp. 50-52.

39. Dennis J. Duncanson, *Government and Revolution in Vietnam* (New York: Oxford, 1968); Allan E. Goodman, *Politics in War: The Bases of Political Community in South Vietnam* (Cambridge, Mass.: Harvard, 1973); and Charles Joiner, *The Politics of Massacre* (Philadelphia: Temple University, 1974); and Nghiem Dang, *Vietnam: Politics and Administration* (Honolulu: East-West Center, 1966).

40. For Galbraith's cable, see The Department of Defense edition, *The Pentagon Papers* (Washington, D. C.: U. S. Government Printing Office, 1971), book 11, pp. 410-8.

41. See Doris Kearnes, *Lyndon Johnson and the American Dream* (New York: Harper and Row, 1976), pp. 251-2.

42. See Loren Bartiz, *Backfire: A History of How American Culture Led Us Into Vietnam and Made Us Fight the Way We Did* (New York: William Morrow, 1985); Leslie Gelb and Raymond Betts, *The Irony of Vietnam: The System Worked* (Washington, D. C.: Brookings Institute, 1979); James William Gibson, *The Perfect War: Technowar in Vietnam* (Boston: The

Atlantic Monthly Press, 1986); David Halberstam, *The Best and the Brightest* (New York: Random House, 1972); Paul Joseph, *Cracks in the Empire: State Politics in the Vietnam War* (New York: Columbia University Press, 1981); Gabriel Kolko, *Anatomy of a War* (New York, Pantheon, 1985); Guenther Lewy, *America In Vietnam* (New York: Oxford University, 1978); Richard Nixon, *No More Vietnams* (New York: Arbor House, 1985); James Thomson, "How Could Vietnam Happen? An Autopsy," *Atlantic Monthly*, 221 (1968), pp. 47-53; Norman Podhoretz, *Why We Were In Vietnam* (New York: Simon and Schuster, 1983); Barbara Tuchman, *The March of Folly: From Troy to Vietnam* (New York: Alfred A. Knopf, 1984). Kim Willenson, et al., *The Bad War: An Oral History of the Vietnam War* (New York: Newsweek, 1987); and William McCloud, *What Should We Tell Our Children About Vietnam?* (Norman, Okla.: University of Oklahoma, 1990) provide additional testimony regarding the war's meaning.

43. Richard Flacks, *Making History: The American Left and the American Mind* (New York: Beacon, 1988); Tod Gitlin, *The Sixties: Years of Hope Days of Rage* (New York: Bantam Books, 1987) and *The Whole World is Watching: Mass Media In the Making and Unmaking of the New Left* (Berkeley, Calif.: University of California, 1980); Maurice Isserman, *If I Had a Hammer* (New York: Basic Books, 1987); and Milton S. Katz, *Ban the Bomb: A History of SANE,* the Committee for a Sane Nuclear Policy (New York: Praeger, 1987).

44. Robert Daniels, *The Year of the Heroic Guerilla: Revolution and Counter-revolution in 1968* (New York: Basic Books, 1989).

45. See Raymond Aron, *The Elusive Revolution: Anatomy of a Student Revolt* (New York: Praeger, 1969); Hervé Bourge, editor, *The French Student Revolt: The Leaders Speak* (New York: Hill & Wang, 1968); *Crisis at Columbia: Report of the Fact-Finding Commission Appointed to Investigate the Disturbances at Columbia University in April and May 1968* (Cox Commission Report, New York: Vintage Books, 1968); Midge Decter, *Liberal Parents, Radical Children* (New York: Coward, McCann & Geoghegan, 1975); Richard Flacks, *Youth and Social Change* (Chicago: University of Chicago, 1971); Ronald Fraser, et al., *1968: A Student Generation in Revolt* (New York: Pantheon, 1988); Kirkpatrich Sale, *SDS* (New York: Boston: 1973); Max Heirich, *The Beginning: Berkeley 1964* (New York: Columbia University, 1971); James S. Kunen, *The Strawberry Statement* (New York: Random House, 1969); Seymour Martin Lipset and Philip G. Altbach, editors, *Students in Revolt* (Boston: Houghton Mifflin, 1969); and David L. Westby, *The Clouded Vision: The Student Movement in the United States in the 1960s* (Lewisburg, Penn.: Bucknell University Press, 1975).

46. Rhoda Lois Blumberg, *Civil Rights: The 1960s Freedom Struggle* (Boston: Twayne, 1984); Clayborne Carson, *In Struggle: SNCC and the Black Awakening of the 1960s* (Cambridge, Mass.: Harvard University,

1981); John H. Clarke, editor, *Malcolm X: The Man and His Times*, (New York: Macmillan, 1969); Eldridge Cleaver, *Soul on Ice* (New York: McGraw-Hill, 1968); Frank I. Donner, *The Age of Surveillance: The Aims and Methods of America's Political Intelligence System* (New York: Vintage, 1981); Philip S. Foner, *The Black Panthers Speak* (Philadelphia: Lippincott, 1970); James Forman, *The Making of Black Revolutionaries: A Personal Account* (New York: Macmillan, 1972); David Garrow, *Bearing the Cross: Martin Luther King, Jr. and the SCLC* (New York: Morrow, 1986); David Garrow, *The FBI and Martin Luther King: From "Solo" to Memphis* (New York: Norton, 1981); Douglas McAdam, *Political Process and the Development of Black Insurgency* (Chicago: University of Chicago, 1982); James M. Washington, editor, *A Testament of Hope: The Essential Writings of Martin Luther King, Jr.* (New York: Harper and Row, 1986); Clyde Taylor, compiler, *Vietnam and Black America: An Anthology of Protest and Resistance* (Garden City, N. Y.: Anchor, 1973); Terry Wallace, *Bloods* (New York: Random House, 1984).

47.   Robert Cooney and Helen Michalowski, *The Power of the People: Active Nonviolence in the United States* (Culver City, Calif.: Peace Press, 1977); David Farber, *Chicago '68* (Chicago: University of Chicago, 1988); and William A. Gordon, *The Fourth of May: Killings and Coverups at Kent State* (New York: Prometheus, 1990); Norman Mailer, *Armies of the Night* (New York: New American Library, 1968); Louis Menashe and Ronald Radosh, editors, *Teach-Ins USA* (New York: Praeger, 1967); and Jim Miller, *Democracy is in the Streets: From Port Huron to the Siege of Chicago* (New York: Simon and Schuster, 1987).

48.   Lawrence M. Baskir and William A. Strauss, *Chance and Circumstances: The War and the Vietnam Generation* (New York: Knopf, 1978); Michael Ferber and Stoughton Lynd, *The Resistance* (Boston: Beacon, 1971); Alice Lynd, *We Won't Go: Personal Accounts for War Objection* (Boston: Beacon, 1968). See also Frank Donner, *The Age of Surveillance* (New York: Knopf, 1980); Jason Epstein, *The Great Conspiracy Trial* (New York: Random House, 1970); Tom Hayden, *Trial* (New York: Holt, Rinehart and Winston, 1970); and Jessica Mitford, *The Trial of Dr. Spock* (New York: Knopf, 1969). A Trotskyite view is provided by Frederick Halstead's, *Out Now: A Participant's Account of the Anti-War Movement Against the Vietnam War* (New York: Anchor, 1978).

49.   Mel Small, *Johnson, Nixon and the Doves* (New Brunswick, N. J.: Rutgers University, 1988).

50.   Jack Whalen and Richard Flacks, *Beyond the Barricades: The Sixties Generation Grows Up* (Philadelphia: Temple University, 1989) and Peter Collier and David Horowitz, *Second Thoughts: Former Radicals Look Back at the Sixties* (New York: Madison, 1989), and David Dellinger, *Vietnam Revisited* (Boston: South End, 1986).

51.   Paul M. Kattenberg, "Reflections on Vietnam: Of Revisionism and Lessons Yet To Learned" in Lloyd J. Mathews and Dale E. Brown, editors, *Assessing the Vietnam War*, pp. 159-170. Joe P. Dunn, in chapter 13 of this volume, thoroughly examines the sources for the study of American military policy in Vietnam.

7

Novels About the "Other Side"

GERALD W. BERKLEY

Historical fiction provides an easy and enjoyable way for students to become involved in a topic and when properly utilized, historical fiction can help to illuminate issues in ways that strictly historical accounts often do not or cannot. Although the reader may ultimately reject a particular author's world-view or value structure, the telling of a tale or the recounting of a personal experience casts a momentary, inherently enjoyable spell.

There are well over one hundred English-language novels that have Vietnam as their primary focus.[1] Unfortunately, what almost all of these works have in common is that their Vietnamese characters are either absent, peripheral, or drawn from Western stereotypes. The main protagonists are usually white soldiers, whose contact with the Vietnamese is limited to a few siliconed, cardboard prostitutes. On the rare occasions when a Vietnamese male is introduced, he is most often depicted as fatalistic, devious, or sadistic. Fortunately, during the early 1980s three novels that transcend these limitations were published: *The Immortal Dragon*,[2] *Saigon*,[3] and *Blue Dragon, White Tiger: A Tet Story*[4]. All three have as a major part of their focus what the Vietnamese experienced during the French and/or American involvement in Vietnam.

THE IMMORTAL DRAGON

The Immortal Dragon was authored by Michael Peterson. A former federal employee who worked on defense contracts, Peterson spent considerable time in Vietnam in the mid-1960s. In 1968, he joined the Marine Corps and was sent back to Vietnam. His writing displays substantial understanding of and empathy for the people of Vietnam. He also provides a rather liberal sprinkling of historical facts throughout the novel.

Strong points of *The Immortal Dragon*, which covers the years 1847 to 1911, include: (1) its discussion of the Imperial Palace in Hue, particularly the grandeur, the intrigues involving eunuchs, concubines, and court favorites, and the isolation of the emperor; (2) the impact of China's nearly one thousand years of occupation, particularly the influence of Confucianism; (3) the role of imperialism, particularly the fact that although the French had initially come for trade and proselytizing they soon developed a desire for more than ports and souls; and (4) the debate among the Vietnamese over the most appropriate means of dealing with the French, that is, whether to try to drive them out or to seek some sort of accommodation that would produce mutual benefits such as trade in exchange for knowledge in the fields of science and technology.

Peterson is also generally successful at characterization. The two major figures in the novel, Ahn Le and Andre Lafabre, are well drawn. Ahn is painted as benevolent, compassionate, and scrupulously just. Lafabre, though presented as somewhat naive, is genuinely concerned with the plight of the Vietnamese and eventually sides with them in their fight for independence. Somewhat more minor figures, such as Louis, the totally decadent son of Andre and his French lover, and Che Lan, the rebel son of Andre and his Vietnamese wife, are also believable. Chien Yu-kuang, however, a Confucian scholar who serves as Ahn's mentor and spiritual adviser, is less realistically drawn. He is given the attributes of the so-called inscrutable Oriental common in Western literature. Chien has visions of "flood waters—swirling and powerful—whose fate was the burning sun and the unquenchable earth [which he sees as] a vast canvas of kaleidoscopic color and scope, a gigantic whirlpool . . ."[5]

The Vietnamese of *The Immortal Dragon* are not peasants, but the elite of Vietnamese society, who are more learned and cultured than their French counterparts. They laugh and joke, quarrel and fight among themselves, share and covet, help and harm—in short, they experience every human emotion that has ever touched a Westerner. The French, while generally naive, are not without merit in the author's eyes. He has Andre Lafabre note:

> Of course I realize some of the terrible things the French have done, but they've done some good things too. Before the French came, Vietnam was a primitive, backward nation ruled by a corrupt mandarinate. Since the French have come, roads and railroads have been built, industry and shipping started, education and medicine spread. Vietnam is finally entering the modern world, and they wouldn't have without the French.[6]

As a final caveat on *The Immortal Dragon*, it should be noted that the novel contains considerable gratuitous sex. In the eyes of some, this may make it less suitable for classroom use.

SAIGON

Anthony Grey, a former Reuters correspondent who was subjected to physical abuse and imprisonment for 26 months by the Red Guards of Beijing, is the author of *Saigon*. In researching this book he traveled to Paris, London, Washington and Cambridge, Massachusetts. On these trips he discussed Vietnam with such notables as Phillippe Devillers, Ralph Smith, William Corson, Frank Snepp and Douglas Pike. The result is a novel that is faithful to historical fact.

Saigon traces the involvement of the Sherman family in Vietnam during the years 1925 to 1975. The major character is Joseph Sherman, who first journeyed to Vietnam at the age of fifteen. He had accompanied his father, an old-style southern senator, on a hunting trip. Joseph, a sensitive youth, was horrified by the French behavior in Vietnam. He was particularly offended by Jacques Devraux, a former officer of the Infanterie Coloniale, who was to later work for the French secret police in Vietnam. As Devraux explained the situation: "The égalité and the fraternité get left at home. But in here colonies France reserves the right to take whatever liberties she chooses."[7] Further, he noted that "the history of the Annamese is full of bloodshed and brutality. There's a cruel streak in these people . . . they are also a deceptive race. They like to mislead with an outward show of passivity."[8]

Joseph subsequently becomes an Asian specialist, and frequently returns to Vietnam. On one of these trips he falls in love with Lan Van Hieu, the daughter of a mandarin who is a "collaborateur"—he cooperated with the French in the exploitation of Vietnam and was generously rewarded for his service. Lan's brother, Tran Van Kim, blazes with the fire of Vietnamese nationalism and eventually becomes a leader in the National Liberation Front.

Other Vietnamese in the novel are Ngo Van Loc and his sons Ngo Van Dong and Ngo Van Hoc. All three develop an intense hatred for the French and end up giving their lives for the revolution.

Major strengths of *Saigon* include the following: (1) an excellent description of Hue, both the architectural beauty and the elaborate court ceremonies; (2) a rather disturbing argument which, while not justifying French imperialism in Vietnam, explains it within the context of the time; (3) a vivid account of the role the British played in Vietnam in 1945 and 1946; and (4) a graphic re-creation of the French plight at Dien Bien Phu.

Easily the most striking aspect of *Saigon* is the depiction of the privations suffered by the Vietnamese who were worked on the French-run rubber plantations. It reads in part:

> A black mantle of pre-dawn darkness still cloaked the jungle and the rubber plantation villages when the Annamese *cai* who assisted the French plantation director and his European staff began sounding clamorous gongs outside the barracks huts. The coolies inside the fetid dens immediately began to stretch their stiffened limbs and drag themselves off their sodden mats, knowing that within minutes the *cai* would be among them flailing heavy staves to rouse the laggards.[9]

In the novel, the coolies begin work before five o'clock, and each completes the first tapping of their 350 trees in the five hours before ten o'clock. Each coolie spends only a minute or so at each tree, draining off dried latex, adjusting the collecting supports and making new incisions through which the day's latex could escape. Poor incisions invariably bring a beating from the *cai* or the French. At ten o'clock the collection of latex begins. The cup on each tree is emptied into carrying cans, and when the cans are full they are deposited at the collection stations. Collection is completed by midday, after seven hours of nonstop toil. A hurried lunch of cold rice follows, and then from one o'clock until sunset the coolies usually work at clearing underbrush and weeds from the rubber groves. Coolies who fail to meet their quota of latex for the day are lashed on the exposed soles of their feet. The novel's readers learn that many Vietnamese who are forced to labor under these conditions do not survive their three-year contracts.

One criticism that might be made of *Saigon* is that the coverage of the 1960s and early 1970s in Vietnam is not nearly as captivating as the attention the author gives the 1940s and 1950s.

BLUE DRAGON, WHITE TIGER: A TET STORY

Tran Van Dinh, author of *Blue Dragon, White Tiger: A Tet Story*, was born into a Confucian/Buddhist, scholar/mandarin family in Hue. He was active in the independence movement against the French, and in 1954 he entered the Vietnamese Foreign Service. His diplomatic assignments included serving as Observer to the United Nations and hargé d'affaires at the Vietnamese embassy in Washington. Since 1971, Tran has taught international politics and communications at Temple University.

The protagonist of Tran's novel is Tran Van Minh, the son of an aristocratic family from Hue. He resigns a diplomatic post in protest of Ngo Dinh Diem's anti-Buddhist policies. He then becomes a professor at "innovative, radical Thomas Paine College" in the United States. At the urging of his family and because of his father's ill health, he returns to Vietnam in 1967 and plunges into the thick of his nation's turmoil. While teaching at Hue University, he is recruited by the Viet Cong. His task is to analyze the American press, and he correctly predicts that a Tet attack on Saigon will result in great disillusionment for the war among the general population in the United States. He later serves as a member of the Viet Cong delegation at the Paris peace talks, and after 1975 he works for the government in both Hanoi and Ho Chi Minh City. He soon becomes disenchanted because of the dogmatism and brutality of Vietnam's new leaders and is particularly upset about the effect communism is having on traditional Vietnamese culture. He joins the boat people and returns to the United States.

Among the more fascinating and moving portrayals in *Blue Dragon, White Tiger* are the description of the Tet celebration; the picture of the transformation of Saigon that the war had caused; the plight of the South Vietnamese army, whose senior officers had served the French colonial army and as a consequence were Vietnamese by name but French by conviction and training; the depiction of life in an underground jungle command post; and sketches of life as a Marxist bureaucrat in Hanoi and Paris. The descriptions and expositions of Buddhist and Vietnamese culture are illuminating and are made even more effective by the extensive use of quotations from Vietnamese poetry and folk tales.

Tran Van Dinh's book has not been well received by many South Vietnamese who are now living in the United States. They see the author as a political manipulator who has presented the National Liberation Front as the only true representative of Vietnamese nationalism. Tran has also been attacked for his portrait of the former presidents of South Vietnam, Ngo Dinh Diem and Nguyen Van Thieu. Both are depicted as self-serving opportunists who were totally out of touch with the general sentiment of their fellow countrymen.

Finally, given the parallels between the author and the main character, the obvious question is the extent to which *Blue Dragon, White Tiger* is autobiographical. Tran Van Dinh answers this with the following quote from the famed eighteenth-century Chinese novel, *The Dream of the Red Chamber*: "When seeming is taken for being; when nothing is taken for something, something becomes nothing."[10]

NOTES

1.   See Tom Colonnese and Jerry Hogan, "Vietnam War Literature, 1958-1979: A First Checklist," *Bulletin of Bibliography* 38, no.1 (January-March 1981), pp. 26-31; and Philip D. Beidler, *American Literature and the Experience of Vietnam* (Athens: University of Georgia, 1982).

   2. Michael Peterson, *The Immortal Dragon* (New York: New
American Library, 1983).
   3. Anthony Grey, *Saigon* (Boston: Little, Brown and Company, 1982).
   4. Tran Van Dinh, *Blue Dragon, White Tiger: A Tet Story*
(Philadelphia: TriAm Press, 1983).
   5. Peterson, *The Immortal Dragon*, p. 156.
   6. Ibid., p. 110.
   7. Grey, *Saigon*, p. 41.
   8. Ibid., p. 256.
   9. Ibid., p. 115.
   10. Tran Van Dinh, *Blue Dragon, White Tiger: A Tet Story*, p. x.

8

Introducing World Literature into a Course on the Vietnam War

JONATHAN GOLDSTEIN

In 1984 and 1987, I participated in a team-taught course on the Vietnam War at West Georgia College.[1] The course used textbooks by Stanley Karnow, Guenter Lewy and George Herring[2], but the vast and still growing body of war-related literary works in French, Vietnamese and English[3] was untapped as a classroom resource. At that time, the value of world literature as a teaching tool in courses on behavior was just beginning to surface, but, like Gerald Berkley, I soon grew impressed by the insights students could gain from such material. Since the West Georgia program pursued an inter-disciplinary approach, I sought to demonstrate to my colleagues that the inclusion of such literary texts could strengthen both pedagogy and student interest across the social science curriculum. It did not, in the end, prove difficult to identify the reasons for or the means of revising our Vietnam course using world literature as a major component of the curriculum.

WHY INCLUDE LITERARY WORKS IN A VIETNAM WAR HISTORY COURSE?

There seem to be two reasons why some of this literature should be incorporated into a Vietnam War history course. The first is a general one that might apply to other history courses. Literary texts, when used as supplements to analytical histories and historical documents, can raise cultural and historical consciousness. They can be used to explore such themes as personal and national aggression, conflict of cultures, dislocation, restless alienation, tradition and modernization, exile, "self" versus "other," "civilized" versus "barbarian," "first" versus "third" world, mother country versus colonial periphery, or metropolis versus hinterland. A speculative approach in which questions are posed before students have read the texts

can prepare students to look for those themes when they read. The texts
then become the materials for finding some of the answers.

A second reason for including literary texts, while particular to the
needs of West Georgia's course on the Vietnam War, may be relevant
elsewhere. When the course was given in 1984 and 1987, no adjunct
literary texts were assigned, nor were students asked to do book reports
using literary works of their own selection. Such lack is a serious
pedagogical shortcoming because the Vietnam War received considerable
attention in both the print and the electronic media. As Robert Elegant,
who reported on Southeast Asia for 20 years, has written in *Encounter*,
"Vietnam was determined not only on the battlefield, but on the printed
page, and above all, on the television screen."[4] At West Georgia in 1984
and 1987, the audio-visual record of the war, especially the Public
Broadcasting System series, was presented and discussed, and therefore
seems to have been validated by the instructor. A student could leave the
course legitimately wondering why no literature had emerged from the
Vietnam War when there were so many movies, newsreels and songs.

I suggested that the 1984 and 1987 syllabi be revised because of general
theoretical and particular pedagogical concerns. All students could be
assigned, as complements to the history texts, readings from the
Vietnamese, French and English literary responses to this war. To
supplement the instructor's choice of texts, each student could be asked to
choose literary works from any of the three relevant groups.

THE REQUIRED READING OF THREE ADJUNCT TEXTS

As in many teaching situations, the instructor's choice of canonical text
is based on considerations of literary worth tempered by such practical
realities as the cost of the books and the amount of time available for the
reading. Given financial and time constraints at West Georgia, three
inexpensive paperbacks, each under three hundred pages, plus a textbook
and book(s) of the student's choosing for book reports, appear to be the
maximum amount of reading that each student can be required to
purchase, read and discuss in class.[5]

Using A Required French Text in Translation

A good text dealing with the French colonial background is Marguerite
Duras's *The Sea Wall*, first published in 1950.[6] Duras's father was a
French colonial official in Vietnam. Her account highlights an aspect of
the French colonial experience that can be overlooked if one focuses on
highly visible confrontations between the *Legion Etrangere* and Viet
nationalists: the fate of the average French agricultural settler who went

out to colonize. According to Duras, the settler was exploited on a different level than the Vietnamese. Before students have read Duras, they can be asked to look in other sources for evidence of Western imperial exploitation. Most will find evidence of exploitation of Vietnamese by the French. After they have read the novel, their perspective can be broadened to encompass familial, inter-generational, and class conflict of French versus French. For example, in the Vietnamese colonial economy, a Michelin plantation executive or owner had as little empathy for the pureblooded French agriculturalist as for a Viet farmer. In telling the story of the trials and tribulations of French settlers Duras portrays exploitation and personal suffering as having universality—a non-nationalistic dimension that can be analyzed in the classroom.

Using A Required English-Language Text

William J. Lederer and Eugene Burdick's *The Ugly American* picks up chronologically where Duras ends. The setting is the mythical Southeast Asian city of Haidho, Sarkan, in the 1940s and early 1950s. France is on its way out, and Americans, Soviets and various political alignments of Sarkanese vie for influence. A liquor-guzzling United States political reject serves as his nation's ambassador. His Machiavellian Soviet counterpart procures Sarkanese goodwill by arranging to have sacks of donated American rice stamped "This is a gift from Russia." The ruse is especially successful since the stamp is in Sarkanese, which most Americans cannot read. There is a single American with a grasp of the language and a non-condescending empathy for the people of Sarkan. Frustrated by the combined efforts of bungling and historically ignorant American bureaucrats, he is beset by the village-level machinations of the communist/nationalist resistance. A poignant irony is that this aid worker's failure is orchestrated by his former Sarkanese comrade from World War II days. Their close personal ties are sundered by ideological disputes over whether gradualist capitalism or revolutionary socialism is the better road to progress for Sarkan.

Like Duras's novel, *The Ugly American* can be used in the classroom to highlight themes of personal, national and international crisis and conflict. Another theme, not present in Duras, concerns how Americans should or should not conduct relations with third world peoples, be they Vietnamese, Iraqis, Central Americans or others. In both the fictionalized and the non-fictionalized parts of *The Ugly American* Lederer and Burdick imply that United States foreign service personnel should have multi-lingual competence and should intensively study the history, geography, economy and culture of the region to which they are assigned. American tours of duty should be lengthened, on the Soviet model, rather than subjected to abrupt, often highly politicized rotation.

The Ugly American was published in 1958, eight years after Duras' book and before any substantial commitment of American ground troops in Vietnam. These were critical years of upheaval and crisis in which the *crème de la crème* of the French military was defeated on the Dien Bien Phu battlefield. During the same eight years, the United States fought Chinese and Korean troops and took on an increasingly militant counterinsurgency posture in Central America, especially in Guatemala. While these broader global conflicts are not explicitly discussed in *The Ugly American*, their causation and parameters are alluded to in Lederer and Burdick's non-fictionalized, didactic last chapter. Like George Orwell's *1984*, *The Ugly American* is timely, foreshadows the future, and stands on its own as a work of literary quality. The characters' concerns become our concerns.

For the more academically motivated students, an alternative text to Lederer and Burdick is Graham Greene's *The Quiet American*.[7] Like Burdick and Lederer, Greene wrote a fast-moving account of what took place just as the French were leaving Indochina and Americans were arriving. There the similarities end. Graham Greene, unlike Lederer and Burdick, resided extensively in Vietnam in the 1950s. He drew on his own experience to create believable characters in a vivid Vietnamese setting rather than cardboard characters in an exotic locale. Greene's protagonist, an English journalist, explores the alleys, boulevards, whorehouses and wharves of Hanoi and Saigon. He visits battlefields and flies a bombing run up Hanoi's Red River valley. Unlike Lederer and Burdick, Greene's cynical correspondent sees no "goodies" and "baddies" and espouses no highly dichotomized, Cold War worldview. He is skeptical of all governmental schemes, especially of the efforts of an idealistic American who wishes to channel aid to a "third force" as France departs. Of this person, the correspondent concludes: "I never knew a man who had better motives for all the trouble he caused."[8]

Using A Required Text in Translation From the Socialist Republic of Vietnam

It is a formidable task to find a readily available inexpensive classroom text coming from or reflective of the viewpoint of the Socialist Republic of Vietnam, hereafter referred to as the SRV. One must distinguish between literature written and published in the SRV versus Vietnamese expatriate literature. Each genre has its own value when used critically in the classroom. The two forms can be juxtaposed much in the way that an American history instructor might contrast literary works by an American Revolutionary and a Tory.

With respect to the literature of the SRV, much has been written in Vietnamese and published there in journalistic fashion. Additionally,

Hanoi's Foreign Languages Publishing House has published in English Nguyen Khac Vien and Hu Ngoc's mammoth, 3-1/2 inch thick anthology *Vietnamese Literature*, and Anh Duc's *Hon Dat*, an example of Vietnamese novels written during the American-Indochina War.[9] For reasons of availability, neither of these works would be appropriate for an American classroom. Relatively little that has been translated into English has found effective distribution in the United States. The card catalog of the National Library in Hanoi lists hundreds of editions of English language works produced by Red River Publishing House and affiliated publishers. Until Sino-Vietnamese hostilities began in 1978-1979, Americans could purchase Vietnamese literature in translation through the semi-official outlet for People's Republic of China publications in the United States, China Books and Periodicals.[10] Since the outbreak of that war, American sources for SRV literature in translation have been largely restricted to the Asia Resource Center, the United States-Vietnam Friendship Association, and the United States-Vietnam Friendship and Aid Association of Southern California.[11] These organizations are staffed mainly by volunteers and are sources for occasional single photocopies, if not class sets of SRV literature.

If and when the United States recognizes the SRV and lifts its embargo on trade with that nation, an important component of the third major linguistic tradition overarches the Vietnam conflict may become more accessible to American teachers and students. Until then one can fall back on autobiography for a text from the SRV. General Vo Nguyen Giap, perhaps the most important military figure in twentieth century Vietnam, published his 110-page autobiographical account *Dien Bien Phu* in Hanoi in approximately 1955. Originally issued by Foreign Language Press, the work has been reprinted in numerous editions. It is available in paperback as pages 131-88 of *People's War People's Army* with a foreword by Roger Hilsman.[12] It is Giap's personal reminiscence of the military and political techniques he used against the French. His theme is an abiding nationalism. He sees native ingenuity as the essential quality that enabled the Vietnamese to defeat the Mongols. The Vietnamese cleverly drove stakes into the Bach Dang River to impale the invaders' warships. An intimate knowledge of terrain helped the Vietnamese achieve what many Westerners perceived as an impossible task: carrying heavy artillery pieces across the mountains to Dien Bien Phu. To Giap, indomitable courage enabled the Vietnamese to mount human-wave suicide charges and to tunnel under French fortifications. Finally, according to him, Marxist ideology and party discipline additionally enabled a victory of a so-called underdeveloped third-world people over a "mighty" first-world foe.[13]

Whether one assigns Giap, Greene, Lederer and Burdick, or Duras, certain teaching strategies can be applied to some or all of these readings. One strategy suggested by Douglas Simon of Drew University is to assign

The Ugly American to students before they have read a single textbook page or have viewed any of the Public Broadcasting System's *Vietnam: A Television History*. Students are asked to write down and discuss the major points, lessons and predictions of the book and then to "file away" these ideas. The class returns to the ideas a couple of weeks later or at the end of the course. At that time students attempt to determine the validity of Lederer and Burdick's major points. How prophetic were these two authors?

A variant on Professor Simon's strategy would be to pose specific speculative questions before students have read their assignments. Were there any pre-1954 lessons from Vietnamese history that should have tempered America's post-1954 policies in that region? Were there any unlearned lessons of the battle of Dien Bien Phu? Younger American officers certainly read Giap's book prior to massive United States involvement and took Giap seriously as a strategist who defeated the French.[14] Giap proceeded to use some of the same strategy against the Americans. Why did Americans not believe that his strategy would succeed against the United States? Was the American role in Vietnam simply wrong on all counts? Do the Vietnamese or American texts contribute any specific information that can help us to better answer that question? These questions can serve as bases for class discussion after the required texts have been read. They broaden a discussion of international relations and raise issues of American ethnocentricity and racism, professional myopia, perceptions of not being a colonial power like France, and over-confidence in having an overwhelmingly favorable balance of military forces.

A BOOK REPORT ON TEXT(S) OF THE STUDENT'S CHOICE

The instructor's selection of three literary texts to complement the textbook has been described as a privileged choice based on practical and financial as well as pedagogical considerations. Each of the three texts has also been chosen for its lucidity. Philip Brown, who used Lederer and Burdick in a Vietnam course at the University of North Carolina at Charlotte, included on his syllabus the phrase "most students have found L & B good reading when they want to relax."[15]

To supplement the canonical choices of the instructor, each student should be asked to select either one full-length novel or two shorter literary works from any of the three groups. He or she would then prepare a four-to-eight-page analysis in which several questions would be answered with reference to the Vietnam War. What subject matter does each author cover? How does each handle this subject matter? What is the major thrust or interpretation of each book? What issues, if any, are

subordinated to bring out the main focus? What are the writer's sources
of information? What are the author's biases? How do you know? What
basic assumptions does each writer make about the indigenous history of
Vietnam? About Westerners in Vietnam? How do you rate the author(s)
in terms of style, clarity, and persuasiveness?

COLLATERAL READING

Three specialized categories of Vietnam War literature from which
students could select collateral reading remain to be discussed: Vietnamese
expatriate texts, episodic novels and texts that lend themselves to
comparative analysis in book report form.

Vietnamese Expatriate Texts

An instructor might wish to recommend one of two translations of
Vietnamese expatriate literary text to more academically motivated
students. Both books are readily available in the United States.

Pham Van Ky's *Blood Brothers* was originally written in 1947 in
French.[16] Ky's major focus is on tradition and change at the village level,
forces personified in the attitudes and behavior of two of the narrator's
"blood brothers." One brother espouses traditional Taoist mysticism, the
Chinese philosophy of inaction (*wu wei*), passivity and asceticism. Another
brother adopts Marxist ideology and joins the Viet Minh. The narrator
finds himself in a dilemma. He is unable to choose not only between
friends and brothers but also between Vietnamese traditionalism and a
radical form of modernization. The second half of his dilemma is also
what Vietnamese society as a whole must confront from 1945 on.

A second Vietnamese expatriate novel that might be considered for
class use has been briefly introduced in Gerald Berkley's chapter: Tran
Van Dinh's *Blue Dragon, White Tiger: A Tet Story*, originally written in
Vietnamese and available in English translation only as a 334-page
hardback.[17] Because of cost and length it may be less appropriate for
classroom use than Ky's shorter and less expensive paperback.

Dinh's work explicates the motif of a "Blue Dragon," representing the
East, spring and tenderness, in conflict with a "White Tiger," symbolizing
the West, winter and force. The novel focuses on the 1960s and 1970s
through the eyes of a Vietnamese diplomat who resigns his post to protest
the anti-Buddhist policies of the Ngo Dinh Diem regime. Minh joins the
Viet Cong and rises to prominence in that organization. Ultimately, he
comes to see the Viet Cong, also, as a force that stifles traditional
Vietnamese culture. He flees Vietnam as one of the "boat people" and
winds up as a refugee in the United States. Dinh includes excerpts from

Vietnamese poetry, songs, inscriptions and histories. In addition to what Dinh includes, a wide variety of these types of non-novelistic Vietnamese literature is readily available in English translation for classroom use.[18]

Episodic Novels

Long, episodic novels can be useful in teaching a Vietnam War course in at least two ways. A primary reason for assigning episodic novels is their lucidity. They have the potential for sustaining less academically motivated students' interest in history—an enthusiasm that may have been kindled by required books like *The Ugly American*. Episodic novels may "turn on" students otherwise "turned off" to history. A second reason for including episodic novels is their substance. All of the novels previously discussed in this paper that were originally written in English (as opposed to novels translated into English) share one characteristic. As Gerald Berkley has pointed out, while there are well over a hundred English-language novels that have Vietnam as their primary focus, in almost all of them Vietnamese characters are either absent, peripheral or drawn from Western stereotypes. He has identified two episodic English-language novels that extensively feature Vietnamese as well as Western experiences during the French and to a lesser extent the American involvements in Vietnam: *The Immortal Dragon* and *Saigon*. My own interpretation of their meaning and value employs somewhat different, though complimentary, points of analysis.

Michael Peterson's *The Immortal Dragon* is an extravaganza of intrigue taking place in France and Vietnam between 1847 and 1914 as the mother country tried to consolidate her Southeast Asian empire.[19] The novel traces the life of Andre, a French *colon*, and his extended French, Vietnamese and mixed-race family. Most prominent among the Vietnamese with whom Andre and his kin interact is Ahn, a mandarin whose fervent nationalism alienates him from Emperor Tu Duc.

Peterson explores the complexity of behavior as Vietnamese try to define and pursue the dragon's virtue. Emperor Tu Duc sees collaboration with France as a means of preserving at least part of his kingdom. That, to him, is a virtue. Ahn defines virtue differently and admonishes the Emperor that "our people will never be subjugated. A thousand years of Chinese (rule) proved that, and these silly pale people from afar have no hope of dominating us."[20] Resistance is the proper course of action.

Peterson's examination of these social conflicts is the strength of his book. On the other hand, he garnishes his tale with almost non-stop sexual and sexist episodes, perhaps gearing his script for a potential television mini-series or for a cinema audience. Berkley is quite correct in noting that the sheer volume of gratuitous sex in *The Immortal Dragon* may make this novel inappropriate for some students, communities or educational systems. From that standpoint alone, the British journalist

Anthony Grey's less sexually explicit *Saigon* may be more appropriate than *The Immortal Dragon*.

Grey picks up roughly where Peterson ends, covering the years 1925 to 1975.[21] He also traces one fictionalized Western family's interaction with Vietnamese counterparts. Beginning with Chuck Sherman's death on a Vietnam hunting expedition in the 1920s and ending with the evacuation of an illegitimate Sherman offspring during the 1975 Battle of Saigon, the novel provides a panorama of urban and rural Vietnamese life, from the elaborate court at Hue to the plantations and villages to the fetid Chinese ghetto of Cholon.

As already noted, Grey and Peterson emphasize the French colonial era. Students who wish to focus more on the American experience, or students who are more academically motivated and who can handle two books rather than reading a single episodic novel, can be given the opportunity to write a comparative book report rather than writing a book report based on a single volume.

A COMPARATIVE BOOK REPORT OF TWO CONTRASTING TEXTS

A student selecting this option would have to select some comparative framework and make it clear to the instructor. The vast and expanding volume of American literature of the Vietnam War makes this approach viable.[22] The literature is sufficiently large that students can crisscross ideological, racial and gender considerations.[23] For example, one can readily contrast, based on literature, pro- and anti-war sensitivities of women who served in Vietnam, both in the military and in the voluntary agencies.[24] Black versus white prisoner of war accounts can be compared.[25]

CONCLUSION

In conclusion, the episodic novel, comparative book report, or three seminal texts representing the major groups of Vietnam war literature can offer students a richer experience than they might have had while restricted to textbooks plus audio-visual accounts. The selection by the instructor of three lucid texts capitalizes on students' enthusiasm and directs it toward clarification of issues that are both highly controversial and relevant in their lives. The addition of an expatriate or episodic novel or other texts that students choose furthers their value-clarification process and mitigates against their adoption of only the worldview presented in texts assigned by the instructor.

Vietnam veteran and education Professor David Berman lamented in an issue of *The Social Studies* that "it is unfortunate that our approach to the teaching of Vietnam is primarily through the American lens."[26] The need that Professor Berman highlights can be filled by juxtaposing Western and non-Western literatures. In that fashion, students' world outlook and empathy for "the other" may be broadened and sensitized. The insertion of world literature into a history course might then, in the long run, even have redeeming features for society as a whole.

NOTES

The copyright on the material in this chapter is held by Jonathan Goldstein and is used here with the author's permission.

1. This chapter is based upon a paper prepared for the panel "Teaching the Vietnam War at the Secondary and Collegiate Levels," Southeast Conference of the Association for Asian Studies (SEC/AAS), Charlotte, North Carolina, January 15, 1988. For criticism of this paper, the author would like to thank Converse College's Joe P. Dunn, who chaired the 1988 panel, as well as Sarah Lawall of the University of Massachusetts at Amherst, William Turley of Southern Illinois University, Douglas W. Simon of Drew University, Lorie Smith of Saint Michael's College, Earl H. Tilford, Jr., of Air University and Don Luce of the Asia Resource Center. That paper was designed to serve as a sequel to an earlier conference presentation entitled "An Interdisciplinary Approach to Teaching the Vietnam War." It should be read in conjunction with that earlier piece. Both papers are descriptions and analyses of an elective course first taught at West Georgia College in 1984. See Jonathan Goldstein, "An Interdisciplinary Experiment in Teaching the American-Indochina War," *Annals* of the Southeast Conference, Association for Asian Studies 7 (1985), pp. 23-30.

2. Stanley Karnow, *Vietnam: A History* (New York: Viking, 1983); Guenter Lewy, *America in Vietnam* (New York: Oxford University Press, 1980); George Herring, *America's Longest War: The United States and Vietnam, 1950-1975* (New York: Knopf, 1986).

3. Joe P. Dunn, "The Vietnam Bookshelf Enters the 1980s," *Naval War College Review* 34, no. 5 (September-October, 1981), pp. 107-13. On Spanish Civil War literature, see Paul Ilie, *Literature and Inner Exile: Authoritarian Spain, 1939-75* (Baltimore, Md.: Johns Hopkins University, 1980).

4. Robert Elegant noted in John Corry, "TV: The Tet Offensive in Vietnam," *The New York Times* (November 8, 1983), sec. c, p. 15.

5. A "buddy system" would be an experimental variant of this strategy. Under such a system, half the class might read text 3A, the other half of the class 3B, and then they might swap the books they have bought.

6. Marguerite Duras, *The Sea Wall*, translated by Herma Briffault (New York: Farrar, Straus and Giroux, 1950, 1976); Marguerite Duras, *A Sea of Troubles*, translated by Antonia White (Harmondsworth, England: Penguin, 1969). The original title of the novel was *Un Barrage contre le Pacifique* (Paris: Gallimard, 1950). For a novel on urban life in French Indochina, a possibility might be Duras's *The Lover*, translated by Barbara Bray (New York: Pantheon, 1985). The original title of this book was *L'amant*. Reviews might suggest which is the better translation and more appropriate choice of subject matter for a particular classroom context.

7. Graham Greene, *The Quiet American* (New York and Harmondsworth, England: Penguin, 1955, 1980). A third alternative to Burdick and Lederer is the Englishman Mark Frankland's semi-autobiographical novel *The Mother-of-Pearl Men* (London: John Murray, 1985), 188 pages; unavailable in paperback as of August 1988.

8. Ibid., p. 60.

9. Nguyen Khac Vien and Hu Ngoc, *Vietnamese Literature* (Hanoi: Foreign Languages Publishing House, 1982); Anh Duc, *Hon Dat*, translated by Robert C. Friend (Hanoi: Foreign Languages Publishing House, 1969). For a general critique of Vietnamese literature, historical and contemporary, see Maurice Durand and Nguyen Tran Huan, *An Introduction to Vietnamese Literature* (New York: Columbia University, 1985), a translation of *Introduction à la Literature Vietnamienne* (1969).

10. China Books and Periodicals, Inc., is registered under the Foreign Agents Registration Act as an agent of the People's Republic of China.

11. Published materials from the Socialist Republic of Vietnam are available in the United States in 1991 from Asia Resource Center, P. O. Box 15275, Washington, D. C. 20003, tele. (202) 547-1114; The U. S.— Vietnam Friendship and Aid Association of Southern California, P. O. Box 453, Murrieta, California, 92362, tele. (714) 677-5905; and The U. S./Vietnam Friendship Association, P. O. Box 5043, San Francisco, California, 94101. The brochure *English-Language Publications from Vietnam* is available from the Murrieta, California, association.

Since 1986 an increasing number of Americans have been visiting Vietnam. American visitors can purchase a wide variety of English-language publications of Xunhasaba-State Enterprise for the Export and Import of Books, Periodicals, and Other Cultural Commodities, 32 Hai Ba Trung, Hanoi, Socialist Republic of Vietnam.

As of 1990, there are excellent prospects for literature from the Socialist Republic of Vietnam becoming more readily available in the United States in the future. The William Joiner Center for the Study of War and Social Consequence, at the University of Massachusetts, Boston, has announced plans for the University of Massachusetts Press to publish five Vietnamese veterans' works in translation. In 1988 the Joiner Center began to co-publish *The Vietnam Forum* in conjunction with Yale University's Council on Southeast Asia Studies. Huynh Sanh Thong, executive editor of the *Forum*, told me on September 19, 1988, of his intention to use the *Forum* increasingly as a publication vehicle for both expatriate Vietnamese writers and writers living and working in Vietnam.

12. Vo Nguyen Giap, *People's War, People's Army* (New York: Bantam, 1968).

13. As a foil to Giap's internationally publicized official history, a professor might wish to assign a contrasting interpretation of the battle. One possibility is a not-for-publication Vietnamese army general staff critique of the battle of Dien Bien Phu, which William Turley discovered in the captured enemy documents collection at the University of Massachusetts, Boston. Turley's discovery is a book of 160 pages, approximately the same length as Giap's. Unlike Giap's, Turley's account was made for teaching Vietnamese army cadres rather than for international distribution. Although it has not been fully translated into English, it holds the potential for classroom usefulness. I am grateful to Kevin Bowen, Co-Director of the Joiner Center at the University of Massachusetts for showing me excerpts from the captured document. See also Ronald H. Spector, "In the Nam and 'Back in the World': American and Vietnamese Sources on the Vietnam War," *The Journal of American History* 75, no. 1 (June 1988), p. 213.

Yet another viewpoint on the battle is provided by the French Marxist historian Alain Ruscio in his article "How Did Our Contemporaries Live the Final Battle of the French War in Indochina," *Vietnam Courier* (Hanoi), no. 6 (1987), pp. 5-9. This article is a translation of excerpts from Ruscio's longer piece, "Dien Bien Phu: du coup de genie a l'aberration," *Revue francaise d'histoire d'outre-mer* (Paris) 72, no. 268 (1985), pp. 335-47. Ruscio deflates a myth that permeated the French press concerning the role of women at Dien Bien Phu. He points out that the much-publicized Florence Nightingale of Dien Bien Phu (Genevieve de Galard) was *not* the only woman to remain in the entrenched camp to the bitter end. The French press rarely mentioned the simultaneous presence of the Vietnamese and North African prostitutes of the *bordels militaires de campagne*. For a more generalized and contrasting Vietnamese expatriate's appraisal of the Democratic Republic of Vietnam's army and the army of the National Liberation Front of South Vietnam, see Truong Nhu Tang's *A Vietcong Memoir* (New York: Vintage, paperback, 1986).

14. See William C. Westmoreland, *A Soldier Reports* (New York: Dell, 1980), pp. 67, 359, 364, 442-45, 536-37.

15. "Vietnam, Spring, 1987, Brown," printed syllabus, History Department, University of North Carolina, Charlotte.

16. Pham Van Ky, *Blood Brothers*, translated by Margaret Maudon (New Haven, Conn.: Council for Southeast Asia Studies, Yale Center for International and Area Studies, 1987). A comprehensive introduction, footnotes, and appendix have been prepared by Lucy Nguyen. This book also includes numerous advertisements for translations into English of other Vietnamese works. This novel was originally published in French as *Frére de sang* (Paris: Editions du Seuil, 1947). On Vietnamese expatriate literature, see articles in *The Vietnam Forum* (New Haven, Connecticut) and David M. Berman, "Vietnam Through Vietnamese Eyes: A Review of the Literature," *Asia Pacific Community* (Spring 1985), pp. 88-104. I am grateful to Professor Berman for insights into Vietnamese literature provided in this article and in his personal commentary during our January 1987 tour of Vietnam.

17. Tranh Van Dinh, *Blue Dragon, White Tiger: A Tet Story* (Philadelphia: TriAm Press, 1983). A second historical novel by Dinh is *No Passenger on the River* (Fort Collins, Colo.: Pratt, 1989).

18. Whether or not one uses Dinh's novel with its excerpts of Vietnamese poetry and songs, the assigning of this type of collateral reading can expand a student's awareness of Vietnamese culture. Among non-novelistic Vietnamese literary works readily available in the United States in English translation are: (1) three collections of historical poetry: Huynh Sanh Thong, translator and editor, *The Heritage of Vietnamese Poetry* (New Haven, Conn.: Yale University Press, 1979); Nguyen Ngoc Bich, translator and editor, with Burton Raffel and W. S. Merwin, *A Thousand Years of Vietnamese Poetry* (New York: Knopf, 1975); and Burton Raffel, translator, *From the Vietnamese: Ten Centuries of Poetry* (New York: October House, 1968); which includes 11 prison poems of Ho Chi Minh; (2) four translations of contemporary Vietnamese poetry: Nhat Hanh and Vo-Dinh, *Zen Poems* (Greensboro, N. C.: Unicorn Press, 1976); Nhat Hanh, *Viet Nam Poems*, translator Nhat Hanh and Helen Coutant (Santa Barbara, Calif.: Unicorn Press, 1972); Thich Nhat Hanh and Vo-Dinh, *The Cry of Vietnam* (Santa Barbara, Calif.: Unicorn Press, 1968); and Don Luce, John C. Schafer, and Jacquelyn Chagnon, editors, *We Promise One Another, Poems from an Asian War* (Washington, D. C.: Indochina Mobile Education project, 1971); (3) a bilingual anthology of Vietnamese folk poetry: John Balaban, translator and editor, *Ca Dao Vietnam: A Bilingual Anthology of Vietnamese Folk Poetry* (Greensboro, N. C.: Unicorn Press, 1980); and (4) a translation of the eighteenth century Vietnamese poet, Nguyen Du: Nguyen Du, *The Tale of Keiu*, translated by Huynh Sanh Thong (New Haven, Conn.: Yale University Press, paperback, 1987, 276 pages). Du is also represented in the aforementioned Nguyen and Hu anthology published in Hanoi and in *We Promise One Another*.

19. Michael Peterson, *The Immortal Dragon* (New York: New American Library, paperback, 1983).

20. Ibid., *Immortal*, p. 163.

21. Anthony Grey, *Saigon* (New York: Dell, paperback, 1983).

22. A student is able to choose from a wide range of available texts to develop his or her comparative framework. Apart from college and public libraries, the B. Dalton bookstore chain has installed a "Vietnam Books" paperback section in its outlets nationwide. There are at least three American book dealers who specialize in Vietnam War literature: Ken Lopez, 51 Huntington Road, Hadley, Massachusetts 01035, tele. (413) 584-4827; Dailey Book Service, 90 Kimball Lane, Christiansburg, Virginia 24073, tele. (703) 382-8949; and Vietnam Bookstore, P.O. Box 469, Collinsville, Connecticut 06022, which also publishes a catalog and newsletter. The bimonthly magazine *Vietnam* (Leesburg, Virginia) includes personal reminiscences of the war and reviews of war literature.

23. To assist students in coming to grips with the abundance of American literature on the Vietnam War, there are several standard references on the subject. Catherine Calloway and Arthur Casciato's bibliographies of criticism of American Vietnam War literature include subsections on poetry, prose and drama: Catherine Calloway, "Vietnam War Literature and Film: A Bibliography of Secondary Sources," *Bulletin of Bibliography* 43, no. 3 (September 1986), pp. 149-58; and Arthur D. Casciato, "Teaching the Literature of the Vietnam War," *Review* (Charlottesville, Va.) 9 (1987), pp. 125-47. Harry Summers's dictionary of the jargon of the American war, *Vietnam War Almanac* (New York: Facts on File, 1985), explicates geographical terms, unit identifications and names of weapons. For listings of titles of Vietnam War literature, students can consult Tom Colonnese and Jerry Hogan's comprehensive bibliography of novels, poetry, plays, short stories and journalistic works containing some fiction, "Vietnam War Literature, 1958-1979: A First Checklist," *Bulletin on Bibliography* 38, no. 1 (January-March 1981), pp. 26-31, 51. They can consult other general literary bibliographies and critiques by John C. Pratt, Edward Palm, John Newman, Margaret E. Stewart, and Philip Beidler: John Clark Pratt, "Bibliographic Commentary," in Timothy Lomperis, *Reading the Wind: The Literature of the Vietnam War* (Durham, N. C.: Duke University Press, 1987); Edward F. Palm, "Novels of Vietnam and the Uses of War Literature," *Marine Corps Gazette* (November 1986), pp. 92-99; John Newman, *Vietnam War Literature* (Metuchen, N. J.: Scarecrow, 1982); Margaret E. Stewart, "Vietnam War Novels in the Classroom," *Teaching History* 6, no. 2 (Fall 1981), pp. 60-66; and Philip D. Beidler, *American Literature and the Experience of Vietnam* (Athens: Georgia: University of Georgia, 1982).

There are also specialized bibliographical resources. Jeffrey Fenn has analyzed American plays pertaining to the Vietnam War, William Ehrhart has anthologized poetry, and Nancy Anisfeld has compiled a reader containing novel and drama excerpts, short stories and poetry: Jeffrey W.

Fenn, "Culture under Stress: American Drama and the Vietnam War," (Ph.D. diss., Theater, University of British Columbia, 1988); William D. Ehrhart, editor, *Carrying the Darkness* (New York: Avon, 1985); and Nancy Anisfeld, editor, *Vietnam Anthology: American War Literature* (Bowling Green, Ohio: Bowling Green State University Popular Press, 1987).

24. On Vietnamese and American women during the Vietnam War, see Patricia L. Walsh, *Forever Sad the Hearts* (New York: Avon, 1982); Linda Van Devanter and Christopher Morgan, *Home Before Morning* (New York: Beaufort, 1983; New York: Warner, 1984); Wendy Larsen and Tran Thi Nga, *Two Women and Vietnam* (New York: Random House, 1986); and Bobbie Ann Mason, *In Country* (New York: Harper and Row, 1985).

25. Pupils who like prisoner of war accounts can find comprehensive bibliographies in Joe P. Dunn's "The POW Chronicles: A Bibliographic Review," *Armed Forces and Society* 9, no. 3 (Spring 1983), pp. 495-514, and in Dunn's "The Vietnam War POW/MIAs: An Annotated Bibliography," *Bulletin of Bibliography* 45, no. 2 (June 1988), pp. 152-57. Students can be directed toward real or fictionalized accounts of American prisoners of war who reached differing conclusions about the war as a result of their incarcerations. Soldiers who emerged from prison more gung ho than they went in, such as United States Air Force Colonel Ted Guy or Navy Apprentice Seaman Douglas Hegdahl, can be juxtaposed with one who emerged as an antiwar activist, such as Army Special Forces Sergeant George Smith. See, for example, James A. Daly and Lee Bergman, *A Hero's Welcome: The Conscience of Sergeant James Daly Versus the United States Army* (Indianapolis: Bobbs-Merrill, 1975); Norman A. McDaniel, *Yet Another Voice* (New York: Hawthorne Books, 1975) or George Smith, *POW: Two Years with the Viet Cong* (Berkeley, Calif.: Ramparts, 1971).

26. David M. Berman, "Perspectives on the Teaching of Vietnam," *The Social Studies* 77, no. 4 (July-August 1986), p. 165.

SELECTED BIBLIOGRAPHY

Anh Duc. *Hon Dat*. Translated by Robert C. Friend. Hanoi: Foreign Languages Publishing House, 1969.

Balaban, John, translator and editor. *Ca Dao Vietnam: A Bilingual Anthology of Vietnamese Folk Poetry*. Greensboro, N. C: Unicorn Press, 1980.

————. *No Passenger on the River*. Fort Collins, Colorado: Pratt, 1989.

Duras, Marguerite. *The Lover*. Translated by Barbara Bray. New York: Pantheon, 1985.

————. *A Sea of Troubles*. Translated by Antonia White. Harmondsworth, England: Penguin, 1969 (1953).

————. *The Sea Wall*. Translated by Herma Briffault. New York: Farrar, Straus and Giroux, 1976 (1950).

Frankland, Mark. *The Mother-of-Pearl Men*. London: John Murray, 1985.

Greene, Graham. *The Quiet American*. New York and Harmondsworth, England: Penguin, 1980 (1955).

Grey, Anthony. *Saigon*. New York: Dell 1983 (1982).

Hilsman, Roger. *People's War, People's Army*. New York: Bantam, 1968.

Larsen, Wendy, and Tran Thi Nga. *Two Women and Vietnam*. New York: Random House, 1986.

Lederer, William J., and Burdick, Eugene. *The Ugly American*. New York: Ballantine, 1985 (1958).

Luce, Don; Schafer, John C.; and Chagnon, Jacquelyn, editors. *We Promise One Another: Poems from an Asian War*. Washington, D. C.: Indochina Mobile Education Project, 1971.

Mason, Bobbie Ann. *In Country: A Novel*. New York: Harper and Row, 1985.

Nguyen Du. *The Tale of Kieu*. Translated by Huynh Sanh Thong. New Haven, Conn.: Yale University Press, 1967.

Nguyen Ngoc Bich, translator and editor, with Burton Raffel and W. S. Merwin. *A Thousand Years of Vietnamese Poetry*. New York: Knopf, 1975.

Nguyen Khac Vien, and Hu Ngoc. *Vietnamese Literature*. Hanoi: Red River Publishing House, 1982.

Nhat Hanh. *Viet Nam Poems*. Translated by Nhat Hanh and Helen Coutant. Santa Barbara, Calif.: Unicorn Press, 1972.

Nhat Hanh and Vo-Dinh. *Zen Poems*. Greensboro, N. C.: Unicorn Press, 1976.

Pham Van, Ky. *Blood Brothers*. Translated by Margaret Maudon. New Haven: Council for Southeast Asia Studies, Yale Center for International and Area Studies, 1987. Introduction, footnotes and appendix by Lucy Nguyen.

Peterson, Michael. *The Immortal Dragon*. New York: New American Library, 1983.

Raffel, Burton, translator. *From the Vietnamese: Ten Centuries of Poetry*. New York: October House, 1968.

Thich Nhat Hanh and Vo-Dinh. *The Cry of Vietnam*. Santa Barbara, Calif.: Unicorn Press, 1968.

Tran Van Dinh. *Blue Dragon, White Tiger, A Tet Story*. Philadelphia: TriAm Press, 1983.

Van Devanter, Linda. *Home Before Morning*. New York: Beaufort, 1983; New York: Warner, 1984.

Vo Nguyen Giap. *Dien Bien Phu*. Hanoi: Foreign Languages Press, 1955.

Walsh, Patricia L. *Forever Sad the Hearts*. New York: Avon, 1982.

9

American Literature and Film of the Vietnam War: Classroom Strategies and Critical Sources
CATHERINE CALLOWAY

In 1973 Julian Smith wrote that the Vietnam War had "produced little popular art: only one major film, *The Green Berets*, one major popular novel, *The Green Berets*, and one popular song, *The Ballad of the Green Berets*."[1] Nearly 50 American novels written during the active years of the war failed to establish themselves as a remarkable literary group,[2] and many of the over 40 Vietnam War films produced during that time avoided combat scenes, treated the returning veteran instead of the soldier at war,[3] or examined the anti-war movement.[4] It was not until after American withdrawal from Southeast Asia that Vietnam became a credible subject for authors and film-makers. In 1977, for the first time since the Tet Offensive in 1968, the movie industry released a "real Vietnam combat film . . . Sidney Furie's *The Boys in Company C*,"[5] and in 1979 Tim O'Brien's Vietnam War novel *Going After Cacciato* received the National Book Award. Now, over a decade after the late 1970s and over 15 years after the anniversary of the fall of Saigon, the war has become a popular topic, with new books or films about Vietnam appearing almost weekly.

PRIMARY SOURCES: LITERATURE

The reader and teacher of the literature of the Vietnam War in the 1990s has a plethora of works from which to choose. One can study or teach literary works by genre and by issue. A genre-oriented approach may include conventional combat novels such as James Webb's *Fields of Fire* (Englewood Cliffs, N. J.: Prentice-Hall, 1978) or John Del Vecchio's *The 13th Valley* (New York: Bantam, 1982), unconventional combat novels such as Gustav Hasford's *The Short-Timers* (New York: Bantam, 1979) or Charles Durden's *No Bugles, No Drums* (New York: Charter, 1976), oral histories such as Al Santoli's *Everything We Had: An Oral History of the*

Vietnam War (New York: Ballantine, 1985) and *To Bear Any Burden* (New York: Ballantine, 1986), "scrapbooks"[6] such as Bernard Edelman's *Dear America: Letters Home from Vietnam* (New York: Pocket Books, 1987) or Laura Palmer's *Shrapnel in the Heart* (New York: Random House, 1987), works of metafiction such as James Park Sloan's *War Games* (New York: Avon, 1973) or Tim O'Brien's *The Things They Carried* (Boston: Houghton Mifflin and Seymour Lawrence, 1990), anthologies of poetry such as W. D. Ehrhart's *Carrying the Darkness* (Lubbock: Texas Tech University, 1988) and *Unaccustomed Mercy: Soldier-Poets of the Vietnam War* (Lubbock: Texas Tech University, 1989), and dramas such as David Rabe's *Streamers* (New York: Knopf, 1977) and *The Basic Training of Pavlo Hummel* (New York: Penguin, 1973).

An issue-oriented approach to the war can also include a variety of literary works. David Willson's *REMF Diary* (Seattle, Wash.: Black Heron, 1988) and Charles Anderson's *Vietnam: The Other War* (New York: Warner, 1990) address the subject of the war in the rear, and Wallace Terry's *Bloods* (New York: Ballantine, 1985), Stanley Goff's *Brothers: Black Soldiers in Nam* (New York: Berkeley, 1986) and John B. Carn's *Vietnam Blues* (Los Angeles, Calif.: Holloway, 1988) focus on the role of minorities in the war. Depictions of women who served in Vietnam can be found in Kathryn Marshall's *In the Combat Zone* (New York: Penguin, 1987), Lynda Van Devanter's *Home Before Morning* (New York: Warner, 1983) and Keith Walker's *A Piece of My Heart* (New York: Ballantine, 1985). Other novels and personal narratives examine the subject of the returning veteran, such as Robert Bausch's *On the Way Home* (New York: Avon, 1982), Philip Caputo's *Indian Country* (New York: Bantam, 1987), Larry Heinemann's *Paco's Story* (New York: Penguin, 1987), Ed Dodge's *Dau* (New York: Berkeley, 1984) or Rick Eilert's *For Self and Country* (New York: Pocket Books, 1984).

Texts such as the above can be used to structure an entire course on the literature of the war or to supplement the required texts in a course of another discipline. A history, political science, communications, or international relations instructor, for example, may wish to include an oral history or personal narrative of the war in a course that focuses on a non-literary aspect of the war or war era.

PRIMARY SOURCES: FILMS

While the Vietnam War has not spawned as many films as it has literary works, there are still a wide range of films available on videocassette for classroom use.[7] An instructor may show movies that fall under the genre of combat films, for example, recent works such as Oliver Stone's *Platoon* (1986), Stanley Kubrick's *Full Metal Jacket* (1987) or John Irvin's

Hamburger Hill (1987).[8] Also useful are the first three combat films to be released almost a decade after John Wayne's *The Green Berets* (1968), films Rick Berg terms "epistemological dramas" because "each attempts to find a means for knowing and understanding the war."[9] These films are Ted Post's *Go Tell the Spartans* (1978), Sidney J. Furie's *The Boys in Company C* (1978) and Francis Ford Coppola's *Apocalypse Now* (1979). Other films, such as Ted Kotcheff's *Uncommon Valor* (1983), Ted Post's *Good Guys Wear Black* (1979) and George P. Cosmatos's *Rambo: First Blood, Part II* (1985), deal with revenge. Movies can also be used to demonstrate the anti-war point of view. Arthur Penn's *Alice's Restaurant* (1969), Richard Rush's *Getting Straight* (1970), Stuart Hagmann's *The Strawberry Statement* (1970) and Anthony Newley's *Summertree* (1971), for instance, capture the flavor of the protest movements of the 1960s.

By far the largest category of Vietnam War films is that which focuses, at least in part, on the returning veteran. Films to choose from in this category include John Flynn's *Rolling Thunder* (1977), Martin Scorsese's *Taxi Driver* (1976), Ted Kotcheff's *First Blood* (1982), T. C. Frank's *Born Losers* (1967) and *Billy Jack* (1971), Michael Cimino's *The Deer Hunter* (1978), Jeremy Paul Kagan's *Heroes* (1977), Hal Ashby's *Coming Home* (1978), Henry Jaglom's *Tracks* (1977), Karl Reisz's *Who'll Stop the Rain* (1978), David Nutter's *Cease Fire* (1985), and Oliver Stone's *Born on the Fourth of July* (1990).

Equally important in the classroom are films that can be classified as documentaries, such as Peter Davis's *Hearts and Minds* (1974), The United States Department of Defense's *Why Viet Nam?* (1965) and Richard Ellison and Stanley Karnow's 13-part series, *Vietnam: A Television History* (1983).[10]

TEACHING METHODS AND STRATEGIES

Using Vietnam War literature and film in the classroom can challenge students' preconceived perceptions of the war and help them to gain a more responsible view of American involvement in Indochina. Unfortunately, some students' only knowledge of the war is derived from the mass media, particularly from the movie industry. Students usually don't know, for instance, that *First Blood* (1982) was a novel authored by David Morrell, a professor at the University of Iowa, before it was a movie starring Sylvester Stallone. Similarly, students are familiar with movies such as *Platoon* and *Full Metal Jacket* before they read novels of initiation such as *Fields of Fire* and *The Short-Timers*. The question is, How do we move students away from their preconceived notions of "Rambomania"[11] and toward a more critical and evaluative attitude toward the war? This goal can be accomplished through the judicious use of literature and film in the classroom.

Certainly literature and film cannot be used in isolation to teach the Vietnam War; they cannot be used as substitutes for the history of the war or as the most authoritative sources for teaching about American involvement in Southeast Asia. It is necessary, therefore, that a student in a course on Vietnam War literature be required to read a history of the Vietnamese conflict and that an instructor of such a course use guest speakers to provide insight into the historical, political and cultural dimensions of the Vietnam War. In like manner, audio-visual material also cannot be relied on as a substitute for, instead of a supplement to, other academic materials. Film must complement and balance other aspects of a course, not overwhelm them.[12] Even an instructor of a course entitled The Vietnam Experience in Film may require readings on Vietnam to accompany visual accounts of the war.[13] But if used in the proper context, Vietnam War literature and film can be valuable classroom aids.

USING WORKS IN PAIRS

One significant way of utilizing literature and film in the classroom is to group works in pairs. A film such as *Hearts and Minds*, for instance, is too graphic to use alone and needs to be used in conjunction with another documentary such as *Why Viet Nam?* so as to lesson the shock value that it has on students. In addition, a more complex novel, such as *Going After Cacciato* (New York: Delta and Seymour Lawrence, 1978), with its tripartate structure and experimental style of writing, may be best taught along with a novel such as David Halberstam's *One Very Hot Day* (New York: Warner, 1984), which follows a more straightforward and linear plot progression.[14] Pairing works can also illuminate the difference between two genres of literature. A conventional combat novel such as *Fields of Fire* can be discussed in relation to an unconventional combat novel such as *No Bugles, No Drums*, thus illustrating two writers' approaches to the war as well as two different types of combat novels. Pairing works that fall into the same genre can demonstrate the many ways that a similar theme can be used by various writers. Films such as *Platoon* and *Full Metal Jacket*, for example, can be paradigmatic of the way that the theme of young men's initiation into war emerges from the Vietnamese conflict as well as from war stories in general. At the same time, these two films afford students the opportunity to debate moral issues. An effective exercise is to have students discuss Michael Pursell's view that "where the plot of *Platoon* suggests the possibilities of moral choice and justice, no such opportunities arise in *Full Metal Jacket*."[15] Is such a statement valid, or is Kubrick's film of more substance than Pursell suggests?

Literary works can also be effectively paired with films. Since many Vietnam War films have been based on fictional works or personal narratives, the opportunity exists for students to comparatively analyze the works of authors and film-makers. A useful assignment is to have students debate, either orally or in writing, which version of *The Short-Timers* is most effective—Hasford's novel or Kubrick's *Full Metal Jacket*, the film. Is Hasford's story any less significant in *Full Metal Jacket* due to the reduction of a three-part novel into a two-part movie, and does the death of Cowboy in the city of Hue instead of the jungles of Vietnam eliminate the moral issues raised in the novel? Similarly, what does Oliver Stone add to Ron Kovic's story in the movie version of *Born on the Fourth of July*, and do these additional events contribute effectively to the movie or damage its credibility? In addition to *Full Metal Jacket* and *Born on the Fourth of July*, a number of other films can be paired with novels or personal narratives. They include Hal Ashby's *Coming Home* (1978) with George Davis's *Coming Home* (New York: Dell, 1975), Norman Jewison's *In Country* (1989) with Bobbie Ann Mason's *In Country* (New York: Harper and Row, 1985), Francis Ford Coppola's *Gardens of Stone* (1987) with Nicholas Proffitt's *Gardens of Stone* (New York: TOR Books, 1984), Ted Kotcheff's *First Blood* (1982) with David Morrell's *First Blood* (New York: Ballantine, 1982), Richard T. Heffron's *A Rumor of War* (1980) with Philip Caputo's *A Rumor of War* (New York: Holt, Rinehart, and Winston, 1977), Mark Robson's *Limbo* (1972) with Joan Silver and Linda Gottlieb's *Limbo* (New York: Pocket Books, 1972), and Bill Couturie's *Dear America: Letters Home from Vietnam* (1987) with Bernard Edelman's *Dear America: Letters Home from Vietnam* (New York: Pocket Books, 1986). Comparatively analyzing such films and books encourages students to evaluate the works, thus helping them develop and hone their critical and analytical skills.

POINTING OUT STEREOTYPES

Through reading literature and viewing films, students can be made aware of stereotypes that have emerged from the Vietnam War. The most popular view of the returning veteran, for instance, has come from the media, which has frequently depicted the typical Vietnam veteran as a raging, shell-shocked lunatic who must be avoided and/or watched carefully to make sure that he does not explode in a paroxysm of unmitigated violence. Movies released in the 1970s, such as *Heroes*, *The Deer Hunter*, *Who'll Stop the Rain*, *Coming Home* and *Apocalypse Now* reinforced media hype and created stereotyped roles for the veteran.[16] In the words of author and veteran Tim O'Brien, "Each of these movies still portrays the Vietnam veteran as something of a flake—baleful, explosive, spiritually exhausted, tormented, with brains like whipped cream."[17] The movies of the 1980s have not helped to erase this stereotype, but instead have reinforced it in an even more violent way. We no longer have just a potentially violent flake, but a killer, like Rambo, whom moviemakers portray with zeal and relish. Through reading novels such as *On the Way Home* and *Indian Country* and viewing films such as *Coming Home* and *Born on the Fourth of July*, students can be led to question why so many veterans are portrayed as being severely traumatized by their war experiences.[18] Also, classes can discuss whether or not these literary works and films accurately depict the majority of our returning veterans. If they do, then why? If they do not, then why not? Does a novel such as *On the Way Home* merely stereotype the veteran as sick, or does Bausch use Michael Sumner, his main character, to disturb the other characters' set perceptions of a returning veteran and of the Vietnam War in general? Students may discuss what a returning veteran is supposed to be like. What is our American definition or our perception of a soldier home from war? Additionally, a discussion of such issues and works can lead to a discussion of the definition and causes of Post Traumatic Stress Disorder (PTSD), another important aspect of the war.

Even such stereotypical films as Joseph Zito's *Missing in Action* (1984), Ted Kotcheff's *Uncommon Valor* (1983) and George P. Cosmatos's *Rambo: First Blood, Part II* (1985) can be effectively used in the classroom as lessons in revisionist history.[19] Through viewing and discussing such works, students can learn to question the validity of different versions of the war and to acknowledge the differences between artistic and historical accounts of the same event. Does any literary work or film show the whole truth of the war? Can absolute truth even be determined? Also, why does a war such as Vietnam generate such fantasy versions? Why do we need to rewrite and win the war through literature and film?

GENDER AWARENESS

The subject of gender awareness can be particularly well addressed through a study of Vietnam War literature and film. Most students are surprised to learn that women actually served in Vietnam in non-combat positions. As Vincent Coppola points out, "The Department of Defense . . . has never kept a record of women veterans, and there are no official studies documenting their readjustment to civilian life."[20] Statistics determining how many women nurses served in Vietnam, for instance, vary considerably; it is estimated that there were between 6,000 and 55,000 American nurses in Southeast Asia during the war.[21] Fortunately, there are now several excellent personal accounts of nurses and other women who served in the war available for classroom use, including such oral histories as Kathryn Marshall's *In the Combat Zone: Vivid Personal Recollections of the Vietnam War from the Women Who Served There* (New York: Penguin, 1987), Keith Walker's *A Piece of My Heart: The Stories of Twenty-Six American Women Who Served in Vietnam* (New York: Ballantine, 1985), Dan Freedman and Jacqueline Rhodes's *Nurses in Vietnam: The Forgotten Veterans* (Lubbock: Texas Monthly, 1987) and Elizabeth Norman's *Women at War: The Story of Fifty Military Nurses Who Served in Vietnam* (Philadelphia: University of Pennsylvania, 1990) as well as personal narratives such as Lynda Van Devanter's *Home Before Morning: The Story of an Army Nurse in Vietnam* (New York: Warner, 1983) and Virginia Elwood-Akers's account of female journalists, *Women War Correspondents in the Vietnam War, 1961-1975* (Metuchen, N. J.: Scarecrow, 1988).

Equally important is the effect that the war had on women who remained on the home front. The effect of the war on those whom psychiatric social worker Shad Meshad calls '"the forgotten wounded,"' the many wives, sisters, mothers, girlfriends and other family members who in some way suffered the disasters of the same war that killed or maimed so many of their husbands, brothers, sons, boyfriends and other loved ones,[22] is revealed in such fictional works as Joan Silver and Linda Gottlieb's *Limbo* (New York: Pocket Books, 1972), Robert Bausch's *On the Way Home* (New York: Avon, 1982), Philip Caputo's *Indian Country* (New York: Bantam, 1987), Bobbie Ann Mason's *In Country* (New York: Harper and Row, 1985), Donald Pfarrer's *Neverlight* (New York: Laurel, 1982) and Jayne Anne Phillips' *Machine Dreams* (New York: Pocket Books, 1984) and personal accounts such as Jim and Sybil Stockdale's *In Love and War: The Story of a Family's Ordeal and Sacrifice During the Vietnam Years* (New York: Bantam, 1985). Students can gain a cross-cultural awareness of the Vietnam War by studying Wendy Larsen and Tran Thi Nga's *Shallow Graves: Two Women and Vietnam* (New York: Random House, 1986; Harper and Row, 1986) and Nguyen Thi Dinh's *No Other Roads to Take: Memoir of Mrs. Nguyen Thi Dinh* (Ithaca, N. Y.: Cornell University Southeast Asia Program, 1976).

The role of women in the war has been especially ignored by the film industry. There are, however, a few films that at least partially address this subject: Mark Robson's *Limbo* (1972), Francis Ford Coppola's *Gardens of Stone* (1987) and Norman Jewison's *In Country* (1989).

CRITICAL SOURCES

In the 25 years since the publication of the first popular American novel about Vietnam, Robin Moore's *The Green Berets*, and the subsequent release of the movie by that title, over six hundred critical articles and books about Vietnam War literature and film have been published. (This figure excludes the thousands of reviews that have appeared in print about individual works.) Teachers and scholars seeking information on these relatively new areas of study thus have a wide variety of sources to turn to for information.

BIBLIOGRAPHIES: PRIMARY SOURCES

Bibliographies are, of course, one of the best sources for an instructor to initially consult for information on both primary and secondary sources of the literature and film of the war. Originally, there were two main bibliographies of primary sources available. Tom Colonnese and Jerry Hogan, "Vietnam War Literature, 1958-1979: A First Checklist," *Bulletin of Bibliography* 38 (January-March 1981), pp. 26-51, lists a number of books and short stories about the war.[23] However, the best list of primary works is John Newman and Ann Hilfinger's *Vietnam War Literature: An Annotated Bibliography of Imaginative Works About Americans Fighting in Vietnam* (Metuchen, N. J.: Scarecrow, 1988, revised from the 1982 edition). Clearly divided by literary genre, this work includes over seven hundred primary sources on drama, fiction and poetry.[24]

Available as well are a number of brief annotated bibliographies and review articles that list primary sources on different literary subjects. Particularly noteworthy are Edward K. Eckert and William J. Searle, "Creative Literature of the Vietnam War: A Selective Bibliography," *Choice* 24 (January 1987), pp. 725-26, 728-35; Philip D. Beidler, "The Vietnam Novel: An Overview with a Brief Checklist of Vietnam War Narrative," *Southern Humanities Review* 12 (Winter 1978), pp. 45-55; Richard W. Grefrath, "Everyday Was Summertime in Vietnam: An Annotated Bibliography of the Best Personal Narratives," *Reference Services Review* 8 (October-December 1980), pp. 23-27; Joe P. Dunn, "The Vietnam War POW/MIAs: An Annotated Bibliography," *Bulletin of Bibliography* 45 (June 1988), pp. 152-57; and John B. Pratt's list of Vietnam War literature in Timothy J. Lomperis, *"Reading the Wind": The Literature of the Vietnam War* (Durham, N. C.: Duke University, 1987).

BIBLIOGRAPHIES: SECONDARY SOURCES

There are also several bibliographies of secondary sources. A brief bibliography of critical literature on Vietnam War fiction and film can be found in James C. Wilson, *Vietnam in Prose and Film* (Jefferson, N. C.: McFarland, 1982) as well as in Susan Jeffords, *The Remasculinization of America: Gender and the Vietnam War* (Bloomington: Indiana University,

1989), and a brief list of sources on poetry and film can be located in Dennis Jackson, Edward A. Nickerson, and James R. Bennett, "The Language of Literature about War: A Selected Annotated Bibliography," *Style* 13 (Winter 1979), pp. 60-88. A more comprehensive list of critical sources on drama, poetry, prose and film is available in Catherine Calloway, "Vietnam War Literature and Film: A Bibliography of Secondary Sources," *Bulletin of Bibliography* 43 (September 1986), pp. 149-58. Since the publication of this source, several hundred more articles and books about Vietnam War literature and film have appeared in print. The following bibliographic citations will attempt to enumerate many of these more recent sources as well as indicate which of the earlier citations are the most substantial.

BOOKS: LITERATURE AND FILM

Book-length studies of Vietnam War literature and film currently number over a dozen.[25] Many of these texts discuss more than one genre and combine discussions of literature and film. The definitive source for Vietnam War literature is Philip D. Beidler, *American Literature and the Experience of Vietnam* (Athens: University of Georgia, 1982), which chronologically surveys four genres—poetry, drama, fiction and nonfiction prose—and identifies characteristics peculiar to Vietnam War literature. An interdisciplinary approach is taken in James C. Wilson, *Vietnam in Prose and Film* (Jefferson, N. C.: McFarland, 1982), which notes the way in which the literature and film reveal how American officials distorted certain aspects of the war, and in John Hellmann, *American Myth and the Legacy of Vietnam* (New York: Columbia University, 1986), which examines Vietnam War literature and film as it fits into the myth of the American frontier hero. Also valuable is Timothy J. Lomperis, *"Reading the Wind": The Literature of the Vietnam War* (Durham, N. C.: Duke University, 1987). Lomperis discusses literary, moral and political issues raised by the Vietnam War and records the results of a national literary conference on the conflict in Southeast Asia. Several of the most recent sources are especially noteworthy. Thomas Myers's *Walking Point: American Narratives of Vietnam* (New York: Oxford University, 1988) studies the literature of the war as divided into several classifications: black humor, realism and mnemonic narrative, for example. A topic-oriented approach, William J. Searle, editor, *Search and Clear: Critical Responses to Selected Literature and Films of the Vietnam War* (Bowling Green, Ohio: Bowling Green State University, 1988) contains 16 essays by individual authors on different genres and issues. Searle's text provides a variety of approaches useful for studying the war, including the quest motif, metafiction and other stylistic and structural devices, women and the war, and the returning veteran.

Most recently, Philip H. Melling's *Vietnam in American Literature* (Boston, Massachusetts: Twayne, 1990), Philip K. Jason's *Fourteen Landing Zones: Approaches to Vietnam War Literature* (Iowa City: University of Iowa, 1991), and Owen W. Gilman, Jr. and Lorrie Smith's *America Rediscovered: Critical Essays on Literature and Film of the Vietnam War* (New York: Garland, 1990) discuss a number of texts, genres, and topics relating to the literature of the war. Gilman and Smith's book includes 25 essays by individual authors on Vietnam War literature and film and American culture.[26]

Several books focus only on film. Julian Smith, *Looking Away: Hollywood and Vietnam* (New York: Scribner's, 1975) and Gilbert Adair, *Vietnam on Film* (New York: Proteus, 1981) examine the earlier films of the war. Two other texts, William J. Palmer's *The Films of the Seventies: A Social History* (Metuchen, N. J.: Scarecrow, 1987) and Lawrence Suid, *Guts and Glory: Great American Movies* (Reading, Mass.: Addison-Wesley, 1978) also contain sections on Vietnam War film.[27] Suid has written one of the very few doctoral dissertations on this subject as well: "The Film Industry and the Vietnam War" (Cleveland, Ohio: Case Western Reserve University, 1980).[28] In addition, Albert Auster and Leonard Quart, *How the War Was Remembered: Hollywood and Vietnam* (New York: Praeger, 1988) discusses the evolution of Vietnam War film from a chronological, thematic and symbolic standpoint.

ADDITIONAL RESOURCES

In addition to the books noted above, there are a large number of other resources available in many areas. The types of Vietnam War literature most frequently analyzed are fiction and personal narratives, and an instructor can find two main types of critical articles on these genres: those providing introductory material on the literature of the war,[29] and those analyzing specific texts.[30] The most neglected genres of Vietnam War literature are poetry and drama. James F. Mersmann's *Out of the Vietnam Vortex: A Study of Poets and Poetry Against the War* (Lawrence: University Press of Kansas, 1974), the one book-length study of Vietnam War poetry, focuses on poets such as Allen Ginsberg, Denise Levertov, Robert Bly and Robert Duncan, who wrote about the war during the 1960s. However, an instructor may consult a variety of individual articles that deal more immediately with the poetry of the war, particularly the poetry written by Vietnam veterans.[31] Currently, no book-length study of Vietnam War drama has been published. While most individual articles on Vietnam War drama treat the plays of David Rabe, there are critical sources available on other dramatists as well as on Rabe.[32]

Like Vietnam War literature, Vietnam War films have been examined in a number of worthwhile articles. In addition to the book-length studies mentioned previously, two types of critical articles on film may be consulted: those citing introductory material on Vietnam War films,[33] and those focusing on specific movies. Many of the earlier articles treat *Apocalypse Now* and *The Deer Hunter*,[34] while the most recent critical commentary deals primarily with *Platoon, Full Metal Jacket*, and *Born on the Fourth of July*.[35]

Certain specific authors or areas are also attracting the attention of Vietnam War scholars. The most extensive criticism on individual Vietnam War writers, for example, deals with Tim O'Brien and David Halberstam. In addition to the critically acclaimed *Going After Cacciato*, O'Brien has written three other novels, one personal narrative, and over 25 short stories, most of which focus on the war in some way, even if as a shadow in the background. O'Brien's numerous writings on Vietnam have generated over two hundred and fifty critical articles and individual reviews.[36] Halberstam, who is perhaps best known for his Vietnam War novel, *One Very Hot Day* and such nonfiction works as *The Best and the Brightest* (New York: Random House, 1972) and *The Making of a Quagmire: America and Vietnam During the Kennedy Era* (New York: McGraw, 1986), has authored a dozen books and over sixty-five articles on Vietnam and other topics. Several hundred articles and reviews have been published about his works.[37]

A focus of much of the current criticism of Vietnam War literature is the subject of gender. Susan Jeffords's *The Remasculinization of America: Gender and the War* (Bloomington: Indiana University, 1989), one of the most recent book-length studies of Vietnam War literature and film, is an excellent source for this topic. Jeffords traces the process of the "the 'remasculinization' of American culture" through a number of literary works and films.[38] Other important sources on women and the Vietnam War have appeared in recent journals.[39] Also significant is the special issue of *Vietnam Generation* 1 (Summer-Fall 1989) that is devoted to gender. This work, edited by Jacqueline Lawson, includes over 20 articles on gender and the war as well as a "Bibliography of Unusual Sources on Women and the Vietnam War."[40] A minimal number of articles have been published on the teaching of Vietnam War literature and film. These sources are useful for their descriptions of classroom strategies and course designs.[41]

By the early 1980s, enough material on Vietnam War literature and film had been published to warrant special journal issues on these topics. Collections of articles on Vietnam War literature and film may be found in special issues of *Critique* 24 (Winter 1983); *Cultural Critique* 3 (Spring 1986); *Genre* 21 (Winter 1988); *Literature-Film Quarterly* 11, no. 1 (1983) and 16, no. 4 (1988); and *Modern Fiction Studies* 30 (Spring 1984). In addition, *Social Education* devoted its January 1988 issue to teaching the war.

By the late 1980s, the study of Vietnam had become such a popular topic that two new journals made the study of war and the Vietnam War era their main focus. *Vietnam Generation*, edited by Kali Tal and published by the American Studies Department at Yale University, deals exclusively with topics relevant to the Vietnam War era, and *War, Literature, and the Arts*, published by the English Department at the United States Air Force Academy, includes articles on Vietnam as well as on war literature in general.[42] Special issues of *Vietnam Generation* have focused on race and the war, gender and the war, Kent State, and Southeast Asian-American communities.

CONCLUSION

The strategies and sources noted above are only a sample of the possibilities available for teaching the literature and film of the Vietnam War. It is imperative that instructors continue to teach the war and the war era and to share their findings with the generations to come so that future instructors will have even more abundant material to draw from.

NOTES

1. Julian Smith, "Look Away, Look Away, Look Away, Movie Land," *Journal of Popular Film* 2 (Winter 1973), p. 29.

2. Peter Leonard Stromberg, "A Long War's Writing: American Novels about the Fighting in Vietnam Written While Americans Fought" (Ph.D. diss., Cornell University, 1974), p. 293.

3. Peter McInerney, "Apocalypse Then: Hollywood Looks Back at Vietnam," *Film Quarterly* 33 (Winter 1979-1980), p. 24.

4. Michael Paris, "The American Film Industry and Vietnam," *History Today* 37 (April 1987), p. 21.

5. Ibid.

6. For a discussion of the "scrapbook" approach to Vietnam War literature, see Kate Beaird Meyers, "Fragmentary Mosaics: Vietnam War 'Histories' and Postmodern Epistemology," *Genre* 21 (Winter 1988), pp. 535-52.

7. The films and documentaries cited are available in many libraries or can be rented or purchased at most local video stores.

8. Like Vietnam War literature, Vietnam War film can be studied by genre. David Whillock, for example, finds four main categories of Vietnam War films, those treating "The Vietnam Veteran; the effects of the war at home; the revenge film (POW film), and the combat film" (p. 246). See

his "Vietnam War Film: In Search of a Genre," *Literature-Film Quarterly* 16, no. 4 (1988), pp. 244-50. For a bibliography of secondary sources on the genre of the war film in general, including Vietnam, see Stephen J. Curley and Frank J. Wetta, "War Film Bibliography," *Journal of Popular Film and Television* 18 (Summer 1990), pp. 72-79.

9. Rick Berg, "Losing Vietnam: Covering the War in an Age of Technology," *Cultural Critique* 3 (Spring 1986), p. 111.

10. For additional Vietnam War films, see Lawrence Thompson, Richard Welch, and Philip Stephens, "A Vietnam Filmography," *Journal of Popular Film and Television* 9 (Spring 1981), pp. 61-67. *Words of War: An Anthology of Vietnam War Literature* compiled by Gordon Hardy (Boston, Mass.: Boston Publishing Co., 1988) includes an annotated list of major Vietnam War films as well. The following recent films about Vietnam and the Vietnam era are also worthy of attention: Barry Levinson's *Good Morning, Vietnam* (1987), Ernest Thompson's *1969* (1988), Patrick Duncan's *84 Charlie Mopic* (1989), and Brian DePalma's *Casualties of War* (1990).

11. For an explanation of the term "Rambomania," see Richard Zoglin, "An Outbreak of Rambomania," *Time,* June 24, 1985, pp. 72-73.

12. As William J. Palmer noted in a July 31, 1990, presentation at a National Endowment for the Humanities summer seminar for teachers at the Indochina Institute at George Mason University, films may be used in clips, particularly if class time is limited or only a portion of a film is relevant to the subject being discussed.

13. For a sample syllabus of a course structured around film, see William Alexander, "A Course Syllabus: Vietnam and the Artist," *Jump Cut* no. 31 (March 1986), p. 62.

14. Adrian Lyne's *Jacob's Ladder* (1990), one of the most recent Vietnam War films, could also be used in conjunction with *Going After Cacciato*. Both works incorporate postmodernist techniques and deal with the theme of the subjective nature of reality.

15. Michael Pursell, "*Full Metal Jacket:* The Unravelling of Patriarchy," *Literature-Film Quarterly* 16, no. 4 (1988), p. 222.

16. Tim O'Brien, "The Violent Vet," *Esquire* 92 (December 1979), p. 96.

17. Ibid.

18. For a discussion of the sick veteran in literature, see William J. Searle, "Walking Wounded: Vietnam War Novels of Return," in William J. Searle, editor, Search and Clear: Critical Responses to Selected Literature and Films of the Vietnam War (Bowling Green, Ohio: Bowling Green State University, 1988), pp. 147-59. The war's effect on Vietnam veterans and their loved ones is discussed in Marilyn Durham, "Narrative Strategies in Recent Vietnam War Fiction," in Owen W. Gilman, Jr., and Lorrie Smith, editors, *America Rediscovered: Critical Essays on Literature and Film of the Vietnam War* (New York: Garland, 1990), pp. 100-8.

19. For a discussion of revisionist history in *Rambo*, see Gaylyn Studlar and David Desser, "Never Having to Say You're Sorry: *Rambo*'s Rewriting of the Vietnam War," *Film Quarterly* 62 (Fall 1988), pp. 9-16.

20. Vincent Coppola, "They Also Served," *Newsweek* 104 (November 12, 1984), p. 35.

21. Lawrence M. Baskir and William A. Strauss estimate that 6,000 women served in non-combatant positions in Vietnam (*Chance and Circumstance* [New York: Knopf, 1978], p. 3). Vincent Coppola states figures as being from "7,000 to 20,000" (*Newsweek*, November 12, 1984, p. 35). Myra MacPherson points out that "official 'guesstimates' range anywhere from 7,500 to 55,000" (*Long Time Passing* [New York: Doubleday, 1984], p. 446).

22. David Behrens, "A Delayed Reaction: Vietnam Casualties at Home," *MS*. 9, September 1980, p. 39.

23. This source is limited in that it is confusingly organized and does not list complete bibliographical information for all entries.

24. Another excellent source of primary works is David A. Willson, *Wilson's Bibliography: War in Southeast Asia*, 3rd ed. (Auburn, Wash.: Green River Community College [98002], 1991).

25. In addition, there are a number of doctoral dissertations, most unpublished, on Vietnam War literature. They include: Michael Omar Bartz, "United States Cultural Movements as Reflected in the Fiction, Journals, and Oral Histories of the Vietnam War," Saint Louis University, 1987; Harvey Ray Brown, Jr., "Modern American War Drama," Lamar University, 1981; Catherine Calloway, "The Vietnam War Novel: A Descent Into Hell," University of South Florida, 1987; Norton Bradley Christie, "Another War and Postmodern Memory: Remembering Vietnam," Duke University, 1988; Youn-Son Chung, "War and Morality: The Search for Meaning in American Novels of World War I, World War II, and the Vietnam War," Emory University, 1985; Mardena Bridges Creek, "Myth, Wound, Accommodation: American Literary Response to the War in Vietnam," Ball State University, 1982; Tom Graydon Colonnese, "The Vietnam War in American Literature," Arizona State University, 1981; David West Furniss, "Making Sense of the War: Vietnam and American Prose," University of Minnesota, 1988; Charles Jamieson Gaspar, Jr., "Reconnecting: Time and History in Narratives of the Vietnam War," The University of Connecticut, 1983; Henry Palmer Hall, Jr., "The Enlisted Man's War: A Study of the Vietnam War Novels," The University of Texas at Austin, 1984; Andrea Brandenburg Heiss, "On Foreign Grounds: Portrayal of Americans in Vietnam," The University of Iowa, 1983; Cletus Keating, "The Rhetoric of Extreme Experience: Michael Herr's Non-Fiction Vietnam Novel, *Dispatches*," University of Denver, 1987; William J. Lennox, Jr., "American War Poetry," Princeton University, 1982; Lloyd Bart Lewis, "The Thousand-Yard Stare: A Socio-Cultural Interpretation of Vietnam

War Narratives," University of Maryland, 1982; Paul Anthony Lister, "War in Norman Mailer's Fiction," Kansas State University, 1974; Anne Malone, "Once Having Marched: American Narratives of the Vietnam War," Indiana University, 1983; James F. Mersmann, "Out of the Vortex: A Study of Poets and Poetry Against the Vietnam War," University of Kansas, 1972; Thomas Robert Myers, "Envisaging a War: Vietnam and the American Historical Novel," Purdue University, 1985; Edward Frederick Palm, "American Heart of Darkness: The Moral Vision of Five Novels of the Vietnam War," University of Pennsylvania, 1983; Kathleen Marie Puhr, "Novelistic Responses to the Vietnam War," Saint Louis University, 1982; Peter Edward Roundy, "Images of Vietnam: *Catch-22*, New Journalism, and the Postmodern Imagination," The Florida State University, 1980; Joseph Elwood Sanders, "Modern American War Plays," University of California, Los Angeles, 1975; Eric James Schroeder, "Truth-Telling and Narrative Form: The Literature of the Vietnam War," University of California, Los Angeles, 1984; Margaret E. Stewart, "Death and Growth: Vietnam-War Novels, Cultural Attitudes, and Literary Traditions," The University of Wisconsin-Madison, 1981; Matthew C. Stewart, "Making Sense of Chaos: Prose Writing, Fictional Kind and the Reality of Vietnam," Emory University, 1988; Kenneth Thompson Stringer, Jr., "A Substitute for Victory?: Fictional Portraits of the American Soldier and Combat in Vietnam," The American University, 1984; Peter Leonard Stromberg, "A Long War's Writing: American Novels About the Fighting in Vietnam Written While Americans Fought," Cornell University, 1974; and Carole Ann Winner, "A Study of American Dramatic Productions Dealing With the War in Vietnam," University of Denver, 1975.

26. Also useful is Lloyd B. Lewis, *The Tainted War: Culture and Identity in Vietnam War Narratives* (Westport, Conn.: Greenwood, 1985) which examines a number of Vietnam War novels, narratives, and oral histories from a sociological standpoint. Lewis' study attempts to answer the question, "*How did the Vietnam War defy interpretation as meaningful combat ritual?*" (p. xii). Two other books partially treat Vietnam War literature and film. Jeffrey Walsh, *American War Literature: 1914 to Vietnam* (New York: St. Martin's, 1982) devotes one chapter to Vietnam War prose, and Jeffrey Walsh and James Aulich, editors, *Vietnam Image: War and Representation* (New York: St. Martin's, 1989) contains a number of individual essays on the literature and film of the war.

27. Palmer's text includes chapters on *Go Tell the Spartans*, *Apocalypse Now*, and an Australian film, *The Odd Angry Shot*. (Palmer is currently working on a new book, *The Films of the Eighties: A Social History*.) Also, Robin Wood's *Hollywood From Vietnam to Reagan* (New York: Columbia University, 1986) alludes to a number of Vietnam War films in its survey of contemporary film and provides an extensive discussion of *The Deer Hunter*.

28. The most recent dissertation on Vietnam War film is Dabney Melissa Hilbish's "Relax, It's Only a Movie: Representations of War in the Vietnam Combat Film," University of Maryland College Park, 1990. See *Dissertation Abstracts International* 51 (November 1990), no. 1667-A.

29. The instructor wishing to acquire introductory material on the prose written about the Vietnam War would do well to consider these excellent contributions to literary criticism: Philip D. Beidler, "Truth-Telling and Literary Values in the Vietnam Novel," *South Atlantic Quarterly* 78 (Spring 1979), pp. 141-56; Mary L. Bellhouse and Lawrence Litchfield, "Vietnam and Loss of Innocence: An Analysis of the Political Implications of the Popular Literature of the Vietnam War," *Journal of Popular Culture* 16 (Winter 1982), pp. 157-74; C. D. B. Bryan, "Barely Suppressed Screams," *Harper's* 268 (June 1984), pp. 67-72; Norman Harris, "Blacks in Vietnam: A Holistic Perspective Through Fiction and Journalism," *The Western Journal of Black Studies* 10, no. 3 (1986), pp. 121-31; Tobey Herzog, "Writing about Vietnam: A Heavy Heart-of-Darkness Trip," *College English* 41 (February 1980), pp. 680-95; Yasuro Hidesaki, "Black Humor and Vietnam War Novels," *Kyushu American Literature* 27 (1986), pp. 97-106; Walter Holbling, "Literary Sense-Making: American Vietnam Fiction," in Jeffrey Walsh and James Aulich, editors, *Vietnam Image: War and Representation* (New York: St. Martin's, 1989), pp. 123-40; John Limon, "War and Play: A Theory of the Vietnam Sports Novel," *Arizona Quarterly* 46 (Autumn 1990), pp. 65-90; Peter McInerney, "'Straight' and 'Secret' History in Vietnam War Literature," *Contemporary Literature* 22 (Spring 1981), pp. 187-204; Edward Frederick Palm, "The Search for a Usable Past: Vietnam Literature and the Separate Peace Syndrome," *The South Atlantic Quarterly* 82 (Spring 1983), pp. 115-28; Donald Ringnalda, "Fighting and Writing: America's Vietnam War Literature," *Journal of American Studies* 22 (April 1988), pp. 25-42; Timothy E. Scheurer, "Myth to Madness: America, Vietnam and Popular Culture," *Journal of American Culture* 4 (Summer 1981), pp. 149-65; William J. Searle, "The Vietnam War Novel and the Reviewers," *Journal of American Culture* 4 (Summer 1981), pp. 83-94; and Gordon O. Taylor, "American Personal Narrative of the War in Vietnam," *American Literature* 52 (May 1980), pp. 294-308.

30. Good examples of articles analyzing specific texts of Vietnam War literature include Cornelius A. Cronin, "Historical Background to Larry Heinemann's *Close Quarters*, *Critique* 24 (Winter 1983), pp. 119-30; John Hellmann, "The New Journalism and Vietnam: Memory as Structure in Michael Herr's *Dispatches*," *The South Atlantic Quarterly* 79 (Spring 1980), pp. 141-51; Maureen Karaguezian, "Irony in Robert Stone's *Dog Soldiers*," *Critique* 24 (Winter 1983), pp. 65-73; Verner D. Mitchell, "I, Too, Sing America: Vietnam as Metaphor in *Coming Home*," *Vietnam Generation* 1 (Spring 1989), pp. 118-24; Thomas Myers, "Dispatches from Ghost Country: The Vietnam Veteran in Recent American Fiction," *Genre* 21

(Winter 1988), pp. 409-28; Edward Frederick Palm, "James Webb's *Fields of Fire*: The Melting Pot Platoon Revisited," *Critique* 24 (Winter 1983), pp. 105-18; Donald Ringnalda, "Chlorophyll Overdose: Stephen Wright's *Meditations in Green*," *Western Humanities Review* 40 (Summer 1986), pp. 125-40; Frank W. Shelton, "Robert Stone's *Dog Soldiers*: Vietnam Comes Home to America," *Critique* 24 (Winter 1983), pp. 74-81; Marshall Van Deusen, "The Unspeakable Language of Life and Death in Michael Herr's *Dispatches*," *Critique* 24 (Winter 1983), pp. 82-87; and Sanroku Yoshida, "Takeshi Kaiko's Paradox of Light and Darkness," *World Literature Today* 62 (Summer 1988), pp. 391-96.

31. Instructors teaching Vietnam War poetry may wish to consult the following critical sources: W. D. Ehrhart, "Soldier-Poets of the Vietnam War," *Virginia Quarterly Review* 63 (Spring 1987), pp. 246-65; John Felstiner, "American Poetry and the War in Vietnam," *Stand* 19, no. 2 (1978), pp. 4-11; Todd Gitlin, "Notes in War Poetry," *Confrontation* 8 (Spring 1974), pp. 145-47; Vincente F. Gotera, "'Depending on the Light': Yusef Komunyakaa's *Dien Cai Dau*," in Owen W. Gilman, Jr., and Lorrie Smith, editors, *America Rediscovered: Critical Essays on Literature and Film of the Vietnam War* (New York: Garland, 1990), pp. 282-300; Deborah H. Holdstein, "Vietnam War Veteran-Poets: The Ideology of Horror," *USA Today* 112 (September 1983), pp. 59-61; Caroline Slocock, "Winning Hearts and Minds: The 1st Casualty Press," *Journal of American Studies 16* (April 1982), pp. 107-17; Stephen Sossaman, "American Poetry from the Indochina Experience," *Long Island Review* 2 (Winter 1973), pp. 30-33; Lorrie Smith, "A Sense-Making Perspective in Recent Poetry by Vietnam Veterans," *American Poetry Review* 15 (November-December 1986), pp. 13-18; and Jeffrey Walsh, "'After Our War': John Balaban's Poetic Images of Vietnam," in Jeffrey Walsh and James Aulich, editors. *Vietnam Image: War and Representation* (New York: St. Martin's, 1989), pp. 141-52.

32. Philip C. Kolin, *David Rabe: A Stage History and a Primary and Secondary Bibliography* (New York: Garland, 1988) lists over a thousand works by and about Rabe, including numerous reviews. See also Norioki Ariizuma, "Vietnam War Plays," in Kenzaburo Ohashi, editor, *The Traditional and the Anti-Traditional: Studies in Contemporary American Literature* (Tokyo: The Tokyo Chapter of the American Literature Society of Japan, 1980), pp. 191-200; Robert Asahina, "The Basic Training of American Playwrights: Theater and the Vietnam War," *Theater* 9 (Spring 1978), pp. 30-37; Pamela Cooper, "David Rabe's *Sticks and Bones*: The Adventures of Ozzie and Harriet," *Modern Drama* 29 (December 1986), pp. 613-25; David De Rose, "*Soldados Razos*: Issues of Race in Vietnam War Drama," *Vietnam Generation* 1 (Spring 1989), pp. 38-55; Weldon B. Durham, "Gone to Flowers: Theatre and Drama of the Vietnam War," in Owen W. Gilman, Jr., and Lorrie Smith, editors *America Rediscovered: Critical Essays on Literature and Film of the Vietnam War* (New York:

Garland, 1990), pp. 332-62; Richard L. Homan, "American Playwrights in the 1970s: Rabe and Shephard," *Critical Quarterly* 24 (Spring 1982), pp. 73-82; Barbara Hurrell, "American Self-Image in David Rabe's Vietnam Trilogy," *Journal of American Culture* 4 (Summer 1981), pp. 95-107; Bonnie Marranca, "David Rabe's Viet Nam Trilogy," *Canadian Theatre Review* 14 (1977), pp. 86-92; David McDonald, "The Mystification of Vietnam: David Rabe's *Sticks and Bones*," *Cultural Critique* 3 (Spring 1986), pp. 211-34; Kate Beaird Meyers, "Bottles of Violence: Fragments of Vietnam in Emily Mann's *Still Life*," in Owen W. Gilman, Jr., and Lorrie Smith, editors, *America Rediscovered: Critical Essays on Literature and Film of the Vietnam War* (New York: Garland, 1990), pp. 238-55; and James A. Robinson, "Soldier's Home: Images of Alienation in *Sticks and Bones*," in William J. Searle, editor, *Search and Clear: Critical Responses to Selected Literature and Films of the Vietnam War* (Bowling Green, Ohio: Bowling Green State University, 1988), pp. 136-46.

33. For introductory material on Vietnam War film, see Al Auster and Leonard Quart, "Hollywood and Vietnam: The Triumph of the Will," *Cineaste* 9 (Spring 1979), pp. 4-9; Tom Buckley, "Hollywood's War," *Harper's* 258 (April 1979), pp. 84-86, 88; M. Cieutat, "Hollywood Films Dealing with the Vietnam War and Related Themes," *Positif* no. 320 (1987), pp. 50-57; James William Gibson, "American Paramilitary Culture and the Reconstitution of the Vietnam War," in Jeffrey Walsh and James Aulich, editors, *Vietnam Image: War and Representation* (New York: St. Martin's, 1989), pp. 10-42; Susan Jeffords, "The New Vietnam Films: Is the Movie Over?" *Journal of Popular Film and Television* 13 (Winter 1986), pp. 186-94; Judy Lee Kinney, "The Mythical Method: Fictionalizing the Vietnam War," *Wide Angle* 75, no. 4 (1985), pp. 35-40; Peter McInerney, "Apocalypse Then: Hollywood Looks Back at Vietnam," *Film Quarterly* 33 (Winter 1979-1980), pp. 21-32; Martin F. Norden, "The Disabled Vietnam Veteran in Hollywood Films," *Journal of Popular Film and Television* 13 (Spring 1985), pp. 16-23; William J. Palmer, "The Vietnam War Films," *Film Library Quarterly* 13, no. 4 (1980), pp. 4-14; Michael Paris, "The American Film Industry and Vietnam," *History Today* 37 (April 1987), pp. 19-26; Marita Sturken, "The Camera as Witness: Documentaries on the Vietnam War," *Film Library Quarterly* 13, no. 4 (1980), pp. 15-20; and Lawrence Suid, "Hollywood and Vietnam," *Journal of American Culture* 4 (Summer 1981), pp. 136-47.

34. Of the many articles published on *Apocalypse Now* and *The Deer Hunter*, the most noteworthy include Ronald L. Bogue, "The Heartless Darkness of *Apocalypse Now*," *The Georgia Review* 35 (Fall 1981), pp. 611-26; P. Chabal and P. Joannides, "Copping out with Coppola," *Cambridge Quarterly* 13, no. 3 (1984), pp. 187-203; R. D. Furia, "*Apocalypse Now*: The Ritual Murder of Art," *Western Humanities Review* 34 (Winter 1980), pp. 85-89; Michael Dempsey, *Apocalypse Now*," *Sight and Sound* 49

(Winter 1979-1980), pp. 5-9; William M. Hagen, "*Apocalypse Now* (1979): Joseph Conrad and the Television War," in Peter C. Rollins, editor, *Hollywood as Historian: American Film in a Cultural Context* (Lexington: University Press of Kentucky, 1983), pp. 230-45; David Boyd, "*The Deer Hunter*: The Hero and the Tradition," *Australian Journal of American Studies* (AJAS) 1, no. 1 (1980), pp. 41-51; Frank Burke, "In Defense of *The Deer Hunter* or: The Knee Jerk Is Quicker than the Eye," *Literature-Film Quarterly* 11, no. 1 (1983), pp. 22-27; Michael Dempsey et al. "Four Shots at *The Deer Hunter*," *Film Quarterly* 32 (Summer 1979), pp. 10-22; Don Francis, "The Regeneration of America: Uses of Landscape in *The Deer Hunter*," *Literature-Film Quarterly* 11, no. 1 (1983), pp. 16-21; and John Hellmann, "Vietnam and the Hollywood Genre Film: Inversions of American Mythology in *The Deer Hunter* and *Apocalypse Now*," *American Quarterly* 34 (Fall 1982), pp. 418-39.

35. Important articles on *Platoon*, *Full Metal Jacket*, and *Born on the Fourth of July* include Don Kunz, "Oliver Stone's Film Adaptation of *Born on the Fourth of July*: Redefining Masculine Heroism," *War, Literature, and the Arts* 2 (Fall 1990), pp. 1-25; Lawrence W. Lichty and Raymond L. Carroll, "Fragments of War: *Platoon* (1986)," in John O'Connor and Martin A. Jackson, editors (and authors of intro.), *American History/American Film: Interpreting the Hollywood Image* (New York: Unger, 1988), pp. 273-287; Devin McKinney, "*Born on the Fourth of July*," *Film Quarterly* 44 (Fall 1990), pp. 44-47; Katrina Porteous, "History Lessons: *Platoon*," in Jeffrey Walsh and James Aulich, editors *Vietnam Image: War and Representation* (New York: St. Martin's, 1989), pp. 153-59; Michael Pursell, "*Full Metal Jacket*: The Unravelling of Patriarchy," *Literature-Film Quarterly* 16, no. 4 (1988), pp. 218-25; Gerri Reaves, "From Hasford's *The Short-Timers* to Kubrick's *Full Metal Jacket*: The Fracturing of Identification," *Literature-Film Quarterly* 16, no. 4 (1988), pp. 232-37; and James A. Stevenson, "Beyond Stephen Crane: *Full Metal Jacket*," *Literature-Film Quarterly* 16, no. 4 (1988), pp. 238-43.

36. Worthwhile articles on *Going After Cacciato* and O'Brien's other works include Milton J. Bates, "Tim O'Brien's Myth of Courage," *Modern Fiction Studies* 33 (Summer 1987), pp. 263-79; G. Thomas Couser, "*Going After Cacciato*: The Romance and the Real War," *Journal of Narrative Technique* 13 (Winter 1983), pp. 1-10; Tobey C. Herzog, "*Going After Cacciato*: The Soldier-Author-Character Seeking Control," *Critique* 24 (Winter 1983), pp. 88-96; Dean McWilliams, "Time in Tim O'Brien's *Going After Cacciato*," *Critique* 29 (Summer 1988), pp. 245-55; Martin Naparsteck, "An Interview With Tim O'Brien," *Contemporary Literature* 32 (Spring 1991), pp. 1-11; Marie Nelson, "Two Consciences: A Reading of Tim O'Brien's Vietnam Trilogy: *If I Die in A Combat Zone, Going After Cacciato*, and *Northern Lights*," in Bernard J. Paris, editor (and author of intro.), *Third Force Psychology and the Study of Literature* (Rutherford, N.

J.: Fairleigh Dickinson University, 1986), pp. 262-79; Michael W. Raymond, "Imagined Responses to Vietnam: Tim O'Brien's *Going After Cacciato*," *Critique* 24 (Winter 1983), pp. 97-104; Arthur M. Saltzman, "The Betrayal of the Imagination: Paul Brodeur's *The Stunt Man* and Tim O'Brien's *Going After Cacciato* 22, no. 1 (1980), pp. 32-38, and Dennis Vannatta, "Theme and Structure in Tim O'Brien's *Going After Cacciato*," *Modern Fiction Studies* 28 (Summer 1982), pp. 242-46. *America Rediscovered: Critical Essays on Literature and Film of the Vietnam War*, Owen W. Gilman, Jr., and Lorrie Smith, editors (New York: Garland, 1990) also contains a number of articles that deal with O'Brien's works. For additional sources, see Catherine Calloway, "Tim O'Brien: A Checklist," forthcoming *Bulletin of Bibliography*, March 1991.

37. I would like to thank Nola Houston for providing the statistics on Halberstam's works.

38. Susan Jeffords, *The Remasculinization of America: Gender and the Vietnam War* (Bloomington: Indiana University, 1989), p. xi.

39. Excellent individual contributions to the study of gender and the Vietnam War include Philip D. Beidler, "The Good Women of Saigon: The Work of Cultural Revision in Gloria Emerson's *Winners and Losers* and Frances Fitzgerald's *Fire in the Lake*," *Genre* 21 (Winter 1988), pp. 523-34; N. Bradley Christie, "What Happened on the Inside: Women Write About Vietnam," Educational Resources Information Center (ERIC) no. ED 296 340 (March 1988), pp. 1-19; Philip K. Jason, "Sexism and Racism in Vietnam War Fiction," *Mosaic* 23 (Summer 1990), pp. 125-37; Jacqueline Lawson, "'She's a pretty woman . . . for a gook': The Misogyny of the Vietnam War," *Journal of American Culture* 12 (Fall 1989), pp. 55-65; Kate Beaird Meyers, "Fragmentary Mosaics: Vietnam War 'Histories' and Postmodern Epistemology," *Genre* 21 (Winter 1988), pp. 535-52; Carol Lynn Mithers, "Missing in Action: Women Warriors in Vietnam," *Cultural Critique* 3 (Spring 1986), pp. 79-90; Kathleen M. Puhr, "Women in Vietnam Novels," in William J. Searle, editor, *Search and Clear: Critical Responses to Selected Literature and Films of the Vietnam War*, (Bowling Green, Ohio: Bowling Green State University, 1988), pp. 172-83; and Kali Tal, "The Mind at War: Images of Women in Vietnam Novels by Combat Veterans," *Contemporary Literature* 31 (Spring 1990), pp. 76-96. Also significant for information on primary sources is Joe P. Dunn, "Women and the Vietnam War: A Bibliographic Review," *Journal of American Culture* 12 (Spring 1989), pp. 79-86.

40. Among the best essays on women and Vietnam War literature in this issue are Renny Christopher, "'I Never Really Became a Woman Veteran Until . . . I Saw the Wall': A Review of Oral Histories and Personal Narratives by Women Veterans of the Vietnam War," pp. 33-45; Cheryl A. Shell, "Making Sense of Vietnam and Telling the Real Story: Military Women *In The Combat Zone*," pp. 59-67; Nancy Anisfield, "Sexist

Subscript in Vietnam Narratives," pp. 109-14; Lorrie Smith, "Back Against the Wall: Anti-Feminist Backlash in Vietnam War Literature," pp. 115-26; and Kali Tal, "Feminist Criticism and the Literature of the Vietnam Combat Veteran," pp. 190-201. Moreover, Susanne Carter, "Visions of Vietnam in Women's Short Fiction," pp. 74-89, is an excellent bibliographic review article of short stories about the war by women writers.

41. See, for instance, William Alexander, "The Holocaust, Vietnam, and the Contemporary Student," *College English* 39 (January 1978), pp. 548-52; D. M. Berman, "Perspectives on the Teaching of Vietnam," *Social Studies* 77 (July-August 1986), pp. 165-68; Arthur D. Casciato, "Teaching the Literature of the Vietnam War," *Review* 9 (1987), pp. 125-47; N. Bradley Christie, "Teaching Our Longest War: Constructive Lessons from Vietnam," *English Journal* 78 (April 1989), pp. 35-38; William Bliss Endres, "Teaching Vietnam: Reflections Beyond the Immediate," *English Journal* 73 (December 1984), pp. 28-30; Perry Oldham, "On Teaching Vietnam War Literature," *English Journal* 75 (February 1986), pp. 55-56; and Margaret Stewart, "Vietnam War Novels in the Classroom," *Teaching History: A Journal of Methods* 6, no. 2 (1981), pp. 60-66.

42. *Vietnam Generation* may be subscribed to by writing to Kali Tal, Editor, *Vietnam Generation*, 10301 Procter Street, Silver Spring, MD 20901. For subscription information on *War, Literature and the Arts*, contact Lt. Col. Donald Anderson, Editor, Department of English, United States Air Force Academy, Colorado 80840-5000.

10

When History Talks Back:
The Voice of the Veteran
KALI TAL

The Vietnam Memorial Wall—the result of a massive effort by veterans to memorialize themselves—acted as a focal point for renewed public discussion and deliberation on the meaning of the Vietnam War. The dedication of the memorial in 1982 brought national attention to veterans' claims that they had been forgotten by their countrymen. "Welcome Home" parades and the dedication of monuments honoring Vietnam veterans became common events across the country. This attention spurred an interest in the writings of veterans, and a number of publishers began to issue and reissue Vietnam War narratives: Avon had begun re-issuing Vietnam novels in 1978 and maintained its rate through 1982, Ballantine began to publish a new category of books labelled Vietnam/Nonfiction; Bantam started focusing on Vietnam in its War/Nonfiction series, and, most recently, the Vintage Contemporaries have begun featuring re-issues of earlier Vietnam novels. Hollywood has also taken a new look at Vietnam, and audiences have flocked to see *Apocalypse Now*, *Platoon*, *Full Metal Jacket*, *Hamburger Hill*, *Off Limits* and *Good Morning Vietnam*. *The New York Times*, on 4 August 1987, claimed that the Vietnam War "has catapulted to the forefront of American culture."[1] In the same article, Philip Caputo called the phenomenon "Vietnam chic."

VIETNAM CHIC

The chic extends beyond popular literature and film and reaches into the classroom. Since 1982 the number of colleges and universities offering courses on various aspects of the Vietnam War and the 1960s decade has exceeded three hundred. Walter Capp's course on the Vietnam War is the most popular class offered at the University of California, Santa Barbara;

almost 1,200 students are turned away from it every year because only 1,100 can fit in the largest campus auditorium. T. R. Kennedy's course on the war at the State University of New York—Stony Brook has also been the largest and most popular course on campus. These courses and many others incorporate talks, lectures and readings by Vietnam veterans into their syllabi. It is the thesis of this chapter that these testimonials, if not properly contextualized, can be an impediment, rather than an aid, to teaching.

I realize that this is an unpopular stand. Along with a revived American interest in the history of the Vietnam War is a new sympathy for the Vietnam veteran. The desperate nature of the veteran's plight—sent off to fight in a hopeless war and then abandoned by the people who sent him—has been conveyed through film and literature. These days, "post traumatic stress disorder" is practically a household word. The failure of the government to provide decent services and benefits for veterans, the publicity surrounding the Agent Orange issue and the natural tendency of the American public to make heroes out of soldiers combine to create a sympathetic atmosphere for veterans who step forward to "tell it like it was."

The crucial question before us is this: Of what use is the testimony of a veteran about traumatic events that happened some twenty years in the past? This, of course, is one of those questions that either has no answer or whose answer is so context dependent that the absence of qualifiers makes a response impossible. Which is exactly my point. I intend to sketch a framework for incorporating veterans' testimony into college and university courses.

The very thing that makes veterans' testimony so attractive to us—the *authenticity* of it—makes that testimony suspect as history. The Vietnam veteran has a tremendous personal investment in his version of the story. Retelling the war is his way of rebuilding personal and national myths that have been shattered by the wartime experience. Vietnam veterans, in this respect, are no different than their Civil War, World War I, World War II or Korean War veteran predecessors. In understanding the complexity of veterans' testimony, it is useful to turn to the work of two men who have already begun to make progress in this direction: Eric Leed and Gerald Linderman.

A QUESTION OF AUTHENTICITY

Leed's *No Man's Land: Combat and Identity in World War I* (New York: Cambridge University, 1979) suggested a new subject for interdisciplinary study—"the transformation of personality in war"—and provided scholars with a new methodological approach. Stating first that his book was neither military history, literary analysis, nor psychohistory, Leed proposed a theory of transformation that incorporated both psychological examination of human response in wartime and the examination of the effect of cultural myth upon human reaction to war. To construct his theory he borrowed concepts from psychiatry, anthropology, history and literary criticism and began to discuss the First World War as a "modernizing experience" that:

> fundamentally altered traditional sources of identity, age-old images of war and men of war. The Great War was a nodal point in the history of industrial civilization because it brought together material realities and "traditional" mentalities in an unexpectedly disillusioning way . . . [T]he disillusioning realization of the inherent similitude of industrial societies and the wars they wage eviscerated, drained, and confounded the logic upon which the moral significance of war and the figure of the warrior had been based.[2]

Leed made good use of an anthropological theory that was articulated by Arnold Van Gennep, who divided rites of passage into three phases: rites of separation that removed an individual or group of individuals from his or their accustomed place; liminal rites, which symbolically fix the character of the "passenger" as one who is between states, places or conditions; and, finally, rites of incorporation (post-liminal rites), which welcome the individual back into the group."[3] Leed claimed that liminality was the condition of the front soldier in World War I and that rather than passing into the post-liminal phase upon his return, the war veteran continued to be a "liminal type": "He derives all of his features from the fact that he has crossed the boundaries of disjunctive social worlds, from peace to war, and back. He has been reshaped by his voyage along the margins of civilization, a voyage in which he has been presented with wonders, curiosities, and monsters—things that can only be guessed at by those who remained at home."[4] The theory of liminality describes a process of symbolic production based on the traumatic experiences of those entering the transition or liminal state. But the symbols generated by liminality are readable only to those familiar with the "alphabet" of trauma; what they represent is not common knowledge and, in fact, symbols that commonly represent a particular idea may be drastically transformed within the mind of the liminal type. (For example, the symbolism inherent in the holocaust survivor poet's description of a bakery's bread oven is entirely different from the same invocation by someone who did not directly experience the holocaust.)

In Leed's estimation, the normal difficulties experienced by the veteran on his return to peacetime society were intensified by the front soldier's perception that those on the home front had benefitted monetarily from his suffering—that capitalists had made profits on the war and that civilians had suffered little or no privations. To support his argument, he pointed to the reorganization of veterans' groups around issues of restitution, benefits and bonuses.[5] The "comradeship" of which veterans spoke was a comradeship of victims, an emotional tie that became the focus of fond memory when the soldier returned to peacetime society and found himself unable to identify with what he found there: "Many ex-soldiers ritualized their liminal status, their position between the front and the home . . . these men 'worked' their war experiences to maintain themselves on the peripheries of society."[6]

Calling World War I "the first holocaust," Leed asserted that it was destined to lead to the Second World War:

> Those who had internalized the War, its peculiar relationship between victims and victimizers, the liminality that it imposed upon combatants, were destined to play a significant part in this repetition. For many could not resolve the ambiguities that defined their identities in war and resume their place in civilian society without acknowledging their status as victims.[7]

World War I provided a crushing blow to the "fictions" by which they lived their lives.

Gerald Linderman advanced a similar argument in his study *Embattled Courage: The Experience of Combat in the American Civil War* (New York: The Free Press, 1987), emphasizing the internal changes undergone by the men who experienced combat. He put an interesting twist on the study by only rarely distinguishing between Union and Confederate soldiers, insisting that the psychological and sociological effects of combat were roughly equivalent in both groups. Linderman divided his book into two sections, the first of which—"Courage's War"—describes the expectations and ideals of the men who joined the Union and Confederate armies. The second section—"A Perilous Education"—deals with the increasing disillusionment and anger of these soldiers when they found that the war was not at all like the war they had imagined. Though he did not use the same terminology as Leed, Linderman characterized liminality in a quite similar manner.

After the Civil War, combat veterans returned to a society that still held those notions about war that soldiers knew, from hard experience, to be outdated (if, indeed, they had ever had any validity). But the new truths that soldiers had discovered were out of place at home: "Killing once again became homicide; foraging was again theft, and incendiarism arson. Even language was a problem: Camp talk had to be cleaned up."[8] In order to cope with the demands and difficulties of everyday life, soldiers had to rewrite their war experiences, smoothing over the difficult parts, revising the unpleasantness:

> While forgetfulness worked to efface painful experience, soldiers construed bad memories in a way that smoothed their departure. When they were able

to discuss the problem among themselves, soldiers ordinarily did so under a rubric—"Time heals all wounds"—revelatory of their assumptions . . . Disturbing memories were to be kept to oneself, not to be aired publicly to relieve the sufferer and certainly not to correct public misapprehension of the nature of combat."[9]

Like Leed, Linderman believes that the soldier who remembered correctly would have been forced to acknowledge his role as a victim. Linderman and Leed also agree that the veteran had a strong role in supporting and encouraging American involvement in a subsequent war. Participating gratefully in commemoration efforts, Civil War veterans benefitted from and supported the revival of American interest in martial matters. According to Linderman, "Although they remained 'men set apart,' their separation had been granted public recognition and their estrangement elevated to civic virtue."[10] Even veterans who had earlier been anti-war and alienated began to take part in and encourage this martial spirit. This revision was so complete that by 1898 the nation enthusiastically applauded the start of the Spanish-American War. The old values were reestablished: "Civil War veterans had become symbols of changelessness—but only by obliterating or amending an experience of combat so convulsive of their values that it had for a time cut the cord of experience."[11]

These two important studies point us in a new direction and urge us toward an understanding of the personal revision process and its interaction with history. We must, as teachers, find a way to cope with the fact that the Vietnam War as depicted by the veterans whom we invite to our classrooms may not be the same Vietnam War that we have uncovered through our research, or even the same war that the soldier himself survived some twenty years earlier. Toward this end, I would like to offer some practical suggestions about inviting Vietnam veteran speakers.

DEMYTHOLOGIZING THE SOLIDER

The most important task of the teacher is to demythologize the soldier. War movies, novels, popular music and stories have given most of our students their ideas about what fighting in a war is all about. Most of the pop culture items focus on the war as a personal growth experience for the soldier, a rite of passage, becoming a man. It is extremely important to introduce students to some of the psychological literature on combat and on military socialization.[12] Combat has deep psychological effects, and it is crucial that students understand some of them. Only then can they listen to the words of the veteran in context, as other than a naively trusting audience.

Students should also be firmly grounded in some of the broader histories of the war.[13] Let students absorb enough information so that they feel confident of their understanding of the war before inviting veterans in to speak to the class. In this way, we can create a situation where students can think critically, where they can analyze a veteran's words and decide whether or not they agree with them.

Exposing students to literature by different Vietnam veterans can also broaden the context in which they understand the veteran who comes to speak. A student who has read Kovic, and Webb and Heinemann is a student who realizes that each veteran can interpret the war in a different, and not necessarily definitive, manner.

If we fail to de-mythologize the veteran, if we fail to provide the student with a context in which to place the veteran speaker, we run the risk of undermining our authority as teachers when we invite the veteran to speak. Rather than having helped our students build a knowledge structure within which the speech of the veteran can be contained, we will be in the position of desperately trying to reclaim critical ground with our students, who will assume that the veteran is the voice of authority because he was there. This may be even more important if the teacher is a Vietnam veteran. If such a teacher does not make it clear that being in Vietnam and understanding the war are two different things, he or she may find himself or herself in the position of pressing students to accept his or her version of the war *because he or she was there*. As any Civil War historian will tell us, this is not a particularly compelling scholarly argument.

Passions about the war still run high, at least among those old enough to remember it—a category which includes most high school and college teachers and everyone else born before 1960. But to us students often seem to us oddly apathetic; for them the war is merely interesting history, like World War II or Korea when we were kids. This lack of passion and moral involvement in the issues of the war means that their real fascination is usually with the soldiers who fought rather than with the causes they fought for. This fascination can work for or against an instructor, depending upon his or her approach. I would like to close with an anecdote about one particularly successful Vietnam War literature course that I taught as a seminar at Yale University.

A COURSE THAT WORKED

The Vietnam Experience: Personal Narratives by Combat Veterans, was taught in the Fall of 1987. The course was a seminar with sixteen students and had nine assigned texts—narratives which included books by Hasford, Herr, Kovic, Webb, Heinemann, Ketwig and others. I also suggested that students purchase a general history of the war that they could use as a reference when they were reading the literature. In addition to the texts, students had the opportunity to watch two Vietnam War films (documentary and fictional) each week. We met once a week, for two hours, to discuss the texts, and students had the option to attend the screenings and discuss the films on one other night each week. In addition, we took advantage of a program of lectures at Columbia University and attended a panel on black soldiers in Vietnam, and one on the Vietnam Memorial Wall.

We began by discussing Michael Herr's *Dispatches*, which for most students was brand new and both shocking and fascinating. *Dispatches* is useful for introducing students to the war because of its tightly written prose and extremely graphic images. Because, for most students, this was their first experience with Vietnam War literature, they approached it naively, accepting that Herr was "telling it like it was." Our initial discussion of the book consisted of students sharing their feelings about the book (which provoked strong emotions in many of them) and then progressed to an exploration of the kind of war that Herr wanted his readers to imagine. We explored his focus, choice of characters and language. The most provocative question was: Who does Michael Herr want you to think he is? That first week, our film showing was a double feature: *Sands of Iwo Jima* (essential viewing for any Vietnam literature class) and *The Green Berets*. The following questions were asked: What is the difference between Michael Herr's vision of war and the vision of war in Wayne's movies? What does Michael Herr think of John Wayne? Can you generate a dialogue between the two?

Each new author we read and each new film we viewed was considered as a voice in an ongoing dialogue about the nature of war in general and the Vietnam War in particular, manhood, duty and culture. Crucial to the students' understanding was the realization that each text (film or printed) had a voice behind it—a voice with a particular interest in being heard in a certain way. The students became very astute at putting together a picture of the author's agenda. And at each discussion session I would introduce some new piece of documentary evidence about the war. One week I brought a six-foot aerial navigation map of Indochina, so that students could locate the places they had been reading about on a map. "Vietnam is so tiny," they exclaimed: each veteran's story had seemed to indicate that the war stretched on forever, in distance and duration. One week I brought a letter from a veteran friend in Arizona who explained why he had gone to war. Another time I brought some of the psychiatric literature on post-traumatic stress disorder, copied from medical journals, so that they could understand that discussion of Vietnam veterans could take place in a completely different context. Yet another time, I read from government hearings on incarcerated veterans.

When I finally decided students were ready to meet and speak to Vietnam veterans about the war, it was arranged through the local veterans' readjustment center, where I was currently teaching a writing workshop. The veterans in one of the rap groups agreed to speak to my students, in groups of four students at a time, during their regular session hours. The first meeting between students and veterans was one I will never forget. Four 18-to-20-year-old men, students at elite Yale University, walked into a room of 12 38-to-45-year-old Vietnam combat veterans (working class, a third of them black, many of them out of work, and several battling drug and alcohol addiction) and took their seats at the round table. The vets were a little hostile. The kids were a little scared. The young men at the table reminded the vets of their 18-year-old selves, but they also reminded them of the college students who had stayed home from the war. The students were having a hard time fitting the sight of a dozen middle-aged men into their images of 19-year-old soldiers. "Why are you here?" grated one of the vets. "Do you want to check us out, and see what kind of freaks we are?" "No," protested one of my students earnestly, "we really want to hear anything you have to say to us." And the tension was broken as questions and answers rolled back and forth, both groups curious about what the other thought. Two hours rushed by, and the session was reluctantly terminated.

I was extremely proud of the way my students had conducted themselves, and each successive group did just as well. I am convinced that the ability of these students to ask and answer difficult questions was based on a firm grounding in the literature of the war, and that they would have had a much more difficult time (the vets would have made sure of that) had they not been so well informed. I also believe that certain important observations (such as, "Hey, some of these guys don't really seem to know a whole lot about the history or politics of the Vietnam War") could never have been made. There is just no substitute for context. I also believe that the experience was made more positive for the participating veterans because these students were educated beyond the point of asking superficial questions that can irritate and offend (such as what is it like to kill somebody?—a question none of my students would have dreamed of asking). Most veteran speakers, I believe, prefer to be regarded as complex human beings rather than as objects for show and tell.

CONCLUSION

The key word here is context. If we can provide our students with a sturdy frame of reference for understanding the Vietnam War, the visits of Vietnam veteran speakers will greatly enrich our history or literature courses on the war. If, however, we fail to provide that context, we may undermine our own authority as teachers and privilege unreasonably the views of veterans. As teachers, we are doing battle with the glib and frequently false images that popular culture sets up for children and teenagers (and even many adults) to absorb. In order to hold our ground, we and our students must have a place to stand.

NOTES

1. "Four Writers Try to Make Sense Of the Vietnam-Book Boom," *The New York Times* (4 August 1987).

2. "Leed, Eric J., *No Man's Land Combat and Identity in World War I* (New York: Cambridge University, 1979), pp. 193-194.

3. Ibid., p. 14.

4. Ibid., p. 194.

5. Ibid., p. 208.

6. Ibid., p. 212.

7. Ibid., p. 213.

8. Linderman, Eric, Embattled Courage: The Experience of Combat in the American Civil War (New York: Free Press, 1987), p. 267.

9. Ibid., p. 268.

10. Ibid.

11. Ibid., p. 280.

12. See, among others, G. Boulanger et al. *Legacies of Vietnam,* volume 4: *Long Term Stress Reactions* (Washington, D. C.: U. S. Government Printing Office, 1981); Gabriel Kolko et al., *Crimes of War* (New York: Random House, 1971); V. Fischer et al., *Myths and Realities: A Study of Attitudes Toward Vietnam Era Veterans* (Washington, D. C.: U. S. Government Printing Office, 1980); P. Karsten, *Law, Soldiers, and Combat* (Westport, Conn.: Greenwood, 1978); Charles Figley, *Trauma and Its Wake* (New York: Brunner/Mazel, 1985); S. Leventman and C. Figley, *Strangers at Home* (New York: Praeger, 1980); and E. Frey-Wouters and R. Laufer, *Legacy of a War: The American Soldier in Vietnam* (New York: M. E. Sharpe, 1986).

13. See, among others, Stanley Karnow, *Vietnam: A History* (New York: Penguin, 1983) and Gabriel Kolko, *Anatomy of a War: Vietnam, the United States, and the Modern Historical Experience* (New York: Pantheon, 1985).

11

The Role of Critical Thinking in a Course on the Vietnam War

MARC JASON GILBERT

A course on the Vietnam War is well-served by the inclusion of material designed to promote the development of analytical or critical-thinking skills. This material can assist in the creation of the active learning environment necessary for students to assimilate the enormous body of knowledge conveyed during any course on the war. As such material can be employed to address a wide variety of topics, it can also assist instructors to achieve a more comprehensive treatment of the war than is otherwise possible. Further, while exercises designed to promote critical thinking, when properly applied, are usually more demanding in terms of student time and creativity than more traditional teaching strategies, students often concede that the effort thus expended is repayed several times over in both knowledge gained and insight acquired. The chief value of integrating the development of critical-thinking skills into the format of a course on the Vietnam War, however, may be the manner in which this teaching strategy opens a safe channel for the passions the war arouses in teachers and students.

THE CENTRALITY OF CRITICAL THINKING

The creation of a course on the Vietnam War is a difficult task. The course must be tailored to its student constituency and modelled for undergraduate, graduate or continuing education instruction. It must be tailored to its mandated length (semester, quarter or short evening course), academic discipline (anthropology, history, literature, political science, or multi-discipline), intended instructional format (lectures, films, team-teaching etc.) and available library, multi-media and human resources, including government document collections, Vietnam veterans and local resettled Vietnamese. Once the course's form and content are established, the instructor must face hard choices regarding the selection of an appropriate text and supplementary readings and decide how much weight should be given to examinations, book reviews and/or research papers in evaluating student performance. To complicate the instructor's tasks, courses on the war are often offered without prerequisites and attended by students with a wide disparity of study skills.

At first glance, such choices and decisions may appear commonplace: most courses require similar attention. As Larry E. Cable notes earlier in this volume, however, the emotion that still overshadows any discussion of the Vietnam War influences and complicates every phase of course formation and preparation. Text choice is, for example, unusually difficult, for unlike texts employed in other areas of study, most Vietnam War texts were written in a state of high emotion. The selection of supplementary course readings, films and videotapes are, for the same reason, equally problematic. Multi-disciplinary and team-taught course strategies have the potential to help diffuse such passions, but they must be structured with particular care lest the students find themselves confronting two wars: the Vietnam War and the war between the academics. Even if these challenges could be met, the assumptions and expectations of instructors and students in today's classrooms would still remain as a formidable obstacle to reasonably well-balanced and well-formed courses.

Though some instructors might jibe at the suggestion that they are unable to maintain their objectivity in the classroom, most would admit that, like most of their generation, they have been too deeply touched by the Vietnam experience to regard a course related to the war as just another preparation. Students, who rarely believe their teachers are objective about any course subject, bring into the classroom their own expectations, which are powerful enough to impose themselves on course structure and conduct. Some students enroll in a course on the war not merely out of a desire to find a context for their own or their parents' actions during the war, but in an effort to seek validation of their own or their parents' wartime activities and post-war opinions. Other students, too young to remember the war, are just as likely to regard such a course as an opportunity to develop or confirm worldviews quite different from those of their parents, while their older war veteran classmates may bring into the lecture hall an equally intense search for new personal meaning.

The mastering of the passions raised by the war is therefore the first priority of many instructors, who, in their effort to remove the obstacles of teacher-student expectations, often rely on two familiar elements of the Socratic method: the examination of the facts and attention to the standards of truth. However, because a fact may only serve as a building block of understanding when it consists of, among other things, the accounts of observers and participants, it can be argued that Vietnam War "facts" are more elusive than usual. We still do not have full access to the enemy's accounts of the war, their records and those records America and its allies left in Vietnam in the wake of their defeat. We have also not been able, due to insufficient staff, security classification and other constraints, to fully examine the enormous collection of official records on the war on file in the National Archives and other national records depositories in Washington, D. C.

Our judgment of key issues, moreover, is clouded by an aspect of official reportage that was symptomatic of our forces in Vietnam. Whether a project in the field was successful or not, it was often essential, for a variety of careerist and bureaucratic reasons, that the field report made it appear effective in the eyes of the superiors who had mandated the project. Such practices formed the first link in the chain of what Larry E. Cable calls the "positive feedback loop" that crippled our war effort. That such demands are human enough and such reportage common in all wars (and during every moment of peace) is cold comfort to teachers who must examine such issues as the performance of the Army of the Republic of Vietnam (ARVN) in the period 1972-1975 or the success of American pacification programs.

The problems engendered by less than optimal historical facts or reports can usually be controlled by tools associated with the search for truth. However, as Douglas Pike has elsewhere observed, "much of the truth" of the Vietnam War is irrelevant or obscured either "because it was the untruths that had the impact, the meaning, that shaped the heritage" or because the "hyperbolic exaggeration that pervades all writings on Vietnam" has undermined our confidence in the general reliability of scholarly assessments that is essential for academic dialogue.[1] The results of Earl H. Tilford, Jr.'s evaluation of early scholarly assessments of the air war in the second chapter of this volume would seem to validate both of Pike's assertions.

The lack of a complete historical record and the state of scholarship on the war has convinced Pike that any effort to assess the war now would be to participate in a "rush to judgment." His solution to the problems facing discourse on the war is as applicable to teaching as it is to research: we should admit to ourselves that we are still "prisoners of competing perceptions" and "devote ourselves to describing them until time permits us to gain a greater knowledge of ourselves and of the other side."[2] Pike believes that the healing effects of the passage of time and the greater access to records that will come with improved relations with Vietnam will ultimately enable us to generate reliable data and arrive at considered and fair judgments. What, however, shall be our guide until that time comes?

Fortunately, classroom techniques that stimulate critical thinking constitute in themselves a guide to course formation and management that can harness rather than restrict the engine of passion and the quest for truth, which notwithstanding Pike's caveat, propels all academic endeavors.

A course on the Vietnam War designed to provide students with lectures, text choices, supplementary reading selections, classroom exercises and research paper topics that are informed by a focus on critical thinking can accomplish much more than the mere creation of a forum for Pike's competing perceptions. Since teaching approaches that stress critical thinking—when properly applied—guarantee a considerable amount of balanced discussion of primary sources or other forms of evidentiary material, teachers and students can engage in considerable intellectual speculation about the war, with the teacher secure in the knowledge that most of his or her students will be prepared to weigh for themselves the truth of *ex parte* statements made on both sides of the lectern. An example related to Earl H. Tilford, Jr.'s work on the air war may serve to illustrate the basic premise and value of a critical-thinking approach to the teaching of the Vietnam War.

No course on the Vietnam War can avoid an examination of the air war. Instructors and students who have any acquaintance with the air war usually have strong opinions on this controversial subject. Prior to a classroom discussion of the this war-within-a-war, an instructor employing a critical-thinking framework can introduce students to an article by Alan Gropman, who argues that if American air power had been unleashed in 1965 as it was in 1972 (Linebacker II), America could have forced the Vietnamese communists to negotiate on terms more favorable to American interests.[3] These same students can also be directed to an article by Tilford in which he contends that Gropman's argument is inaccurate and ahistorical and fails to account for the changed international climate in the wake of Nixon's visit to China, which had reduced the likelihood of global war or Chinese intervention that had earlier "tied the hands" of President Johnson and his pilots.[4] Finally, students can also be asked to study the comments of Douglas Pike, who, while sharing Gropman's belief that a less restrictive bombing policy in the period 1965-1969 would have led to earlier negotiations, suggests that these negotiations may not have immediately ended the war but merely continued it in another form.[5] Subsequent discussion of the air war may feature the instructor's own evaluation of the air war and an airing of students' views.

A critical-thinking approach, however, extends beyond course reading assignments and an open forum classroom discussion. Armed by their background reading, students could be assigned to defend a position on the air war in a debate. Examinations devoted to evaluating student command and comprehension of this subject can ask students to identify and discuss the three perspectives advanced in their readings. Research papers exploring this subject, like those devoted to all other research topics, can conform to guidelines that indicate to the students that, while they may defend any position taken on the air war, papers that fail to analyze competing lines of thought will not receive a satisfactory grade.[6]

Five years after graduation, students who have taken a course so designed may no longer remember what is meant by the term Linebacker II, but such exercises are likely to have honed their reasoning abilities. Students will, more immediately, have become better able to judge for themselves the value of their instructor's opinions and have gained an appreciation of the value of John K. Fairbank's remark that "the lessons of history are never simple. Whoever thinks he sees one should probably keep on with his reading."[7]

Some instructors may contend that, while the development of critical thinking serves a laudable purpose, they possess neither the time nor the resources to construct a unit around it, let alone an entire course. There are, however, more ways of making the development of critical-thinking skills an integral part of a course on the war than might be imagined. There are also great incentives for secondary school and college teachers to make use of these skills as a means of maintaining an active learning environment. For example, due to the notoriously short historical memory of American students, so much class time must be devoted to explanatory material (such as a description of the Cold War) that unless students are given the opportunity to interact with the course material, even so compelling a tale as Vietnam can become a bore. Of the many methods currently employed to avoid such a dismal development, the most dramatic involve various forms of simulation, or role-playing.

DECISION-MAKING SIMULATIONS AND ALTERNATIVE EXERCISES

It is possible to construct a course around a form of role-playing that, while directly employing the energies of only a few students in a large class, has the capacity to reach and excite all students enrolled in the course. During the first few class meetings the instructor solicits volunteers to serve in one of several study groups that will be formed to devote special study to a key decision or turning point of the war. Students who do not volunteer must complete a written assignment that places an equivalent demand on student time. Not all students can volunteer as the size of student groups is limited and only a fraction of the class will be in the study groups. Each member of a study group creates an essay in the form of a policy position paper prepared by the head of one of the government agencies or another individual directly involved in the decision under study. For example, one student might seek to simulate the report of the director of the Central Intelligence Agency on the possible success of a coup d'etat confronting Ngo Dinh Diem, while other students might represent the views on this subject of the American ambassador in Saigon, the secretary of state, the national security advisor, Ngo Dinh Diem himself, and so forth. The group meets with the instructor, who helps them to define their roles and obtain source material. They later meet privately for a group debate. This debate is conducted along the lines of a meeting with the president during which each party attempts to persuade their chief that the course they propose should be adopted. Having thus honed their skills and knowledge, these students then orally argue their case before the class. The class responds with arguments and opinions of their own and plays the arguments of one group member against another, much as John F. Kennedy did during meetings with his White House staff. William Duiker, who has taught a survey course on Vietnam using this method for some time, often devotes a considerable number of class hours to such exercises, but finds the returns well worth the sacrifice. It would seem that instructors who have the luxury of teaching a small survey class or a seminar on the war could employ this method throughout the course with equally good results.

Instructors with large classes who approve of the above idea, but are not willing or able to devote six or seven class sessions to such exercises, or who teach a course in which the Vietnam War is but a part, might wish to reserve such treatment for a few key turning points, such as America's response to Ho Chi Minh's letters to Truman in 1945. Such an exercise might be considered for use in developing a Vietnam component of a course on the Cold War, a course on recent American history or a survey of world civilization. The single role-playing session Cecil B. Currey uses to introduce his students to the mind-set of revolutionaries and their tactics, described in the third chapter of this volume, would seem to be as well suited to a course on comparative politics or revolution as to a survey of the Vietnam War. Such sessions, perhaps best called round tables, need not focus on key decisions, single events or policy-making. Their greatest value may rest in the light they can shed on those more general issues that are central to the war but are difficult to bring into the classroom.

RACE AND GENDER ROUND TABLE

Today's students may be less inclined than their predecessors to ask "What did you do in the Class War, Daddy?"[8] They are, however, quite eager to know more about the role of ethnic minorities and women in the war. This should come as no surprise: women and ethnic minorities constitute well over half the general student population and account for a growing proportion of enrollments in courses on the war. Interest in this topic has, moreover, been stimulated by the large number of ethnic minorities and women involved in Operation Desert Storm. While issues of race and gender are only just beginning to emerge in the scholarship of the Vietnam War, sufficient materials exist to allow students to investigate and discuss the role of these groups in the war and the war's impact upon them.[9]

Instructors who convene a round table on gender issues may wish to direct students to *Vietnam Generation* 1, nos. 1-4 (1989). This volume, composed of the first four numbers of that year's issues under a single cover, is devoted to the exploration of this subject and includes an invaluable "Bibliography of Unusual Sources on Women and the Vietnam War" (pp. 274-77), which references works on women experiencing post-traumatic stress disorder as well as studies on and memoirs of Vietnamese women.

CAMBODIA AND LAOS ROUND TABLE

While teachers are becoming more aware of the Vietnamese dimension of the American war in Vietnam, they often devote little attention to Cambodia and Laos, which were important factors in the occasioning and conduct of America's involvement in Southeast Asia. There are today sufficient sources to enable a student to explore early Cambodian and Laotian culture, the French presence and communism in both countries, the career of Norodom Sianoukh, the Khmer Rouge, the "secret" air war in Cambodia and Laos, the Cambodian holocaust and its survivors, the role of Cambodia and Laos in the Third Indochinese War, and the "second chance" that this war, or rather the search for a means of ending it, offers America in Southeast Asia.[10]

VIETNAMESE ROUND TABLE

Most instructors recognize that America's inability to understand Vietnamese political culture was a major contributing factor to the failure of American policy in Southeast Asia. They often find it difficult, however, to discuss this aspect of the war due to a perceived lack of time. A round table on Vietnamese leaders may constitute one solution to this problem. A class may be assigned appropriate background reading in one or more of the large number of autobiographical and biographical works on the lives of Vietnamese touched by the war and asked to contribute to a single classroom discussion of the ideals and actions of the Vietnamese they studied. The lives of members of the Viet Cong, leaders of the Hanoi and Saigon regimes and Vietnamese peasants and refugees are currently well-represented in works highly accessible to the student reader.[11]

ANTIWAR ROUND TABLE

The literature on the anti-war movement is so rich that it is possible to explore its relationship to the campaign for nuclear disarmament, New Left internationalism, the civil rights movement, the student revolt and counter-cultural and intergenerational conflict, opposition to the draft, and the movement's impact on the war. The task of preparing students to address the antiwar movement has been greatly eased by the appearance of the late Charles DeBeneditti's final and seminal work, *An American Ordeal: The Antiwar Movement of the Vietnam Era* (Syracuse, N. Y.: Syracuse University, 1990). Though only just now reaching the market, *An American Ordeal* is already being touted as the best and most comprehensive account of the movement. Yet, despite the plethora of resources, it remains difficult to convey to students even basic elements of antiwar behavior, such as the reluctance of antiwar activists to criticize the policies or behavior of the North Vietnamese or the Viet Cong. Only by immersing a class in the origins and nature of the anti-war movement can such issues be resolved and the broad scope of this movement's ideology and the diversity of its membership be correctly understood. Lois Horton of George Mason University has proposed one method by which this object can be achieved. She suggests enlivening a course on the Vietnam War or any course on modern American society with a class session in which each student, following the model provided by Duiker, takes the position of one of the many segments of the anti-war movement (pacifists, feminists, internationalists, military men, Vietnam Veterans Against the War, draft resisters, civil rights leaders, etc.). Such an exercise should help students understand American opposition to the war and work to prevent the repetition of the "America: love it or leave it" sloganeering that even today can erupt in the classroom when the anti-war movement is discussed.[12]

HISTORY TALKS BACK

A minor variation of the role-playing theme involves assigning students to master biographical material on individual representatives of the "Vietnam experience." When his or her research is complete, each student addresses the class at an appropriate time during the course in the character of that individual or as a spokesman for that actor in history. It would seem that a class that was merely engaged in the act of contemplating hearing and quizzing Ho Chi Minh, Ngo Dinh Diem, Edward Lansdale, John Kerry or Abbie Hoffman is already engaged in a learning experience.

OPPOSING VIEWPOINTS

Another related role-playing technique exploits the controversial nature of so many of the war's key incidents, individuals and policies. Students are paired. Each pair is assigned material supporting one of two opposing sides of a still hotly debated issue related to the war. One member of each pair is selected to defend one of the two sides of the argument before the class as if they were members of a competing debating team. William Dudley and David Bender, editors, *Opposing Viewpoints: Vietnam* (San Diego, Calif.: Greenhaven Press, 2nd rev. ed., 1990) is useful for this purpose. The better anthologies on the war, discussed below, are rich in resources for such exercises. This approach must, however, be pursued with care. As Douglas Pike has pointed out, "on the one hand [the employment of an opposing viewpoints strategy] helps do what education is supposed to do: teach students how to think. On the other, it adds little factual knowledge, leaving only a mind filled with conflicting perceptions wondering what is the truth?"[13] The approach is thus more effectively employed as a touchstone for introducing new issues for study or for the discussion of issues students have already had an opportunity to explore rather than in lieu of the study of the issues themselves.

MOOT COURT

The considerable research materials now available on the trials of the Chicago Seven and Lieutenant William Calley as well as on the hearings into the killings at Kent State University have encouraged several professors to recreate these inquiries in the classroom.[14] Such projects might be conducted by teams of students taking the roles of lawyers and witnesses on both sides of the courtroom or argued in the form of a moot court. The "cases" could be "tried" before the rest of the class or before the student body at large.

TOTAL IMMERSION

Some teachers seek to totally emerse students in the Vietnam era in order to provide them with a better understanding of the war and the period in which it took place. Such a transformation can be quite complete and reach beyond a single class to the general student body. For example, the school band can play music from the era at sporting events, and school dances can have a "sixties" theme. The advantages of such a program, even one less fully realized, might be substantial if carefully managed. A visit to local graves of soldiers killed in the war, a viewing of contemporary films and television programs and a reading of contemporary newspapers (including student newspapers) might help students gain insight into the era's Cold War concerns and sense of innocence lost that is often hard to communicate through the use of traditional classroom strategies.

Paul Davis of Union High School in South Carolina is currently conducting one such program entitled "The Vietnam Project." The scope of the project is quite broad. It embraces the entire student body and the surrounding community and pursues a calendar of events that spans an entire year. During that year, speakers with diverse backgrounds ranging from prisoners of war to antiwar leaders will visit the campus. Students have already begun publishing a project newsletter and have hosted a local radio program. An anthology will be published of the best student interviews with Vietnam era veterans and their families. A Vietnam Veterans Day will be observed and feature a display of art work created by the veterans themselves. A map of Southeast Asia on display at the school features an overlay of pictures of local veterans that indicates the date and location of their service. Links have been established with neighboring schools, and the faculty of local colleges and universities have been enlisted to assist in the program. A locally funded grant will be awarded to the teacher who most effectively integrates Vietnam war material into his or her courses. Those instructors who wish to benefit from Mr. Davis's experience and expertise may write to him at Union High School, Peach Orchard Road, Union, South Carolina 29379 or call (803) 429-1753.

ALICE'S RESTAURANT

Lynda Boose of Dartmouth College simulates the introduction of the draft lottery by creating a lottery of her own. Dates of birth are chosen by lot and read out until one-third of her class has received numbers rendering them liable to the draft. These students leave the classroom as their numbers are called. The discussion that follows this exercise is, by all accounts, quite lively.

THE THINGS THEY CARRIED

There is one variant of role-playing that takes the active form of critical-thinking exercises to its logical extreme. Kathryn Terrill of Mt. Hood Community College in Gresham, Oregon has utilized the services of a Vietnam veteran to recreate on campus a night-time patrol, replete with booby traps and other requisite alarms and excursions. The students who share "walking point" and the rest of their classmates all come back to the classroom in one piece, but all are touched by the experience. The scope of such simulations is limited: few colleges would or should allow students to be fired upon with live ammunition or experience the sufferings of Vietnamese non-combatants touched by the war. Yet, to cite another more benign example, teachers who are able to take their students on a ride in a "Huey" speak well of such experiences.

SCENARIOS

There are means of engaging minds through role-playing that do not occur in the classroom and its aerial or nocturnal environs. Larry E. Cable provides his students with a detailed scenario that translates the crises of the Vietnam War into parallel events occurring in a mythical Latin American state. This scenario is in the form of a briefing paper that summarizes all available intelligence reports and governmental department views of conditions "in country." Each student is identified in the briefing paper as an adviser to the president on national security issues. A terse note at the top of the document indicates that the chief requires this analyst's opinion as soon as possible. That opinion is to be informed by the analyst's own conception of the lessons of Vietnam and is submitted in lieu of a research paper at the end of the course. The scenario is too lengthy to be reproduced here; however, less detailed variants of this exercise are readily available.[15] Cable uses his students' written replies as the basis of their entire grade in his course. Other instructors who employ this method treat it as only one element of the course grading scheme.

COURSE JOURNALS

There are a wide range of alternatives to role-playing. Among the most popular of these exercises is the keeping of a course journal. Like role-playing schemes, course journals can take many forms.[16] The most common form of journal preparation is based on a syllabus that identifies questions students are to answer on the basis of their impressions of course lectures, films, readings and classroom visits by Vietnam War veterans and other guests. These questions can be highly inventive and can transcend the course material itself. Students may be asked to evaluate their knowledge of America's recent past, measure any growth of an understanding of the war's complexity and record any personal sense of tragedy, triumph, sadness, or pride arising from their experience of the course. Instructors who have read journals that record their students' reactions to viewing films such as *Hearts and Minds* or the equally visceral, though less polemical, Home Box Office video program *Dear America: Letters Home from Vietnam* are convinced of the utility of this exercise.

ORAL HISTORY INTERVIEWS

The availability of subjects for oral history interviews in most urban areas and many rural areas of the country has led many instructors to use oral history as a means of galvanizing student interest and promoting intellectual growth. Students are assigned extensive background readings relevant to the subject of their interview (anti-war activists, infantrymen, women who served in the military or in the auxiliary services in Vietnam, air force personnel, etc.), provided with direction in the conduct of oral history interviews, and required to give a classroom report on the results of their interviews at an appropriate time during the course. Most teachers who employ this technique are sensitive to the concerns raised by Kali Tal in her contribution to this volume, for an oral history interview with a veteran is a visit by a veteran to a class with an enrollment of one. Classroom visits by Vietnam veterans are, of course, a common occurrence in courses on the war and, as Kali Tal has demonstrated, when they are appropriately managed they can be a powerful stimulus to critical thinking.

A FAMILY AFFAIR

Some instructors ask students to complete a history of their own families during the Vietnam era. This exercise would work well in a course held in the American South due to the high concentration of professional military families, Reserve Officer Training programs and military bases. However, few American families of the era were not affected by the war, though they may have experienced it less directly. Those students whose families were untouched by the war can be assigned to examine the published accounts of Vietnam era American or Vietnamese families, or asked to flesh out a biography of a fictional American or Vietnamese family whose history is provided in outline form by the instructor.

WORLD HISTORY ANALYSES

Students may be asked to trace one of the many currents of world history that shaped the course of both revolution in Vietnam and the American response to it. They may, for example, be asked to examine the ideological roots of Vietnamese culture, nationalism, communism, military strategy and post-war security policy. When Lynda Boose and Douglas Haynes team-teach a course on the Vietnam War at Dartmouth College, they ask their students to analyze Vietnamese revolutionary ideology in the light of other revolutionary ideologies, including the anti-Marxist ideology of Mohandas Karamchand Gandhi. They also invite their students to compare American policy in the Philippines with American policy in Vietnam, or America's overall Asian policy with the many variants of European imperial administration in the region.

The place of the antiwar movement in the global political movements of the day can also be examined. Students can compare the agendas of antiwar leaders with those of their counterparts in Paris in 1968 and in China during the Great Proletarian Cultural Revolution, and examine these movements for common sources and any mutual influences. Robert V. Daniels, *Year of the Heroic Guerrilla: World Revolution and Counterrevolution in 1968* (New York: Basic Books, 1989) provides both an exhaustive treatment of this subject and a superb bibliography of contemporary American and foreign social movements.

The Vietnam War clearly had a global reach. Students may be directed to investigate the degree to which the war effected the shape of Asian politics and American and Vietnamese political institutions. They may choose to study the impact of the war on the international community through such events as the international response to the fate of the "boat people" and the plight of Cambodia. They can also study the impact of the war on the Association of Southeast Asian Nations (ASEAN) or the parallels alleged to exist between the American experience in Vietnam and the Soviet experience in Afghanistan.[17]

VIETNAM IN AMERICA: AMERICA IN VIETNAM

Students may benefit from an assignment that requires them to examine the Cambodian, Hmong, Laotian and Vietnamese communities in the United States or to compare American policy toward refugees from Southeast Asia with U. S. policy toward refugees and immigrants from other countries. They may also be asked to study and report on the Amerasian community in Vietnam.[18]

MEDIA ANALYSIS

Another popular exercise entails the use of newspaper and journal accounts in a fashion similar to that advocated by Melford Wilson, Jr., and Steve Potts. Students are given a list of key wartime decisions or events, directed to contemporary periodical accounts of those events, and are asked to compare them to the coverage of these same occurrences provided by the course text, lectures and other course materials. The results are submitted in written form or in written and oral form at an appropriate moment in the course. One variant of this approach would direct students to compare American and foreign press reports of events in Southeast Asia.

Alternatively, students can be assigned readings in the growing literature on coverage of the war by the news media and asked to analyze or defend the positions on this issue taken by critics and defenders of the role of the media in America's defeat. Scholarship on the role of the media in the war has much improved of late, as has access to a wide spectrum of opinions on its impact. There are now two reliable surveys of that role, Daniel Hallin's *The Uncensored War: The Media and Vietnam* (New York: Oxford University, 1986) and William Hammond's *Public Affairs: The Military and the Media* (Washington, D. C.: Center for Military History, United States Army, 1989). Most of the more recent Vietnam war course readers and anthologies offer excellent material for the study of the news media's coverage of the war.

LITERATURE

As Gerald Berkley, Jonathan Goldstein and Catherine Calloway have made clear in their contributions to this volume, the literature of the Vietnam War is a major pedagogical tool suitable for use in any course examining the war. The most common means of employing this resource to stimulate critical thinking in such courses is the assigning of works to students for comparison and review. By coordinating these reviews with the discussion of important issues, students get the benefit of entering into the hyper-reality of fiction that, in the view of some, is a corrective to the desensitized and sanitized version of reality often contained in historical memoirs and official accounts. There is no question that the literature of the Vietnam War cannot help but lend insight into what the war meant to those who experienced it first hand. Such is the variety of that literature that there is not a phase or aspect of the war that cannot be illuminated by a literary work used in support of course lectures and text. For example William Lederer and Eugene Burdick's, *The Ugly American* (America comes to Vietnam); Graham Greene's *The Quiet American* (advice and support); Philip Caputo's *Rumor of War* (America takes charge); Jack Broughton's *Thud Ridge* and *Going Downtown* (the air war); Robert Mason's *Chickenhawk* (airmobile warfare); Tran Van Dinh's *Blue Dragon, White Tiger* (Tet); and so forth. While some instructors make liberal use of literary sources, many are quite selective, employing only two or three works of fiction (most commonly *Rumor of War* or Tim O'Brien's *Going After Cacciato*). Some employ these sources extensively, but in the form of excerpts. Thanks to the newer Vietnam readers and anthologies described immediately below, this may be done with considerable success, though

there is no substitute for the experience of reading an artist's work as he
or she intended it to be read.

ANTHOLOGY INTERACTIONS

As mentioned above, there are now some excellent anthology and
document collections available that are, in some cases, not only excellent
sources for critical-thinking exercises, but whose readings are designed to
constitute such an exercise. Jeffery P. Kimball, editor, *To Reason Why: The
Debate Over the Causes of U.S. Involvement in the Vietnam War* (New York:
McGraw Hill, 1990), Robert J. McMahon, editor, *Major Problems in the
History of the Vietnam War* (New York: D. C. Heath, 1990), John Norton
Moore, *The Vietnam Debate: A Fresh Look at the Arguments* (Lanham, Md.:
University Press of America, 1990) offer students a variety of viewpoints
expressed in essays and documents. Harrison Salisbury, editor, *Vietnam
Reconsidered: Lessons from a War* (New York: Harper and Row, 1984),
Grace Sevy, editor, *The American Experience in Vietnam* (Norman, Okla.:
University of Oklahoma Press, 1989) and John C. Warren, editor, *American
Intervention in Vietnam: An Anthology* (White Plains, N. Y.: Longmans,
1987) offer so wide a range of opposing viewpoints and perspectives that
no campus library supporting a course on the war should be without them.
In chapter 13 of this volume, Joe P. Dunn draws attention to the large
number of document collections now available to those teaching about the
Vietnam War. Yet, no reader or documents collection yet produced is
without pedogoical flaw or egregious omission. Instructors seeking a
reader will no doubt find that the best course to follow is to have students
purchase the reader deemed best suited to the overall needs of the course
and assign them additional readings as required in selections drawn from
other readers or original sources placed on reserve in the library.

"TALKING ABOUT VIETNAM"

The popularity of mainstream academic courses on the Vietnam War
and the concurrent re-opening of public dialogue about the war has led
many schools and some public institutions to sponsor evening study groups
and public seminars that are intended to bring the study of the war to as
many Americans as possible. Several California academic and public
institutions, including its public library system and the Indochina Project
at the University of California, Berkeley have joined together to create
what may prove to be a model for such courses. Those engaged in similar
work will certainly benefit from an examination of the separate guides for
instructors and participants prepared for the "Talking about Vietnam"

series of seminars that will be held in California public libraries in the near future. Information about the program may be obtained by writing to Talking about Vietnam, Rhea Joyce Rubin, Project Director, Peninsular Library System, San Mateo, California 94402-4000 or by calling (415) 349-5538.

CONCLUSION

Those instructors who employ exercises designed to improve the critical-thinking skills of their students rarely use one exercise exclusively or stay with a single exercise indefinitely. For example, John M. Gates of the College of Wooster has long mixed the use of a single high impact novel (*Rumor of War*) with a course journal. He has recently decided to abandon the journal assignment in order to keep his own interest alive, and is searching for a replacement format. Fortunately, the key to these exercises is not the individual format employed. It will be remembered that they were initially exemplified here in a form as prosaic as a reading assignment. The true keys to success in the development of critical-thinking skills are the recognition by the instructor of what critical-thinking exercises can contribute to course cohesion and comprehensiveness and his or her willingness to engage students in a quest for knowledge that can stimulate within them a love of learning.

NOTES

1. Douglas Pike, "The Status of Scholarship on the War," in John Schlight, editor, *Second Indochina War Symposium: Papers and Commentary* (Washington, D. C.: Center for Military History, United States Army, 1986), p. 269.

2. Ibid., p. 270.

3. Alan P. Gropman, "Lost Opportunities: The Air War in Vietnam, 1961-1973," in Lawrence E. Gunter and Peter M. Dunn, editors, *The American War in Vietnam: Lessons, Legacies and Implications for Future Conflicts* (Westport, Conn.: Greenwood, 1987), pp. 49-67.

4. Earl H. Tilford, Jr., "Air Power in Vietnam: The Hubris of Power," Lawrence E. Grinter and Peter M. Dunn, *The American War in Vietnam*, pp. 69-83.

5. Douglas Pike made these remarks in a discussion pursuant to presentation of his paper "The Other Side," in Peter Braestrup, editor, *Vietnam as History: Ten Years after the Paris Peace Accords* (Washington, D. C.: University Press of America, 1984), pp. 86-87.

6. Among those research topics amenable to a "critical thinking" emphasis are: American Women and the War; African Americans and the War; the Air War; the Anti-War Movement; Operation Cedar Falls; the Civilian Action Program; Counterinsurgency; the Fall of Diem; Ho Chi Minh; the Hmong and the War; The Killings at Kent State University; My Lai; Operation Ranch Hand; Prelude to Vietnam—The United States in the Philippines; Vietnamese Refugees in America; Vietnamese Women and the War; Prince Norodom Sianoukh; the Veterans Administration Hospital System and the Vietnam War; the Viet Cong; Vietnamization; William Westmoreland as a War Leader; and Vo Nguyen Giap. Among those topics that most often result in descriptive papers, but need not do so if carefully supervised, are: Special Forces in Vietnam; Airmobility, Medical Services in Vietnam and Naval Operations in Vietnam.

7. See Noel C. Eggleston, "On Lessons: A Critique of the Summers Thesis," in Grinter and Dunn, editors, *The American War In Vietnam*, p. 111.

8. James Fallows, "What Did You Do in the Class War, Daddy?" *The Washington Monthly*, 7 (Oct. 1975), pp. 5-19.

9. For the role and impact of women on the war, see Barthy Bird, *Home Front: Women and Vietnam* (Berkeley, Calif.: Shameless Hussy Press, 1986); Virginia Elwood-Akers, *Women War Correspondents in the Vietnam War, 1961-1975* (Metuchen, N. J.: Scarecrow Press, 1988): Dan Freeman and Jacqueline Rhodes, *Nurses in Vietnam: The Forgotten Veterans* (Lubbock, Tex.: Texas Monthly Press, 1987); Ley Li Hayslip with Jay Wurts, *When Heaven and Earth Changed Places* (New York: Doubleday, 1989); Jann Jansen, *Paper Bridges: From Vietnam With Love* (New York: Penguin, 1990); Wendy Larsen and Tran Thi Nga, *Shallow Graves: Two Women and Vietnam* (New York: Random House, 1986); Kathryn Marshall, *In A Combat Zone: Vivid Personal Recollections of the Vietnam War from the Women Who Served There* (New York: Penguin, 1987); Bobby Ann Mason, *In Country* (New York: Harper and Row, 1985); Nguyen Thi Dinh, *No Other Road to Take: Memoir of Mrs. Nguyen Thi Dinh* (Ithaca, N. Y.: Cornell University Southeast Asia Program, 1976); Joan Silver, *Limbo* (New York: Pocket Books, 1972); James and Sybil Stockdale, *In Love and War: The Family's Ordeal and Sacrifice During the Vietnam Years* (New York: Bantam, 1985); Lynda Van Devanter, *Home Before Morning: The Story of an Army Nurse in Vietnam* ((New York: Warner, 1983); and Keith Walker, *A Piece of My Heart: The Stories of Twenty-Six American Women Who Served in Vietnam* (New York: Ballantine, 1985).

The literature on ethnic minorities is very limited and certainly no source can tell us that, in terms of the number who served in relation to their total population, a larger percentage of Micronesians from Guam fought in Vietnam than any other American ethnic group. The best and most widely available work an instructor can use to introduce the issue of race into a class on the war are Wallace Terry, *Bloods: An Oral History of the Vietnam War by Black Veterans* (New York: Random House, 1984); Stanley Goff and Robert Sanders with Clark Smith, *Brothers: Black Soldiers in the Nam* (Novato, Calif.: Presido, 1982, Berkeley, 1985); and Clyde Taylor, editor, *Vietnam and Black America: An Anthology of Protest and Resistance* (Garden City, N. Y.: Doubleday, 1973). Also of use are several articles on the subject collected in *Vietnam Generation* 1, no. 2, (1989). For further discussion of sources on race and gender issues, see chapter nine, pp. 140, 144-5, and 149; chapter six, p. 103; chapter eight, p. 129; chatper 11, pp. 176-7; and chapter 13, pp. 217-8.

10.   See Frederick Z. Brown, *Second Chance: The United States in Indochina in the 1990s* (New York: Council on Foreign Relations Press, 1989). For a discussion of sources on Cambodia and Laos see chapter six, pp. 97-99.

11. For sources on Vietnam's early history and modern leadership, see chapter six, pp. 89-97.

12. For a fuller discussion of sources for the study of the anti-war movement, see chapter six, pp. 102-3.

13. Douglas Pike, review of William Dudley and David Bender, *The Vietnam War: Opposing Viewpoints* (San Diego, Calif.: Greenhaven, 2nd rev. ed., 1990), in *Indochina Chronology* 9, no. 4 (October-December 1990), p. 19.

14. William L. Calley, *Body Count: Lieutenant Calley's Story as Told to John Sack* (London: Hutchinson, 1971); Peter Davies, *The Truth About Kent State: A Challenge in the American Conscience* (New York: Farrar Straus and Giroux, 1973); David Farber, *Chicago '68* (Chicago: University of Chicago, 1988); William A. Gordon, *The Fourth of May: Killings and Coverups at Kent State* (New York: Prometheus, 1990); Richard Hammer, *One Morning in the War: The Tragedy at Son My* (New York: Coward, McCann and Geoghegan, 1970) and *The Trial of Lt. Calley* (New York: Coward, McCann and Geoghegan, 1971); Seymour Hersh, *Cover-Up* (New York: Random House, 1972) and *My Lai 4: A Report on the Massacre and Its Aftermath* (New York: Random House, 1970); James Michener, *Kent State: What Happened and Why* (New York: Random House, 1971); and William R. Peers, *The My Lai Inquiry* (New York: Norton, 1976). See also p. 248 of the appendix to this volume.

15. See appendix, pp. 240-1. Bruce Siggson of Xavier University in New Orleans employs a one-page diplomatic cable headed "Top Secret," dated Paris, March 8, 1969 and addressed to Le Duan, Secretary General, Lao Dong Workers Party in Hanoi. The author of the cable, Le Duc Tho, writes "Tet War military failure. How long before we see military goals achieve political goals? What if Uncle Ho dies? Can we continue without him? Dr. Kissinger threatens new and intense bombing of cities. What should be our strategy?   Consider please: The American antiwar

movement; the American will to continue the war; the new American presidential administration; the new American bombing campaign; the role of America's allies; the state of world opinion; the role of the NLF; and action to be taken if American forces attack sanctuaries in Laos and Cambodia. Need reply soon. Talks resume tomorrow."

16. See David Skidmore, "A Vietnam War Syllabus," Foreign Policy Analysis Notes 17, no. 2 (Summer 1990), pp. 3-8, and pp. 242, 285-6, and 288 of the appendix to this volume.

17. See Gennady Bocharov, *Russian Roulette: Afghanistan Through Russian Eyes* (New York: Harper Collins, 1990); Esther B. Fein "Veterans from Two Armies and Two Wars Finding Shared Wounds in Moscow," *The New York Times*, October 3, 1988, International edition, p. 6; and *The New York Times*, August 9, 1990, sec. a, p. 7.

18. See Nathan Caplan, John K. Whitmore and Marcella H. Choy, *The Boat People and Achievement in America: A Study of Economic and Educational Success* (Ann Arbor, Mich.: University of Michigan, 1989) and David Haines, editor, *Refugees As Immigrants: Cambodians, Laotians and Vietnamese in America* (Totowa, N. J.: Rowman and Littlefield, 1989).

12

Using Primary Sources
STEVE POTTS

For those who teach high school or college history courses, the presence of the Vietnam War, a conflict that ended before many of our students were born, is inescapable. This presence is uncomfortable. The recent and continuing outpouring of movies, television programs, and books about the war engage students' curiosity. That is fine. Their questions about the war, however, force teachers to face how they will teach a subject that many of them lived through as either participants or observers. That is uncomfortable. Teaching their own experiences forces them to question their assumptions and come to terms with an often painful part of their past.

Come to terms we must, though, because the war and its effects are rapidly becoming grist for the educational mill: witness the explosion of courses at both secondary and college levels dealing with the war. By one recent count, several hundred secondary schools and colleges now offer classes on the war. As interest builds in finding a permanent place for the war in the classroom, teachers must seriously address how they will incorporate the history of the 1960s into the curriculum of the 1990s. One approach is to use primary documents in the classroom.

WHY USE DOCUMENTS?

With the flood of secondary works now available, teachers struggling to approach the war in the classroom may wonder why they should delve into primary documents. Many instructors may feel uncomfortable using sources with which they are not very familiar, and they may also wonder where such materials may be obtained. The case for using primary sources as valuable classroom tools can be made through four arguments.

The typical high school history survey text devotes little space to the war. This condensed approach to a very important segment of American history is rarely comprehensive, accurate or objective. The judicious use of primary sources can extend the textbook's coverage as well as offer the beginnings of a thorough, balanced approach to the war. Documents may, for example, introduce differing viewpoints concerning issues raised by the war. They may also introduce new perspectives—those of women, minorities, and the Vietnamese themselves—which are lacking in most texts.

Second, most students find the primary documents, even if they feature stilted language and are dense and cryptic in style, far more intriguing than their textbooks. These texts are often uninspiring collections of simply written and poorly formatted facts and figures. One teacher has compared reading the survey texts to the combat experience: long stretches of boredom punctuated by occasional moments of action. The same teacher, however, noted that his students found primary sources, materials written by participants in and observers of the war, far more interesting. Documents can work wonders at catching and holding the attention of otherwise indifferent students.

The last two reasons for using documents in the classroom are the most substantive. Historians are forced to come to terms with their own subjectivity, the emotional baggage they bring to the study of their subjects. This phenomenon is nowhere more apparent than among the scholars who study the Vietnam War; their written salvos flit across the page long after the battlefield guns were stilled. Students, too, will eventually have to make up their own minds regarding the war. Why not confront them actively in the classroom with the same differing opinions and conflicting evidence they will face in their lives outside of the classroom? If students are to receive a balanced view of the war, it is imperative that they be exposed to a wide range of opinions concerning the war.

As has been suggested in chapter 11, this confrontation with conflicting thoughts, facts and emotions may also result in the very effect teachers hope to produce—the development of critical-thinking skills. The Vietnam War offers an excellent chance for teachers to introduce the process of critical thinking to students. The process historians use— formulating a thesis, amassing sources, selecting and evaluating evidence—is the same pattern teachers hope their students will learn. Students' abilities to write and think logically, organize their thoughts and critically assess arguments can all be approached through using primary sources.

Once a rationale for using primary documents has been reached, the classroom teacher still needs to determine what sources to use and what sources are available. Although miles of microfilm and mountains of paper documents exist, few teachers have either time to develop or access to these resources. There are, however, numerous printed sources now available for teachers who wish to use primary documents in their classes. Although the following section describes only a small sampling of what is available, these sources are appropriate to the objectives of most instructors who regularly teach courses on the war—they provide comprehensive coverage, they engage and hold students' interest, and they provide many opportunities to develop critical-thinking skills.

SOURCES

Sources such as Gareth Porter's *Vietnam: A History in Documents* (New York: New American Library, 1981) and his *Vietnam: The Definitive Documentation of Human Decisions,* 2 volumes, (Stanfordville, N. Y.: Earl H. Coleman Enterprises, 1979) and Steven Cohen's *Vietnam: Anthology and Guide to A Television History* (New York: Knopf, 1983), which was developed for use with the PBS series, contain a series of documents and attached commentary that are valuable for the student and the beginning teacher as well. Additional sources which many instructors have found useful include Allan W. Cameron, editor, *Viet-Nam Crisis: A Documentary History 1940-1956,* (Ithaca, N. Y.: Cornell University Press, 1971) and Allan B. Cole, *Conflict in Indo-China and International Repercussions: A Documentary History, 1945-1955* (Ithaca, N. Y.: Cornell University, 1956). Although somewhat dated, both collections include valuable materials on Japanese, French, and early American involvement in Indochina. The U. S. Senate Committee on Foreign Relations' *Background Information Relating to Southeast Asia and Vietnam* extends the documentary record from 1950 to 1975 and includes a useful chronology. The best available current text on the war which relies heavily on documents is *Major Problems in the History of the Vietnam War* (Lexington, Mass.: D. C. Heath, 1990) edited by Robert J. McMahon. This volume contains documents spanning the development of modern Vietnamese nationalism in the 1900s to contemporary reflections on the Vietnam War's importance to America. Documents are accompanied by interpretive essays by leading Vietnam scholars that reflect the very divergent views on the war. John Clark Pratt's *Vietnam Voices: Perspectives on the War Years, 1941-1982* (New York: Viking, 1984) is a potpourri of nonfiction and fictional responses from a wide range of sources about the war. James Banerian's *Losers Are Pirates* (Phoenix, Ariz.: Sphinx, 1985), though chiefly a critique of the Public Broadcasting System's *Vietnam: A Television History,* contains valuable short excerpts in translation from Vietnamese works.

Students usually find a representative sample of Vietnamese communist documents valuable. Writings by Ho Chi Minh, Vo Nguyen Giap, Le Duan, Pham Van Dong, and Truong Chinh, available in translation from the Foreign Languages Publishing House in Hanoi, tell us much about their authors and their philosophy of Marxism and revolution. Recent issues of *Vietnamese Studies* and the *Vietnam Courier*, both written in English and printed in Hanoi, contain material that help students understand life in contemporary Vietnam as well as help them gather information on art, history, literature and science in socialist Vietnam. Both of these periodicals also contain editorials that provide a teacher with a good opportunity to discuss the forms and uses of propaganda and language in Marxist countries. The sources for early Vietnamese nationalism, nationalist poetry and memoirs of communist and non-communist leaders are discussed in chapter six. Teachers seeking to employ documents in the classroom will, however, find *Breaking Our Chains: Documents on the Vietnamese Revolution of 1945* (Hanoi: Foreign Languages Press, 1960) particularly valuable. The State Department's Foreign Relations of the United States (FRUS) series contains a documentary record of our diplomatic relations with Indochina. Three recent volumes in the series focus specifically on America's deepening commitment to maintain a viable government in South Vietnam: *Foreign Relations of the United States, 1955-1957;* volume 1, *Vietnam* (Washington, D. C.: U. S. Government Printing Office, 1985); *Foreign Relations of the United States, 1958-1960;* volume 1, *Vietnam* (Washington, D. C.: U. S. Government Printing Office, 1986); and *Foreign Relations of the United States, 1961-1963;* volume 1, *Vietnam* (Washington, D. C.: U. S. Government Printing Press Office, 1988). More recent material is contained in publications issued by the government (Foreign Broadcast Information Service (FBIS) and Joint Publications Research Service [JPRS]) and in *Indochina Chronology*, a quarterly compilation of current materials on Laos, Vietnam and Cambodia edited by Douglas Pike and produced by the Indochina Project at the University of California at Berkeley. Pike includes a list of recent books, articles and audio-visual materials on Indochina and the Vietnam War in his chronology, and this is undoubtedly the best resource available for the classroom teacher. Finally, America's early involvement in Indochina is recounted through documents in the 12-volume U. S. Department of Defense's *United States-Vietnam Relations, 1945-1967* (Washington, D. C.: U. S. Government Printing Office, 1971), better known as the *Pentagon Papers* that can be found in Gerald Gold, Allan M. Siegel and Samuel Abt, editors, *The Pentagon Papers as Published by The New York Times* (New York: Quadrangle Books, 1971); and Senator Mike Gravel, editor, *The Pentagon Papers: The Defense Department History of United States Decision-Making on Vietnam*, 5 volumes (Boston: Beacon Press, 1971-1972).

Examples of several primary documents and how they are employed in the classroom may illustrate the many uses of primary documents. Ho Chi Minh's call for support for his newly created Revolutionary League for the Independence in June 1941 is very useful and can be found in Steven

Cohen, *Vietnam: An Anthology and Guide to a Television History* (New York: Knopf, 1983), p. 14. Students can be assigned to read this document after they have seen a film and heard several lectures about conditions in Indochina at the outbreak of World War II. Students can then be asked to analyze the appeals that Ho Chi Minh is making to attract support. What are his goals? What kind of language does he employ in making his appeal? How does he tie his group to the Vietnamese past and to national feelings?

This document's appeals to patriotism, to a united front against fascism and to revolution seem very strident, especially when placed next to the second document students may read, the Vietnamese Declaration of Independence issued in September 1945. Students can be asked to compare this document with the American Declaration of Independence. The ensuing discussion may often focus on the similarities in content and structure between the two declarations: both were products of a people angry with their colonial rulers. Both, too, are essentially a list of grievances framed by lofty oratory. Students can also learn that in both Vietnam in 1945 and America in 1776, substantial numbers of people were opposed to the goals outlined in the respective declarations.

American involvement in Indochina can also be studied by examining the letters exchanged between Ho Chi Minh and Lyndon Johnson in the winter of 1967, that, like Ho Chi Minh's call for support for the Revolutionary League, can be found in Steven Cohen's *Vietnam: Anthology and Guide to A Television History*, pp. 143-6. Students can be asked to outline the positions that both North Vietnam and the United States held regarding negotiations. What did the United States want out of negotiations? What were the North Vietnamese goals? Why were Johnson and Ho unable to reach agreement on negotiations? The answers to these questions can spur lengthy discussions on the personalities of the various people involved, the process by which executive decisions are reached and the differing goals and perceptions that each side in the Vietnam War had of the other.

Discussions of the war's pivotal moments or issues often can be aided by examining documentary evidence. For example, one might examine the Gulf of Tonkin Resolution, the "blank check" that Congress gave the president in August 1964 (see John Clark Pratt, compiler, *Vietnam Voices: Perspectives on the War Years, 1941-1982* (New York: Viking, 1984), pp. 173-4. After a discussion of how Johnson obtained Congress's cooperation in passing the resolution, students may begin looking at just what powers the resolution gave the president. What military options did Johnson have? Why didn't Congress declare war? Was the war legal? Was the resolution constitutionally sound? Why was it repealed? Primary documents can provide the basis for extended discussions on a wide variety of issues connected with the war, complex and detailed political, moral and legal questions that textbooks often ignore.

CONCLUSION

Although the hundreds of memoirs, oral histories, slide collections, videotapes and novels that might also be considered primary documents have not been mentioned, this small sample of available resources suggests a teaching approach that promises a lively, vital discussion of a complex historical event. While teachers cannot expect students to master the complexities of an event that historians find overwhelming, teachers can encourage their students to objectively evaluate their country's involvement in Southeast Asia. By using primary sources, by letting the events and people of history speak for themselves, teachers can finally find a place for Vietnam in the curriculum.

SOURCE LIST

Banerian, James, translator and editor. *Vietnamese Short Stores: An Introduction.* Phoenix, Arizona: Sphinx Publishing, 1986.

Breaking Our Chains: Documents on the Vietnamese Revolution of August 1945. Hanoi, Foreign Languages Publishing House, 1960.

Cameron, Allan W., editor. *Viet-Nam Crisis: A Documentary History 1940-1956.* Ithaca, New York: Cornell University Press, 1971.

Cohen, Steven. *Vietnam: Anthology and Guide to a Television History.* New York: Knopf, 1983.

Cole, Allan B. *Conflict In Indo-China and International Repercussions: A Documentary History, 1945-1955.* Ithaca, New York: Cornell University Press, 1956.

The Failure of "Special War 1961-1965." *Vietnamese Studies* no. 11. Hanoi: Xunhasaba, n.d.

Foreign Relations of the United States, 1955-1957, volume 1, *Vietnam.* Washington, D. C.: U. S. Government Printing Office, 1985.

Foreign Relations of the United States, 1958-1960, volume 1, *Vietnam.* Washington, D. C.: U. S. Government Printing Office, 1986.

Foreign Relations of the United States, 1961-1963, volume 1, *Vietnam.* Washington, D. C.: U. S. Government Printing Office, 1988.

Gold, Gerald, Allan M. Siegel, and Samuel Abt, editors. *The Pentagon Papers as published by The New York Times.* New York: Quadrangle Books, 1971.

Ho Chi Minh. *Selected Writings (1920-1969).* Hanoi: Foreign Languages Publishing House, 1977.

Huynh Sanh Thong, translator. *The Quarrel of the Six Beasts.* The Lac-Viet Series No. 4. New Haven: Yale Southeast Asia Studies, 1988.

———, translator and editor. *To Be Made Over: Tales of Socialist Re-education in Vietnam.* The Lack-Viet Series No. 5. New Haven: Yale Southeast Asia Studies, 1988.

———, translator. *The Tale of Kieu,* by Nguyen Du. New Haven: Yale University Press, 1979.

Le Duan. *Selected Writings,* Hanoi: Foreign Languages Publishing House, 1977.

McMahon, Robert J., editor. *Major Problems in the History of the Vietnam War.* Lexington, Massachusetts: D. C. Heath and Company, 1990.

Nguyen Chi Thien. *Flowers From Hell.* Selected and translated by Huynh Sanh Thong. The Lac-Viet Series no. 1. New Haven: Yale Southeast Asia Studies, 1984.

Nguyen Khac Vien, editor. "American Failure." *Vietnamese Studies* Number 20. Hanoi: Xunhasaba, 1968. [This issue looks at the Tet Offensive from the North vietnamese viewpoint, including battles at Hue, Khe Sanh, and Saigon. It includes detailed maps of North Vietnamese campaigns.]

———, editor. *In Face of American Aggression 1965-1967.* Vietnamese Studies no. 16. Hanoi: Xunhasaba, n.d.

———, editor. *Indochina 1971-1972.* Vietnamese Studies no. 33. Hanoi: Xunhasaba, 1972.

———, editor. *The Long Resistance (1858-1975).* Hanoi: Foreign Languages Publishing House, 1975.

———, editor. *Vietnam, Laos, Cambodia, 1969-70*. Vietnamese Studies no. 28. Hanoi: Xunhasaba, 1970.

———, editor. "The Year 1968." *Vietnamese Studies* no. 22. Hanoi: Xunhasaba, n.d.

Nguyen Ngoc Bich, editor. *War and Exile: A Vietnamese Anthology*. N.p.: Vietnamese PEN Abroad, East Coast U.S.A., 1989.

———, translator and editor. *A Thousand Years of Vietnamese Poetry*. New York: Knopf, 1975.

Nguyen Thi Thu-Lan, with Edith Kreisler and Sandra Christenson. *Fallen Leaves*. The Lac-Viet Series no. 11. New Haven: Yale Southeast Asia Studies, 1989.

The Pentagon Papers: The Senator Gravel Edition: The Defense Department History of the United States Decision-making on Vietnam. 5 volumes. Boston: Beacon Press, 1971-1972.

Pham Van Dong. *Selected Writings*. Hanoi: Foreign Languages Publishing House, 1977.

Pham Van Ky. *Blood Brothers*. Translated by Margaret Mauldon. The Lac-Viet Series no. 7. New Haven: Yale Southeast Asia Studies, 1987.

Porter, Gareth, editor. *Vietnam: A History in Documents*. New York: New American Library, 1981.

———. *Vietnam: The Definitive Documentation of Human Decisions*. 2 volumes. Stanfordville, N. Y.: Earl H. Coleman Enterprises, 1979.

Pratt, John Clark, compiler. *Vietnam Voices: Perspectives on the War Years, 1941-1982*. New York: Viking, 1984.

Public Papers of the Presidents of the United States, Dwight D. Eisenhower. 8 volumes. Washington, D. C.: U. S. Government Printing Office, 1960-1961.

Public Papers of the Presidents of the United States, John F. Kennedy. 3 volumes. Washington, D. C.: U. S. Government Printing Office, 1962-1964.

Public Papers of the Presidents of the United States, Lyndon B. Johnson.
10 volumes. Washington, D. C.: U. S. Government Printing Office,
1965-1970.

Public Papers of the Presidents of the United States, Richard Nixon.
6 volumes. Washington, D. C.: U. S. Government Printing Office, 1971-
1975.

Public Papers of the Presidents of the United States, Gerald R. Ford.
6 volumes. Washington, D. C.: U. S. Government Printing Office, 1975-
1979.

"South Vietnam '64." *Vietnamese Studies.* No. 1. Hanoi: Foreign
Languages Publishing House, n.d.

Tran Van Tra. *Ending the 30 Years War.* Ho Chi Minh City: Literature
Publishing House, 1982.

Troung Chinh. *Selected Writings.* Hanoi: Foreign Languages Publishing
House, 1977.

U. S. Congress, Senate Committee on Foreign Relations. *Background
Information Relating to Southeast Asia and Vietnam.* 7th rev. ed. 93rd
Congress, 2d sess. Washington, D. C.: U. S. Government Printing
Office, 1975.

U. S. Department of Defense. *United States-Vietnam Relations, 1945-67.*
12 volumes. Washington, D. C.: U. S. Government Printing Office,
1971.

Van Tien Dung. *Our Great Spring Victory: An Account of the Liberation
of South Vietnam.* New York: Monthly Review Press, 1977.

Vietnam Courier.

Vietnam Forum.

Vietnamese Studies.

Vo Nguyen Giap. *Selected Writings.* Hanoi: Foreign Languages Publishing
House, 1977.

Vo Phien. *Intact.* Translated by James Banerian. Victoria, Australia:
Vietnamese Language & Culture Publications, 1990.

13

Texts and Auxiliary Resources
JOE P. DUNN

Ronald Spector questions whether we can adequately study Vietnam at this stage since the number of scholars with true expertise is so small and so little basic scholarly research is available.[1] Admittedly, much of what passes today for courses on the war is superficial, cliché-ridden, or pop culture-oriented. Even granting Spector's argument, we do not have the luxury of waiting until we are better prepared to treat the subject. Across the country, students are taking courses on the war. As colleges scramble to introduce classes, the number of offerings is expanding rapidly, and the subject tends to draw large enrollments. Interest level is stimulated by a number of high-profile Vietnam movies, television series and other such potentially transient factors, but the desire to understand has a deeper footing. Vietnam is repeatedly referred to in contemporary cultural and political life, Vietnam veterans are becoming highly visible, and today's students are trying to understand their parents' generation. We have a sound basis to believe that the quest for understanding Vietnam will continue. Both colleges and high schools have good reasons to address this interest in the war.[2]

Whether the number of courses specifically on the war will expand or subside is less important than that the subject takes its place in the basic curriculum, as case study in survey-level courses and as specialized upper-division courses in history, political science, and other areas. At the high school level, textbooks are giving more attention to the war than they did just a few years ago, and in another ten years it will be as inconceivable to ignore the Vietnam War in the high school classroom as it would to overlook the American Revolution or World War II. To accomplish this goal at both college and high school levels, many teachers will have to prepare themselves in areas outside their basic expertise. Among their first tasks will be the selection of a course text or texts, the creation of a supplementary reading list tailored to support their course's focus and the gaining of command of those bibliographies and reference materials that serve to identify further resources for course reading assignments.

SELECTING A TEXT: A REVIEW OF THE LITERATURE

The explosion of interest in the Vietnam War in the 1980s led to the emergence of a growing number of fine texts on the subject. This was not the case in the 1970s, when good texts on the war did not exist. The 1960s standards, Joseph Buttinger, *Vietnam: A Political History* (1968) and George McT. Kahin and John W. Lewis, *The United States in Vietnam* (rev. ed., 1969), the very popular early anti-war text, were out of print. Chester L. Cooper, *The Lost Crusade: America in Vietnam* (1970, 1972) was in print only briefly in mid-decade. Although it was a combination memoir and history by an Asian specialist career diplomat rather than a text, the book served in the absence of other alternatives for the few who taught Vietnam courses during that period.

The few texts available in the 1970s were summarial and superficial. These included Peter A. Poole, *Eight Presidents and Indochina* (1978); Alexander Kendrick, *The Wound Within* (1974); Hugh Higgins, *Vietnam* (1975); Allan R. Millett, *A Short History of the Vietnam War* (1978), actually a series of 1975 *Washington Post* articles that looked back on the war from an immediate post-war perspective; and British diplomat J. Davidson's *Indochina: Signposts in a Storm* (1979), a brief overview of the interrelationship of events in all of Indochina since World War II.

Two other volumes published in the late 1970s were not written as textbooks, but both continue to be used as texts today: Dave Richard Palmer's *Summons of the Trumpet: A History of the Vietnam War from a Military Man's Viewpoint* (Novato, Calif.: Presidio, 1978; Ballantine, 1984) and Guenter Lewy's *America in Vietnam* (New York: Oxford University Press, 1978; 1980). Palmer, an active-duty army brigadier general when he wrote the book, provided the first military history of the war directed at a lay audience. The book is a straightforward, readable and clear presentation of the military's frustrations and Palmer's own strong critique of the Westmoreland strategy. Lewy's book was at the time of its publication (and to some extent it remains) one of the most controversial written on the war. A political philosopher who specializes in moral questions, Lewy was the first to gain access to Defense Department records in order to address the question of the morality of America's involvement in and conduct of the war. Lewy is not generally favorable toward American involvement in Vietnam, and he excoriates many aspects of the military performance; but he concludes that American involvement and actions were moral. Lewy presents one of the most detailed accounts of the military conduct of the war and the complex moral questions and controversies raised. It is a sophisticated work not particularly suitable for the novice; however, it can serve as a useful text for advanced students.

George C. Herring's *America's Longest War: The United States and Vietnam, 1950-1975* (New York: Knopf, 1979, 2nd ed., 1986) was the first of a new generation of Vietnam texts. One of the most widely used of the available texts, the book is short, readable, soundly documented and balanced in its interpretation. Herring is one of the nation's leading diplomatic historians, and the text emphasizes political decision-making and diplomacy. Because his account starts in 1950, as the United States began to support the French in the First Indochina War, it does not provide the necessary background in Vietnamese politics of the first half of the twentieth century. An understanding of Vietnamese nationalist movements of the 1920s and 1930s is important to determining the appeal of the revolutionary forces later, and World War II is essential to comprehending all that transpired in the 1950s and early 1960s. The book should have at least a chapter on these topics. Despite this drawback, the book is an outstanding contribution, and it deserves the many accolades that it has received.

Three other texts were published shortly after Herring's original edition. Two of them still have considerable merit. Paul M. Kattenburg, *The Vietnam Trauma in American Foreign Policy, 1945-1975* (New Brunswick, N. J.: Transaction Books, 1981) can serve well in some situations, especially for advanced students who can ask and address larger policy questions. Kattenburg headed the State Department Vietnam Desk in the 1950s and headed the Vietnam Interdepartmental Working Group in the Kennedy administration. He was the first American official on record at a high-level policy-making meeting (National Security Council, August 31, 1963) to propose that the United States pull out of Vietnam. The book reflects the author's inside experience and his insight as a political scientist.

Kattenburg approaches the subject in analytical chapters such as "Ten Fateful Decisions on Vietnam, 1961-75," "Winning Without Winning, 1961-75" and "Losing Without Losing, 1961-75," which develop topics such as the role of toughness and force; the premium on action, determination, and persistence; the failure of policy analysis; the triumph of management; the heyday of the managerial approach; the domestic and foreign consensus of support; and closed-system decision-making. His "Disengagement from Indochina" and "Vietnam as Lesson of History" are outstanding retrospectives. If some of his points seem a bit dated now, he was among the first to raise many of these issues. James Pinckney Harrison, *The Endless War: Vietnam's Struggle for Independence* (Riverside, N. J.: The Free Press, 1982; McGraw-Hill, 1983) views the war from the Vietnamese perspective. An expert on the Chinese communist revolution, Harrison explains the background and evolution of the Vietnamese revolution and why the communists defeated both the French and the Americans. He provides an excellent introduction to Vietnamese politics, culture and the power of nationalism, ideology, organization and practice in the communist movement. Although one of the best sources for understanding the revolutionary movement, the book is skimpy on American decisions and involvement. Employed in combination with a book that concentrates upon the American half of the war, this can be an excellent text.

Michael Maclear's *The Ten Thousand Day War: Vietnam, 1945-1975* (New York: St. Martin's, 1981), the companion volume for the 26-part Canadian series on the war, has a readable text and contains a large number of excellent pictures, but this anti-war popular history has been supplanted today both by more balanced scholarly texts and by better popular histories.

The Public Broadcasting System's 13-part *Vietnam: A Television History*, broadcast in 1983, spurred general interest in the war and in Vietnam courses. A number of very fine texts emerged to meet the new demand. The most famous, and possibly the most used text today, Stanley Karnow's *Vietnam: A History* (New York: Viking, 1983; Penguin, 1984) was published as a companion volume for the television series. Journalist Karnow, a polished writer with considerable experience in Southeast Asia, strives for balance, fairness and comprehensiveness. The volume is a readable mixture of solid history and anecdotal insights that encompasses two thousand years of Vietnamese history as background before concentrating intensely upon the period from 1940 to the aftermath of 1975.

Vietnam: A History has been praised and damned excessively. While the book has many positive attributes, it is not, as some reviewers assert, the definitive work. Asianists point out that the presentation of Vietnamese culture is journalistic rather than substantive. Treatment of policy-making is anecdotal rather than analytical. Several interpretations are subject to question. Conservatives find the book too liberal, and some liberals believe that it is just the opposite. The 1973-1975 period is too highly compressed. But the most practical problem with Karnow as a possible text is that its 700-page length may limit other readings in the course.

Another popular history, one of more manageable length, is Thomas D. Boettcher's *Vietnam: The Valor and the Sorrow* (Boston: Little, Brown, 1985). Boettcher, a free-lance writer who served as an air force public information officer in Vietnam, did not set out to write a text. He conceived his volume as a popular history for the layman, somewhat of a single-volume condensation of *The Vietnam Experience* (a multi-volume work, cast in the mold of the Time-Life serial publications, that will be discussed later). Boettcher's journalistic narrative is augmented by 550 annotated pictures, many fascinating sidebars and a wealth of interesting statistical information. After early favorable reviews, the publisher marketed the volume as a textbook. Boettcher is not a Vietnam scholar; several of his interpretations probably would not stand up to intense scrutiny, and the emphasis is heavily upon the military conduct of the war. Vietnamese are seen primarily through American eyes. However, the book is fascinating reading that students enjoy. It is strong on the fighting of the war, especially on the air war, on which it is one of the best sources available. Boettcher's sympathies with American soldiers and fliers are evident. Although the book needs to be augmented to cover other aspects of the war, it is a valuable tool for novice teachers as well as students. Used properly, it is one of the best texts available.

My other personal favorite text is quite different. William S. Turley, *The Second Indochina War: A Short Political and Military History, 1954-75* (Boulder, Colo.: Westview, 1986; Mentor, 1987) is a remarkable little book. Turley, a leading expert on Vietnamese communism, combines original research, thorough knowledge of the literature, his own insight from several trips to Vietnam during and since the war, and sound interpretation into an amazingly succinct and well-crafted 200-page narrative that provides balanced treatment of both the Vietnamese and the American sides of the war. Useful maps, charts, tables, a fine chronology and an excellent brief bibliographic essay complement the volume. At its current price, a mere $4.95, the paperback copy of the text is an exceptional financial bargain.

Also highly recommended is Timothy J. Lomperis, *Vietnam: The War Everyone Lost—and Won: America's Intervention in Vietnam's Twin Struggles* (Baton Rouge, La: Louisiana State University, 1984; Congressional Quarterly, 1987). The product of Lomperis's award-winning doctoral dissertation, the book was not written as text but as an innovative interpretation of the war. However, the new paperback edition is being marketed as a textbook, and for advanced students this thoughtful and provocative study can be a very good text. Lomperis's study of revolution and the struggle for legitimacy is a very sophisticated analysis of both the Vietnamese and the American conceptions and conduct of the war, which the author places in the context of a narrative history.

Definitely worth consideration is Anthony James Joes, *The War for South Viet Nam: 1954-1975* (New York: Praeger, 1989), a relatively short, readable volume written for the novice audience. Unlike Turley and Lomperis, Joes is not a Vietnam expert but a generalist who has written books on several areas of political history. The book's merits include that it provides good background in Vietnamese history, politics, and the origins of the conflict for understanding the context of American involvement; it gives balanced insight into the communist forces; and it is strong on military strategy issues. Joes's interpretations are bold, provocative, and well argued, bound to stimulate debate.

Instructors seeking a text will also want to examine three surveys that have only just recently come onto the market. Two of these texts, George Donelson Moss, *Vietnam: An American Ordeal* (Englewood Cliffs, N. J.: Prentice-Hall, 1990) and James S. Olson and Randy Roberts, *Where the Domino Fell: America and Vietnam, 1945 to 1990* (New York: St. Martin's, 1991) have many similarities. Both are based on secondary sources and are written for novice students by non-specialists. However, both books demonstrate good command of the literature; and each is a balanced, interesting account which blends political, diplomatic, military and social history. Each gives necessary attention to Vietnamese culture and heritage prior to World War II, but focus primarily upon the United States side of the equation. Moss is significantly longer, more detailed, and it ends in 1975. Olson and Roberts's concluding chapter on the 1975-1990 period concentrates upon the images expressed in the growing number of Vietnam movies. Both of these books are solid texts worthy of examination.

Gary R. Hess, author of *Vietnam and the United States: Origins and Legacy of War* (Boston: Twayne, 1990), is one of the nation's leading diplomatic historians and students of American-Asian relations. His new text is a brief, well-written interpretative synthesis that provides balance between the background of the war, the years of America's intensive diplomatic and military involvement and postwar events. Half the narrative treats the years prior to 1965. The American war years are capsuled but insightful, and Hess gives fair treatment to the Vietnamese on both sides of the conflict. One of the volume's unique features is the emphasis on United States-Vietnamese relations since 1975. An epilogue, "Reflections on the War," surveys the two "schools," dubbed the "winnable" and the "unwinnable" analyses, on why America was not successful in fulfilling its objectives.

I do not recommend Gabriel Kolko, *Anatomy of a War: Vietnam, the United States, and the Modern Historical Experience* (New York: Pantheon, 1985; 1986), a provocative, intense, vintage New Left analysis. True, the volume attempts to get beyond surface narrative to explore the underlying political and social structures that explain the war, and Kolko's extensive employment of North Vietnamese documents is impressive. But portrayals of the United States and South Vietnamese are trite, the NLF and North Vietnamese are stereotypic heroes, and a simplistic, dogmatic tone prevails throughout. Kolko has changed his perspectives little since the 1960s despite overwhelming evidence, much released by the North Vietnamese themselves, that many of his sacred articles of faith are simply wrong. Finally, the massive 600-page tome is boringly overwritten in long, excessive sentences. Although I do not recommend this book as a text, faculty members need to familiarize students with this genre of interpretation. Paul Joseph's *Cracks in the Empire: State Politics in the Vietnam War* (Boston: South End Press, 1981; New York: Columbia University Press, 1987), which approaches the war from a simplistic radical analysis, is at least readable and would introduce students to this perspective.

Three other texts, Martin F. Herz, *The Vietnam War in Retrospect* (Washington, D. C.: Georgetown University School of Foreign Service, 1984); William J. Duiker, *Vietnam: Nation in Revolution* (Boulder, Colo.: Westview, 1983); and Melanie Beresford, *Vietnam: Politics, Economics and Society* (London and New York: Pinter, 1988), have limited but important functions. In his slim, 71-page volume, which consists of four lectures that he gave to prospective diplomats at the Georgetown School of Foreign Service, the now-deceased Herz covers the expanse of the war and emphasizes the lessons of the American experience. The lectures are spirited, outspoken, incisive, and fair. Herz argues that the United States had little choice but to assist the South Vietnamese; however, he lambasts the sloppy thinking, lack of historical perspective, self-delusion and ineptitude that characterized American involvement. Whatever one may think of Herz's interpretations, they are clearly stated and cogently argued. While the coverage is far too limited to use the book as a single text for a Vietnam course, it functions well in courses such as American history survey, diplomatic history or introductory international relations, which treat the war as one of several topics. Because of Herz's clarity and brevity, the book is well suited for use in a high school class. Duiker's volume, which appears in the Westview "Nations of Contemporary Asia" series, is a comprehensive but succinct introduction to Vietnam for the general reader. The book's eight chapters include description and analysis of the historical context, the origins of the revolution, and the economy, culture and society, as well as the foreign relations of Vietnam. The book is an excellent vehicle for introducing the country in a course on the war, and for those courses on the war that approach it from the perspective of Asian history. It is now available in what by today's standards is a moderately priced paperback edition (approximately $15.00 to $19.00). Beresford's volume, in the "Marxist Regimes Series," is somewhat like Duiker's, although longer and for more advanced students. It provides many valuable tables of basic data and units on history and political traditions, the social system, the political systems, the economy and current domestic and foreign policies.

Two recent texts are written specifically for the high school market. Thomas Whittemore, *The Vietnam War: A Text for Students* (Cambridge, Mass.: Cambridgeport Press, 1988) is a nondescript 150-page paperback with a basic, straightforward, non-controversial narrative that features section and chapter reviews, key terms, discussion questions and eight short biographical notes. Jerold A. Starr, editor, *The Lessons of the Vietnam War* (Pittsburgh: Center for Social Studies Education, revised edition, 1991) is an ambitious undertaking consisting of 12 self-contained units written by different authors and designed especially for high school students or lay audiences. Published in notebook form to facilitate photocopy for classroom use, the units include pedagogical activities, maps, photographs, and other study aids. The authors are a mixed bag. Vietnam scholars such as William Duiker, George Herring, Charles DeBenedetti, Fred Wilcox, Steven Cohen and myself are interspersed with high school teachers, veterans and professional writers. An ambitious marketing effort has attracted considerable attention to the product, but the anthology is overrated. Conversely, high school teacher John C. Warren's *America's Intervention in Vietnam: An Anthology* (White Plains, N. Y.: Longman, 1987) is a fine, balanced collection well suited for secondary or college students.

Of the several non-text histories, three deserve special attention. One covers a limited period, the second is an attempt at a nearly comprehensive history, and the third is the best military history of the war now available. The first two are too exhaustive to contemplate as texts, but they will have profound impact upon the way that the war is understood in the next decade. When the last volume becomes available in paperback, it should be the standard military history text, and it too will have a major impact upon our continuing reassessment of the war.   George McT. Kahin's *Intervention: How America Became Involved in Vietnam* (New York: Random House, 1986) is the most detailed, intensely documented study available on American involvement from 1946 to 1966. Through the use of the Freedom of Information Act, Kahin won release of thousands of classified documents that provide the basic source of his research. Although much more sophisticated in this present work, Kahin's view has not changed significantly from his famous text of the 1960s. He still emphasizes the indigenous roots of the war, although he now admits that the NLF was not completely independent from the Lao Dong Party, the North Vietnamese communists. He rejects Hanoi's post-war claim that it controlled the southern movement from the first; rather he sees the North hesitantly and belatedly assuming control over a spontaneous uprising in the South.

Kahin continues to attack American involvement on both moral and strategic grounds.   His argument that the prime motivation was an excessive fear of monolithic communism is largely unchanged from the late 1960s. He implies that had the United States stayed out of the war, an autonomous, neutralist Vietnam could have been possible.   However, Kahin judges Lyndon Johnson much less harshly than do other scholars. He places the heaviest blame on the Eisenhower and Kennedy administrations, and he depicts Johnson as a dove, a prudent and cautious president gravely concerned about escalation but surrounded by hawkish advisors who misled and in some cases deceived him. Thus there is an interesting convergence between Kahin and the conservative revisionist critics who blame Johnson for undue caution and reticence rather than decisive leadership in prosecuting the war.

Kahin's most emphatic point is his challenge to the revisionists who argue that had America had stronger will or better military strategy, victory could have been achieved. On the contrary, he emphasizes that the United States was battling a truly Vietnamese nationalist movement. The history of the area made the chances for establishing a Western client state nearly impossible. Thus Diem and his successors were doomed from the first, which no amount of American power could change.

R. B. Smith's *An International History of the Vietnam War*, 4 volumes (New York: St. Martin's, 1984-1990) presents a very different interpretation from Kahin's. Smith, a world-renowned Southeast Asia specialist at the University of London, presents the Vietnam War as part of a global pattern of conflict best analyzed in global terms. In the first two volumes, *Revolution Versus Containment, 1955-61* (1984) and *The Kennedy Strategy* (1985), he challenges most of the views that Kahin expresses. Smith takes seriously the North Vietnamese claims that they controlled the southern insurgency from the first, and he places the blame for the war squarely upon the North Vietnamese and their Soviet and Chinese allies. The conflict must be understood, he maintains, in terms of the global contest for power that we generally refer to as the Cold War. Thus, the United States had little choice but to respond to the challenge in Southeast Asia. He rejects contentions of blind anti-communism or naive overcommitment in nation building. The United States had vital and legitimate economic and strategic interests in the region; hence our involvement was realistic and warranted. Smith believes that greater application of power was necessary and feasible, and might have mitigated against the failure of American military strategy in the war. Lest one conclude that Smith's viewpoint is merely unreconstructed Cold War hawkishness, it should be noted that this is a very sophisticated study that tries to get at the dynamics of the complex interrelationships of all the parties involved in the war, and it is in line with the best post-revisionist Cold War literature. The volumes have received high praise by scholars of differing perspectives.[3]

Phillip B. Davidson, *Vietnam at War: The History, 1946-1975* (Novato, Calif.: Presidio, 1988) concurs with most of Smith's interpretations. General Davidson served as MACV J-2 (1967-1979), the highest-ranking military intelligence officer in Vietnam, under commanding generals William Westmoreland and Creighton Abrams. The insight from this position combined with his astute talents as a military historian and former professor at West Point are evident in this massive volume, the product of 11 years of research and writing.

Davidson debunks many myths as he explains how and why the war was fought as it was, the mistakes made, the successes and failures, and the misinterpretations rendered by the media, political figures, and other commentators. He gives a very good history of the French Indochina War; offers rare insight into the minds of Westmoreland and Abrams; and is equally insightful about individuals such as Presidents Johnson, Nixon, and Thieu, as well as Robert McNamara, Henry Kissinger, Robert Komer, and Vietnamese generals on both sides. However, General Vo Nguyen Giap, whose career the author analyzes through the three stages of the war, receives the greatest attention. One of the book's strongest aspects is the material about the communist side gained from captured documents, interrogation of former enemy soldiers and recent Vietnamese writings.

Candid, incisive and fair, Davidson speaks forthrightly, but the shrillness, rancor and absolute sureness present in many high-ranking memoirs is absent. His concluding chapter on why the U. S. lost the war is one of the best analyses in print on the subject. While many may challenge Davidson's perspectives and points, this cogently argued and well-written study is an outstanding military history for scholar and layman alike. It is a very useful classroom source. A sequel volume, *Secrets of the Vietnam War* (Novato, Calif: Presidio, 1990), expands upon why the war was fought as it was, causes for the failures in strategy, the implications of political and military decisions, persistent Vietnam myths and further analysis of why the United States was not successful.

A relatively recent text suitable for courses that focus on the causes and background of the war is Anthony Short's *The Origins of the Vietnam War* (New York: Longman, 1989), a volume in the fine British series on the well-springs of modern wars. Although a bit dry, it is a good survey that traces the long evolution of the conflict in its international context up to 1965.

Finally, Wilbur H. Morrison, *The Elephant and the Tiger: The Full Story of the Vietnam War* (New York: Hippocrene Books, 1990), an ambitious anecdotal military history placed in larger political context, is a fascinating, if unsatisfactory, volume. Armed with strong convictions and the omnipresent theme that the war could have been won, the author editorializes excessively. Some of his judgments may have validity, but they are personal opinions and assertions without documentation. Based entirely upon published materials, particularly official military histories and memoirs, the book cites no attribution. It offers some insight into how the war was fought, and it is most engaging reading. However, it needs to be read with acute discernment.

AUXILIARY RESOURCES

The number of potential auxiliary books is vast. As with textbooks, the teacher must select readings according to the purpose each is to serve and the relation to the other sources employed. The following is a brief listing of my suggestions of the better auxiliary readings.

ILLUSTRATED HISTORIES AND PICTORIALS

Vietnam was the most visually recorded event in American history. All who lived through the war have certain images burned into our minds. For a generation of students inclined to process information visually, pictures are important. To a degree this explains the important role that films have played in the teaching of the war. A few of the more important pictorial accounts of the war are noted below.

Two multi-volume illustrated histories are valuable sources. *The Vietnam Experience* (Boston: Boston Publishing Company, 1981-1989) is a 25-volume illustrated history with multiple authors under editor-in-chief Robert Manning (former Assistant Secretary of State for Public Affairs in the Kennedy and Johnson administrations and former editor of *Atlantic Monthly*). The series includes both chronological and topical volumes.

Each book is approximately two hundred pages of interesting text built around hundreds of black-and-white and color pictures, maps, charts, sidebars and chronologies. The volumes have excellent bibliographies, indexes and lists of names, terms and acronyms. Unfortunately, they are published only in hardback and the price is prohibitive for classroom use. But the series is essential for any library, either for browsing or as a reference. *The Illustrated History of the Vietnam War* (New York: Bantam, 1987-1991) is a paperback combat pictorial series organized topically with titles such as *Marines, Khe Sanh, Armor, Artillery, Riverine Force, Rangers, Skyraider*, and so forth. Written for the layman by authors with expertise on the particular topic, the volumes have abundant pictures, maps, charts, sidebars and glossaries. Although much less expensive than the series above, neither are these books appropriate as student texts, but they too are fine browsing or reference sources. Lou Drendel's multi-volume *Air War over Southeast Asia* (Carrollton, Tex.: Squadron/Signal Publications, 1982-1984) has more limited appeal.

Single-volume illustrated histories include Ray Bonds, editor, *The Vietnam War: The Illustrated History of the Conflict in Southeast Asia* (New York: Crown, 1979); Douglas Welsh, *The History of the Vietnam War* (New York: Bison/Exetor Books, 1981); George Esper and the Associated Press, *The Eyewitness History of the Vietnam War, 1961-1975* (New York: Ballantine, 1983); Carl Berger, *The United States Air Force in Southeast Asia, 1961-1973: An Illustrated Account* (Washington, D. C.: Office of Air Force History, 1984); Brian Beckett, *The History of the Vietnam War* (New York: Gallery Books, 1985); Kevin M. Generous, *Vietnam: The Secret War* (New York: Gallery, 1985); Joel D. Meyerson, *Images of a Lengthy War: The United States Army in Vietnam* (Washington, D. C.: Center of Military History, 1986); Richard F. Newcomb, *A Picture History of the Vietnam War* (Garden City, N. Y.: Doubleday, 1987); Tom Carhart, *Battles and Campaigns: Vietnam, 1954-1984* (Greenwich, Conn.: Bison, 1987); Phil Chinnery, *Air War Vietnam* (New York: Bison, 1987); Ian Beckett, *Conflict in 20th Century: Vietnam: From 1945* (New York: Gallery, 1987); Clark Dougan, et al., *The American Experience in Vietnam* (New York: Norton, 1988); Jeremy Barnes, *The Pictorial History of the Vietnam War* (New York: Gallery Books, 1988); Charles T. Kamps, *The History of the Vietnam War: An Illustrated History of the War in South East Asia* (New York: The Military Press, 1988); and F. Clifton Berry, Jr., *The Illustrated History of the Vietnam War: Air Cav* (New York: Bantam, 1988).

Tim Page's *Nam* (New York: Knopf, 1983), *Ten Years Later: Vietnam Today* (New York: Knopf, 1987), and (with John Pimlott) *NAM: The Vietnam Experience* (New York: Mallard Press, 1988); James N. McJunkin and Max D. Crace, *Visions of Vietnam* (Navato, Calif.: Presidio, 1983); Mark Jury's *The Vietnam Photo Book* (New York: Vintage, 1986); Geoffrey Clifford and John Balaban, *Vietnam: The Land We Never Knew* (San Francisco: Chronicle Books, 1989); and Susan D. Moeller, *Shooting War: Photography and the American Experience of Combat* (New York: Basic

Books, 1990) are classic photo albums that capture much of the essence of the experience.

Edward Clinton Ezell, *Reflections on the Wall: The Vietnam Veterans Memorial* (Harrisburg, Penn.: Stackpole Books, 1987) and Michael Katakis, *The Vietnam Veterans Memorial* (New York: Crown Publishers, 1989) are two of the best of several pictorials on the subject. Jerry and Sandra Straight, *Vietnam War Memorials: An Illustrated Reference to Veterans' Tributes Throughout the United States* (Jefferson, N. C.: McFarland, 1988) treats the wider scope.

DOCUMENT COLLECTIONS

As Steve Potts has demonstrated in the previous chapter, document collections are crucial, in teaching a course. While myriads of documents are available on the war, only a few published collections that can be used as texts exist. Unfortunately, the inexpensive, single-volume paperback edition of *The Pentagon Papers*, with commentary by Neil Sheehan, Hedrick Smith, E. W. Kenworthy, and Fox Butterfield (New York: Bantam, 1971), an exceptionally valuable source, is no longer available. Other earlier collections are also out of print.

Among available collections, three stand out. Gareth Porter, *Vietnam, A History in Documents* (New York: New American Library, 1981) has full texts of documents from both sides, usually internal documents rather than published declarations. William A. Williams, et al., *America in Vietnam: A Documentary History* (New York: Anchor/Doubleday, 1985) contains 84 documents divided into four chronological periods from the 1840s to 1975. A lengthy introductory essay heads each section, and short commentaries illuminate the individual documents. Marvin E. Gettleman, et al., *Vietnam and America: A Documented History* (New York: Grove, 1985) is much the same. The selection of documents in each volume reflects their anti-war orientation.

Steven Cohen's *Vietnam: Anthology and Guide to a Television History* (New York: Knopf, 1983), produced to support the PBS *Vietnam: A Television History* series, contains a broad assortment of documents providing a range of views and interpretations. Unlike the collections above, which concentrate upon previously classified government documents, many of the pieces in this collection are excerpted public statements, speeches and published writings by journalists or scholars. Historical summaries, chronologies, glossaries, discussion questions and bibliographies support the documents. Since the volume is closely tied to the television history, it is less valuable if used alone. Robert J. McMahon's *Major Problems in the History of the Vietnam War: Documents and Essays* (Lexington, Mass.: D. C. Heath, 1990); and George Donelson Moss, *A Vietnam Reader: Sources and Essays* (Englewood Cliffs, N. J.:

Prentice-Hall, 1991), which provides sixty documents and five provocative original essays, are very useful new sources.

One other collection deserves mention: Bernard Edelman, *Dear America: Letters Home from Vietnam* (New York: Norton, 1985; Pocket Books, 1986) fills a special niche in Vietnam literature. No one knows how many millions of pieces of personal correspondence flowed to and from Vietnam during the years of American involvement. In response to a public appeal, families submitted over 3,000 pieces of Vietnam correspondence for consideration in this volume, and 208 letters by 125 different authors are included. Edited to eliminate repetitious, private and tangential information, to regularize spelling, and to indent paragraphs, these epistles from ordinary soldiers written at different times and places and in different conditions in the war retain their powerful authenticity. Many of the letters are particularly poignant because the author did not return from his or her tour. This may not be the most important collection of documents or the most profound book on the war, but it relates much about how the war was experienced, and it is a book worth considering as a source for students. A video based on the book, also titled *Dear America*, first appeared on Home Box Office television and is now available in cassette. It uses scenes from Vietnam and the contemporary music of the time as overlay over the reading of the letters. Exceptionally well done, it is one of the best video sources available about the war.

SUPPLEMENTARY READINGS

Michael Charlton and Anthony Moncrieff, *Many Reasons Why: The American Involvement in Vietnam* (New York: Hill and Wang, 1978), a series of interviews conducted by two British journalists with policy-makers about the evolution of American involvement in Vietnam from World War I through 1975, serves as a fine collateral text. These question-and-answer sessions with individuals such as George Ball, William Bundy, William Colby, Tran Van Don, Daniel Ellsberg, Nguyen Cao Ky, Edward Lansdale, Henry Cabot Lodge, Graham Martin, Walt Rostow, Dean Rusk, Maxwell Taylor, and William Westmoreland, illuminate the thinking of decision-makers.

Another favorite auxiliary source is journalist Myra MacPherson's *Long Time Passing: Vietnam and the Haunted Generation* (New York: Doubleday, 1985; New American Library, 1985), an eclectic, anecdotal, rambling *tour de force* of vignettes based upon interviews with over 500 of the Vietnam generation—soldiers, resisters, evaders, deserters, expatriates, heroes, wounded veterans, protestors, and so forth. The resultant compendium of perspectives, ideas, emotions, hopes, dreams, angers and despairs is impressionistic, emotional and argumentative. The volume would have been better if the author had moderated her own strong anti-war stance, but MacPherson writes with flare and passion, and the book is powerful, disturbing and thought-provoking. It serves a good role in providing an overview of how the war affected a wide range of people. Despite its almost 700-page length, students find it engrossing, and it does read quickly.

Two excellent older anthologies worth considering are Bernard B. Fall, *Last Reflections on a War* (New York: Doubleday, 1967; Schocken, 1972), a collection of essays, several previously unpublished, by the man who was the world's most knowledgeable expert on Vietnam prior to his untimely death while on combat patrol in 1967, and John Clark Pratt, *Vietnam Voices: Perspectives on the War Years, 1941-1982* (New York: Viking Penguin, 1984), a chronologically arranged, balanced collection of documents, histories, memoirs, fiction and other sources.   Both are excellent sources. Among the best recent anthologies are Grace Sevy, *The American Experience in Vietnam: A Reader* (Norman: University of Oklahoma, 1989); Jeffrey Kimball, *To Reason Why: The Debate about the Causes of U.S. Involvement in the Vietnam War* (New York: McGraw-Hill, 1990); Andrew J. Rotter, *Light at the End of the Tunnel: A Vietnam War Anthology* (New York: St. Martin's, 1990); and the volumes by Robert J. McMahon and George Donelson Moss noted in the section devoted to document collections.

No discussion of auxiliary readings should fail to mention the two award-winning best-sellers of the early 1970s, even if both are somewhat out of favor today. David Halberstam's *The Best and the Brightest* (New York: Random House, 1969; Fawcett, 1972), the classic liberal, "mistake," "quagmire" thesis with emphasis upon failure in the policy process and men who made American foreign policy, is lively and absorbing. A story of heroes and villains, it remains an arguable thesis with which I have some sympathy, although the interpretation is considered passé by some commentators. It may be best employed along the lines pursued by John James MacDougall in chapter four of this volume—in conjuction with more detailed studies, such as Larry Berman's *Planning a Tragedy* (discussed below).   Frances Fitzgerald's *Fire in the Lake: The Vietnamese and the Americans in Vietnam* (Boston: Little, Brown, 1972) won the Pulitzer Prize, National Book Award, and Bancroft Prize in History, and was one of the most acclaimed books of the 1970s. Although a flawed work that understood neither the Vietnamese nor American policy and action as well as the author alleged, the book is provocative and often insightful. With proper caveats, the book still merits attention.

Flawed in other ways but profitable for presenting the "conservative revisionist" interpretation of the war are Norman Podhoretz, *Why We Were in Vietnam* (New York: Simon and Schuster, 1982; Touchstone, 1983) and Richard Nixon, *No More Vietnams* (New York: Arbor House, 1985; Avon, 1986). Both provide counterpoint against other interpretations, and they forcefully argue a position that students should confront. But both are quite self-serving, and few scholars would endorse many of their contentions. As with most overly simplistic interpretations of either the left or the right, the authors' combative certainty has a seductive appeal to novice students.

Harry G. Summers, Jr., *On Strategy: The Vietnam War in Context* (Novato, Calif.: Presidio, 1982; Dell, 1984) offers a more sophisticated revisionist interpretation. Like other revisionists, Summers believes that the war was honorable and winnable. He condemns the hesitant, vacillating civilian leadership exhibited by the McNamara coterie and Lyndon Johnson. However, the real reason for failure, he claims, came from within the military itself. Summers denounces the military's acceptance of "management mentality," its failure to do the necessary pre-intervention strategic planning, the reluctance of the Joint Chiefs of Staff to stand up courageously against pernicious directions, and General Westmoreland's ill-conceived, improvisational war strategy. According to Summers, the United States focused upon the wrong enemy, since it judged the war as "revolutionary" and the Viet Cong as the primary adversary rather than North Vietnam as the real enemy in a conventional war. Self-deceived about the true nature of the war, the military had no clear objective and could not formulate sound strategy. Bad strategy led to faulty military operations in the field and ultimately to loss of the war.

The "Summers thesis" is one of the important controversies in the study of the war, and the volume is, or at least for a period of time was, popular as a source in Vietnam courses. However, the book and the argument have many critics.[4] Lawrence E. Grinter and Peter M. Dunn, editors, *The American War in Vietnam* (cited below in the section devoted to bibliographies) provides some of the best critiques of Summers's arguments and other issues about how the war was fought. Unfortunately, the book, which would be a good classroom resource, is only available in an inordinately expensive hardcover edition.

Of the many fine books that deal with decision-making, none are better or more suited for a course with this orientation than Larry Berman's two excellent studies, *Planning a Tragedy: The Americanization of the War in Vietnam* (New York: Norton, 1982) and *Lyndon Johnson's War: The Road to Stalemate in Vietnam* (New York: Norton, 1989). Neil Sheenhan's Pulitzer Prize winner, *A Bright Shining Lie: John Paul Vann and America in Vietnam* (New York: Random House, 1988), is a monumental work on the American policy process. Unfortunately, it is far too long and discursive to be used in many courses.

Two outstanding, available paperback volumes are John Schlight, editor, *The Second Indochina War Symposium: Papers and Commentary* (Washington, D. C.: Army Center of Military History, 1986) and Lloyd J. Matthews and Dale E. Brown, editors, *Assessing the Vietnam War: A Collection from the Journal of the U.S. Army War College* (McLean, Va: Pergamon Brassey, 1987). Douglas Kinnard, *The War Managers* (Hanover, N. H.: University Press of New England, 1977; Avery Publishers, 1985), the result of a survey of the 173 general officers who served in Vietnam between 1965 and 1972, offers good, brief, readable commentary on the military conduct of the war.

James William Gibson's *The Perfect War: Technowar in Vietnam* (Boston: Atlantic Monthly Press, 1986, subtitled in the paperback edition *The War We Couldn't Lose and How We Did*, Vintage, 1987) deserves mention, but not recommendation. Gibson develops a model of the war as a "corporate production system" with men and high technology employed to impose American values upon another culture. Although the argument is spirited and the book full of interesting, if not always reliable, detail, the author pushes the metaphor far beyond reason and his interpretation of the war is, in my opinion, absurd. The book proceeds from a faulty premise and builds its case on half-truths and perverse interpretations of data. The choice of sources is quite narrow, and they are employed most selectively. Gibson himself appears to have little understanding of military operations. In sum, the book is provocative and has some nuggets of insight, but as reviewer Allan Millett asserts, it is "a shallow, ardent account of the Vietnam war that can be ignored by serious students of the conflict, whatever their political persuasion."[5]

Noted cultural historian Loren Baritz's *Backfire: A History of How American Culture Led Us into Vietnam and Made Us Fight the Way We Did* (New York: William Morrow, 1985; Ballantine, 1986), one of the best known interpretative works, is a better effort at holistic analysis. Well written, reflective and engaging, this blend of historical narrative, anecdote and social analysis has some value. However, like Gibson, Baritz's strong assumptions color all that he sees, and the book promises more than it delivers.

Memoirs and novels written in the form of memoirs give us insight into the nature of the war and its impact upon participants. They are a particularly useful source for the classroom. A whole volume could be written on the hundreds of fictional and nonfictional narratives. The reader's attention is called to the specialized bibliographies noted above that survey this literature, especially Timothy Lomperis's *Reading the Wind*. Despite the volume of literature, three books continue to stand out: Philip Caputo's *A Rumor of War* (New York: Holt, Rinehart, and Winston, 1977; Ballantine, 1978), a memoir written as novel; Michael Herr's *Dispatches* (New York: Knopf, 1977; Avon, 1978), which captures the argot, place and mood of combat in the 1967-1968 frame; and John M. Del Vecchio's *The 13th Valley* (New York: Bantam, 1982), in my opinion still the best war novel to come out of Vietnam.

Collective memoirs are quite valuable for students since they expose the reader to a wide range of experiences. The best of this genre are Al Santoli's *Everything We Had: An Oral History of the Vietnam War by Thirty-Three American Soldiers Who Fought It* (New York: Random House, 1981; Ballantine, 1982) and *To Bear Any Burden: The Vietnam War and Its Aftermath in the Words of Americans and Southeast Asians* (New York: Dutton, 1985; Ballantine, 1986); Peter Goldman and Tony Fuller, *Charlie*

Company: What Vietnam Did to Us (New York: Morrow, 1983; Ballantine, 1984); Joe Klein, *Payback: Five Marines and Vietnam* (New York: Knopf, 1984; Ballantine, 1985); Kim Willenson, *The Bad War: An Oral History of the Vietnam Conflict* (New York: New American Library, 1987); Thomas Myers, *Walking Point: American Narratives of Vietnam* (New York: Oxford, 1988); and Harry Maurer, *Strange Ground: Americans in Vietnam, 1945-1975, An Oral History* (New York: Henry Holt and Company, 1989). Mark Baker's *Nam: The Vietnam War in the Words of the Men and Women Who Fought There* (New York: Morrow, 1981; Berkeley, 1986) is less satisfactory since it relies upon unattributed quotes without identifying individuals and it focuses almost exclusively upon the most unsavory aspects of the war.

Among specialized collective memoirs, the 20 veterans interviewed in Wallace Terry's *Bloods: An Oral History of the Vietnam War by Black Veterans* (New York: Random House, 1984; Ballantine, 1985) and Stanley Goff and Robert Sanders (with Clark Smith), *Brothers: Black Soldiers in the Nam* (Novato, Calif.: Presidio, 1982; Berkeley, 1985) reflect a cross-section of the Black experience in the war. The best collective memoirs about POWs are: Stephen A. Rowan, *They Wouldn't Let Us Die: The Prisoners of War Tell Their Story* (Middle Village, N. Y.: Jonathan David, 1973); Zalin Grant, *Survivors* (New York: Norton, 1975; Berkley, 1985); and John G. Hubbell, et al., *POW: A Definitive History of the American Prisoner of War Experience in Vietnam, 1964-1973* (New York: Reader's Digest Press, 1976).[6] The role of women in Vietnam, until recently a neglected subject, has begun to attract attention. A question even exists as to how many women served in Vietnam. According to the Department of Defense, 7,465 women served as active duty military in Vietnam, but the Veterans Administration puts the number at 11,000.[7] While no accurate figures on non-military women are available, estimates place the number who served as civilian nurses, missionaries, teachers, journalists, entertainers, Red Cross or Special Services personnel and as private business employees as high as 50,000. At least eight military women and an undetermined number of civilian women died in the war. My own work, "Women and the Vietnam War: A Bibliographic Review," cited above in the section devoted to specialized bibliographies, is a comprehensive overview of the extant literature on the subject.

Collective memoirs of women's experiences are found in three invaluable books: Keith Walker, *A Piece of My Heart: The Stories of 26 American Women Who Served in Vietnam* (Novato, Calif.: Presidio, 1986; Ballantine, 1987); Kathryn Marshall, *In the Combat Zone: An Oral History of American Women in Vietnam, 1966-1975* (Boston: Little, Brown, 1987; Penguin, 1988), the testimonies of 20 women; and Dan Freedman and Jacqueline Rhoads, *Nurses in Vietnam: The Forgotten Veterans* (Austin, Tex.: Texas Monthly Press, 1987).

The best individual accounts are Lynda Van Devanter's *Home Before Morning: The Story of an Army Nurse in Vietnam* (New York: Beaufort Books, 1983; Warner, 1984), the first book to attract attention to female

Vietnam veterans; and Patricia Walsh's *Forever Sad the Hearts* (New York: Avon, 1984), a novel based upon Walsh's experiences as a civilian nurse in Vietnam. Van Devanter's activism in veterans' affairs and high media profile has attracted considerable attention to her story; it is a valuable book for students to read. Walsh's novel, though, is an even better source, one of the most moving personal accounts available on the war.

Two other books about women merit consideration as readings in a Vietnam course: Wendy Wilder Larsen and Tran Thi Nga, *Shallow Graves: Two Women and Vietnam* (New York: Random House, 1986; Harper and Row, 1986) and Bobbie Ann Mason's acclaimed novel, *In Country* (New York: Harper and Row, 1985). Written in *truyen*, a literary form of Vietnamese short prose poems, *Shallow Graves* provides an American woman's glimpses of Vietnamese life and a Vietnamese woman's family and personal history. The segment by Madame Nga, one of the few memoirs by a Vietnamese woman, is a moving and illuminating introduction to Buddhist traditions and culture, life amidst war and the dislocation of the refugee. In all the literature on the war, this is a unique book. *In Country*, a clever double entendre for service in Vietnam and residence in rural mid-America, is the story a teen-age girl's attempt to understand the impact of Vietnam upon all of those around her. Although the book is more about the sterility of rural, small-town teenage popular culture in the 1980s, it affords insight into (to play on MacPherson) the post-Vietnam haunted generation that will be a long time in passing. A piece of fine literature, the novel helps students to understand that their own generation continues to be affected by this war that transpired so long ago.

Students need to get beyond an exclusively American vision to appreciate the Vietnamese, their culture, political milieu and perspectives. Chapters six through nine and chapter thirteen of this volume identify a wide range of resources for and means of bringing Vietnam into the classroom that will well-equip instructors to assist their students accomplish this task. Three of the many works that can be employed for this purpose are, however, under-appreciated or easily over-looked. Tom Mangold and John Penycate, *The Tunnels of Cu Chi* (New York: Random House, 1985; Berkley, 1986) is one of the most absorbing books in all the literature. It introduces Viet Cong soldiers who fought in and out of the tunnels in the South as well as the American "tunnel rats" who engaged them in the dark recesses of this nether world. As well as any other source, the book explains why the United States was unable to subdue such determination, courage and self-sacrifice through high technology. Tran Tri Vu (pseudonym), *Lost Years: My 1632 Days in Vietnamese Re-education Camps* (Berkeley, Calif.: Institute of East Asian Studies, 1989) and Thomas Taylor, *Where the Orange Blooms: One Man's War and Escape in Vietnam* (New York: McGraw-Hill, 1989), the memoirs of soldier and fugitive Ben Cai Lam, are accounts of life in South Vietnam after Hanoi's triumph that have so recently come onto the market that some instructors might be unaware of their existence.

BIBLIOGRAPHIES AND REFERENCE RESOURCES

As the above discussion of texts and auxiliary reading would suggest that, despite Spector's assertion of the dearth of real scholarship on the war, the literature available is overwhelming. The recent explosion of fiction now numbers hundreds of volumes; nonfiction, including a growing amount of solid scholarship, registers thousands of books and articles. The teacher venturing into this complex area should consult a number of very good bibliographies, several of which are annotated. The most comprehensive, up-to-date are: Richard Dean Burns and Milton Leitenberg, *The Wars in Vietnam, Cambodia, and Laos, 1945-1982: A Bibliographic Guide* (Santa Barbara, Calif: ABC-Clio, 1984), which contains 6,000 entries, including Congressional publications, in several languages arranged by topics and subtopics, and Louis A. Peake, *The United States in the Vietnam War, 1954-1975: A Selected Annotated Bibliography* (New York: Garland, 1986), a topically arranged volume of English language sources.

Christopher L. Sugnet, John T. Hickey, and Robert Crispino, *Vietnam War Bibliography: Selected from Cornell University's Echols Collection* (Lexington, Mass.: Lexington Books, 1983) emphasizes Vietnamese titles in its 4,000 entries, which include manuscripts, reports, correspondence, documents, and articles. John H. M. Chen, *Vietnam: A Comprehensive Bibliography* (Metuchen, N. J.: Scarecrow, 1973) and Roy Jumper, *Vietnam: An Annotated Bibliography* (Salisbury, N. C.: Documentary Publishers, 1980) are now quite dated. Jane L. Cohen, Sarah L. Chapman, and Bonnie G. Klein, *A New Kind of War: The Vietnamese Conflict and the United States* (Heidelburg, FRG: HQs, U. S. Army, Europe and 7th Army, 1986) has limited distribution, but it is useful as it includes fiction, microfilm materials, indexes and audio-visual materials.

Michael Cotter, *Vietnam: A Guide to Reference Sources* (Boston: G. K. Hall, 1977) is good but dated. The most useful of this genre is Ronald H. Spector, *Researching the Vietnam Experience* (Washington, D. C.: U. S. Army Center of Military History, 1984), an invaluable introduction to the topic that includes government records, memoirs, oral histories, and public and private collections. Charles Ralston, "The Vietnam War in Books and Periodicals," *Antiquarian Bookman Weekly* 79 (June 29, 1987), pp. 2885-2892, is a good introduction to bibliographies, reference works, document collections and official histories.

Several Vietnam texts have very extensive bibliographies or bibliographic essays. But the best sources are annotated essay articles which attempt to put the literature into categories or some analytical framework. The first systematic attempts along these lines were Peter Braestrup, "Vietnam as History," *The Washington Quarterly* 1 (Spring 1978), pp. 178-87, and my own article, "In Search of Lessons: The Development of a Vietnam Historiography," *Parameters: The Journal of the U.S. Army War College* 9 (December 1979), pp. 28-40. My continuing efforts to deal with the ever-increasing literature include "The Vietnam Bookshelf Enters the 1980s," *Naval War College Review* 34 (September-October), pp. 107-12; "Teaching Vietnam as History," *Teaching History: A Journal of Methods* 6 (Fall 1981), pp. 50-59; "Our Changing Vietnam Retrospect," *Air University Review* 37 (March-April, 1986), pp. 115-23; and "On Legacies and Lessons: The Literature and the Debate," in Lawrence E. Grinter and Peter M. Dunn, editors, *The American War in Vietnam: Lessons, Legacies, and Implications for Future Conflicts* (Westport, Conn.: Greenwood, 1987), pp. 3-12.

Other significant bibliographic essays include David P. Chandler, "Post Mortes on the Wars in Indochina—A Review Article," *Journal of Asian Studies* 40 (November 1980), pp. 77-86; Richard K. Betts, Douglas Pike, and Harry G. Summers, "Vietnam as the Past," (three separately written essays that include bibliographies) *The Wilson Quarterly* 6 (Summer 1983), pp. 95-139; Fox Butterfield, "The New Vietnam Scholarship," *The New York Times Magazine* (February 13, 1983), pp. 26-35, 45-61; Steven P. Soper, "Perspectives and Prejudices: Writing on the Vietnam War," *Teaching Political Science: Politics in Perspective 11* (Spring 1984), pp. 130-41; James Fetzer, "The United States and the Vietnam War: A Selected Bibliography," *American-East Asian Relations Newsletter* 4 (December 1984), pp. 47-52; Edward Eckert, "The Vietnam War: A Selective Bibliography," *Choice* 24 (September 1986), pp. 51-71; and Christopher C. Lovett, "We Held the Day in the Palm of Our Hand: A Review of Recent Sources on the War in Vietnam," *Military Affairs* 51 (April 1987), pp. 67-72.

Although they do not survey large numbers of books, the following essays develop important analytical frameworks for dealing with the literature: George C. Herring's three articles, "America's Strategy in Vietnam: The Postwar Debate," *Military Affairs* 46 (April 1982), pp. 57-63; "Vietnam Remembered," *Journal of American History* 73 (June 1986), pp. 152-64; and "America and Vietnam: The Debate Continues," *American Historical Review* 92 (April 1987); and Robert A. Divine, "Vietnam Reconsidered," *Diplomatic History* 12 (Winter 1988), pp. 79-93.

For specialized bibliographies and essays on the military services, see *The Marines in Vietnam, 1954-1973: An Anthology and Annotated Bibliography* (Washington, D. C.: History and Museums Division, HQs, U. S. Marine Corps, 1979); Myron J. Smith, *Air War, Southeast Asia, 1961-1973: An Annotated Bibliography and 16mm Film Guide* (Metuchen, N. J.: Scarecrow, 1979); and Edward J. Marolda and G. Wesley Pryce, III, *A Select Bibliography of the United States Navy and the Southeast Asian Conflict, 1950-1975* (Washington, D. C.: Naval Historical Center, 1982).

The following specialized bibliographies are self-explanatory: Richard W. Grefrath, "Everyday Was Summertime in Vietnam: An Annotated Bibliography of the Best Personal Narratives," *Reference Service Review* 8 (October-November 1980), pp. 23-27; Merritt Clifton, *Those Who Were*

There: Eyewitness Accounts of the War in Southeast Asia, 1956-1975 and Aftermath: Annotated Bibliography of Books, Articles and Topic-Related Magazines, Covering Writings Both Factual and Imaginative (Paradise, Calif.: Dust Books, 1984); Lawrence F. Ashmun, *Resettlement of Indochinese Refugees in the United States: A Selective and Annotated Bibliography* (DeKalb, Ill.: Center for Southeast Asian Studies, Northern Illinois University, 1984); Caroline D. Harnly, *Agent Orange and Vietnam: An Annotated Bibliography* (Meutchen, N. J.: Scarecrow, 1988); F. C. Brown, *POW/MIA Indochina, 1946-1986: An Annotated Bibliography of Nonfiction Works Dealing with Prisoners of War/Missing in Action* (San Francisco: Rice Paddy Press, 1988); and three articles by this writer: "The P.O.W. Chronicles: A Bibliographic Review," *Armed Forces and Society* 9 (Spring 1983), pp. 495-514; "The Vietnam War POW/MIAs: An Annotated Bibliography," *Bulletin of Bibliography* 45 (June 1988), pp. 152-57; and "Women and the Vietnam War: A Bibliographic Review," *Journal of American Culture* 12 (Spring 1989), pp. 85-92. Specialized bibliographies in *Vietnam Generation* include: "A Bibliography of Unusual Sources on Women and the Vietnam War," 1 (Summer-Fall, 1989), pp. 274-77; William King, "Bibliography of Sources Dealing with Minority Issues," 1 (Spring 1989), pp. 151-59; and Skip DeLano, "Selected Bibliography: GI and Veterans' Movement Against the War, 1965-1975," 2, no. 1, pp. 110-18.

The explosion of fictional literature has led to a growth of bibliographies and review essays focusing upon literature and film. The older sources include Tom Colonnese and Jerry Hogan, "Vietnam War Literature, 1958-1979: A First Checklist," *Bulletin of Bibliography* 38 (January-March 1981), pp. 26-51; James C. Wilson, *Vietnam in Prose and Film* (Jefferson, N. C.: McFarland, 1981); Gilbert Adair, *Vietnam on Film* (New York: Proteus Books, 1981); Margaret E. Stewart, "Vietnam-War Novels in the Classroom," *Teaching History: A Journal of Methods* 6 (Fall 1981), pp. 60-66; Neil Baldwin, "Going after the War," *Publishers Weekly* (February 11, 1983), pp. 34-38; and C. D. B. Bryan, "Barely Suppressed Screams: Getting a Bead on Vietnam Literature," *Harpers* 268 (June 1984), pp. 67-72.

Among recent sources are these excellent contributions: F. C. Brown and B. Laurie, *Annotated Bibliography of Vietnam Fiction: 500 Titles Dealing with the Conflict in Vietnam, Cambodia, and Laos* (San Francisco: Rice Paddy Press, 1986); Catherine Calloway, "Vietnam War Literature and Film: A Bibliography of Secondary Sources," *Bulletin of Bibliography* 43 (September 1986), pp. 149-58, a marvelous work; Major Edward F. Palm, "Novels of Vietnam and the Uses of War Literature," *Marine Corps Gazette* (November 1986); Edward K. Eckert and William J. Searle, "Creative Literature of the Vietnam War: A Selective Bibliography," *Choice* 24 (January 1987), pp. 725-35; and Arthur D. Casciato, "Teaching the Literature of the Vietnam War," *Review* (Charlottesville, Va.) 9 (1987), pp. 125-47. The latest and best are John Newman, *Vietnam War Literature:*

An Annotated Bibliography of Imaginative Works About Americans Fighting in Vietnam, 2nd ed. (Metuchen, N. J.: Scarecrow, 1988), an updated, greatly expanded edition of the original 1982 publication which now includes 752 capsule reviews of 429 novels, 192 short stories and collections, 73 poetry works, and 20 plays; and Sandra M. Wittman, *Writing About Vietnam: A Bibliography of the Literature of the Vietnam Conflict* (Boston, Mass.: G. K. Hall, 1989).

Timothy J. Lomperis, editor, *Reading the Wind: The Literature of the Vietnam War, an Interpretative Critique* (Durham, N. C.: Duke University Press, 1987), the product of an Asia Society-sponsored conference, is an exceptional work. John Clark Pratt's summary essay, which characterizes the literature by time periods, is the best source in print on this topic. Albert Auster and Leonard Quart, *How the War Was Remembered: Hollywood & Vietnam* (New York: Praeger, 1988) and Jack Colldeweih, "Napalm in the Morning: The Vietnam War Film," *A Vietnam Reader: Sources and Essays*, edited by George Donelson Moss (Englewood Cliffs, N. J.: Prentice-Hall, 1991), pp. 217-44, attempt the same chronological and analytical assessment of film. Victoria E. Johnson, compiler, *Vietnam on Film and Television: Documentaries in the Library of Congress* (Washington, D. C.: Library of Congress, July 1989) is extremely useful.

Although dozens of reference books, general and specialized, are available on the war, the following are the most important for the classroom teacher. Shelby M. Stanton, *Vietnam Order of Battle: A Complete Illustrated Reference to the U.S. Army Ground Forces in Vietnam, 1961-1973* (Washington, D. C.: U. S. News and World Report Books, 1982), is *the* source on the military organization in Vietnam, unit histories, battles, campaigns, insignia and other antiquarian interests. Leroy Thompson, *The US Army in Vietnam* (Devon, United Kingdom: David and Charles, 1990) is more compact and useful for the novice. Harry G. Summers, Jr., *The Vietnam War Almanac* (New York: Facts on File, 1985) is a valuable glossary of names, places, military units and terms. John Bowman, *The Vietnam War: An Almanac* (New York: World Almanac Publications, 1985) has a detailed almost daily chronology, biographical sketches and illustrated features on several topics. Bowman's updated *The Vietnam War: Day by Day* (New York: Mallard Books, 1989) is an even more detailed coffee table version. James S. Olson, *Dictionary of the Vietnam War* (Westport, Conn.: Greenwood, 1988) includes more than nine hundred brief descriptive essays written for the novice by 28 non-specialists. William J. Duiker, *Historical Dictionary of Vietnam* (Metuchen, N. J.: Scarecrow, 1989) provides cross-referenced dictionary items, maps, chronologies, tables and bibliography. All these volumes are valuable for developing lectures or for other aspects of teacher preparation.

Thomas C. Thayer, *War Without Fronts: The American Experience in Vietnam* (Boulder, Colo.: Westview, 1985), a statistical analysis of the war with 121 tables and a finely honed text, is one of the single most important sources for interpreting the military conduct of the war. Thayer addresses a number of fascinating questions, and he draws penetrating conclusions. Despite the statistical orientation, the book is accessible to even the least quantitative layman.

Several "fact books" have some value as ready references: *Vietnam Fact Book* (Springfield, Va.: Joint Publications Research Service, SEA Report 85-121, August 7, 1985); John Musgrave and Michael Clodfelter, *The Vietnam Years* (Boston: Quinlin Press, 1986), which contains one thousand questions and answers; Alan Dawson, *The Official Vietnam Trivia Book* (Bangkok, Thailand: Thai Watana Press, 1987), whose 420 questions and answers are light but informative; Erhard Konerding, *Vietnam War Facts Quiz: The Truth and Drama of American Involvement* (Middleton, Conn.: Southfarm Press, 1986), with a multiple choice and true/false format; Jeff Stein, *The Vietnam Fact Book* (New York: Dell, 1987), an inexpensive paperback with question-and-answer units on politics, names and places, units and insignia, weapons, the ground and air war, the war at home and Vietnam in books, movies and music—interesting tidbits that can spice up lectures; and R. E. Armstrong, *The Vietnam Veterans Trivia Book* (Oklahoma City: Vietnam Veterans of America, Chapter 291, 1989) with two hundred questions and answers. Gregory R. Clark, *Words of the Vietnam War: The Slang, Jargon, Abbreviations, Acronyms, Nomenclature, Nicknames, Pseudonyms, Slogans, Specs, Euphemisms, Doubte-talk, Chants, and Names and Places of the Era of United States Involvement in Vietnam* (Jefferson, N. C.: McFarland, 1990) has ten thousand entries. Linda Reinberg, *In the Field: The Language of the Vietnam War* (New York: Facts on File, 1991) is a bit less ambitious with five thousand entries.

CONCLUSION

Student interest in Vietnam is clearly evident, and materials for the classroom teacher are abundant. For those venturing into this field, diligent preparation is imperative. If we are to garner any value from this tragic war, we must allow the next generation the opportunity to address the meaning, legacies and lessons of this major event in American history.

NOTES

1. Ronald H. Spector, "What Did You Do in the War, Professor: Reflections on Teaching about Vietnam," *American Heritage* 38 (December 1986), pp. 98-102.

2. Arguments for teaching a Vietnam course and some of the rationales, purposes, means and sources are found in Joe P. Dunn, "Teaching Vietnam as History," *Teaching History: A Journal of Methods* 6,

Fall 1981, pp. 50-59; Sandra C. Taylor with Rex Casillas, "Dealing with Defeat: Teaching the Vietnam War," *Newsletter of the Society for Historians of American Foreign Relations* 11 (December 1980), pp. 8-16, and 12 (March 1981), pp. 1-9; Sandra C. Taylor, "Teaching the Vietnam War," *The History Teacher* 15 (November 1981), pp. 57-66; Walter H. Capps, "On Teaching Today's Students about the Vietnam War," *Federation Review* 8 (May/June 1985), pp. 10-13; Jonathan Goldstein, "Teaching the American-Indochina War: An Interdisciplinary Experiment," *Teaching History: A Journal of Methods* 12 (Spring 1987), pp. 3-9 and "Using Literature in a Course on the Vietnam War," *College Teaching* 37 (Summer 1989), pp. 91-95; and R. Steven Daniels and Carolyn L. Clarke-Daniels, "Teaching the Vietnam War: An Examination of History, Policy, and Impact," *The Political Science Teacher* 3 (Fall 1990), pp. 13-16. Special issues devoted to teaching Vietnam in *Teaching Political Science: Politics in Perspective* 12 (Summer 1985); *Social Education* 52 (January 1988); and a forthcoming edition of *Vietnam Generation* each contain several articles. Also see Jonathan Goldstein, "Educators' Tour to Vietnam, January 1987," *Organization of American Historians Newsletter* 16 (February 1988), pp. 14-15 and Thomas Banit, "Vietnam Education in New England," *New England Journal of History* 47 (Spring 1990), pp. 56-64. On teaching Vietnam at the high school level, see William I. Griffin and John Marciano, *Teaching the Vietnam War* (Montclair, N. J.: Allenheld, Osman, 1979); Joe P. Dunn, "On Teaching Recent History: An Exchange," *Teaching History: A Journal of Methods* 6 (Fall 1981), pp. 94-95; Dan B. Fleming and Ronald J. Nurse, "Vietnam Revised: Are Our Textbooks Changing?," *Social Education* 46 (May 1982), pp. 338-43; Joe P. Dunn, "Teaching the Vietnam War in High School," *The Social Studies* 74 (September-October 1983), pp. 198-200; Alvin P. Sanoff, "Vietnam Comes of Age," *U.S. News and World Report* 102 (February 2, 1987), pp. 58-59; several of the articles in *Social Education* 52 (January 1988); David M. Berman, "In Cold Blood: Vietnam in Textbooks," *Vietnam Generation* 1 (1989), pp. 61-80; Karen Franklin, "Making Peace with Vietnam," *Teacher Magazine* (March 1990), pp. 30-33; and Karen Franklin, "Everything I Need to Know I Learned in Vietnam," *Veteran* 10 (May 1990), pp. 15-17.

The question of what should be taught is discussed in H. Bruce Franklin, "Teaching the Vietnam War Today: Who Won and Why? *The Chronicle of Higher Education* 23 (November 4, 1981), p. 64, and letters in response in the December 9 and 16, 1981, issues; Dunn, "On Teaching Recent History," pp. 94-95; Sanoff, "Vietnam Comes of Age," pp. 58-59; Fox Butterfield, "Disparity in College Courses on Vietnam," *New York Times*, April 27, 1988, sec. b, p. 11; Frederick Z. Brown, "Myth and Misperception Abound in our Courses on the War in Vietnam," *The Chronicle of Higher Education* 34 (May 25, 1988), sec. a, p. 48; Bill McCloud, "What Should We Tell Our Children About Vietnam?"

American Heritage 39 (May-June 1988), pp. 55-77; Stephen Goode, "Taking a Trip Back to the Sixties," *Insight on the News* 4 (August 15, 1988), pp. 50-52; Allan Goodman, "Scholars Must Give More Serious Thought to How They Teach and Write about the War in Vietnam," *The Chronicle of Higher Education* 36 (July 25, 1990), sec. a, p. 36; numerous syndicated newspaper articles on teaching the subject.

3. See the excellent review article on Kahin, Smith, and Kolko: George C. Herring, "America and Vietnam: The Debate Continues," *American Historical Review* 92 (April 1987) pp. 350-62.

4. General Bruce Palmer, Jr., *The 25-Year War: America's Military Role in Vietnam* (Lexington, Ky: University of Kentucky Press, 1984; New York: New American Library, 1985) makes points similar to Summers's in a much better written and more balanced book. See the excellent review article on the two books, Gary R. Hess, "The Military Perspective on Strategy in Vietnam," *Diplomatic History* 10 (Winter 1986), pp. 91-106. Admiral U. S. Grant Sharp's *Strategy for Defeat: Vietnam in Retrospect* (Novato, Calif.: Presidio, 1978; 1986) is a forceful expression of the "we weren't allowed to win" thesis. George C. Herring, "America's Strategy in Vietnam: The Postwar Debate," *Military Affairs* 46 (April 1982), pp. 57-63, addresses the Sharp and Summers/Palmer variants of the revisionist approach. Andrew F. Krepinevich, Jr., *The Army and Vietnam* (Baltimore: Johns Hopkins University Press, 1986) is a perceptive critique of both positions. Also see Larry E. Cable, *Conflict of Myths: The Development of American Counterinsurgency Doctrine and the Vietnam War* (New York: New York University Press, 1986); F. Charles Parker IV, *Vietnam: Strategy for a Stalemate* (New York: Paragon House, 1989); and Larry Berman, *Lyndon Johnson's War: The Road to Stalemate in Vietnam* (New York: Norton, 1989) for perceptive critiques of the Johnson military strategy or, more accurately, non-strategy. Finally, Bob Buzzanco, "The American Military's Rationale Against the Vietnam War," *Political Science Quarterly* 101, no. 4 (1986), pp. 559-76, treats high-ranking military officers who opposed not only the strategy of the war but the conflict itself.

5. Allan R. Millett, review of James William Gibson, *The Perfect War: Technowar in Vietnam* (Boston: Atlantic Monthly Press, 1986) in *The American Historical Review* 93 (April 1988), p. 528.

6. For more information on the POW literature, see my two bibliographic articles on the subject cited in the section of this chapter devoted to bibliographies.

7. Some of this discrepancy arises from what constituted being "in Vietnam." The Department of Defense figures, for instance, do not count navy women who served on board hospital ships off the coast of South Vietnam or air force nurses stationed in Japan, Okinawa, or the Philippines who regularly flew into the country on evacuation flights.

14

A Guide to Curriculum Development Resources
MARC JASON GILBERT

The Vietnam War began in earnest for the United States over 25 years ago. Given that Southeast Asian studies programs were active on American university campuses at the war's onset and that the current resurgence of interest in this conflict began over a decade ago, it would be logical to expect that curriculum development resources on the Vietnam War would by now be plentiful. Unfortunately, for a wide variety of reasons, including the priority given to Chinese and Japanese area studies since the war, there is a paucity of materials that can serve as guides to course formation or as models against which instructors may measure their own efforts. Yet, though small in number, these resources are worthy of close examination.

SYLLABI COLLECTIONS

One of the earliest efforts to assist in the process of Vietnam War course development was prepared under the direction of Nguyen Manh Hung, the director of the Indochina Institute at George Mason University and released as a *Report on the Survey of Courses on Vietnam Era Events.* This survey, which was updated to 1986 and is currently being updated to 1990, features the comments of teachers responsible for the more than 90 courses on the war and on the Vietnam era. It can be obtained by writing to the Indochina Institute, George Mason University, 4400 University Drive, Fairfax, Virginia 22030-4444.

Another early effort to further the process of course development, Ronald D. Renard, et al., editors, *Southeast Asia Course Outlines: A Collection,* is now available in a second edition (1988). It is produced by the Center for Southeast Asian Studies of the School of Hawaiian, Asian and Pacific Studies, University of Hawaii at Manoa. This work contains

over 130 course outlines, reading lists and a bibliography, though only
some of the outlines and a portion of the bibliography pertain directly to
Vietnam, Cambodia and Laos. Of possible greater utility in structuring a
course in the Vietnam War is Grant Goodman, editor, *Asian History* (New
York: Markus Weiner, 1986). This volume, one of a well-known series of
syllabi collections from this publisher, contains model syllabi entitled
"Southeast Asia," "The United States in Vietnam," and "The Vietnam War:
1944-1975" prepared by Craig Lockard, A. Grunfeld and Roger Dingman,
respectively. This syllabi collection can be obtained by writing to Markus
Wiener, Inc., Order Department, Suite 911, 225 Lafayette St., New York,
New York 10012, or by calling the publisher's order fulfillment center at
(212) 941-1324. The journal *Vietnam Generation* 3, no. 4 (Spring 1991)
features a further selection of course syllabi. David Skidmore of Drake
University has published a course syllabus on the war in *Foreign Policy
Analysis Notes* 17, no. 2 (Summer 1990), pp. 3-8, that includes very detailed
instructions to students on the keeping of a course journal.

CULTURE GUIDES

While it may also serve as a text, Huynh Dinh Te's extremely useful *The
Indochinese and Their Culture* was devised as a teaching guide. As noted
elsewhere in this volume, *The Indochinese and Their Culture* and
forthcoming separate guides by Te and others to Cambodian, Laotian and
Vietnamese cultures can be obtained by writing to Van Le, Consultant,
TPRC Coordinator, Bilingual Education Office, California State
Department of Education, P.O. Box 944272, Sacramento, California 94244.

A VIDEOCASSETTE GUIDE AND A WORKBOOK

One of the most recent entries into the field of syllabus development
is a video presentation in which 50 master teachers responsible for courses
on the Vietnam War share their classroom strategies and experiences. This
cassette, entitled *Teaching the Vietnam War: Classroom Strategies* (1990), is
produced by the Center for Social Studies Education, 115 Mayfair Drive,
Pittsburg, Pennsylvania 15228. The Center for Social Studies Education
also publishes *The Lessons of the Vietnam War* (1988), a related workbook
edited by Jerold Starr. This volume, about to appear in a second edition,
is prepared in a notebook format and contains a wide variety of classroom
materials and learning exercises prepared by a very diverse group of
contributors. While its overall tenor and some of its individual sections
has failed to please all of its users and even some of those who contributed

to it, many instructors have found the workbook to be a valuable classroom resource.

MAP RESOURCES

In the 1960s, Vietnam was described as a theater of war that most Americans could not find on a map. There are now some map resources that make it less likely that students studying the war will have the same problem. The Defense Mapping Agency's Tactical Pilotage Charts (TPC) of Southeast Asia are full color relief maps of reasonable detail (1:500,000) and fine clarity. Approximately three feet by four feet in size and less than $4.00 each, these sectional maps can be joined together to form a very impressive and inexpensive visual aid. The sections required to construct a map of all of Vietnam are K-10A, K-10B, K-10C, K-10D, J-11A and J-11D. By adding sections J-10C (northwestern Laos) and K-9B (a small section of extreme western Cambodia) all the combatants can be represented in their entirety. Alternatively, by using the Defense Mapping Agency's Operational Navigation Chart (ONC) series, it is possible to build a single eight foot by six foot map of Vietnam from ONC sections J-11 and K-10. A slightly larger map of Vietnam, Laos and Cambodia can be created by the addition of sections J-10 and K-9. The Operational Navigational Chart series is, however, scaled at 1:1,000,000 and thus lacks some of the drama associated with the Tactical Pilotage maps. Both series are obtainable by writing to The Map Store, 1636 Eye Street, N.W., Washington, D. C. 20006 or calling (800) 544-2659.

Hammond Incorporated has recently produced a 25 inch by 38 inch wall map entitled "The Vietnam Conflict" (no. 0315-6). The map does not demarcate provincial boundaries, but has many useful features, including a chronology and a locator identifying the sites of major air strikes and military operations. At the current price of $3.95 each for the student edition, it is worthy of consideration for course adoption. Hammond also produces an 11 inch by 17 inch student project map of Southeast Asia (no. 8682-5) that indicates mountains, rivers and boundaries at a cost of approximately $0.25 each. These maps can be obtained by writing to the Hammond offices at 515 Valley Street, Maplewood, New Jersey 07040-9976 or by calling (800) 526-4953.

PERIODICAL LITERATURE

Joe P. Dunn's bibliographic essay features a lengthy reference to the growing periodical literature on the teaching of the war. One of the most noteworthy of these sources is Dunn's own "Teaching Teachers to Teach the Vietnam War," *Social Education* 52, no. 1 (January 1988), pp. 37-38. Jonathan Goldstein's article, "An Interdisciplinary Experiment in Teaching the American-Indochina War," in the *Annals of the Southeast Conference, Association for Asian Studies* 7 (1985), pp. 23-30, remains a model of its kind. Instructors may also wish to make use of the Educational Resources Information Center (ERIC) data base. It currently lists 24 journal articles and reports under various search command headings, including "Vietnam Syllabi Curriculum Development." ERIC is available at most college libraries. The educational reports cited in ERIC are on file at some college and most university libraries.

MONOGRAPHS

There are a few monographs that address the subject of teaching the war. The title of William L. Griffen and John Marciano, *Teaching the Vietnam War: A Critical Examination of School Texts and Interpretive Comparative History Utilizing the Pentagon Papers and Other Documents* (Montclair, N. J.: Allanheld, Osman, 1979), is self-descriptive. Joe P. Dunn's *Teaching the Vietnam War: Resources and Assessments* (Los Angeles: Center for the Study of Armament and Disarmament, California State University at Los Angeles, 1990) is a handy 90-page handbook that draws upon the author's experience as an author and frequent reviewer of works published on the subject. William McCloud's *What Shall We Tell Our Children About Vietnam* (Norman, Okla.: University of Oklahoma Press, 1990) is a fuller presentation of the data presented in McCloud's article of the same name in *American Heritage* 39 (May-June 1988), pp. 55-77. It provides instructors with a collection of thought-provoking answers to the question posed in the work's title offered by Americans drawn from many different walks of life. While not intended as a teaching guide, McCloud's volume is a very useful resource for teachers addressing the war's legacy and meaning. Finally, a special issue of the Asia Society's *Focus on Asia* magazine (Fall 1983) on the teaching of the war has been kept in print in monographic form as *Vietnam—A Teacher's Guide*. This work, obtainable for approximately $5.00, contains articles on the French in Indochina, the growth of America's involvement in Southeast Asia, Vietnamization and the home front. It also contains a resource guide and brief remarks on teaching Vietnamese culture and history. It may be ordered from the Asia Society, 725 Park Avenue, New York, New York 10021 or by calling the Society's Education office at (212) 288-6400. Instructors who are teaching a course involving Southeast Asia for the first time may profit from reading another Asia Society publication, Seymour Fersh's *Teaching About Asia* (1987).

BULLETINS AND NEWSLETTERS

Instructors wishing to keep abreast of classroom resources may avail themselves of the services and publications provided by institutions serving the field. *Indochina Chronology* is a quarterly publication associated with the University of California's Indochina Project and Indochina Archive. It contains numerous book reviews and notices of new teaching aids and is distributed at no cost to professionals. It can be obtained by writing to the editor, Douglas Pike, at the Institute of East Asian Studies, University of California, Berkeley, California 94720. Instructors may also wish to place their names on the mailing lists of the *Indochina Interchange*, the bulletin of the U.S.-Indochina Reconciliation Project (5808 Greene Street, Philadelphia, Pennsylvania 19144) and the very useful bulletin of the Asia Resource Center (P. O. Box 15275, Washington, D. C. 20003). The Indochina Institute of George Mason University, mentioned above, produces a quarterly newsletter at a price of $22.00 a year that repays its cost with news items regarding recent developments in Vietnam, Laos and Cambodia and brief reviews of publications of value to teachers in the field.

ACADEMIC CENTERS AND ASSOCIATIONS

There are many academic centers and institutes for the promotion of Asian and Southeast Asian Studies in the United States. Most of these institutions are staffed by personnel who can direct instructors to local film, book and document collections on the war and direct instructors to local Veterans groups and resettled Southeast Asian refugee communities. Only a few of these institutions, however, have developed formal programs to assist those responsible for teaching courses on the Vietnam War, and the majority of these limit participation in their programs to teachers active in their region. All the more welcome then are the small number of regional and national centers that offer outreach services nationwide.

The Center for Southeast Asian Studies of the University of Wisconsin, Madison, can supply teachers interested in Southeast Asia with a list of free sources of information, a bibliography, a quick reference chart, a list of films, a list of *National Geographic* materials on Southeast Asia, a map of Southeast Asia, a map of Laos, Kampuchea and Vietnam, materials on European influence in Southeast Asia, and materials on Southeast Asian independence movements and governments. Instructors wishing to obtain these aids need only send a covering letter and a stamped self-addressed envelope for every two of the items listed above to the Outreach Coordinator, Center for Southeast Asian Studies, 4115 Helen C. White Building, 600 North Park Street, Madison, Wisconsin 53706. Further information about the outreach program can be obtained by calling (608) 263-1755.

The Center for Southeast Asian Studies of the School of Hawaiian, Asian and Pacific Studies, University of Hawaii at Manoa (416 Moore Hall, 1890 East-West Road, Honolulu, Hawaii 96822-2383) has prepared detailed teaching packets for K-12 educators. The packets address the following topics: Southeast Asia; Southeast Asia, The Colonial Period; Modern Southeast Asia; Hot Spots in Southeast Asia; Burma and Cambodia; Update Indochina (Kampuchea and Laos); Vietnam; and Vietnam, Opening Doors. Each packet contains descriptive information, bibliographies, blank and labeled maps, quizzes, discussion questions, chronologies, film lists, background articles, lesson plans and numerous activity sheets. Each packet is priced at $4.00 (inclusive of mailing costs). Checks should be made payable to the Southeast Asia Outreach Program. The Center can also be reached by calling (808) 948-6085.

The recently established Center for the Study of the Vietnam Conflict at Texas Tech University (P. O. Box 4529, Lubbock, Texas 79409-1013) and the newly founded Center for the Study of American Wars (write in care of Dr. Peter Rollins, English Department, Oklahoma State University, Stillwater, Oklahoma 74078) will in the near future begin to offer a wide range of services and resources for teachers. The previously mentioned Indochina Institute at George Mason University intends to expand its services to include regular workshops such as the one it conducted for college teachers in the summer of 1990 with the support of the National Endowment for the Humanities. The staff of the Indochina Archive (6701 San Pablo Ave., Oakland, California 94608), operating under the auspices of the University of California, Berkeley, stands ready to assist any teacher or scholar interested in the Vietnam War. The Center for International Studies of Ohio University (Athens, Ohio 45701) maintains an outreach program for the Ohio Valley region that embraces Southeast Asia.

The Association for Asian Studies and its regional affiliates often conduct teacher-training workshops on the Vietnam War at their annual meetings. Information regarding such programs and the location of the nearest Center for Asian or Southeast Asian Studies can be obtained by writing to the Association for Asian Studies, Inc., 1 Lane Hall, University of Michigan, Ann Arbor, Michigan 48109 or by calling (313) 665-2490.

Two other academic associations are also committed to the sponsorship of teaching panels on the Vietnam War. The World History Association has recently lent support to the study of the place of Southeast Asia and the Vietnam War in world history. Further information can be obtained by writing to the World History Association's Executive Director, Richard Rosen, at the Department of History and Politics, Drexel University, Philadelphia, Pennsylvannia 19104. The annual meeting of the Popular Culture Association has often been the venue for the presentation of challenging and speculative research on the Vietnam War. They have also been the venue for teaching workshops that have addressed such issues as teaching about pre-1964 Indochina, creating the Vietnam experience in the classroom and teaching the literature of the war. Information regarding such workshops can be obtained by writing to The Center for Popular Culture, Bowling Green State University, Bowling Green, Kentucky 43403-0220.

CONCLUSION

The material currently available to those seeking to improve the quality of teaching about the Vietnam War is not as well-developed or as readily available as instructors might wish. There is, however, every reason to believe that the number of teaching guides, classroom materials and workshops will expand to meet the need for such resources created by the contemporary increase in interest in a war that has left an indelible mark on modern history.

Appendix:
Selected Course Syllabi

HISTORY 369: THE VIETNAM WAR
UNITED STATES AIR FORCE ACADEMY
MAJOR MARK CLODFELTER

Nature and Purpose of the Course

Clausewitz was the first military thinker to place warfare in its proper position within the general flow of human affairs, and his perspective will govern our examination of the Vietnam War. War, Clausewitz asserted, is an extension of politics. To undertake warfare for any other reason is absurd. Armed conflict is one of many tools that a government may use to achieve national objectives, but since war carries great human and economic costs, its objectives must be worthwhile, realistic, and achievable. Moreover, a nation must assure that it has sufficient material and moral strength to sustain itself over the course of a conflict. Many factors enter into success or failure in war: leadership, fighting qualities, logistics, economics, the home front, luck and the ever present "fog of war" are only a few. Throughout war's trials and tribulations, the political objective must always be kept firmly in mind, for it must govern the course and nature of combat if personal and national sacrifices are to make any sense. War, then, is a means to further national objectives, and to understand why it succeeds or fails, the true student of war must look to its many dimensions. Our central question in this course is: How well did the United States government understand and practice this view of warfare in Vietnam?

Each of you holds a special interest and motivation for taking this course. You must be prepared, however, to examine a number of aspects relating to the war that you might not investigate yourself. Battlefield tactics and campaigns will be an important part of our study, as well as the political pressures experienced by national leaders. The many frustrations of the war will also demand your attention, and you will be asked to explain why the war was so misjudged by American leaders and the general population. "The Vietnam War" will be an exciting course that will give you an unsurpassed experience in understanding the nature of warfare as it applies to our nation and its goals. In the end, you will come away far better equipped to serve as an Air Force officer.

Course Objectives

To determine the political motivations behind America's involvement in Vietnam; to understand the American military's approach to war-fighting in Vietnam and the approach taken by the Viet Minh, Viet Cong, and North Vietnamese; to gain an appreciation for the geography, culture, and history of Indochina; and to understand the complex nature of limited war in the modern era.

The true test of an education is the ability to communicate knowledge. Therefore, a great amount of emphasis in this course will be placed on analysis and writing. Your ideas, no matter how brilliant, are useless if you cannot communicate them to someone else.

Course Calendar

DATES	LESSON	TITLE	ASSIGNMENT
5-6 Jan	1	Administration and Introduction	
8-9 Jan	2	Clausewitz and Warfare	Handout: Crowl Harmon Lecture
10-11 Jan	3	Geography of Indochina	Handout: *Vietnam War Almanac*, 1-12
12-16 Jan	4	Vietnamese Culture *Geography Quiz*	Handout: *Tradition*, 15-41
17-18 Jan	5	Early Vietnamese History	Karnow, 89-127
19-22 Jan	6	French Colonialism and Japanese Occupation	Karnow, 128-160
23-24 Jan	7	War with the French	Karnow, 161-188

<u>DATES</u>	<u>LESSON</u>	<u>TITLE</u>	<u>ASSIGNMENT</u>
25-26 Jan	8	The French Failure	Karnow, 188-205 Maurer, 68-79
29-30 Jan	9	Nation Building, North and South	Karnow, 206-239 Truong, Chap 5,7
31 Jan-1 Feb	10	Kennedy and Diem *First Written* *Assignment Due*	Karnow, 240-69 Truong, Chap 8 *Maurer, 99-107
2-5 Feb	11	Diem's Demise	Karnow, 270-311 Maurer, 89-99
6-7 Feb	12	LBJ Takes Over	Karnow, 312-348 Truong, Chap 9
8-9 Feb	13	Disorder and Decisions: From the Tonkin Gulf to the Eve of Sustained Involvement	Karnow, 349-386
12-13 Feb	14	LBJ Goes to War—Or Does He?	Karnow, 387-415
14-15 Feb	15	*GR-1* (Common GR Period, 14 Feb. Lectinars TBD)	
16-20 Feb	16	Enclaves and Escalation	Karnow, 415-426 Lewy, 50-56
21-22 Feb	17	Air Mobile and the Ia Drang (Guest Speaker)	Maurer, 137-148
23-26 Feb	18	Bombs, Bridges, MiGs, Pauses, Oil, Electricity, and Frustration	Handout, Clodfelter, 1-25
27-28 Feb	19	A Pilot's View of the Air War (Guest Speaker)	Maurer, 365-371 381-393, 426-436
1-2 Mar	20	The Ground War, 1966-1967	Lewy, 56-76

DATES	LESSON	TITLE	ASSIGNMENT
5-6 Mar	21	The Ground War: A Personal View (Guest Speaker)	Maurer, 158-195
7-8 Mar	22	The Enemy's View of the War (Guest Speaker) *Second Written Assignment Due*	Truong, Chaps 10,14
9-12 Mar	23	The War's Impact on the South	Maurer, 289-309, 329-339
13-14 Mar	24	On the Eve of the Storm	Karnow, 474-514
15-16 Mar	25	Tet: American Victory?	Karnow, 515-545
19-20 Mar	26	Tet: American Defeat?	Karnow, 545-566
21-22 Mar	27	*GR-2* (Common GR Period, 22 Mar. Lectinars TBD)	
23 Mar-2 Apr	28	US Special Ops in Vietnam (Guest Speaker)	Maurer, 340-364
3-4 Apr	29	Nixon's War	Karnow, 567-601
5-6 Apr	30	Vietnamization	Lewy, 190-195 Maurer, 520-525
9-10 Apr	31	Invasions of Cambodia and Laos	Karnow, 601-636
11-12 Apr	32	The Easter Offensive the ARVN, and American CAS (Guest Speaker)	Lewy, 196-201
13-16 Apr	33	Mining, Linebacker I, and Linebacker II	Maurer, 542-551 Clodfelter Handout, 25-37

DATES	LESSON	TITLE	ASSIGNMENT
17-18 Apr	34	America's Declining Role (Guest Speaker) *Third Written Assignment Due*	Maurer, 249-271, 504-519
19-20 Apr	35	The American POW Experience (Guest Speaker)	Lewy, 332-342 Maurer, 408-427
23-24 Apr	36	A Decent Interval and Collapse	Karnow, 655-670 Maurer, 606-613 *Truong, Chap 21
25-26 Apr	37	The Summers Thesis: A Critique	Summers and Porter Handouts
30 Apr-1 May	38	My Lai and War Crimes	Lewy, 307-331, 356-364
2-3 May	39	The War's Impact on the United States	Karnow, 1-27
4-7 May	40	The War's Impact on the American Military	Maurer, 445-465
8-9 May	41	The Lessons of Vietnam?	*Foreign Affairs* Handouts
10-11 May	42	The Historiography of the War	

* Denotes Optional Reading Assignment

Course Materials

a. Stanley Karnow, *Vietnam: A History*

b. Guenter Lewy, *America in Vietnam*

c. Harry Maurer, *Strange Ground: Americans in Vietnam 1945-1975, An Oral History*

d. Truong Nhu Tang, *A Viet Cong Memoir*

e. Jack Broughton, *Thud Ridge* (This book is to be read on your own during the semester, and your knowledge of it will be tested on the final exam.)

f. Numerous handouts provided by the instructor

Assignment Instructions

All written assignments will be structured and documented according to Kate Turabian's *A Student Guide To Writing Term Papers:*

a. *Written Assignment 1 (150 points)*
    Date Due: Lesson 10, beginning of class

It is 1 May 1954. You are a senior-level advisor to President Dwight D. Eisenhower. You have known Eisenhower for many years—you served as an Army brigadier general on his SHAPE staff in World War II—and he has complete faith in your judgment. The President has come to you seeking advice on how he—and the United States—should respond to the French request for assistance at Dien Bien Phu. He presents you with several cables and transcripts that he has recently received on the French crisis and asks you to "give it your best shot." Using these materials and your own intuition, draft a 2-3 page proposal that you think "Ike" would find acceptable.
The President will be especially interested in the logic of your idea, as well as the manner in which you organize your thoughts and your clarity of expression. Spelling or grammatical errors irritate him more than double-bogeying on a par 5.

b. *Written Assignment 2 (175 points)*
    Date Due: Lesson 22, beginning of class

It is 20 July 1965. You are a personal friend of President Lyndon Johnson, and the President highly respects your opinions. Like him, you are a native Texan, and you campaigned hard for his successful Senate bid in 1948. Because you are such a close friend, he has come to you to seek your advice on what to do in Vietnam. Secretary of Defense Robert S. McNamara has just returned from a visit to Saigon to review the situation in South Vietnam. The President has given you a copy of McNamara's report, as well as several other studies by high-ranking political and military figures. He wants your advice on precisely what the United States should do in Southeast Asia—should it escalate the war, continue at the same level of intensity, or perhaps get out? Given the reports you have received, and your own knowledge of

Johnson's ambitions and his manner of dealing with problems, suggest a response that you think he would accept.

The President has stressed above all that your response must be logical, well-organized, easy-to-understand, and no more than 4 typed pages. He especially despises those Harvard-types who write only in bureaucratic jargon. Yet he has also said he wants something "more than a sixth-grade level that has a misspelled word every other line."

c. *Written Assignment 3 (200 points)*
    Date Due: Lesson 34, beginning of class

It is 27 March 1968. Once more President Johnson faces a dilemma over Vietnam, and he has returned for advice to his old friend who provided him with sound guidance in the summer of 1965. The Tet Offensive has now wreaked havoc throughout South Vietnam, American troops are besieged at Khe Sanh, public protest against the war is at a fever pitch, and Johnson has only narrowly defeated "peace candidate" Eugene McCarthy in the New Hampshire primary. The President again provides you with documents from high-level civilian and military officials. He asks you to review their suggestions and then develop a recommendation of your own. You are aware that Johnson is in an extremely somber mood, and because of your friendship, any suggestion that you make regarding Vietnam is likely to have a profound impact. Given the gravity of the situation, prepare a response that you believe Lyndon Johnson would find acceptable.

He has told you to be forthright, but to justify your recommendation fully in a 4-5 page report. As always, he is interested in the most logical alternative you can provide, and he wants it soundly organized, clearly written, and error free.

HISTORY 301: AMERICA'S VIETNAM WAR
COLLEGE OF WOOSTER
JOHN M. GATES

Course Purpose

The course will focus on a number of questions such as: why did the United States become so deeply involved in a war that proved so frustrating and divisive; what was the nature of the war, particularly for the people participating in it or living in the zone of conflict; why did the United States fail so completely in Vietnam; and what lessons can Americans learn from the Vietnam experience?

Course Core Readings

Core reading is provided by the following books available at the bookstore: Philip Caputo, *A Rumor of War*; Stanley Karnow, *Vietnam: A History*; and Gareth Porter, editor, *Vietnam: A History in Documents*.

Course Evaluation

Students are expected to keep a journal which will count approximately 50-60% of the course grade. Another 20-25% will be based on participation in class discussions and quizzes or other written exercises where appropriate. The individual reading project report and final paper (described on the last page of the syllabus) will count for the remaining 20-25%.

The Course Journal

Each student is to keep a journal in which he or she will make regular, dated entries. The journal entries should be thoughtful, reflective comments on the assigned work of the course (both the reading and the in-class work, including the TV documentaries shown in class) and on additional work undertaken independently by the student. Students are expected to read widely and think extensively about the war in Vietnam and its legacy. The journal is to be a record of results of that work in which the reactions to and thoughts about the material are presented coherently in a series of written comments.

Journals are to be brought to class each day. They may be collected and evaluated at any time and should be kept up to date. Comments on reading assignments should be written *before* the class in which the reading is to be discussed.

The journals will be evaluated primarily on the quality of the comments contained in them and not on the quantity of writing. A perceptive analytical comment that demonstrates considerable thought is better than a long, rambling summary of one's reading.

Late journals or other written work will not be accepted nor make-up exams given unless the student has a written and verifiable excuse signed by the Dean of Students or the Dean of the College stating that incapacitating illness, hospitalization, incarceration or some other unanticipated catastrophe prevented completion of the assignment on time.

Attendance

Regular attendance is expected, and cutting will result in a lower grade.

Television Documentaries

Episodes of the documentary television series, "Vietnam: A Television History," are on reserve in the audio-visual section of the library. You are responsible for arranging to view each of them at your own convenience before the class following each *Documentary* date indicated in the "Schedule of Classes and Assignments" which begins on p. 3 of the syllabus. Each video tape contains two episodes, so you need to be careful to make certain you are viewing the correct cassette.

The episodes will also be shown in the Film Preview Room of the library or the Blue Room (check schedule) at 7:00 p.m. on the days marked *Documentary* in accordance with the following schedule:

Tues., Jan. 16—episode 1 (tape 1/1st half), "The Roots of War."

Tues., Jan. 30—episode 2 (tape 1/2d half), "The First Vietnam War."

Tues., Feb. 6—episode 3 (tape 2/1st half), "America's Mandarin."

Thur., Feb. 15—episode 4 (tape 2/2d half), "LBJ Goes to War."

Thur., Feb. 22—episode 5 (tape 3/1st half), "America Takes Charge."

Sun., Feb. 25—episode 6 (tape 3/2d half), "With America's Enemy."

Tues., Mar. 20—episode 7 (tape 4/1st half), "Tet, 1968."

Thur., Mar. 22—episode 9 (tape 5/1st half), "No Neutral Ground."

Sun., Mar. 25—episode 8 (tape 4/2d half), "Vietnamizing the War."

Thur., Apr. 5—episode 11 (tape 6/1st half), "Homefront, U.S.A."

Thur., Apr. 12—episode 10 (tape 5/2d half), "Peace Is at Hand."

Sun., Apr. 15—episode 12 (tape 6/2d half), "The End of the Tunnel."

Tues., Apr. 17—episode 13 (tape 7), "Legacies."

Schedule of Classes and Assignments
Americans Thrown into War

Mon., Jan. 8—   Introduction to the course.

Wed., Jan. 10—   Read the first half of Caputo (about 125 pp. of easy
                  reading). Why has the author created the work you are
                  reading? What is the author trying to tell us? What
                  techniques are used to accomplish that end?

Fri., Jan. 12—   Finish Caputo (another 125 pp. of easy reading). What
                  does the book tell you about (1) the nature of the war,
                  (2) the people fighting in it, (3) their own view of their
                  role? After finishing the book, what is your opinion of
                  American behavior in Vietnam? Why do you think the
                  United States was involved in the war?

                  Select the one quotation from the book that you believe
                  best characterizes the nature of the war for the
                  Americans participating in it.

Mon., Jan. 15—   Karnow, ch. 1 (45 pp.). What are the key issues and
                  questions that Karnow identifies? How are they related
                  to the material contained in Caputo?

How Did the U.S. Become Involved in Vietnam?

Tues., Jan. 16—   *Documentary*, Blue Room, episode 1 (tape 1/1st half),
                  "The Roots of War."

Wed., Jan. 17—   Karnow, ch. 2 & ch. 3 to p. 118 (64 pp.). Why was
                  France able to control its Southeast Asian colony for so
                  long? What were the roots of Vietnamese opposition
                  to French colonialism and when did they develop?

Fri., Jan. 19—   Karnow, ch. 3, pp. 118-127 & ch. 4 (42 pp.). How did
                  effective Vietnamese opposition to French colonialism
                  develop? Why were the French unable to prevent the
                  Vietnamese revolution from developing? What might
                  the French have done to prevent the revolution?

Mon., Jan. 22—   Porter, documents #1-28 (42 pp.). Be prepared to
                  identify the most relevant passages from the documents
                  in the assignment that you believe provide the best
                  answer to these questions: (1) What were the goals of
                  the Vietminh? (2) What were the goals of the French?
                  (3) What were the goals of the U.S.? Given the
                  situation in Vietnam, what do you believe U.S. policy
                  should have been at the end of World War II?

Wed., Jan. 24—   Porter, documents #29-57 (43 pp.). Select the relevant
                  passages from the three documents that you believe
                  provide the best answer to the above questions for the
                  period from 1946 to early 1950.

Fri., Jan. 26—   *Media Assignment*: Using newspapers, news magazines,
                  and other periodicals published at the time and readily

available to the general public, be prepared to describe the impression the average American might have had of the war in Indochina in the period from 1950 to the end of 1953.

Mon., Jan. 29— Porter, documents #58-84 (42 pp.). Comparing the documents with those read earlier, answer the following questions: (1) How did U. S. policy regarding Indochina change between 1945 and 1954? (2) Why did those changes take place? (3) What policy do you believe the U. S. should have followed and why?

Tues., Jan. 30— *Documentary*, Blue Room, episode 2 (tape 1/2d half), "The First Vietnam War, 1946-1954."

Wed., Jan. 31— Karnow, ch. 5 (45 pp.). How do you explain the French failure and the Vietminh success? What might the French have done to be more successful?

Fri., Feb. 2— Porter, documents #85-108 (38 pp.). Select specific passages to answer the following questions: Was South Vietnam created as a sovereign nation? What was the status of North and South Vietnam under the agreement reached at Geneva? What promises did the U. S. make at Geneva?

Mon., Feb. 5— Porter, documents #109-130 (40 pp.). Using references from the documents answer the following questions: Why were the elections mentioned in the Geneva accords not held? When did the war between the Saigon government and the guerrillas begin again? Why? Who do you believe was responsible for irritating it?

Tues., Feb. 6— *Documentary*, Blue Room, episode 3 (tape 2/1st half), "America's Mandarin, 1954-1953."

Wed., Feb. 7— Karnow, ch. 6 (34 pp.). What problems faced the Saigon government in its attempt to establish an independent nation in South Vietnam? What alternative policies might have been pursued to improve the situation?

An American War in Vietnam

Fri., Feb. 9— Karnow, ch. 7 & Porter, documents #131-49 (59 pp.). What led the Kennedy administration to break the Geneva ceiling on military advisors and become more deeply involved in Vietnam?

Mon., Feb. 12—   Karnow, ch. 8 & Porter, documents #150-63 (60 pp.).
                  Why did the Kennedy administration support the
                  military coup against Diem? Was that a wise decision?

Wed., Feb. 14—   Karnow, ch. 9 & Porter, documents #164-76 (63 pp.).
                  What was the situation in Vietnam following the coup
                  against Diem? Why did the Johnson administration
                  believe the U. S. should get more deeply involved in the
                  war? Was that a wise decision? What other options
                  existed? What chance did the Seaborn mission have;
                  could a peace agreement have been negotiated in 1964?

Thur., Feb. 15—   *Documentary*, Film Preview Room, episode 4 (tape 2/2d
                  half), "LBJ Goes to War, 1964-1965."

Fri., Feb. 16—   Karnow, ch. 10 & Porter, documents #177-93 (61 pp.).
                  What happened in the Gulf of Tonkin? Did Lyndon
                  Johnson deceive Congress and the American people?

Mon., Feb. 19—   *Media Assignment*: Answer the following questions using
                  newspapers and periodicals from the time surrounding
                  the Gulf of Tonkin incident in 1964 and the beginning
                  of the U. S. bombing of North Vietnam. How accurate
                  was the press coverage of the events (compared to
                  material read for Feb. 16)? How was the U. S.
                  commitment in Vietnam explained to the American
                  people? How did the press react to Johnson's
                  escalation of the war? Were any Americans protesting
                  American involvement in Vietnam?

Wed., Feb. 21—   Karnow, ch. 11 & Porter, documents #194-210 (66 pp.).
                  Why did the Johnson Administration begin a sustained
                  bombing campaign against North Vietnam? What did
                  the Johnson Administration believe it might accomplish
                  by greater involvement? What problems confronted the
                  Americans trying to fight in Vietnam?

Thur., Feb. 22—   *Documentary*, Film Preview Room, episode 5 (tape 3/1st
                  half), "America Takes Charge, 1965-1967."

Fri., Feb. 23—   Karnow, ch. 12 (47 pp.). How did the U. S. plan to win
                  the war in Vietnam? Be prepared to describe the
                  American strategy in Vietnam. What were the strengths
                  and weaknesses of the U. S. approach?

Sun., Feb. 25—   *Documentary*, Film Preview Room, episode 6 (tape 3/2d
                  half), "With America's Enemy."

Mon., Feb. 26—   Using information from the documentary and the
                  following documents from Porter, come to class
                  prepared to give an intelligence briefing on "The
                  Communist Enemy in Vietnam," citing specific
                  documents to support your findings. Use Porter

documents #s 109, 113, 115, 122, 123, 124, 125, 126, 128, 130, 147, 151, 164, 177, 186, 187, 191, 194, 201, 203, & 209. In particular, be prepared to describe the communist strategy and note its strengths and weaknesses.

Wed., Feb. 28— Karnow, ch. 13 (41 pp.). What was the situation in Vietnam in 1966-1967? Why do you think the Americans took the approach they did to fighting the war? How wise was the American policy? What alternatives would have been better?

Fri., Mar. 2— Porter, documents #211-27 (32 pp.). Why could peace negotiations not be arranged? What did the Johnson Administration hope would happen in Vietnam? What was the actual situation by the end of 1967?

Spring Break: Mar. 3-18.

Mon., Mar. 19— Karnow, ch. 14 & Porter, documents #228-36 (65 pp.). What happened at Khe Sanh and in the rest of Vietnam at Tet? What did the Communists hope to achieve? What did they achieve? How would you characterize the situation in Vietnam in the months after Tet? In the U. S.?

Tues., Mar. 20— *Documentary*, Blue Room, episode 7 (tape 4/1st half), "Tet, 1968."

Wed., Mar. 21— *Media Assignment*: The reporting of the Khe Sanh battle and the Communist Tet offensive has provoked a continuing debate. Using newspaper and magazine articles covering the period January through March 1968, assess the reports. What kind of response do you believe the coverage would evoke in the readers? Does the coverage have an antiwar bias? Did it fit the facts in the documents or presented in Karnow, ch. 14?

Thur., Mar. 22— *Documentary*, Film Preview Room, episode 9 (tape 5/1st half), "No Neutral Ground: Cambodia and Laos."

Fri., Mar. 23— The United States dropped more bombs in Vietnam, Laos, and Cambodia than it dropped in World War II. The value of the bombing is one topic that continues to be debated by individuals attempting to evaluate the American approach to the war. Use scholarly journals or chapters in individual books in the library, prepare to debate the following resolutions: (1) The American bombing campaign in Indochina hurt the U. S. cause more than it helped, and (2) The bombing campaign

could have worked to end the war had it been
implemented correctly.

The Shock of Failure

Sun., Mar. 25— *Documentary*, Film Preview Room, episode 8 (tape 4/2d
half), "Vietnamizing the War, 1969-1973."

Mon., Mar. 26— Karnow, ch. 15 & Porter, documents #237-43 (67 pp.).
How did the Nixon administration's approach to the war
differ from that of the Johnson administration?

Wed., Mar. 28— *Media Assignment*: In November 1969 the American
public received the shocking news of an incredible
atrocity of war, the My Lai Massacre. Starting with the
news in November, follow the story of the massacre, the
trial of Lt. Calley and Capt. Medina, and the
investigation of the attempt to cover up the event. Why
had the massacre occurred?

Fri., Mar. 30— *No Class* (Prof. at out of town meeting.)

Mon., Apr. 2— *Mock Trial*: Was Lt. Calley guilty of a war crime? Were
the realities of the war in Vietnam a mitigating
circumstance? Come to class prepared to prosecute or
defend Calley. Also have notes that will enable you to
play the role of any of the individuals you have read
about who might have been called as a witness.

Wed., Apr. 4— *Media Assignment*: A second shock to the nation came
with the invasion of Cambodia only a few months after
the My Lai story. It was accompanied by protests in
which college students at Kent State University were
killed. For Americans reading newspaper and magazine
accounts of the invasion, protests, and killings in May
1970, what would appear to be the answers to the
following questions: Why had the Nixon administration
invaded Cambodia? Why were the students protesting?
How widespread were the protests? Why had students
been killed?

Thur., Apr. 5— *Documentary*, Film Preview Room, episode 11
(tape 6/1st half), "Homefront U.S.A."

Fri., Apr. 6— Cohen "Documents" (36 pp. *on closed reserve in the
library*). Which side of the antiwar debate would you
have taken in 1969? What reasoning would you have
used to support your views? What would you have
answered to the question, "Should the U. S. withdraw
from the war in Vietnam?"

Mon., Apr. 9—   *Media Assignment*: A third shock came with the
                 publication of the "Pentagon Papers" in the *New York
                 Times* starting on June 13, 1971. What would readers
                 have learned about the American war in Vietnam and
                 the government's role in it from the stories that flowed
                 from the release of the secret documents contained in
                 the "Pentagon Papers" stories? If you had been an
                 editor at the *NYT* would you have printed the secret
                 documents? If you had been a judge would you have
                 supported the government's attempt to prevent
                 publication of the "Pentagon Papers" or the *NYT's* right
                 to publish them?

Wed., Apr. 11—   Karnow, pp. 623-55 & Porter, documents #244-262
                 (66 pp.). Why did the Nixon administration sign the
                 Paris accord? What were the terms of the agreement?
                 Was it "peace with honor" as the President had
                 promised, or had the U. S. "sold out" South Vietnam?

Thur., Apr. 12— *Documentary*, Film Preview Room, episode 10 (tape 5/2d
                 half), "Peace Is at Hand."

Fri., Apr. 13—   *Media Assignment*: In December 1972 the Nixon
                 administration authorized extremely heavy bombing of
                 North Vietnam. Reading newspaper and magazine
                 accounts in late December 1972 and in January 1973,
                 what would Americans have known about the bombing
                 campaign? What was the reaction of editors and
                 reporters to the event? How did the Nixon
                 administration explain the bombing?

Sun., Apr. 15—   *Documentary*, Film Preview Room, episode 12 (tape 6/2d
                 half), "The End of the Tunnel."

Mon., Apr. 16—   Karnow, pp. 655-70 & Porter, documents #263-end of
                 book (39 pp.). Why did the U. S. completely abandon
                 South Vietnam in 1975? Did the U. S. betray South
                 Vietnam?

The Lessons and the Legacy of Vietnam's War

Tue., Apr. 17—   *Documentary*, Blue Room, episode 13 (7th tape),
                 "Legacies."

NOTE: The last journal entry required is for the next class. After
                 that all your effort should be devoted to the final paper
                 and journal entries are no longer required.

Wed., Apr. 18— Xerox articles by Col. Harry Summers, Jr. & John M. Gates evaluating the U. S. approach to the war (16 double pp. *on closed reserve in the library*). What are the differences of interpretation evident in the two articles? How do you explain those differences? What are the implications of each author's view as far as the development of future American policy is concerned?

Fri., Apr. 20— Come to class with a written statement of your topic for the *individual reading projects* and a tentative bibliography of your proposed reading. The topic should be one that was not covered by the assigned reading. Examples of the kind of topics one might study include (1) disagreements over the war's lessons such as that identified in the reading for Apr. 18, (2) problems veterans have faced upon their return to the U. S., (3) the problems facing any of the countries of Indochina following the war, (4) the "killing fields" phenomenon in Cambodia, (5) the policy legacy of the war (the War Powers Act, for example).

Mon., Apr. 23— Reports on individual reading projects.
Wed., Apr. 25— Reports on individual reading projects.
Fri., Apr. 27— Reports on individual reading projects.
Final Paper— Write a critical essay of no more than 10 typed, double-spaced pages on "The Lessons of America's Vietnam War" as they relate to your individual reading. Your conclusions should be supported by specific examples (with accompanying references to the specific pages in the sources read during the term indicated by footnotes).

The final paper is due in the instructor's office before 9:30 p.m., Tues., May 1 (the end of the second hour of the regularly scheduled exam time for the course).

HISTORY 341-01, THE U.S./VIETNAM WAR
UNIVERSITY OF ALABAMA
INSTRUCTORS: H. JONES AND R. ROBEL

Required Readings and Textbooks

Stanley Karnow, *Vietnam, A History*; Bernard Fall, *Hell in A Very Small Place: The Siege of Dien Bien Phu*; David Halberstam, *Ho*; and Truong Nhu Tang, *A Viet Cong Memoir*.

Examinations

There will be two examinations given for this course. The Mid-term examination will cover materials in Karnow from Chapters 1 through 7. The final examination will cover materials for the remainder of the text and also will include a special section dealing with Truong's A Viet Cong Memoir. The examinations must be written in ink or ball point (pencil is not permitted). These examinations MUST BE TAKEN ON THE DATES SCHEDULED! Any exceptions to this schedule must be truly extraordinary and MUST be approved by BOTH instructors PRIOR to the examination period.

Book Reviews

Two Book Reviews are required and they will be on Fall's *Hell in a Very Small Place* and Halberstam's *Ho*. The reviews must follow accepted guidelines . . . about 600 words, typed, and double-space. Examples of proper reviews will be provided for reference.

Both reviews MUST be presented on the scheduled dates and there will be no exceptions. Failure to present the reviews on these dates will result in an "F" grade for the review.

> *Hell in a Very Small Place* is due on Sept. 14th
> *Ho* is due on Oct. 26

The reviews are to be presented as a First Draft on the scheduled dates, yet every effort should be made to prepare them as if they were a finished product! They will be corrected and returned to the students for a Second Draft submission. A deadline will be announced later as concerns this Second Draft and this draft should reflect all recommendations for changes. Only the Second Draft will be evaluated, but the First Draft must be appended to the Second Draft so that we can check the results of this whole project.

Map Assignment

A map assignment will be given, but there will be no evaluation of this for the final grade. Yet, it must be accomplished for successful completion of this course.

Final Grade Determination

Undergraduate Students:

Mid-term Examination	35%
Final Examination	35%
Book Reviews	30%

Graduate Students:

Mid-term Examination	35%
Final Examination	35%
Term Paper	15%
Book Reviews	15%

Graduate Student Credit

All students who take this course for Graduate Credit will be required to write a major research paper in addition to all that is required for undergraduate students. This paper will entail newspaper/periodical research. The nature of the project is to attempt to "re-live" some particular event in the Vietnam War period by consulting the newspaper coverage of this event as well as investigating the periodical and editorial assessment of this event. The event should not extend beyond a two week period, although periodical coverage may extend beyond the two-week limit. The purpose of the paper is to make some effort to assess what might be the understanding, awareness and appreciation of the general American public as relates to this event at the time it took place. Careful documentation will be required and will be thoroughly investigated by the instructors. All topics must be approved by the instructors prior to commencing work on them.

Tentative Lecture Schedule

CLASS MTG.	DATE	LECTURER	TOPIC
1. August	26	J&R	Orientation
2.	28	R	Asian Historical Setting (Karnow, Ch. 1)
3.	31	R	Vietnam to 1850 (Karnow, Ch. 2)
4. September	2	J	Foundations of America's Asian Policy: Image and Reality

CLASS MTG.	DATE	LECTURER	TOPIC
5. September	4	R	France in Indochina, 1850-1940 (Karnow, Ch. 3)
6.	9	R	French Colonial Rule & Role of Vietnamese
7.	11	R	Development of Vietnamese Resistance
8.	14	J	WW II in Asia: A Racial War?
9.	16	R	WW II in Asia: The Asian Perspective
10.	18	J	WW II America's Initial Interest in Indochina
11.	21	R	WW II Indochina
12.	23	R	Ho Chi Minh and the Vietminh
13.	25	J	America's Lost Opportunity? Ho Chi Minh, Archimedes Patti & the Return of France to Indochina (Karnow, Ch. 4)
14.	28	R	Asian Developments, 1945-1953
15.	30	J	The First Indochinese War: Truman's Pledge to France (Karnow, Ch. 5)
16. October	2	J	The First Indochinese War: Eisenhower, Dien Bien Phu & The Geneva Accords of 1954
17.	5	J	Nation Building in South Vietnam, I (Karnow, Ch. 6)
18.	7	J	Nation Building in South Vietnam, II
19.	9	R	Asia & Vietnam in the 1950's (Karnow, Ch. 7)

CLASS MTG.	DATE	LECTURER	TOPIC
20. October	12		MID-TERM EXAMINATION PART I
21.	14		MID-TERM EXAMINATION PART II
22.	16	R	Asia in the 1960's
23.	19	J	Perils of a Mandarin: The Second Vietnam War & Kennedy's Commitment to Diem (Karnow, Ch. 8)
24.	21	J	The Buddhist Crisis & Assassination of Diem
25.	23	R	Vietnam in the early 1960's
26.	26	J	Toward Total Commitment: Gulf of Tonkin Controversy (Karnow, Ch. 9 and 10)
27.	28	J	Holding the Line: "Rolling Thunder" & the 1st American Combat Troops in Vietnam
28.	30	J	Americanizing the War (Karnow, Chs. 11 & 12)
29. November	2	J	The American Peace Offensive (Ch. 13)
30.	4	J	Retreat from Commitment: Tet & the Beginnings of Vietnamization (Karnow, Ch. 14)
31.	6	J&R	Film Presentation
32.	9	R	Vietnam, 1965-1968 Part I
33.	11	R	Vietnam, 1965-1968 Part II
34.	13	R	Protest Movement in the USA in the 1960's

CLASS MTG.	DATE	LECTURER	TOPIC
35. November	16	J	The Nixon-Kissinger Policy of Detente: Vietnamization and Cambodia (Karnow, Ch. 15)
36.	18	J	Toward "Peace with Honor": My Lai, The Pentagon Papers & C o n t i n u e d Disillusionment
37.	20	R	Vietnam, 1968-1970
38.	23	R	Cambodia and Laos, 1970-1975
39.	25	R	Vietnam, 1970-1975
40. December	2	J	Paris Cease-Fire Agreement of Jan. 27, 1973 (Karnow, Ch. 16, pp. 625-55)
41.	4	J	The 3rd Indochina War: Fall of Saigon & the End of the American Experience in Vietnam (Karnow, Ch. 16, pp. 655-70)
42.	7	R	"Postwar" Vietnam: The Legacy
43.	9	J	"Postwar" United States: The Legacy
44.	11	J&R	"Lesson of Vietnam" (re-read Karnow, Ch. 1)
45.	15		FINAL EXAMINATION 8:00 - 10:30 AM

HISTORY 158: THE VIETNAM WAR AND AMERICA
EMORY UNIVERSITY
DR. WILLIAMS

Course Description

This course will include lectures, discussions and film, focusing on the American phase of the Vietnam conflict. We will review the political and diplomatic circumstances of American participation in Vietnam, explore military planning and execution, and look at the results of the war on the homefront.

Course Requirements and Evaluation

Grades will be determined by a midterm and a final. The
Grading scale is: 100-93 A; 92-90 A-; 89-87 B+; 86-83 B;
                      82-80 B-; 79-77 C+; 76-73 C; 72-70 C-;
                      69-67 D+; 66-60 D; 59-F

Midterm Exam: Friday, March 9, 40% of grade
Final Exam: Wednesday, May 9, 8:30-11:00 am,
                   60% of grade.

Students may submit a paper to substitute for the midterm exam. The topic of the paper must be approved by the instructor before the end of the third week of classes. The paper (approximately 10-15 pages in length) is due on the last day of classes, April 30. The paper may be submitted to fulfill the College writing requirement, but only if the student has informed the instructor of his/her intention of doing so before the end of the third week of classes.

Students may also submit a paper which will fulfill the junior or senior paper requirements for the history department. See the instructor for approval of topic, deadlines, length, and percent of course credit.

P*L*E*A*S*E N*O*T*E! On the title page of your paper indicate which requirements it is designed to fulfill. You will not receive College or departmental credit for having fulfilled writing requirements unless you have: *informed the instructor and received topic approval before the end of the third week,* and *indicated on the title page of your paper which requirements it is designed to fulfill.*

Course Reading and Guest Lectures

Eight books are required and are available at the university bookstore.

Frances Fitzgerald, *Fire in the Lake*
Tim O'Brien, *If I Die in a Combat Zone*
Michael Herr, *Dispatches*
Baskir and Strauss, *Chance and Circumstance*
Norman Mailer, *Armies of the Night*
Gloria Emerson, *Winners and Losers*
Stephen Cohen, *Vietnam*
Al Santoli, *Everything We Had*

Reading

Week of Monday:

Jan.	30	Herr, all; Cohen, Ch. 1.
Feb.	13	Santoli, all; Cohen, Chs. 2, 3.
	27	O'Brien, all; Cohen, Chs. 4, 5.
Mar.	12	Fitzgerald 1-230; Cohen, Chs. 6, 7.
	26	Mailer, all; Cohen, Chs. 8, 9.
Apr.	9	Baskir and Strauss, all; Cohen, Chs. 10, 11.
	23	Emerson, Parts I, III, VI; Cohen, Chs. 12, 13.

Film

The course includes the recent 13-part PBS series on the Vietnam War. It will be shown on Jan. 30; Feb. 13, 27; Mar. 12, 26; Apr. 9, 23. The films will be shown in White Hall 206, *with the exception of Jan. 30 when White Hall 207 will be used*. The films will be shown at 4:30 p.m.; you may attend either showing.

HISTORY 100: THE HISTORY OF THE VIETNAM WAR
UNIVERSITY OF CALIFORNIA, BERKELEY
INDOCHINA PROJECT
DOUGLAS PIKE

Scope of the Course

This is an undergraduate/upper division course designed for students interested in the Vietnam War with no particular background in or knowledge of the war. Lectures will deal chiefly with the contending forces; the major events of the war with special attention to certain aspects (i.e., press, anti-war movements, political settlement efforts, etc.);

assessment of the war's outcome; postwar historical meaning. There are no prerequisites.

Course Requirements

The text to be used, which each student is expected to obtain *History of Vietnam: Reader*, Douglas Pike (editor), (*Copymat*, 2560 Bancroft). It is a combination reference work and collection of historical and contemporary articles about Vietnam War. An extensive bibliography titled *Vietnam War Reading Suggestions* will be distributed *gratis*. There are no required readings as such. Students are expected to familiarize themselves with the contents of the *Reader* and to draw on it as well as on the *Reading Suggestions* as needed to meet course requirements.

Course Grading

There will be an objective take-home midterm examination March 22 designed to test knowledge of the war and familiarity with the major contending forces and more significant events. It will count for 20 percent of the final grade. The final examination will be essay type open book and will be theme oriented. It will count for 40 percent of the final grade. The course term paper, which will count for 40 percent of the final grade, should be from 20 to 25 typewritten pages (hand-written papers are not acceptable). It may be descriptive, analytical or discursive although, given the brevity, of necessity should be fairly delimited in scope. It should raise some inquiry about a specific aspect of the war; after briefly setting down necessary background, it should draw a conclusion (or provide an answer). A list of suggested topics will be made available early in the course although students need not confine their choice to the list. Students are encouraged to consult the lecturer prior to beginning research for advice and suggestions on source materials. Deadline for papers: May 22nd.

Course Lecture Schedule

CLASS NO.	DATE	TITLE	ACTIVITY
1	Jan. 2	Organization of Class	Introduction
2	Jan. 25	"Vietnam War: Historical Overview"	Lecture
3	Jan. 30	"Culture of Indochina: Overview"	Lecture
4	Feb. 1	"Geo-Politics in Indochina's History"	Lecture
5	Feb. 6	"Vietnam: Major Historical Influences"	Lecture
6	Feb. 8	"Major Historical Influences" (cont.)	Lecture

CLASS NO.	DATE	TITLE	ACTIVITY
7	Feb. 13	"Philosophical/Theoretical Construct of the Vietnam War"	Lecture
8	Feb. 15	"Bibliography of the Vietnam War"	Lecture
9	Feb. 20	"Personalities, Major Figures in the Vietnam War"	Lecture
10	Feb. 22	"Competing Perceptions of the Vietnam War"	Lecture
11	Feb. 27	"Competing Perceptions...." (cont.)	Lecture
12	March 1	"Strategic Nature of the Vietnam War"	Lecture
13	March 6	"Strategic Nature of the War" (cont.)	Lecture
14	March 8	"Early Years of the Vietnam War"	Lecture
15	March 13	"Early Years of the War" (cont.)	Lecture
16	March 15	"Middle Years of the Vietnam War"	Lecture
17	March 20	"Middle Years of the War" (cont.)	Lecture
18	March 22	"Final Years of the Vietnam War"	Lecture

Spring Recess - Take Home Midterm

CLASS NO.	DATE	TITLE	ACTIVITY
19	April 3	"Final Years of the War" (cont.)	Lecture
20	April 5	"Paris and the Negotiated Settlement"	Lecture
21	April 10	"Researching the Vietnam War" (opt.)	Field Trip
22	April 12	"The Vietnam War Inside the Washington Beltway"	Lecture
23	April 17	"The Vietnam War Outside the Beltway"	Lecture
24	April 19	"The War, Mass Media & Public Opinion"	Lecture
25	April 24	"Historical Assessment of the War"	Lecture
26	April 26	"Assessment of the Vietnam War" (cont.)	Lecture
27	May 1	"Aftermath of the Vietnam War"	Lecture
28	May 3	"Aftermath" (cont.)	Lecture
29	May 8	Review/clean up	Dead Week
30	May 10	Review/clean up	Dead Week
31	May 19	Final Exam (Papers due)	Examination

FILM SHOWINGS (OPTIONAL): Wednesdays, 3-5 p.m., Room 26, Dwinelle Hall

HISTORY 480: TOPICS IN ASIAN HISTORY - VIETNAM
UNIVERSITY OF GUAM
GERALD BERKLEY

Course Purpose

Relatively few students know much about Vietnam or the character of United States participation in Asian affairs. The purpose of this course will be, at least partially, to rectify this. Vietnam will be examined, and this examination will be based on facts and careful analysis, on historical evaluation and critical regard for truth, and on awareness that policies are not abstractions, but realities that translate themselves into concrete actions and consequences, ultimate success or failure, possible tragedy and destruction.

Readings

The following volumes are to be purchased: Duiker, William, *Vietnam: Nation in Revolution*; Herring, George, *America's Longest War: The United States and Vietnam 1950-1975*; Caputo, Phillip, *A Rumor of War*.

Requirements

Students will be held responsible for all the material covered in the course: lectures, guest speakers, discussion, audio-visual material, and readings. The final grade will be determined in the basis of three (3) examinations - 30% each; and a research paper - 10%.

SCHEDULE: *READINGS*:

Aug. 21 -	The Vietnamese and	Duiker, pp. 1-48; 72-77
Sept. 16	French Colonialism	97-100; and 116-129
Sept. 18	EXAM I	
Sept 20 -	U. S. Involvement	Duiker, pp. 49-64; 77-89;
Oct. 27		1950-1968, 100-105; and
		129-131; Herring, pp. 3-220
Oct. 30	EXAM II	
Nov. 1 -	U. S. Involvement	Duiker, pp. 88-96; 106-115;
Dec. 1		and 131-155; Herring,
		pp. 221-281; Caputo, all
Dec. 5	FINAL	

HISTORY 500: THE VIETNAM WAR
TROY STATE UNIVERSITY
EARL H. TILFORD

Course Purpose

This seminar will introduce the graduate student to the Vietnam War. We will seek a balance between study of military, political, and social aspects of the war but, obviously, our focus will be on military history with an emphasis on the aerial dimensions of the conflict. Each student will do considerable supplemental reading. One should expect to read two books every three weeks. A 400 to 500 word review will be written for each book. The reviews will be typed, double-spaced, and reproduced so that all the students can benefit from your efforts. These reviews will be handy when you study for the comprehensive examinations.

Required Texts

George Herring, *America's Longest War*
Guenter Lewy, *America in Vietnam*
John Clark Pratt, *Vietnam Voices*

Conducting the Seminar

Every four-hour meeting period will begin with a lecture to set the focus for the evening's discussion. The lecture will be testable as will, in a sense, the discussion that follows. In the remaining time, comprising two or three 50-minute periods, seminar members will lead the discussion focusing on the books read for that evening. Books will be assigned at least two weeks in advance so that every student will have an opportunity to prepare adequately for the discussion and to write the accompanying review. Be prepared to talk about your book, the issues it raises, its place in the historiography, and its relative importance. Your report and the discussion should last 15 to 20 minutes. Book reviews count 1/3rd of your final grade.

Grading

I have a three-tiered grading policy which is designed to let the student develop his or her interest to the maximum extent possible.

Option A

This option is for the student with an interest in learning as much from the reading as possible. I recommend it for those who have a peripheral interest in Vietnam and who do not know a lot about the war.

Book reviews: 1/3rd of final grade
Final exam: 2/3rd of final grade

Option B

I recommend this option for students with stronger interests in the Vietnam War and for those who have some experience at graduate education. It involves a research paper as well as the flexibility of taking a final examination to balance your overall grade.

Book reviews: 1/3rd of final grade
Term paper: 1/3rd of final grade
Final exam: 1/3rd of final grade

The paper should be rather narrow in focus, concentrating on a special event of amplifying your interest in a certain area. It will be 15 to 20 pages in length.

Option C

This option is for the student with an interest in Vietnam, experience at graduate research, and a possible desire to pursue doctoral work. It involves doing a research paper of 25 to 35 pages in length. The paper should be of high quality, showing sophistication in handling sources as well as excellence in presentation.

Book reviews: 1/3rd of final grade
Research paper: 2/3rd of final grade

Papers will be typed, double-spaced and *will conform* with Kate Turabian's *A Manual for Writers* (4th edition).
Discuss your topic with me before you get started. While the possibilities are great, time is somewhat of a factor so do not dawdle.

Final Examination

The final examination will be comprehensive. Those choosing Option A will take a final examination twice as long as those selecting Option B.

Examinations will include fill in the blank items, map questions, a matching section requiring knowledge of authors and books, and essay questions which will test your mastery of the bibliography.

This course is demanding and qualifies in every way as an advanced, graduate-level experience. It is also interesting and fun if you prepare adequately.

Date/Lesson	Topic	Reading
24 March	Indochina Background	

hour 1: Administration and introductions

hour 2: Course overview and discussion

hour 3: Vietnam, 200 B.C. to 1900

hour 4: Vietnam, 200 B.C. to 1900

---

31 March	The French Indochina War	Pratt, pp. 1-62

hour 1: Lecture

hour 2: *The First Vietnam War*, Peter M. Dunn
      Why Vietnam, Archimedes Patti

hour 3: *Street Without Joy*, Bernard Fall
      Hell in a Very Small Place, Bernard Fall

hour 4: *The Struggle for Indochina, 1940-1955*,
      Ellen J. Hammer
      The Battle of Dien Bien Phu, Jules Roy

---

7 April	Truman and Eisenhower Years	Pratt, pp. 65-89
		Lewy, pp. 1-18
		Herring, pp. 1-72

hour 1: Lecture

hour 2: Lecture

Date/Lesson   Topic   Reading

hour 3: *In the Midst of Wars*, Edward Lansdale
        Anatomy of a Crisis, Bernard Fall
        Conflict in Laos, Arthur Dommen

hour 4: *The Ugly American*, Burdek and Lederer
        The Best and the Brightest, David Halberstam

---

14 April   Kennedy Years and the   Pratt, pp. 89-152
              Advisory Effort   Lewy, pp.   1-18
                                              Herring, pp. 73-107

hour 1: Lecture

hour 2: Movie, "Vietnam, How We Got In.
        Can We Get Out?"

hour 3: *Kennedy in Vietnam*, William J. Rust
        *Viet Cong: National Liberation Front of
          Vietnam*, Douglas Pike
        The Pathet Lao, Herbert Zasloff

hour 4: *U.S. Air Force in Southeast Asia: The
          Advisory Years*, R. Futrell
        Operation Ranch Hand, William A. Buckingham, Jr.
        The Making of a Quagmire, David Halberstam

April 21   Commitment and Stalemate   Pratt, pp. 157-253
                                              Lewy, pp. 42-126

hour 1: Lecture

hour 2: *Summons of the Trumpet*, Dave Richard Palmer
        *The Rise and Fall of an American
          Army*, Shelby Stanton

hour 3: *A Soldier Reports*, William Westmoreland
        Fire in the Lake, Francis Fitzgerald

hour 4: *Battles in the Monsoon*, S. L. A. Marshall
        The Two Vietnams, Bernard Fall

Date/Lesson	Topic	Reading

28 April   Air Power, 1961-68   Herring, pp. 108-181;
                                                    Pratt, pp. 254-323;
                                                    Lewy, pp. 374-417

hour 1: Lecture

hour 2: Movie, "There Is a Way"

hour 3: *Strategy for Defeat*, U. S. Grant Sharp
         Thud Ridge, Jack Broughton
         Rolling Thunder, James Clay Thompson

hour 4: *Pak Six*, G. I. Basel Discussion

5 May   Tet, Withdrawal, the   Lewy, pp. 126-161
                Anti-War Movement   Pratt, pp. 327-393
                                                    Herring, pp. 183-216

hour 1: Lecture

hour 2: Lecture

hour 3: *Backfire*, Loren Baritz
         War Without Fronts, Thomas C. Thayer
         *The Irony of Vietnam: The System
             Worked*, Leslie Gelb and Richard K. Betts

hour 4: *Lyndon Johnson and the American Dream*,
             Doris Kearns
         Tet, Don Oberdorfer

12 May   Nixon's War and   Pratt, pp. 393-548
                Vietnamization   Lewy, pp. 162-222

hour 1: Lecture

hour 2: *On Strategy*, Harry G. Summers, Jr.
         Self-Destruction, Cecil B. Currey (Cincinnatus)

Date/Lesson   Topic   Reading

hour 3: *The Laotian Fragments*, John Clark Pratt
        My Secret War, James Drury

hour 4: Movie, "Defend the Night"

---

19 May   1972 to the Fall   Herring, pp. 216-27
                                                Pratt, pp. 549-63

hour 1: Lecture

hour 2: *Sideshow*, William Shawcross
        Silence Was a Weapon, Stuart Herrington
        Twenty Years and Twenty Days, Nguyen Cao Ky

hour 3: *Decent Interval*, Frank Snepp
        Peace With Honor? Stuart Herrington
        The Final Collapse, Cao Van Vien

hour 4: Discussion

---

26 May   Reflections and   Pratt, pp. 641-669
            Conclusions

hour 1: Discussion and questions

hours 2-4: Final examination

POLITICAL SCIENCE 385/585: THE VIETNAM EXPERIENCE
CONVERSE COLLEGE
JOE P. DUNN

Introduction

We are in the midst of a resurgence of interest in the Vietnam War, a good time for the ambitious enterprise which I propose. Vietnam remains one of the most complex and controversial events in American history, one in which passion and polemic often prevail over scholarly assessment and rational discourse. While we will not eschew passion entirely, we will strive for objectivity, accuracy, fairness, and reasoned interpretation. We will attempt to get beyond some of the simplistic views of the war to appreciate the complexity of the multi-faceted experience. We will cover a long span of history, deal with both Asian society and our own, and cross many disciplinary lines, e.g. history, political science, sociology, anthropology, religion, economics, journalism, and more. We will view the war from many perspectives, Vietnamese and American, not to mention those of other participants and/or observers. In this process, I hope that you will gain something about recent American history, Asian culture and society, colonialism and anti-colonialism, the process of foreign policy/national security decision-making, American society and politics, and ourselves as a people.

I have been thinking, reading, and writing about the Vietnam War for a long time, and I have some definite views (which are always in a process of reevaluation); but my goal is not to convince you of my interpretations and views. Rather I will pose many questions and I hope a few dilemmas. Vietnam was a kaleidoscope, a multi-sided prism with many conflicting truths. The goal is for you of the post-Vietnam generation to come to your own conceptions, your analysis of the lessons, and your determination of the meaning of the experience for the present and the future.

Objectives

(1) Survey the long history of Vietnam to better appreciate another cultural heritage.

(2) Understand the impact of European colonialism and the resultant forces of nationalism, anti-imperialism, revolution, and Marxist appeal in the Third World.

(3) Focus upon the origins and evolution of American involvement from the end of World War II through the First and Second Indochina Wars.

(4) Examine the national security decision process in each succeeding Presidential administration and critically assess performance.

(5) Evaluate the military conduction of the war, discuss the controversies, and concentrate upon the question of why we were not successful in our objectives.

(6) Update events in Indochina since the end of American involvement.

(7) Review the impact of the war upon the American nation at the time and since.

(8) Introduce the historiography of the war, and debate the lessons, legacy, and implications of the war.

Readings

Thomas D. Boettcher, *Vietnam: The Valor and The Sorrow*
    (1985)
William S. Turley, *The Second Indochina War: A Short
    Political and Military History,* 1954-1975 (1986)
Troung Nhu Tang, *A Viet Cong Memoir* (1985)
Lawrence E. Grinter and Peter M. Dunn, *The American War
    in Vietnam: Lessons, Legacies, and Implications For Future Conflicts*
    (1987)
Thomas C. Thayer, *War Without Fronts: The American
    Experience in Vietnam* (1985)
Lynda Van Devanter, *Home Before Morning: The Story of
    an Army Nurse in Vietnam* (1983)
        or
Patricia Walsh, *Forever Sad the Hearts* (1984)
Jim and Sybil Stockdale, *In Love and War* (1984)

Grade Requirements

There will be a mid-term (3 hrs. objective and essay); a second exam (1 hr. objective near end); a readings essay or research paper; and a final exam (3 hrs. essay).

Junior-Senior Papers

All history and politics majors must do a major research paper in one of their major courses during both their junior and senior years. If you chose to do your paper in this course, *it is due no later than November 25.* The paper may be substituted for the Readings Essay.

Graduate Requirements

Graduate students will do the Research Paper as well as the Readings Essay. On all work, graduate students will be held accountable to standards appropriate to their advanced standing.

COURSE OUTLINE:

I.   A SURVEY OF VIETNAMESE HISTORY FROM
      ANTIQUITY TO THE FRENCH

Sample Mid-Term Questions

(1) You are a former French government health services administrator. Your grandfather first came to Vietnam as a minor bureaucratic official. Your parents owned a small rubber plantation near Saigon and had other holdings in mining and commerce around the country. You went into government service working in various areas of the country including time in montagnard areas in the Central Highlands and in Cao Dai areas near Tay Ninh City. Finally, you became the administrator of the largest hospital in Hanoi during the 1940s through the mid-1950s. One of your brothers became a military officer serving with the French Expeditory Forces. Your sister became a nun. Your other brother ran the family business and expanded into factory operations in Hue and Danang. He remained in Vietnam through the early 1960s.

Write a brief history of the events of your family members' lives during these turbulent times. Your essay will be evaluated upon the basis of historical accuracy, creativity, and the degree to which it captures the breadth and complexity of the Vietnamese political and social climate during the first half of the 20th century.

(2) You come from a long line of Vietnamese nationalists. Your grandfather, a low-level mandarin from Hanoi, was very active politically from the 1880s through the 1920s. Your father was an administrator in Hoa Hao area near the Cambodia border in the late 1930s through the 1950s. You are a Buddhist lawyer from Saigon involved in politics during the 1950s and early 1960s. You are writing a family history for your daughter to explain to her the complexity of Vietnamese politics over this span and your family's involvement in nationalist resistance activity. Your essay will be evaluated on the same criteria as above.

Sample Final Exam Questions

(1) "If Americans had the same appreciation for history, ability to learn from it, and cultural sensitivity as do the Vietnamese, things would have been different in our involvement in Vietnam." Comment on this statement.

(2) "From the American professional soldier's perspective, the most frustrating aspect of the Vietnam conflict is that the U. S. armed forces did everything they were supposed to do, winning every major battle of the war, yet North Vietnam, rather than the United States, triumphed in the end. How could U. S. troops have succeeded so well, but the war effort have failed so miserably?" Comment on this statement and attempt to explain the dilemma.

POLITICAL SCIENCE 147J: THE VIETNAM EXPERIENCE
DREW UNIVERSITY
DOUGLAS SIMON

Course Purpose

The Vietnam War was one of the most complex and controversial events in American history. Perspectives and evaluations at the time were often more passionate and polemical than scholarly. Some of the passion has now subsided, but the controversy remains. At least today we appear more able to appreciate the complexity of the multi-faceted experience, and some of the more simplistic interpretations have disappeared.

The purpose of this course is to offer an indepth analysis of America's involvement in Southeast Asia. While not strictly an historical survey, the time span to be covered runs from 1944 to the fall of Saigon in 1975. The course will include analysis from several perspectives: analysis of the policy process whereby the United States committed itself to the region and eventually conducted its own war there; the evolution of the independence movement in Indochina; the conduct of the war; the impact of the war on the Vietnamese and American government and society and an assessment of the affect of the war on subsequent U. S. foreign policy.

Requirements

Attendance is mandatory.

There will be 3 examinations on designated dates. They will not be cumulative in content.

Each student will prepare a written and oral book review. The written review will be 3-5 pages and the class presentation will be 7-10 minutes. Copies of each book review will be provided to each member of the class and the instructor.

Each student will prepare a 3-5 page thought paper during the final week of the course.

The Killing Fields will be shown on the evening of January 19 in LC-30 with an introduction and discussion following.

Grading

3 Examinations	60%
Book Report	20%
Thought Paper	20%

Texts

Stanley Karnow, *Vietnam: A History*
Al Santoli, *Everything We Had*

Book Reports

Book reports should be chosen from the subjects and books listed below. Subjects are listed in order of presentation and specific dates are listed in the schedule.

Subject	Book
War in the Villages	Jeffery Race, *War Comes to Long An* or Jonathan Schell, *The Village of Ben Suc*
Bombing in N. Vietnam	James C. Thompson, *Rolling Thunder*

Subject	Book
The My Lai Massacre	Seymour Hersh, *Cover Up*
	Lt. Gen. W. R. Peers, *The My Lai Inquiry*
The Tunnel War	Tom Mangold and John Penycate, *The Tunnels of Cu Chi*
An Advisor's World	David Donavan, *Once A Warrior King*
DRV Perspective	Trung Nhu Tang, *A Viet Cong Memoir*
The Black Experience	Wallace Terry, *Bloods*
Freeing Prisoners	Benjamin Schemmer, *The Raid*
A Military Critique of the Military in Vietnam	Harry G. Summers, Jr., *On Strategy*
Cambodian Tragedy	Molyda Szymusiak, *The Stones Cry Out*
	Francois Ponchard, *Cambodian Year Zero*
U.S. - Cambodia	William Shawcross, *Sideshow*
The POWs	Jim and Sybil Stockdale, *In Love and War*
	Scott Blakely, *Prisoner At War: The Survival of Commander Richard A. Stratton*
The Fall of Saigon	Tiziano Tarzan, *Giai Phong: The Fall and Liberation of Saigon*
	Frank Snepp, *Decent Interval*
Agent Orange	Fred Wilcox, *Waiting For An Army To Die*
The Boat People	Bruce Grant, *The Boat People*
System Failure?	Leslie Gelb and Richard Betts, *The Irony of Vietnam: The System Worked*
A Conservative Critique	Norman Podhoretz, *Why We Were in Vietnam*

Lecture Schedule

Jan 5   *Introduction and Overview*
Monday

        Reading: Karnow, Ch. 1 "The War Nobody Wanted"

        Videotape: "Roots of War"

Jan 6   *Early History*
Tuesday
        Reading: Karnow, Ch. 2 "Piety and Power"
                        Karnow, Ch. 2 "The Heritage of
                                 Vietnamese Nationalism"

Jan 7   *The War with the French*
Wednesday
        Reading: Karnow, Ch. 4 "The War with the
                                 French"
                        Karnow, Ch. 5 "The Light that Failed"
        Videotape: "The First Vietnam War"

Jan 8   *Geneva Through Kennedy '54-63*
Thursday
        First Quiz: Karnow Chapters 1-5
        Reading: Karnow, Ch. 6 "America's Mandarin"
                        Karnow, Ch. 7 "Vietnam is the Place"
                        Karnow, Ch. 8 "The End of Diem"
        Videotape: "American's Mandarian"

Jan 12   *The Johnson Years 1964-68*
Monday
        Reading: Karnow, Ch. 9 "The Commitment
                               Deepens"
        Videotape: "The Commitment Deepens"
        Reports: War in to the Villages
                        Bombing the North

Jan 13   *The Johnson Years, cont.*
Tuesday
        Reading: Karnow, Ch. 10 "Disorder and Decision"
                        Karnow, Ch. 11 "LBJ Goes to War"
        Videotape: "America Takes Charge"
        Reports: The My Lai Massacre
                      The Tunnel War
                      An Advisor's Life

Jan 14   *The NLF and DRV*
Wednesday
        Second Quiz: Karnow, Chapters 6-11
        Reading: Karnow, Ch. 12 "Escalation"
                        Karnow, Ch. 13 "Debate, Diplomacy,
                               Doubt"
        Videotape: "With America's Enemy"
        Report: DRV Perspective

Jan 15   The Tet Offensive
Thursday

     Reading: Karnow, Ch. 14 "Tet"
     Videotape: "Tet, 1968"
     Reports: The Black Experience in Vietnam

Jan 19   The Nixon Administration
Monday

     Reading: Karnow, Ch. 15
     Videotape: "Vietnamizing the War"
     Report: Freeing Prisoners of War
               Military Critique of the Military
     Evening Presentation: "The Killing Fields"
          LC-30 7:00 p.m.

Jan 20   Cambodia/Laos
Tuesday

     Report: The U.S. and Cambodia
               The POWs
     Videotape: "No Neutral Ground: Cambodia and
               Laos"
     Report: The Cambodian Tragedy The U.S. and
               Cambodia

Jan 21   The Paris Peace Negotiations
Wednesday

     Reading: Karnow, Ch. 16 "The Peace That Never
               Was"
     Videotape: "Peace Is at Hand"
     Report: The POWs

Jan 22   The War at Home
Thursday

     Report: Kent State
     Videotapes: "Homefront USA"
               "Hearts and Minds"

Jan 26   The Final Collapse
Monday

     Third Examination: Karnow, Chapters 12-16
     Videotape: "The End of the Tunnel"
     Report: The Fall of Saigon

Jan 27   The Legacies of Vietnam
Tuesday
          Report: Agent Orange
                           The Boat People
          Videotape: "Legacies"
                           "Vietnam 10 Years Later"
Jan 28   Vietnam in Retrospect
Wednesday
          Videotape: Critique of the Vietnam Television
                           History Series
          Report: System Failure?
                           A Conservative View

POLITICAL SCIENCE 462: GOVERNMENT AND POLITICS OF VIETNAM
SOUTHERN ILLINOIS UNIVERSITY
PROFESSOR WILLIAM S. TURLEY

Course Purpose

This course is designed to provide students with an opportunity to study in depth the politics of a nation that has passed through one of the most important revolutions in the 20th century. The world's fourteenth largest country, Vietnam is the third largest to be governed by a Marxist-Leninist party. Some attention will be given to history and the impact of colonial rule, but the primary focus will be on the politics of the "divided states" that existed from 1954 to 1975 and the problems faced by the unified Socialist Republic since war's end. Though not a "Vietnam war course," the war and the U. S. role in it will be one of the subjects discussed.

An additional major objective will be to place Vietnam in comparative perspective, with special regard to revolutionary change, conflict, economic and political "development," and the politics of communist systems. In pursuit of this objective, we will study Vietnam's efforts to reform its socialist system, efforts which resemble those now occurring in the Soviet Union and China but which have the potential to change profoundly the character and institutions of the entire Marxist-Leninist world.

Required texts

William J. Duiker, *Vietnam Since the Fall of Saigon*
Samuel L. Popkin, *The Rational Peasant*
William S. Turley, *The Second Indochina War*

Additional required reading marked in the course outline below with an asterisk will be on library reserve.

Course requirements

1. A 3 to 5 page review of Popkin, due one week after discussion of this book is completed in class. Exact due date will be set later (20 percent of course grade).

2. A term paper, 10 to 15 pages in length (20pp. for graduate students), due 5 p.m. 26 April. Students are to choose their own topics. A 1 or 2 page outline and list of sources are due 5 p.m. 24 March. Use solid sources, not TIME and NEWSWEEK. Consult bibliography below (but you are by no means limited to sources cited here). PAPERS OR OUTLINES SUBMITTED AFTER DEADLINE WILL RESULT IN REDUCTION OF GRADE FOR THE PAPER ONE FULL LETTER FOR EACH DAY THAT THEY ARE LATE. (50 percent of course grade).

3. A final exam. (30 percent of course grade). The following books, useful as supplementary readings and term paper research, have been placed on three day reserve:

Huynh Kim Khanh, *Vietnamese Communism 1926-1945*
David Elliott (editor), *The Third Indochina Conflict*
William Duiker, *The Communist Road to Power in Vietnam*
Gareth Porter (editor), *Vietnam: The Definitive History of Human Decisions*, 2 volumes. (NOTE: This is a very large collection of key documents from the war)
Jeffrey Race, *War Comes to Long An*
Alexander Woodside, *Community and Revolution in Modern Vietnam*

Other titles may be added to this list as the term progresses.

Course Outline and Readings

1. Land and people

    Duiker, *Vietnam: Nation in Revolution*, pp. 1-12.

2. Political economy of an ararian society

    Popkin, pp. 1-82

3. Colonial rule

>Popkin, pp. 133-183

4. Sectarian and political subcultures

>Popkin, pp. 184-242

5. Agrarian revolt and communist revolution

>Popkin, pp. 184-267
>Ho Chi Minh, "The Path Which Led Me to Leninism"
>Ho Chi Minh, "Founding of the Communist Party of Indochina (1930)"

6. The regimes of North and South

>Turley, pp. 1-35

>Edwin Moise, "'Classism' in North Vietnam," in Turley (editor), *Vietnamese Communism in Comparative Perspective.*

7. Intervention and militarization

>Turley, pp. 37-98

8. Ending the War

>Turley, pp. 99-206

9. Socialist transformation: ideology and practice

>Duiker, pp. 3-88

>Turley, "Socialist Republic of Vietnam," in Delury (editor), *World Encyclopedia of Political Systems & Parties*, volume 2 (Facts on File, 1987), pp. 1263-73.
>Nayan Chanda, "The New Revolution," *Far Eastern Economic Review* (10 April 1986).

10.   Special problems

>Arthur W. Westing, "The Environmental Aftermath of Warfare in Viet Nam," *SIPRI Yearbook* (1982), pp. 363-387.

Sophie Quinn-Judge, "Vietnamese Women: Neglected Promises,"
Indochina Issues, No. 42 (December 1983).

Stewart E. Fraser, "Vietnam Struggles with Exploding
Population," *Indochina Issues*, no. 57 (May 1985).

David Marr, "Church and State in Vietnam," *Indochina Issues*,
no. 74 (April 1987).

11.   Post War international relations

Duiker, pp. 91-164

Paul Quinn-Judge, "The Vietnam-China Split: Old Ties Remain,"
Indochina Issues, no. 53 (January 1985).

12.   Vietnam and security in Asia

Duiker, pp. 165-175

Turley, "Vietnam's Challenge to Southeast Asia Regional Order,"
in Kihl and Grinter (editors), *Asian-Pacific Security* (Lynne
Rienner, 1986).

POLITICAL SCIENCE 384/584: THE VIETNAM WAR
HISTORY 384/584: THE VIETNAM WAR
UNIVERSITY OF WISCONSIN
LEONARD GAMBRELL AND STEPHEN GOSCH

Purpose of the Course

This multidisciplinary and television-assisted course explores and reviews
the actions and decisions of various individuals, groups and governments
in the development, initiation and conduct of the wars in Vietnam, 1945-
1975. These conflicts are analyzed from the perspectives of two different
but related disciplines: political science and history.

There is dual purpose in the review and analysis of policies, decisions
and actions. First, we seek to learn what actually happened in the past and
how searching for this knowledge can illuminate the present. Secondly, we
search for knowledge about the American political behavior, political
patterns and values as we explore policies, decisions and actions. In *both*
cases we will discover there is conflicting evidence as to what actually
happened and what it says about our behavior patterns and values.
Students should explore all aspects of the conflicts in Vietnam and develop
comprehensive knowledge and opinions supported by evidence.

NOTE: General William C. Westmoreland, who commanded American military forces in Vietnam from 1964 to 1968, will be speaking at UW-EC on December 7 as a part of the Forum Series. His lecture, which everyone enrolled in this course is required to attend, is entitled, "The True History of the Vietnam War." In addition, we hope that General Westmoreland will be able to visit this class prior to his Forum lecture; the readings assigned for that day have been selected with this in mind.

Textbooks

George C. Herring, *America's Longest War*. 2nd ed. Available from
    Textbook Services.
Marvin E. Gettleman, et al. *Vietnam and America: A Documentary History*.
    On sale in the University Bookstore.
Graham Greene. *The Quiet American*. University Bookstore.
Robert Mason. *Chickenhawk*. University Bookstore.

Topics to be Considered:

Sept. 7:   Introduction to the Course: Who are the Vietnamese?

Sept. 14: Vietnam in the French Empire, 1862-1940
Reading: Gettleman, General Introduction & Part I.
           Documents distributed on September 7.

Sept. 21: Vietnam and World War II
Reading: Gettleman, pp. 27-30; 36-47

Sept. 28: The First Vietnam War, 1945-1954, and the American Policy of
           Containment
Reading: Gettleman, pp. 30-36; 47-66
           Herring, chapter I

Oct. 5:   The Collapse of the Geneva Settlement, 1954-1961
Reading: Herring, chapter II
           Gettleman, pp. 69-95; 100-132
           Essay due on *The Quiet American*
           Essay question: Compare and contrast the views of
           Fowler and Pyle toward Vietnam and the Vietnamese. With
           whose views do you tend to identify? Explain.

Oct. 12:   The New Frontier and the Collapse of "Nation-Building"
Reading: Herring, chapter III
           Gettleman, pp. 135-234

Oct. 19: The Americanization of the War, 1964-1965
Reading: Herring, chapter IV
          Gettleman, 237-273

Oct. 26: The Escalation of the War, 1965-1968
Reading: Herring, chapter V
          Gettleman, pp. 273-288
          Mid-semester examination.

Nov. 2:   The Decisive Year, 1968
Reading: Herring, chapter VI
          Gettleman, pp. 335-355, 373-402

Nov. 9:   The Impact of the War on Vietnam and the Vietnamese
Reading: Gettleman, pp. 403-17; 461-69
          Truong Nhu Tang, *A Vietcong Memoir*, chapter 14
          E. W. Pfeiffer, "Operation Ranch Hand"

Nov. 16: A War for Peace, 1969-72
Reading: Herring, chapter VII
          Gettleman, pp. 421-51; 458-61

Nov. 23: The American Soldier in Vietnam
Reading: Gettleman, pp. 315-31; 451-58
          Essay due on *Chickenhawk*.
          Essay question: How did the war affect Robert Mason?

Nov. 30: The Movement Against the War
Reading: Gettleman, Part VI
          Berkeley Vietnam Day Committee, "Attention All Military
            Personnel," October 1965
          Michael Fellner, "The Untold Story," Parts I and II, *Wisconsin,*
          The Milwaukee Journal Magazine, May 18 & 26, 1986

Dec. 7:   A Visit with General William C. Westmoreland
Reading: William C. Westmoreland, *A Soldier Reports*, excerpts. (This
          book is also on reserve in the library.)
          Gettleman, pp. 335-355.

Dec. 14: The "Postwar War," 1973-1975, and The Legacy of the War
Reading: Herring, chapter VIII
          Gettleman, pp. 469-502
          Noam Chomsky, "Intervention in Vietnam and Central America:
          Parallels and Differences."

Course Requirements and Grading

Essays: 40%
Mid-Semester Exam: 30%
Final Examination: 30%

Essay Assignments

Two brief essays (not more than two typewritten pages), the first based on Graham Greene's novel, *The Quiet American*, and the second on Robert Mason's memoir, *Chickenhawk*, are required of all students in this course. The essays should discuss the extent to which the books contribute to one's understanding of the Vietnam war. In addition, the essays should address the specific questions listed above. The papers will be evaluated according to the following criteria:

1. Does your essay indicate that you have read the book with care?

2. Is the essay original and thoughtful? On original work: Do not read anything about the book or the author. Base your essay solely on the book in question.

3. Is your essay free of grammatical, spelling and typographical errors?

4. Was the essay turned in on time? Late papers will be penalized.

Make-up Examinations

Students who fail to take an examination at the regularly scheduled time will receive a "0" grade for that exam unless prior arrangements have been made with the instructors. Make-up exams will be available only when it is clear to the instructors that some serious circumstance has made it impossible for the student to take the exam at the scheduled time. A request for a make-up exam should be made promptly.

Graduate Students

Graduate students should meet with the instructors to discuss an additional assignment.

HONORS 49013G: THE LITERATURE OF THE VIETNAM WAR
ARKANSAS STATE UNIVERSITY
CATHERINE CALLOWAY

Course Description

This course examines the wide range of literature that has emerged from America's involvement in the Vietnam War. Students need to learn about and understand a period of recent history that had—and continues to have—a profound effect on American society. Reading the literature spawned by the Vietnam War not only aids students in developing an awareness of the impact of these literary works on contemporary literature in general, but also expands students' knowledge of the social, psychological, historical, political, cultural and geographical aspects of the war.

Course Objectives

1. To gain an understanding of America's longest and most diverse war and to discuss its impact on literature as well as on American culture and society.
2. To identify the different types of literary works that have emerged from the Vietnam War.
3. To identify the main themes and motifs contained in these literary works.
4. To gain an awareness of the way in which writers have interpreted the significance of the Vietnam War.
5. To understand the various structural patterns used to translate a diverse and complex war into literature.

Required Textbooks

Edelman, Bernard, editor. *Dear America: Letters Home from Vietnam.* New York: Pocket Books, 1987.

Ehrhart, W. D., editor. *Carrying the Darkness: The Poetry of the Vietnam War.* Lubbock, Texas: Texas Tech University Press, 1985.

Hasford, Gustav. *The Short-Timers.* New York: Bantam, 1979.

Herr, Michael. *Dispatches.* New York: Avon, 1977.

Kovic, Ron. *Born on the Fourth of July.* New York: Pocket Books, 1976.

Marshall, Kathryn. *In the Combat Zone: Vivid Personal Recollections of the Vietnam War from the Women Who Served There*. New York: Penguin, 1987.

Mason, Bobbie Ann. *In Country*. New York: Harper and Row, 1985.

O'Brien, Tim. *Going After Cacciato*. New York: Delta and Seymour Lawrence, 1978.

——. *If I Die in a Combat Zone/Box Me Up and Ship Me Home*. New York: Dell, 1973.

Rotter, Andrew J. *Light at the End of the Tunnel: A Vietnam War Anthology*. New York: St. Martin's, 1991.

Webb, James. *Fields of Fire*. New York: Bantam, 1978.

Tentative Reading Schedule

January 10	Introduction to the course
12	Introduction to the course
	Rotter, "Introduction," pp. 1-25
	"Chronology," pp. 579-586 (Rotter)
15	Video: *Why Viet Nam?*
17	THE PERSONAL NARRATIVE
	Parmet, "No 'Non-Essential Areas',"
	pp. 125-136 (Rotter)
	O'Brien, *If I Die*
19	O'Brien, *If I Die*
22	O'Brien, *If I Die*
	Herring, "LBJ Goes to War,"
	pp. 137-151 (Rotter)
	Berman, "The Tet Offensive,"
	pp. 152-164 (Rotter)
	Caputo, "Getting Hit,"
	pp. 291-296 (Rotter)
24	THE CONVENTIONAL COMBAT NOVEL
	Webb, *Fields of Fire*
	Karnow, "Nixon's War,"
	pp. 179-189 (Rotter)
26	Webb, *Fields of Fire*
29	Webb, *Fields of Fire*

30 Marshall, *In the Combat Zone*
    MacPherson, "Women at the Barricades, Then
       and Now," pp. 493-503 (Rotter)
    Hayslip, "Letting Go,"
       pp. 569-578 (Rotter)
    Fitzgerald, "A Clash of Cultures,"
       pp. 379-399 (Rotter)

April 2 Guest Speaker: Political Scientist
       4 THE EXPERIMENTAL NOVEL
          O'Brien, *Going After Cacciato*
       6 O'Brien, *Going After Cacciato*
       9 O'Brien, *Going After Cacciato*
      11 O'Brien, Going After Cacciato
      13 LITERATURE OF THE RETURN
          Kovic, *Born on the Fourth of July*
      16 Kovic, *Born on the Fourth of July*
      18 Kovic, *Born on the Fourth of July*
      20 Film Clip: *Born on the Fourth of July*
      23 Guest Speaker: Vietnam Veteran
          Mason, *In Country*
      25 Mason, *In Country*
      27 Mason, *In Country*
      30 Film Clip: *In Country*

Attendance Policy

This is an honors seminar. You will need to attend each class session,
complete all of the required reading (prior to our discussion of the
material in class), think about the literary and other relevant issues
involved, and participate in the discussion of ideas. It is important that
you be prepared to not only discuss the issues that emerge from the
reading but also to critique the stance of the writer and to formulate your
own ideas. Class participation will count one-sixth of the final grade;
therefore, it is to your advantage to attend class regularly.

Assignments

The Journal: Since many Vietnam War writers began their novels or
memoirs by keeping a journal during the war, it is only appropriate that
readers of these works also keep a journal. Journal entries (a minimum
of two or three a week) may take the form of reactions to the literary
works, films or television shows about the war, guest speakers, and class
discussions, for example, or of original poems or fiction. The journals

will be collected at least once before midterm and again before finals and will count one-sixth of the final grade.

Papers: Students will be required to write two analytical and/or critical papers (six to eight typed pages) dealing with some aspect of the literature of the war. A project may be substituted for one of the papers. A project may involve writing a short story about the war, dramatizing a portion of a literary work, or preparing a sample Vietnamese meal for the class, for example. Papers and/or projects will count one third of the final grade.

Exams: Two major exams, consisting of both objective and discussion questions, will constitute approximately one third of the final grade. Exam dates will be announced in class in advance, and students are expected to be present in class on those days.

Oral Report: The reading required for this class represents only a minute fragment of the hundreds of literary works spawned by the Vietnam War. It would be presumptuous to argue that the works read in this course are the best and/or most representative works of this canon of literature. For this reason, each student will give a brief (5 or 10 minute) report on a work of Vietnam War literature not included on the syllabus. These reports will provide students with the opportunity to study works in their areas of special interest and will provide the class with additional insight into the literature of the war. The oral report will count as fifty percent of the class participation grade.

Additional Requirements for Graduate Students: In addition to the above assignments, graduate students will compile a bibliography of the primary and secondary sources of a major Vietnam War writer. Also, the length of the two papers will be ten to fifteen pages instead of six to eight pages. Each assignment for the course will count one-seventh of the final grade instead of one-sixth.

Grading Scale: 100-90=A
                                                   89-80=B
                                                   79-70=C
                                                   69-60=D
                                             Below 60=F

Sample Exam Questions

Identification: oral history
New Journalism
metafiction
TET Offensive
walking point
free fire zone
melting pot platoon
Khe Sahn

Discussion:

1. Pretend that you are writing an introduction to an anthology on Vietnam War literature. What information on the war and its literature would you provide for the reader of this anthology? How would you characterize this literature overall? What are its strengths and weaknesses? What elements make it a unique genre of literature?

2. A number of critics have commented on the difficulty that the Vietnam War writer has faced in trying to write structured works about a diverse and complex war that was chaotic and unstructured. Discuss the ways in which writers have handled this problem with technique and form.

3. The works that we have examined have touched on a number of different aspects of the war and involve fields such as history, political science, psychology, sociology, geography, women's studies and Vietnamese culture. Discuss the interdisciplinary nature of the war, citing specific examples from the literature that we read to support your ideas.

VIETNAM WAR NARRATIVES:
AN INTERDISCIPLINARY APPROACH
YALE UNIVERSITY
KALI TAL

Required Readings

David Dellinger, *Vietnam Revisited: Action from Invasion to Reconstruction* (New York: South End Press, 1986).
Gustav Hasford, *The Short-Timers* (New York: Harper & Row, 1983).

Stanley Kubrick, Michael Herr, Gustav Hasford, *Full Metal Jacket* (New York: Knopf, 1987).

Michael Herr, *Dispatches* (New York: Bantam, 1986).

Charles Clements, M.D., *Witness to War: An American Doctor in El Salvador* (New York: Bantam, 1984).

A. R. Flowers, *De Mojo Blues* (New York: E. P. Dutton, 1986).

Wendy Wilder Larsen, *Tran Thi Nga, Shallow Graves: Two Women and Vietnam* (New York: Harper and Row, 1986).

Renata Adler, *Reckless Disregard: Westmoreland vs. CBS et al., Sharon vs. Time* (New York: Vintage, 1986).

Nayan Chanda, *Brother Enemy, the War After the War: A History of Indochina since the Fall of Saigon* (New York: Collier, 1986).

Arthur Egendorf, *Healing From The War* (Boston: Houghton Mifflin, 1985).

A reader containing various critical articles, oral histories, poems, cartoons and essays will be available from Kinko's.

Required Films

Full Metal Jacket
Alamo Bay
Bloods
Good Morning Vietnam!
Apocalypse Now
A Program for Vietnam Veterans
Boys in Company C
Tet Offensive/CBS Series

Course Requirements

Journal: Students are required to keep a journal of their responses to readings, course materials and discussions. An unusual requirement of this journal, however, is that it be kept by a pair of students and each student must address the other student's comments and questions. The journal must be exchanged at least once a week and handed in at the end of each class meeting. The journals can be picked up again the day after class.

Oral History: Each student must interview at le. st one Vietnam veteran and one Vietnamese emigrant or refugee. This assignment must be completed by the sixth week of the course.

Final Paper: The final paper will be a major research paper in which the student will use an inter-disciplinary methodology to explore some aspect of the Vietnam War. Examples of this might be: a paper which uses both psychological approaches to post-traumatic stress disorder in Vietnam veterans and a literary critical analysis of fiction by Vietnam Veterans; a paper which examines the historical accuracy of encyclopedia entries about the Vietnam War and examines those entries as popular culture texts; a paper which examines contemporary films about the Vietnam War and interprets public response to those films within a sociological framework. The final paper will be a minimum of 20 pages. It will be due the final week of the course.

Course Outline

Week 1:   Introduction to the course. Contextualizing the Vietnam War—Geography, history, politics, ethnohistory. Discussion of historiography of the Vietnam War—competing schools of history, the process of historical revisionism. Reading: *Vietnam Revisited*, selections from the reader.

Week 2:   Psychological approaches to Vietnam veterans and the Vietnam War "experience." Post-traumatic stress disorder, agent orange, and veterans' benefits. The Winter Soldier Investigations and the Song My Massacre. Reading: *Healing from the War*, selections from the reader. Film: *A Program for Vietnam Vets*.

Week 3:   Vietnam as an individual experience. The grunt's-eye view of the war. Combat experience. Journalists and soldiers. Experiences of Black, Asian-American, Hispanic and American Indian soldiers. Reading: *Dispatches*, selections from the reader. Film: *Bloods*.

Week 4:   Storytelling and Vietnam. Discussion of the "Literature of Trauma"—Holocaust Literature, World War I Literature, and Vietnam Literature. Literature as a method of interpretation of war experience. Reading: *De Mojo Blues*, selections from the reader.

Week 5:   Life after Wartime. The politics of Vietnam veterans.
               The Vietnam Memorial—*James Webb and The Statue vs.
               Jan Scruggs and the Wall*. Vietnam veterans against the
               war. Central America and Vietnam. Reading: *Witness to
               War*, selections from the Reader. Film: Apocalypse Now.

Week 6:   The meeting of Vietnamese and American Culture.
               American perceptions of Vietnam. Vietnamese
               perceptions of Americans. Montagnards and Hmong
               Tribesmen. Discussion of problems and challenges of
               overcoming ethnocentricism. Reading: *Shallow Graves*,
               and selections from the reader.

Week 7:   History of Indochina since 1975. World politics goes on,
               even though American popular culture is still fighting the
               war. Vietnamese in America, refugee communities.
               Reading: *Brother Enemy*, and selections from the reader.
               Film: *Alamo Bay*.

Week 8:   The press and the Vietnam War. Press coverage of the
               1968 Tet Offensive. *Westmoreland vs. CBS*. Discussion of
               the underground press. Effect of television on news
               reporting of the war. Reading: *Reckless Disregard*, and
               selections from the reader. Film: *Tet Offensive*.

Week 9:   From *The Short-Timers* to *Full Metal Jacket*: The
               transformation of novel by Vietnam Veteran Hasford to
               film by world-acclaimed director Stanley Kubrick through
               the medium of journalist Michael Herr. Reading: *The
               Short-Timers, Full Metal Jacket*, and selections from the
               reader. Film: *Full Metal Jacket*.

Week 10:   Final discussion. Students will have the opportunity to
               tell each other about their papers, and to share selections
               from their journals.

Index

About the Contributors

GERALD W. BERKLEY is Associate Professor of Asian History and the Chair of the Division of Humanities and Social Sciences at the University of Guam, Mangilao, Guam. From 1979 to 1986, he taught Asian history, including courses on Vietnam, at both the Auburn and Montgomery campuses of Auburn University. His publications include scholarly articles in *The Air University Review, Annals of the Southeast Conference of the Association for Asian Studies, Modern China* and *Republican China*.

LARRY E. CABLE is Associate Professor of History at the University of North Carolina at Wilmington. He received his doctorate from the University of Houston. He served in, and is now an acknowledged academic expert on, Vietnam era military intelligence and unconventional warfare. His recent books, *Conflict of Myths: The Development of American Counterinsurgency Doctrine and the Vietnam War* (New York: New York University, 1986) and *Unholy Grail: The U. S. and the Wars in Vietnam, 1965-1968* (New York: Routledge, 1991) are major contributions to this field.

CATHERINE CALLOWAY is Assistant Professor of English and the acting director of the graduate program in English at Arkansas State University, Jonesboro, Arkansas. She received her doctorate from the University of South Florida at Tampa. She teaches an honors course on the literature of the Vietnam War and has published numerous articles and bibliographies on Vietnam War literature and film. In 1989, she received a faculty research grant from Arkansas State University to study the role of women in the Vietnam War, and most recently she participated in the 1990 National Endowment for the Humanities Summer Institute on Teaching the Vietnam War at the Indochina Institute at George Mason University in Fairfax, Virginia.

CECIL B. CURREY is Professor of History at the University of South Florida at Tampa and an Army Reserve chaplain with the rank of colonel. He received his doctorate from the University of Kansas. He is the author of nine books, including *Edward Lansdale: The Unquiet American* (Boston: Houghton Mifflin, 1988) and *Self-Destruction: The Disintegration and Decay of the United States Army During the Vietnam Era* (New York: Norton, 1981), which he wrote under the pseudonym of "Cincinnatus." He is currently completing a biography of the Vietnamese General Vo Nguyen Giap, a project which has taken him to Vietnam three times in the last two years. He is particularly interested in low-intensity conflicts and people's wars of national liberation and has regularly lectured to various military commands on the tactics of such conflicts.

JOE P. DUNN is Professor of History and Politics at Converse College, Converse, South Carolina. He received his doctorate in history from the University of Missouri and did post-doctorate work in political science at Duke University. He served as a sergeant in Vietnam with the 199th Infantry Brigade. Teaching the Vietnam War has been the primary focus of his many published professional articles and his national conference presentations. He has conducted teacher-training workshops on Vietnam across the country and has administered his own grant-funded Vietnam War Institute to prepare high school teachers to teach about the war.

MARC JASON GILBERT is Professor of History at North Georgia College, Dahlonega, Georgia. He received his doctorate in South and Southeast Asian history from the University of California, Los Angeles. During the Vietnam War, he served as a staff assistant to a conflict resolution study-team unique among its think-tank contemporaries in that it was funded by the Department of Defense and won the approval of the anti-war Students for a Democratic Society. He has contributed to many regional and national conferences on the study and teaching of the Vietnam War, including a 1990 symposium on the war held at the United States Air Force Academy. A specialist in nationalism and imperialism in Asia, his most recent publications have been directed toward illuminating the place of Southeast Asia and the Pacific in world history.

JONATHAN GOLDSTEIN is Associate Professor of History at West Georgia College, Carrollton, Georgia, and a Research Associate of Harvard University's John K. Fairbank Center for East Asian Research. He received his doctorate in Chinese and American history from the University of Pennsylvania. He is the author of several monographs and articles on the subject of America's relations with Asia, including "Indochina War on Campus: The Summit/Spicerack Controversy at the University of Pennsylvannia, 1965-67," published in the *Annals of the Southeast Conference of the Association for Asian Studies 4* (1983), pp. 78-79. He is one of only a few American scholars who visited Vietnam between 1975 and 1988.

JOHN JAMES MACDOUGALL is Associate Professor of Political Science at the University of Alabama in Huntsville. He received his doctorate in history from the University of Michigan. In 1970-1972, he was a contract research analyst studying Vietnamization for the Bendix Corporation and the United States Department of Defense. He has since published extensively in the field of Southeast Asian politics, with emphasis on Indonesia.

STEVE POTTS teaches American and Asian history at Hibbing Community College, Hibbing, Minnesota. The recipient of the 1991-1992 Chancellor's Doctoral Fellowship at the University of Nebraska, he is currently on leave to work on a doctorate in history. He has taught courses on the Vietnam War in a variety of settings and has published several articles on teaching the war. His current research interests include American corporate investment in Indochina and the anti-war movement's impact upon two Minnesota communities.

KALI TAL is the general editor of *Vietnam Generation: A Journal of Recent History and Contemporary Issues* and president of Vietnam Generation, Inc., a non-profit corporation dedicated to promoting education and literature about the Vietnam War era and generation. She is also completing a dissertation in American studies at Yale University. She has published in the fields of American studies, women's studies and Afro-American studies, and considers herself a "radical generalist."

EARL H. TILFORD, JR. (USAF, Ret.) served in Southeast Asia during the Vietnam War as an United States Air Force intelligence officer. He earned his doctorate in military history at George Washington University and is the author of *A History of Air Force Search and Rescue Operations in Southeast Asia, 1961-1975*, (Washington, D. C.: Office of Air Force History, 1982) and *Setup: What the Air Force did in Vietnam, and Why* (Maxwell Air Force Base, Ala.: Air University, 1991). He is Professor Emeritus of Military History at Air University and has taught courses on the Vietnam War at a variety of institutions of higher learning, including the Air War College, the Air Command and Staff College and the University of Alabama.

MELFORD WILSON, JR. is Professor of Political Science at Winthrop College, Rock Hill, South Carolina. He received his doctorate in International Relations at American University. A frequent scholar-visitor to Asia, he is the author of three textbooks on international relations currently in use in China.